Operations

Management

Operations
Management

Andrew Greasley

JOHN WILEY & SONS, LTD

Other Wiley Editorial Offices

John Wiley & Sons, Inc., 111 River Street, Hoboken, NJ 07030, USA

Jossey-Bass, 989 Market Street, San Francisco, CA 94103-1741, USA

Wiley-VCH Verlag GmbH, Boschstr. 12, D-69469 Weinheim, Germany

John Wiley & Sons Australia Ltd, 42 McDougall Street, Milton, Queensland 4064, Australia

John Wiley & Sons (Asia) Pte Ltd, 2 Clementi Loop #02-01, Jin Xing Distripark, Singapore 129809

John Wiley & Sons Canada Ltd, 22 Worcester Road, Etobicoke, Ontario, Canada M9W 1L1

Wiley also publishes its books in a variety of electronic formats. Some content that appears
in print may not be available in electronic books.

Library of Congress Cataloging-in-Publication Data

Operations Management / Andrew Greasley
p. cm.
Includes index.
ISBN 0-470-01209-9
1. Production management.   2. Process control.   I. Title.
TS155.G817 2005
658.5 – dc22   2005022610

British Library Cataloguing in Publication Data

A catalogue record for this book is available from the British Library

ISBN-13 978-0-470-01209-3
ISBN-10 0-470-01209-9

Project management by Originator, Gt Yarmouth, Norfolk (typeset in 9/13pt Garamond ITC).
Printed and bound in Great Britain by Scotprint, Haddington, East Lothian.
This book is printed on acid-free paper responsibly manufactured from sustainable forestry
in which at least two trees are planted for each one used for paper production.

CONTENTS

DETAILED CONTENTS

PART 2 DESIGN   58

3 Process Types   60

4 Layout Design   72

5 Facility Design and Location   93

6 Process Technology   115

7 Product and Service Design   135

8 Process Design   160

13 Lean Operations and JIT   297

14 Enterprise Resource Planning   318

17 Quality

18 Improvement

PREFACE

Operations management deals with the management of the creation of goods and the delivery of services to the customer. It thus plays an essential role in the success of any organization. The aim of this book is to provide a clear and concise treatment of this large field of study, focusing on the main areas of operations strategy, the design of the operations system, the management of the operations over time and operations improvement. Both qualitative and quantitative aspects of the subject are covered, as well as established and relatively new areas such as Six Sigma and e-commerce.

As an introduction to operations management, this book aims to cover all these relevant areas in the field but in such a manner that students are not overwhelmed by the amount of material presented. The text and its accompanying resources have been designed with the student in mind at all times, in order to provide a focused and accessible learning experience.

The target audience is undergraduates on business studies and joint degrees where no prior knowledge of the subject area is required. The book will also interest postgraduate students on MBA and specialist masters programmes.

Contents of the Book

After an *introductory chapter* the book is structured into three main parts: strategy, design and management. Within this part structure the book consists of 18 chapters. This design has been used in order to maximize the clarity of the presentation of material.

Chapter 1 provides an introduction to the field of operations management, defines the role of operations in the organization and discusses the increasing role and importance of service operations.

Chapter 2 covers the area of operations strategy. The vital role of operations in providing the capability to implement an organization's strategy is covered as well as guidance on how to formulate a successful operations strategy.

The role of design in operations is covered in *Chapters 3–9*. Areas covered include the configuration of processes in manufacturing and services firms, the design and location of operations facilities, technology used in the operations process, product and service design, the design of the processes that deliver services and the design of jobs. An emphasis on service design is provided in this part by covering topics such as business process management and service blueprinting.

The management of operations is covered in *Chapters 10–16*. Areas covered include operations planning and control, capacity management, inventory management, lean operations and JIT, enterprise resource planning, supply chain management and project management. The impact of e-commerce on operations is covered using topics such as e-procurement.

Chapters 17–18 cover topics such as total quality management, continuous and breakthrough improvement approaches, statistical process control and acceptance sampling. The growing influence of Six Sigma programmes is also covered.

Learning Aids for Students

The text provides a number of features to help student learning:

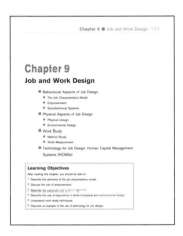

■ Each chapter begins with a list of the main learning objectives for the material covered.

■ Case study boxes provide international, real-life details of operations concepts, with questions to encourage critical reflection on the key issues.

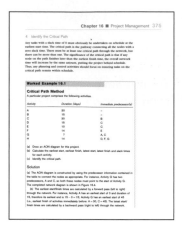

■ Worked examples provide a step-by-step guide to the procedure to solve quantitative problems.

■ End-of-chapter exercises provide topics for discussion and examples to help develop practical skills.
■ References and Further Reading are supplied to enable students to explore topics in greater depth.
■ Annotated weblinks are provided as an extra resource to assist students in locating further additional material.

Lecturer Resources

Lecturers who adopt this text can obtain the following resources to support their teaching on the supporting web site at *www.wiley.com/go/operations*:

■ Powerpoint slides for each chapter.
■ Suggested solutions for all case study questions.
■ Suggested solutions for all end-of-chapter exercises.

Student Resources

Students are provided with multiple-choice quizzes for each chapter that they can use to check their understanding. The further reading and weblinks for each chapter are also available online, as well as the entire glossary.

ABOUT THE AUTHOR

Andrew Greasley is a lecturer at the Aston Business School, Aston University, Birmingham, UK. He lectures in Operations Management and is a member of the Technology and Operations Management research group at Aston. He is author of *Simulation Modelling for Business* published by Ashgate Ltd and is co-author of *Business Information Systems: Technology, Development and Management for the E-business* published by Pearson Education Ltd. His research interest is in the area of simulation modelling. He has over 50 publications, including papers in journals such as the *International Journal of Operations and Production Management, Journal of the Operational Research Society, Simulation, Technovation* and *Business Process Management Journal.* He has undertaken a number of teaching and consultancy projects in the area of simulation in the UK, Europe and Africa.

ACKNOWLEDGEMENTS

The author would like to thank the assistance of the team at John Wiley & Sons Ltd. in the compilation of this book. Special thanks go to Sarah Booth and Deborah Egleton. The author would also like to thank the team of reviewers for their constructive comments which have helped develop the book.

Part 1
Introduction

Chapter 1

Introduction

■ What Is Operations Management?

■ The History of Operations Management

■ The Role of Operations Management

■ Operations within the Organization

● The Process View of Operations

■ The Nature of Operations Management

● Service Operations Management

● Types of Service Operations

● The Strategic Role of Operations

● Technology and Operations Management

Learning Objectives

After reading this chapter, you should be able to:

1 Define the term 'operations management'.

2 Understand the role of operations in transforming the organization's inputs into finished goods and services.

3 Describe the process view of organizations.

4 Define the main types of service operations.

5 Understand the distinction between front-office and back-office tasks.

6 Understand the strategic role of operations.

7 Explain the relationship between technology and operations.

Introduction

Operations management decisions directly affect the size, shape, quantity, quality, price, profitability and speed of delivery of a company's output, whether the company produces a manufactured product such as a car or delivers a service such as insurance. This chapter introduces the concept of operations management and describes some of the decision areas it covers. Operations is examined in terms of its components and its role in the organization. The operations activity is defined as a transformation process and as such occurs throughout the organization. The operations function itself is defined as being concerned with transformation processes that provide goods and services for customers. Some key themes of operations management are also explored – namely, service operations management, the strategic role of operations and the use of technology in operations.

What Is Operations Management?

Operations management is about the management of the processes that produce or deliver goods and services. Not every organization will have a functional department called 'operations', but they will all undertake operations activities because every organization produces goods and/or delivers services.

Operations management has made a significant contribution to society by playing a role in areas such as increasing productivity, providing better quality goods and services and improving working conditions. Productivity has been increased through such measures as the use of technology (Chapter 6) and new production methods (Chapter 13). Increased productivity permits the more efficient production of goods and services and so helps raise living standards. Better quality goods and services are available through the use of quality initiatives such as Total Quality Management (TQM) (Chapter 17). The rate of improvement in quality levels is reflected in such programmes as Six Sigma (Chapter 17). Improved working conditions are an outcome of the realization that the contribution of people is vital to an organization's success. Job design (Chapter 9) is used to help enable the full potential of employees.

OPERATIONS MANAGEMENT:
the management of the processes that produce or deliver goods and services.

The operations manager will have responsibility for managing resources involved in this process. Positions involved in operations have a variety of names, and may differ between the manufacturing and service sectors. Examples of job titles involved in manufacturing include logistics manager and industrial engineer. Examples in service industry include operations control manager (scheduling flights for an airline), quality manager, hotel manager and retail manager. People involved in operations participate in a wide variety of decision areas in the organization, examples of which are given in Table 1.1.

Table 1.1   Decision Areas in Operations Management

Chapter	Decision area	Example decision
2	Operations Strategy	What strategy should be followed?
3	Process Types	How do we configure the process which will deliver our service to customers?
4	Layout Design	How do we organize the physical layout of our facilities and people?
5	Facility Design	What is the location of our operations facilities?
6	Process Technology	What role should technology have in the transformation of materials in the operations system?
7	Product and Service Design	What products and services should the organization provide?
8	Process Design	How do we design the service delivery process?
9	Job Design	How do we motivate our employees?
10	Planning and Control	How do we deploy our staff day-to-day?
11	Capacity Management	How do we ensure that our service is reliably available to our customers?
12	Inventory Management	How can we keep track of our inventory?
13	Lean Operations and JIT	How do we implement lean operations?
14	Enterprise Resource Planning	How do we organize the movement of goods across the supply chain?
15	Supply Chain Management	What benefits could e-procurement bring to our operations?
16	Project Management	How do we ensure our projects finish on time and within budget?
17	Improving Performance	How can we implement a TQM programme?
18	Measuring Performance	What role could Statistical Process Control (SPC) have in our operation?

The scale and importance, and hopefully the excitement, of operations management is indicated by the range of decision areas shown in Table 1.1. Like many texts on the subject area of operations management, this book is structured around these decision areas (see chapter references in Table 1.1). The overall organization of the book is also divided into sections on strategy (Chapter 2), design (Chapters 3–9), management (Chapters 10–16) and improvement (Chapters 17–18), to aid clarity.

Job Description for Operations Director (salary circa £65,000)

Operations Director

This company has established itself as a leading manufacturer within an industry sector where growth is encouraging overseas competitors to venture into the UK market. Profitable yet aware of the need to change, a plan has been put into place that will allow greater cohesiveness between manufacturing and commercial operations. Increased flexibility in production techniques is also on the corporate agenda with the development of new products associated with initiatives in this area. This is a key position within the executive team carrying responsibility for all aspects of company activity with the exception of finance and commercial functions.

The Role

- Devise and implement a business operations strategy that secures the achievement of profit and loss (p&l) objectives that are in line with the overall business plan.
- Management, motivation and development of the workforce (circa 120) through a period of change whilst ensuring continuous improvement of quality and operational efficiency.
- Create a culture of customer awareness that leads to collaborative product development and prompt resolution of issues that might affect perceptions of customer service.
- Influence the future direction of the business by being a fully participative member of the executive board.

The Candidate

- Graduate, operations or general manager of a customer-focused manufacturing business.
- Adept leader of change, able to devise innovative ways of working and ensure employee buy-in.

- Has implemented, or at the very least explored the feasibiity of, the transfer of some manufacturing activities to lower cost offshore alternatives.
- Clear communicator, numerate. Committed to achieving objectives and determined in overcoming obstacles.

The History of Operations Management

Operations management did not emerge as a formal field until the 1950s and 1960s when textbooks specifically dealing with operations management were published. Major developments up to this point impacting on the field of operations management start with the Industrial Revolution of the 18th century. Before this time products were made individually by skilled craftspeople in their homes and so were relatively expensive to produce. Inventions such as the steam engine (by James Watt in England in 1764) and concepts such as the use of interchangeable parts (Eli Whitney, 1790) and the division of labour (described by Adam Smith, 1776) led to the move to volume production. Here mechanization (provided by steam power) was combined with the use of low-skilled labour (people were given small, simple tasks using the concept of the division of labour) to produce standard parts in high volumes which could be assembled into products. These ideas were refined and the use of scientific management, developed by Frederick W. Taylor and incorporating such elements as time study (Chapter 9), and the invention of the moving assembly line, first used by the car manufacturer Henry Ford in 1913, led to the era of mass production at the start of the 20th century. This represented a major breakthrough in the ability of production systems to offer goods to a large number of customers at a price they could afford.

An additional element in the make-up of operations management occurred during World War II when the need to solve complex problems of logistics and weapons system design led to the development of the area of operations research. A number of the techniques developed then are still part of the operations management field today. As stated earlier, operations management as a discipline then began to emerge in the 1960s and has continued to develop since.

The 1970s saw the use of computers in Materials Requirements Planning (MRP) software (Chapter 14) for inventory control and scheduling. The 1980s saw the emergence of the Just-In-Time (JIT) philosophy (Chapter 13) from Japan which transformed the way businesses deliver goods and services. In response to the need to improve the quality of goods and service the ideas of Total Quality Management (TQM) (Chapter 17) were widely adopted in the 1980s. The 1990s saw the emergence of such concepts as supply chain management (Chapter 15) and Business Process Reengineering (BPR) (Chapter 17). Most recently, the use of the Internet to conduct transactions or e-commerce (Chapter 6) has changed the way operations management is performed.

The history of operations shows how the field has adapted and continues to change as it tries to respond to an ever greater range of challenges, from the needs of customers who require high-quality, low-price goods delivered quickly to managing the impacts of global competition and addressing environmental concerns.

The Role of Operations Management

We will start by considering that the role of operations management is to manage the transformation of an organization's inputs into finished goods and services (Figure 1.1).

The input activity involves two categories of resources. Transforming resources are the elements that act on, or carry out, the transformation process on other elements. The two main types of transforming resources are:

■ Facilities, such as building, equipment and process technology. The management of these operations' resources are covered in Chapters 3–8. The use of process technology to transform material, information and customer resources is covered in Chapter 6.
■ Staff, all the people involved in the operations process. In services the customer may well be involved as a transforming resource. Think of a fast-food restaurant where the customer is expected to order the food and take it to their table and clear up afterwards. The management of human resources in operations is covered in Chapter 9.

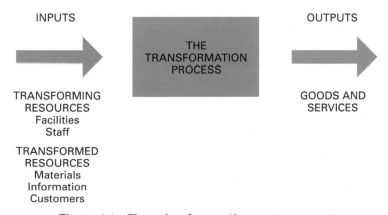

Figure 1.1   The role of operations management

The nature and mix of the transforming resources will differ between operations. The transformed resources, which are the elements acted on by the transforming resources, give the operations system its purpose or goal. The three main types of transformed resource are:

- *Materials* – these can be transformed either physically (e.g., manufacturing), by location (e.g., transportation), by ownership (e.g., retail) or by storage (e.g., warehousing).
- *Information* – this can be transformed by property (e.g., accountants), by possession (e.g., market research), by storage (e.g., libraries) or by location (e.g., telecommunications).
- *Customers* – they can be transformed either physically (e.g., hairdresser), by storage (e.g., hotels), by location (e.g., airlines), by physiological state (e.g., hospitals) or by psychological state (e.g., entertainment).

The transformation process itself will transform the material, information and customer resources in the way described above in order to produce goods and services.

Operations within the Organization

So far, we have dealt with providing an overview of operations itself. This section discusses the role of operations in relation to other areas within the organization. Three of the most important functional areas in an organization can be classified as the operations, marketing and finance functions. The marketing function works to find and create demand for the company's goods and services by understanding customer needs and developing new markets. The need for marketing and operations to work closely together is particularly important as the marketing function will provide the forecast of demand from which operations can plan sufficient capacity in order to deliver goods and services on time. The finance function is responsible for the obtaining and controlling of funds and covering decisions such as investment in equipment and other operations resources such as personnel and materials.

Other functions which play a supporting role in the organization include the Human Resources (HR) function which will play a role in regard to recruitment and labour relations, the Research and Development (R&D) function which generates and investigates the potential of new ideas and the Information Technology (IT) department which supplies and co-ordinates the computer-based information needs of the organization.

The relationship between functions can be seen as a number of sub-systems within the system called the 'organization'. Thus, each function (e.g., marketing) can be treated using the same input/process/output transformation model as the operations function. In other words, each function within the organization can be treated as performing an operations activity, as they are transforming inputs into outputs. This implies every part of the organization is involved in the operations activity (to an internal or external customer) and, thus, the theory of operations covered in this book is relevant to them.

The Process View of Operations

There has been criticism of the view of the organization as a number of functions. Melan (1993) considers the following conditions are usually built into the functional structure:

■ Rewards systems that promote values and support the objectives of the functional department rather than the business in its entirety.
■ Group behaviour, which encourages a strong loyalty within the department and an us versus them attitude toward other departments within the firm.
■ A high degree of decentralization, creating firms within the firm, each with its own agenda.

These and other deficiencies of the functional organization have led to a move away from considering business as a set of discrete functional areas towards a view of the organization as consisting of sets of processes which link together in order to meet customer needs. Each process can be treated using the input/process/output transformation model as with the functional perspective, but there is a clear emphasis on breaking down the barriers between departments and ensuring that output meets customer requirements. Processes can be carried out by separate individuals (individual processes), contained within a department (functional processes) or occur in several functional areas (cross-functional processes). An example of a process view of an organization is shown in Figure 1.2.

In functional terms, the processes would be situated in areas such as operations, marketing and finance, but from the customer's view the value they gain is dependent on the performance of the set of linked processes involved in the delivery of the product/service. The term 'value added' is used to denote the amount of value a process creates for its internal or external customer. The set of processes used to create value for a customer is often called the **value chain**. The value chain includes primary processes that directly create the value the customer perceives and support processes that assist the primary process in adding value. The key issue is that the configuration of the value chain should be aligned with the particular way the organization provides value to the customer.

VALUE CHAIN:
the set of processes used to create value for a customer.

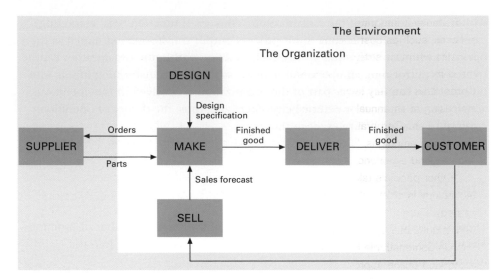

Figure 1.2   Process view of an organization

Card Corporation

Founded in 1988 by Ivor Jacobs, Card Corporation aims to plug a market gap by producing short-run print items such as business stationery. It can only achieve its aim by being a seamless end-to-end e-business – internally integrated and open to its supply chain partners. Its own systems focus on providing a cost-effective, high-quality service and eliminating many of the costs and delays associated with communication and the transfer of information. This integrated approach to technology has given the company a single system that offers:

☐ online ordering, design, approval, dispatch and order tracking;
☐ automatic data capture;
☐ the conversion of designs from low resolution (on the website) to high resolution (in print);
☐ the rendering of material into a press-ready format;
☐ digital printing;
☐ automated guillotining and finishing.

Having built its own technology infrastructure, the company is also well placed to amend its processes in response to customer requests. "Whenever a customer or supplier comes to us and says they'd like a certain feature to be added, we go back and write it in. They're the people who are using it, so we have to take their suggestions on board," says Ivor.

Because it integrated technology from the start, many of the traditional measures of success, such as cost savings or increased sales, don't apply to Card Corporation. The benefits are more straightforward – technology made the company possible. It enabled the company to meet an unanswered demand and to do so very profitably. Card Corporation has very few direct competitors and, with sales snowballing, turnover is increasing at an annual rate of 80–90%. Its pioneering role in the industry has also allowed Card Corporation to grow through word of mouth, rather than through extensive marketing campaigns. "People tell other people about our site because they've had such a good experience from it," says Ivor.

"Other people's take-up of faster bandwidths and general misunderstanding of what technology is all about is a barrier," admits Ivor. As an early adopter of an e-business strategy, Card Corporation's response is to help move its trading partners forward as well. It does this by building simple but powerful features into its system that will provide demonstrable benefits to clients. For example, the company has set up an automated online approval tool and has built sufficient flexibility into its system so that it can develop new offerings in response to client requests. This adaptability helps clients see the benefits of technology and encourages them to e-enable their businesses. Although cost is a major consideration for all businesses, Ivor feels that you have to be patient about when you will see a return on your investment: "You have to be persistent and push through any financial obstacles."

Ivor sees consumer adoption of broadband as the next significant step for the growth of the company and for e-business generally. "We're hoping that more customers embrace broadband – as we do a lot of image swapping, broadband would speed up the process markedly for us," he explains.

Source: Department of Trade and Industry. www.dti.gov.uk
Crown copyright material is reproduced with the permission of HMSO and the Queen's Printer for Scotland

1   Describe the main processes at the Card Corporation.

2   How are the resources transformed by the processes at the Card Corporation?

**Case Study 1.1
Questions**

The Nature of Operations Management

Operations management is constantly changing and here are some of the key themes:

■ The role of services in operations management.
■ The strategic role of operations.
■ The role of technology in operations management.

Service Operations Management

Although historically associated with manufacturing industry there has been a shift in the theory and practice of operations management to incorporate service systems. This is partly due to the importance of the service industry which accounts for an increasing proportion of the output of industrialized economies. In developed countries, manufacturing output has fallen steadily as a proportion of GDP from 28.9% in 1960 to 18.9% in 2000 (UNCTAD, 2003). Employment in manufacturing as a share of total employment in developed countries has also fallen from 26.5% of the workforce to 17.3% in 2000 (UNCTAD, 2003). In the European Union between 1995 and 2001, four service sectors (other business activities, health and social work, computer activities and education) created 6.7 million new jobs; the equivalent of 58% of total job creation (www.dti.gov.uk/ewt/servgen.htm).

There is some disagreement about what constitutes the service sector, but in the widest sense it can be seen as organizations that do not fall into what the economists call the primary sector (farming, forestry and fishing) or secondary sector (industries including manufacturing, mining and construction). Table 1.2 provides some examples of service and non-service operations systems.

Table 1.2 Examples of service and non-service operations

Services		*Non-services*	
Transportation	Postal Airlines Trucks	Agriculture	Crops Livestock Fishing
Utilities	Electric Gas Water	Manufacturing	Electronic goods Cars Aircraft
Retail	Food Furniture Eating	Mining	Coal Oil Gas
Financial	Banks Insurance Estate agents	Construction	Buildings Roads
Personal services	Hotels Cinema Car maintenance		
Social services	Health Education Charities		

The rise to prominence of the service sector in the economies of developed countries is due to an increase in what are termed 'consumer services and producer services'.

Consumer services are services aimed at the final consumers and these have risen in line with people's increasing disposable income in developed countries. Once expenditure on essentials such as food and shelter have been accounted for, people will then spend on purchases such as travel, hotels, restaurants and other social and personal services.

Producer services are used in the production and delivery of goods and services and constitute firms providing services such as consultancy advice, legal advice, IT support, transportation and maintenance facilities. The rise of producer services indicates that although the share of manufacturing is declining, it still plays an important part in a nation's economy. This is because many of the producer services are actually in business to provide services to manufacturers. Also, many of these services that are being provided were once undertaken by manufacturers themselves and were thus classified as part of the manufacturing sector!

Manufacturing also dominates trade between countries in the EU. The public and private service sectors account for almost 70% of EU employment and just over 70% of gross value added, but just 20% of intra-EU trade. This is partly due to the 'non-tradability' of some services, but it is also due to barriers to cross-border service provision between Member States. The poor performance of services may explain part of the difference in competitiveness between the EU and the USA (www.dti.gov.uk/ewt/servgen.htm). Although there has been much discussion regarding the loss of manufacturing jobs in developed countries there is also evidence that service jobs are subject to being moved abroad also (see Case Study 1.2).

CASE STUDY 1.2

More European Companies Moving Services Offshore

European companies, especially British ones, are increasingly following their US counterparts in shifting service operations abroad, according to a survey published yesterday. Nearly half the companies questioned – drawn from Europe's top 500 – planned to move more services offshore in the next few years, driven primarily by the need to cut costs to maintain competitiveness. However, the survey, conducted jointly by the United Nations Conference on Trade and Development (UNCTAD) in Geneva and Munich-based Roland Berger Strategy Consultants, also shows that Europe, including the UK, is a favoured destination for many European companies seeking to relocate service activities.

British companies were the source of 61% of the total number of service jobs moved offshore, followed by Germany and the Benelux countries, with 14% each. Top destinations were Asia, mostly India, with 37% of projects, western Europe with 29% and eastern Europe with 22%. In western Europe the main locations were the UK, Ireland, Spain and Portugal; in eastern Europe, Poland, Hungary and Romania. In terms of jobs rather than projects, India was by far the most important offshore destination because the projects sent there tended to be larger, according to the survey.

Companies said cost reduction was the main motive for going offshore, typically reporting savings between 20 and 40%. In all, about 80% said their projects had been successful, with only 3% dissatisfied. About 60% of current or planned projects involved 'back-office' services such as finance, accounting, information technology support and human resources functions. About a third had moved or were considering moving 'front-office' services such as customer call centres. Despite the favourable experience of those companies that were already moving services offshore, about half the European companies surveyed had no plans to do so.

Source: Frances Williams, FT.com, June 15, 2004. © **The Financial Times Ltd**

Case Study 1.2 Question

1   What are the advantages and disadvantages of moving service operations abroad?

Types of Service Operations

In order to assess the challenges for operations in managing services it is useful to determine the characteristics of different services. It is useful to distinguish between the design of the service (Chapter 7) and the design of the system that delivers the service (Chapter 8). Services themselves can be classified by their tangibility, while the way they are delivered can be classified by their simultaneity.

Tangibility

TANGIBILITY:

if goods are tangible, they are a physical thing you can touch. A service is intangible and can be seen as a process that is activated on demand.

This is the most commonly used distinction between goods and services. Goods are **tangible**, they are a physical thing you can touch. A service is intangible and can be seen as a process that is activated on demand. In reality, however, both goods and services have both tangible and intangible elements and can be placed on a continuum ranging from low to high intangibility. For example, the food in a fast-food restaurant is a major tangible element of the service. The food in a restaurant is still an important element, but other intangible elements such as waiter service and décor are important factors too. In fact, most operations systems produce a mixture of goods and services. Most goods have some supporting service element (e.g., a maintenance contract with a new washing machine), called a facilitating service, while many services will have supporting goods (e.g., a report provided by a management consultant), termed a facilitating good. More information on the design of the service package (the bundle of goods and services) is given in Chapter 7 on product and service design.

The fact that services are intangible implies another important characteristic of **perishability**. Because a service is not a physical thing that can be stored, but is a process, it must be consumed when it is produced or it will perish. The service provided by an empty seat in a restaurant or by an empty seat on an aircraft cannot be stored for use later. Thus, revenue lost from these unused resources can never be recovered. This would not be a problem if the demand (in terms of volume and timing) for a service could be accurately determined and service capacity provided to match this. However, this is unlikely to be the case and unlike most goods, which can be stored if demand is lower than capacity to be used when demand is greater than capacity, services must always attempt to match supply and demand. This topic is considered in more detail in Chapter 11 on capacity management.

> **PERISHABILITY:** because a service is not a physical thing that can be stored, but is a process, it must be consumed when it is produced or it will perish.

Simultaneity

Simultaneity relates to the characteristic that services are produced and consumed simultaneously. This means the service provider and customer will interact during the service delivery process. The amount of interaction is termed the **degree of customer contact**. In fact, the customer is unlikely to be a passive receiver of the service, but will be involved to a greater or lesser extent in the actual delivery of the service itself. For instance, a supermarket requires the customer to choose and transport the goods around the store and queue at an appropriate checkout till. However, it should not be assumed that all employees in a service operation have to deal directly with a customer. For the supermarket example, the checkout till is an example of high customer contact, but stores personnel may not have to deal directly with the customer at all. This distinction in services is denoted by 'back-office' tasks which add value to the inputs of the service operation (e.g., stocktaking) and 'front-office' tasks which deal with the customer both as an input and output of the operation (Figure 1.3).

> **SIMULTANEITY:** characteristic of services that are produced and consumed at the same time.

> **DEGREE OF CUSTOMER CONTACT:** the amount of interaction between the service provider and customer during the service delivery process.

Different organizations will have a different balance between front- and back-office operations. A front-office-based operation will be focused on the service experience of the customer and this is where most value will be added. Some traditional back-office-focused organizations, such as manufacturers, are increasing the role of service experience and, thus, their front-office operations. This is because they judge that the ability to differentiate on the service aspect of their offering may provide a longer term source of competitive advantage than they can achieve by differentiating with the goods themselves. Some other organizations are, however, moving in the opposite direction and recognizing that customer

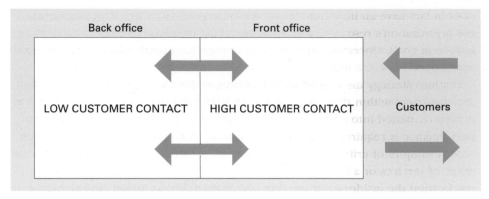

Figure 1.3   Front office and back office in operations management

value is being added by the tangible aspect of the service package delivered by the back-office operations. For example, budget airlines have eliminated many front-line service aspects of the flight experience and focused on the transportation of the customer process itself.

The fact that services require simultaneity and are produced and consumed simultaneously, implies another important characteristic of **heterogeneity**. This refers to the interaction of the customer, service provider and surroundings causing variability in the performance of the service. From the perspective of the service provider, humans by their nature are likely to vary their actions and sometimes make mistakes. Also, individual customers will perceive the quality of the service differently and the context of the service encounter (e.g., the existence of queues or weather conditions) may also impact on the service. This variability in performance and perceptions may lead to difficulties in maintaining a consistent level of service quality.

Some services, termed 'mass services', which operate at high volume and low variety of outcome, attempt to reduce variability due to heterogeneity by standardizing the service. This can be achieved by using approaches such as training staff to follow standard procedures and using equipment to support the service delivery process. This approach may not, however, be appropriate for professional services, which operate at low volume and high variety because here the customer requires high levels of contact with the service provider and a customized service. Service types such as mass service and professional service are covered in more detail in Chapter 3 'Process Types'.

HETEROGENEITY:
the interaction of the customer, service provider and surroundings causing variability in the performance of the service.

The Strategic Role of Operations

Despite the termed 'operations', operations management is not simply about the day-to-day (i.e., operational) running of an organization. Operations management does in fact have an important strategic role in ensuring that the management of the organization's resources and processes move the organization closer to its long-term goals. Operations strategy can be seen from market-based and resource-based perspectives. Using a **market-based operations strategy** approach to operations strategy the organization makes a decision regarding the markets and the customers within those markets that it intends to target. This market position is then translated into a list of criteria or objectives which define what kind of performance is required in order to successfully compete in the markets chosen. Some examples of criteria for performance are terms such as fast delivery, a wide range of services or a low price. A **resource-based operations strategy** view works from the inside-out of the firm, rather than the outside-in perspective of the market-based approach. Here an assessment of the operation's tangible and intangible resources and processes leads to a view of the operations capability. More detail on operations strategy is provided in Chapter 2 'Operations Strategy'.

MARKET-BASED OPERATIONS STRATEGY: the organization makes a decision regarding the markets and the customers within those markets that it intends to target.

RESOURCE-BASED OPERATIONS STRATEGY: an assessment of the operation's tangible and intangible resources and processes leads to a view of the operations capability.

Technology and Operations Management

Technology plays a key role in the transformation process for which operations is responsible. **Process technology** is used to help transform the three main categories of transformed resources, which are materials, customers and information. One of the most widely used and useful process technologies is Computer-Aided Design (CAD) which allows testing of product and service designs using computer-based drawings. Customer processing technology such as automated teller machines can reduce or eliminate the need for employee contact in customer-facing operations. Information technologies such as e-business systems are having a major effect on how firms organize their supply chains and utilize their capacity. More details on process technology are provided in Chapter 6 'Process Technologies'.

PROCESS TECHNOLOGY: used to help transform the three main categories of transformed resources, which are materials, customers and information.

CASE STUDY 1.3

'First Bank' PLC

'First Bank' has recently begun to offer Internet banking to extend their range of services to the customer and decrease the demand on their branch personnel. However, the web site has been experiencing difficulties with a slow response rate to customer inquiries. Demand for the Internet service has also been much lower than expected. As Operations Manager the company requires your view on the following issues.

1   What are the competitive consequences of 'pulling out' of Internet banking for the company?

2   What impact will a decision to 'pull out' of Internet banking have on the company in terms of future technology-based initiatives.

3   How can the bank improve customer take-up of its Internet banking initiative?

Summary

1   Operations management is about the management of the processes that produce or deliver goods and services.

2   The operations system can be seen as a transformation process. It converts inputs known as transformed resources (classified as materials, information and customers) using transforming resources (classified as staff and facility) into finished goods and services.

3   An alternative to the functional perspective of an organization is a process view in which the organization is seen as consisting of a set of processes which link together to meet customer needs.

4   Service organizations can be classified by their tangibility (the extent to which they incorporate a physical thing you can touch). The way services are delivered can be classified by their simultaneity (the extent to which the service is produced and consumed at the same time).

5   Service operations can be denoted by front-office tasks which deal directly with the customer and back-office tasks which add value to the inputs of the service operation.

6   Operations management has an important strategic role in ensuring that the management of the organization's resources and processes direct the organization closer to its long-term goals.

7   Technology plays a key role in the transformation of materials, customers and information for which operations is responsible.

Exercises

1. Look at a recruitment web site or the recruitment section of a newspaper and locate three operations roles in job advertisements in the manufacturing industry and three in the service industry.

2. How would you distinguish between the fields of operations management and operations research?

3. Identify the main transformed and transforming resources for the types of organizations below:

☐ fast-food restaurant;

☐ hotel;

☐ university;

☐ food retailer;

☐ car manufacturer.

4. Explain the use of the process view of organizations.

5. What are the implications of moving tasks between the front-office and back-office areas of a service operation?

6. Explain the term 'heterogeneity' as applied to service operations.

References

Melan, E.H. (1993), *Process Management: Methods for Improving Products and Services*, McGraw-Hill.

Porter, M.E. and Millar, V.E. (1985), How information gives you competitive advantage, *Harvard Business Review*, July/August, 149–160.

UNCTAD (2003), *Trade and Development Report: Capital Accumulation, Growth and Structural Change*, available online at **www.unctad.org**

Web link: **www.dti.gov.uk/ewt/servgen.htm**

Further Reading

Gaither, N. and Frazier, N. (2002), *Operations Management*, 9th Edition, South-Western College Publishing.

Johnston, R. and Clark, G. (2005), *Service Operations Management: Improving Service Delivery*, Pearson Education Ltd.

Slack, N. and Lewis, M. (2006), *Operations Strategy*, 2nd Edition, Pearson Education Ltd.

Slack, N., Chambers, S. and Johnston, R. (2004), *Operations Management*, 4th Edition, Pearson Education Ltd.

Van Looy, B., Gemmel, P. and Van Dierdonck, R.V. (eds) (2003), *Services Management: An Integrated Approach*, 2nd Edition, Pearson Education Ltd.

Vonderembse, M.A. and White, G.P. (2004), *Core Concepts of Operations Management*, John Wiley & Sons.

Web Links

Selected List of Operations Management Web Sites

www.euroma-online.org/associations/euroma/index.asp European Operations Management Association (EUROMA). Leading association for operations managers. Contains information on conferences, workshops and publications.

www.eisam.org European Institute for Advanced Studies in Management (EISAM). International network for management research and teaching.

www.iomnet.org.uk Institute of Operations Management. A professional body for those involved in operations management in the UK. Contains links to online resources.

www.informs.org/resources Institute for Operations Research and Management Science. Resources such as web guides, journals and links to societies in the field of Operations Research.

www.poms.org Production and Operations Management Society. International society providing resources such as journals and encylopedias of operations management terms.

www.mas.dti.gov.uk/home.jsp Manufacturing Advisory Service. DTI site for UK manufacturers.

www.manu-online.co.uk The Manufacturing Institute. Contains news and events on manufacturing in the UK.

www.apics.org The Association for Operations Management. Resources such as industry news in operations management.

www.mhhe.com/omc/index.html Operations Management Center. Resources regarding operations management for students and professionals.

www.brint.com An extensive search engine for business technology resources.

www.unctad.org United Nations Conference on Trade and Development. Provides links to a number of reports regarding world trade and economic development issues.

www.ame.org The Association for Manufacturing Excellence. Events and publications aimed at improving productivity.

Selected List of Operations Management Academic Journals

www.emeraldinsight.com/ijpom *International Journal of Operations and Production Management (IJOPM)*

www.sciencedirect.com/science/journal/02726963 *Journal of Operations Management (JOM)*

www.poms.org/POMSWebsite/Journal.html *Production and Operations Management (POM)*

www.msom.org *Manufacturing and Service Operations Management*

www.jsr.sagepub.com/ *Journal of Service Research*

www.sciencedirect.com/science/journal/01664972 *Technovation*

www.pdma.org/journal and **http://www.sciencedirect.com/science/journal/07376782** *Journal of Product Innovation Management*

www.sciencedirect.com/science/journal/02637863 *International Journal of Project Management*

www.sciencedirect.com/science/journal/09255273 *International Journal of Production Economics*

www.sciencedirect.com/science/journal/09697012 *European Journal of Purchasing and Supply Management*

Chapter 2
Operations Strategy

- ■ **What is Strategy?**
  - ● Levels of Strategy
- ■ **Judging the Contribution of Operations to Strategy**
- ■ **Measuring the Contribution of Operations to Strategy: The Performance Objectives**
  - ● Quality
  - ● Speed
  - ● Dependability
  - ● Flexibility
  - ● Cost
  - ● The Performance Objectives from an Internal and External Perspective
- ■ **Operations Strategy Approaches**
  - ● Market-based Approach to Operations Strategy
  - ● Resource-based Approach to Operations Strategy
  - ● Reconciling the Market-based Approach and Resource-based Strategy Approaches

■ Operations Strategy Formulation

- ● Step 1 Corporate Objectives
- ● Step 2 Marketing Strategy
- ● Step 3 How Do Products Win Orders in the Market Place?
- ● Step 4 Delivery System Choice (Structural Decisions)
- ● Step 5 Infrastructure Choice (Infrastructural Decisions)

■ Achieving Strategic Fit – Trade-offs, Focus and Agility

- ● Trade-offs
- ● Focus
- ● Agile Operations

Learning Objectives

After reading this chapter, you should be able to:

1 Explain how strategy can exist at three levels within the organization.

2 Discuss the five performance objectives.

3 Contrast the market-based and resource-based approaches to operations strategy.

4 Discuss the Hill framework for operations strategy formulation.

5 Discuss two measurements systems to identify the relative importance of the competitive factors.

6 Explain the concept of trade-offs in operations.

7 Explain the concept of focus in operations.

8 Explain the concept of agile operations.

Introduction

Operations management includes all the activities that are required to create or deliver a product or service. Operations engages the majority of the people employed and assets deployed in most organizations. Thus, the way operations is managed in the long term, the operations strategy, is likely to be a vital element of an organization's success. This chapter describes the role and formulation of operations strategy in the organization and discusses the increasing importance of the role of operations strategy. The purpose of operations in terms of an organization's strategy has often been seen as supportive, while functions such as marketing provide a competitive edge. Operations can, however, provide the basis of a firm's competitive strategy. The purpose of an operations strategy is to interpret the overall business strategy, which will be concerned with goals such as growth and profitability, into goals that direct how operations will be managed. These goals may be defined by the five operations performance objectives of quality, speed, dependability, flexibility and cost. In this chapter an approach to developing a strategy to achieve these goals is considered which is concerned with matching internal operations capability with external competitive market requirements.

What Is Strategy?

STRATEGY:
the direction and scope
of an organization over
the long term.

Strategy can be defined as follows (Johnson *et al.*, 2005):

> *Strategy is the direction and scope of an organization over the long term: ideally, which matches its resources to its changing environment, and, in particular, its markets, customers or clients so as to meet stakeholder expectations.*

Thus, strategic decisions occur as a result of an evaluation of the external and internal environment. The external evaluation may reveal market opportunities or

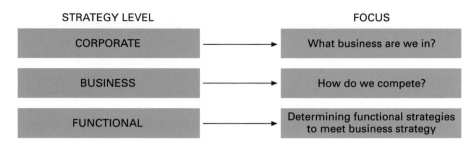

Figure 2.1 Levels of strategy

threats from competitors. The evaluation of the internal environment may reveal limitations in capabilities relative to competitors. Strategy is seen as complex in nature due to factors such as the high level of uncertainty in future consequences arriving from decisions, the need for integration of both long-term and day-to-day activities across the business and the fact that major change may have to be implemented as a consequence of strategic choices made.

Levels of Strategy

Strategy can be seen to exist at three main levels of corporate, business and functional within the organization (Figure 2.1).

Corporate Level Strategy

At the highest or **corporate level** the strategy provides long-range guidance for the whole organization, often expressed as a statement of its mission. The mission statement should define the key **stakeholders** whom the corporation will seek to satisfy and describe the overall strategy it will pursue to meet their objectives. Stakeholders can be defined as anyone with an interest in the activities of the organization and can be divided into three main groups:

■ Internal stakeholders include the organization's managers and employees. Employees will be concerned with issues such as job security, rewards, recognition and job satisfaction. In addition to these concerns, one of the key roles of management is to try to reconcile the competing interests of stakeholder groups of customers, investors and employees.
■ Connected stakeholders are parties with a direct connection with the organization such as customers, investors, shareholders, money lenders, distributors and suppliers. These will all have a variety of needs from the organization. For example, customers will be interested in the price, quality and

CORPORATE LEVEL STRATEGY: provides long-range guidance on the direction of the whole organization.

STAKEHOLDERS: anyone with an interest in the activities of an organization such as employees, customers and government.

service level of the goods and services that the organization delivers to the marketplace.

■ External stakeholders cover other parties that can impact on the organization, the most important of which is usually the government. Governments are involved in such activities as setting regulations in areas such as health and safety and environmental policies. Government grants may be available in certain geographical areas which may affect the operations location decision. Other external stakeholders include the local community and pressure groups.

Using the stakeholder model the goal of the organization should be to satisfy the needs of stakeholders which are necessary for the success of the organization in the long term.

CASE STUDY 2.1

Findus Foods

Here is an example of a vision/mission statement from a company web site.

The Findus Vision

We have a common purpose within the company to make the following 'Visions' a reality and these statements reflect the culture of the organization we are trying to develop. People make success, and so we want everyone to believe in our visions and work to achieve them.

Purpose

Findus will be one of the premier frozen food companies in Europe. Our consumers, employees, shareholders and communities will know us by the improvements we are making to their quality of life, through our superior products and the responsible way we create them.

Visions

☐ Findus products will be the consumer's first choice due to their superiority in taste, freshness and goodness.

☐ Findus will constantly lead the growth of the frozen food category at a pace never seen before.

☐ Findus will be the preferred supplier to all our customers.

☐ Findus will be a good place to work.

☐ Findus will set a new standard for corporate responsibility in the food industry.

☐ Findus will be organized to meet our business needs and will focus on the achievement of perfect customer and consumer service.

☐ Findus – The One Company.

Source: www.findus.com

1   Identify the stakeholder groups that are incorporated in the Findus vision statement.

Business Level Strategy

The second level of strategy is termed a 'business strategy' and may be for the organization or at the Strategic Business Unit (SBU) level in larger diversified companies. Here, the concern is with the products and services that should be offered in the market defined at the corporate level. The SBU must develop a strategy at this level which defines a competitive advantage for its products or services in the market. Competitive advantage may be achieved by strategies such as low cost, product innovation, or customization of a service to a niche market.

> **BUSINESS LEVEL STRATEGY:**
> strategy at the organizational or Strategic Business Unit (SBU) level in large companies. The strategy is concerned with the products and services that should be offered in the marked defined at the corporate level.

Functional Level Strategy

The third level of strategy is termed the operational or functional strategy where the functions of the business (e.g., operations, marketing, finance) make long-range plans which support the competitive advantage being pursued by the business strategy.

> **FUNCTIONAL LEVEL STRATEGY:**
> where the functions of the business (e.g., operations, marketing, finance) make long-range plans which support the competitive advantage being pursued by the business level strategy.

   The 'levels of strategy' model implies a 'top-down' structured approach to strategy formulation in which corporate goals are communicated down to business and then functional areas. Although there has always been interaction within this hierarchy in both directions, the role of functional areas such as operations in setting the framework for how a company can compete from the 'bottom-up' is being recognized. For example, the theory of emergent strategies (Mintzberg and Waters, 1995) shows how the implementation of strategy, rather than following a structure determined by a long-term plan, emerges from day-to-day experience at an operational level.

   The contribution of operations to strategy development and its relationship to the levels in the organization where strategy is developed is the focus of discussion in this chapter.

Judging the Contribution of Operations to Strategy

As stated, the contribution that operations can make to strategy development and implementation is being recognized. Hayes and Wheelwright (1988) assert that the success of organizations is dependent on their overall operations capability and so

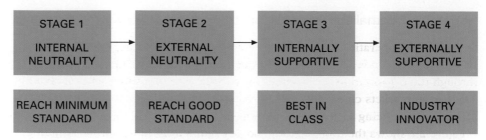

Figure 2.2 Four stages of judging operations contribution to strategy

provide a model which enables managers to identify operations' current strategic role and the changes needed in order to improve competitiveness. The four-stage model traces the contribution of the operations function from a largely reactive role in Stage 1 to a proactive element in competitive success in Stage 4 (Figure 2.2).

The stages are described as follows:

Stage 1   Internal Neutrality

Here, the operations function has very little to contribute to competitive success and is seen as a barrier to better competitive performance by other functions. The operations function is simply attempting to reach a minimum acceptable standard required by the rest of the organization whilst avoiding any major mistakes, hence the term 'internal neutrality'. However, a major mistake by operations could still have serious consequences for the rest of the organization (e.g., product recall).

Stage 2   External Neutrality

Here, the operations function begins to focus on comparing its performance with competitor organizations. Although it may not be innovative enough to be in the 'first division' of companies in its market, by taking the best ideas and attempting to match the performance of competitors it is attempting to be externally neutral.

Stage 3   Internally Supportive

Here, the operations function is one of the best in their market area and aspires to be the best in market. The operations function will thus be organizing and developing the operations capabilities to meet the strategic requirements of the organization. Thus, operations is taking a role in the implementation of strategy and being 'internally supportive'.

Stage 4   Externally Supportive

In Stage 4 the operations function is becoming central to strategy making and providing the foundation for future competitive success. This may be delivered through the organization of resources in ways that are innovative and capable of adapting as markets change. When operations is in the role of the long-term driver of strategy it is being 'externally' supportive.

Figure 2.2 shows the four stages of judging operations contribution to strategy and the corresponding role of the operations function in delivering the organization's strategy. As the organization moves from Stage 1 to Stage 4 its role moves from being reactive in response to strategic objectives passed down to it, to ensuring resources are developed to support the strategy, to (in Stage 4) providing the business with its competitive advantage.

Measuring the Contribution of Operations to Strategy: The Performance Objectives

The five basic **operations performance objectives** (Slack *et al.*, 2004) allow the organization to measure its operations performance in achieving its strategic goals. The operations performance objectives are:

■ quality;
■ speed;
■ dependability;
■ flexibility;
■ cost.

> **OPERATIONS PERFORMANCE OBJECTIVES:**
> can be measured by the five performance objectives of quality, speed, dependability, flexibility and cost.

Each one of these objectives will be discussed in terms of how they are measured and their significance to organizational competitiveness.

Quality

Quality (Chapter 17) covers both the quality of the design of the product or service itself (Chapter 7) and the quality of the process that delivers the product or service (Chapters 3, 6 and 8). From a customer perspective, quality characteristics include reliability, performance and aesthetics. From an operations viewpoint quality is related to how closely the product or service meets the specification required by the design, termed the 'quality of conformance'. In terms

> **QUALITY:**
> the product or service itself and the processes that produce the product or service.

of measurement, quality can be measured by the 'cost of quality' model covered in Chapter 17. Here, quality costs are categorized as either the cost of achieving good quality (the cost of quality assurance) or the cost of poor-quality products (the costs of not conforming to specifications). The advantages of good quality on competitiveness include:

- *Increased dependability* – fewer problems due to poor quality means a more reliable delivery process.
- *Reduced costs* – if things are done right first time, expenditure is saved on scrap and correcting mistakes.
- *Improved customer service* – a consistently high-quality product or service will lead to high customer satisfaction.

Speed

SPEED:
the time delay between a customer request for a product or service and then receiving that product or service.

Speed is the time delay between a customer request for a product or service and then receiving that product or service. The activities triggered from a customer request for a product or service will be dependent on whether a make-to-stock or customer-to-order delivery system is in place. The concept of $P:D$ ratios (Chapter 11) compares the demand time D (from customer request to receipt of goods or services) to the total throughput time P of the purchase, make and delivery stages. Thus, in a make-to-stock system D is basically the delivery time, but for a customer-to-order system (e.g., a service system) the customer demand time is equal to the purchase, make and delivery stages (P). In this case, the speed of the internal processes of purchase and make will directly affect the delivery time experienced by the customer.

Although the use of a make-to-stock system may reduce the delivery time as seen by the customer, it cannot be used for services and has disadvantages associated with producing for future demand in manufacturing. These include the risk of the products becoming obsolete, inaccurate forecasting of demand leading to stock-out or unwanted stock, the cost of any stock in terms of working capital and the decreased ability to react quickly to changes in customer requirements. Thus, the advantage of speed is that it can be used to both reduce costs (by eliminating the costs associated with make-to-stock systems) and reducing delivery time leading to better customer service.

DEPENDABILITY:
consistently meeting a promised delivery time for a product or service to a customer.

Dependability

Dependability refers to consistently meeting a promised delivery time for a product or service to a customer. Thus, an increase in delivery speed may not lead to customer satisfaction if it is not produced in a consistent manner. Dependability can be measured by the percentage of customers that receive a product or service within the delivery time promised. In some instances it may even be important to deliver not too quickly, but only at the time required (e.g., a consignment of wet concrete for construction!). Dependability leads to better customer service when the customer can trust that the product or service will be delivered when expected. Dependability can also lead to lower cost, in that progress checking and other activities designed to ensure things happen on time can be reduced within the organization. Key activities needed to increase dependability include planning and control mechanisms to ensure problems are uncovered early, and making dependability a key performance measure.

Flexibility

Flexibility is the ability of the organization to change what it does quickly. This can mean the ability to offer a wide variety of products or services to the customer and to be able to change these products or services quickly. Flexibility is needed so the organization can adapt to changing customer needs in terms of product range and varying demand and to cope with capacity shortfalls due to equipment breakdown or component shortage. The following types of flexibility can be identified:

> **FLEXIBILITY:**
> the ability of the organization to change what it does quickly. In terms of products or services this can relate to introducing new designs, changing the mix, changing the overall volume and changing the delivery timing.

■ *Product or service* – to be able to quickly act in response to changing customer needs with new product or service designs.
■ *Mix* – to be able to provide a wide range of products or services.
■ *Volume* – to be able to decrease or increase output in response to changes in demand. Volume flexibility may be needed for seasonal changes in demand. Services may have to react to demand changes minute by minute.
■ *Delivery* – this is the ability to react to changes in the timing of a delivery. This may involve the ability to change delivery priorities between orders and still deliver on time.

Flexibility can be measured in terms of range (the amount of the change) and response (the speed of the change). Table 2.1 outlines the range and response dimensions for the four flexibility types of product or service, mix, volume and delivery.

The range and response dimensions are connected in the sense that the more something is changed (range) the longer it will take (response). The relationship between the two can be observed by constructing range–response curves.

	Range flexibility	Response flexibility
Table 2.1 The range and response dimensions for the four system flexibility types		
Product or service flexibility	The range of products and services which the company has the capability to produce.	The time necessary to develop or modify the products and services and processes which produce them to the point where regular delivery can start.
Mix flexibility	The range of products and services which the company can deliver within a given time period.	The time necessary to adjust the mix of products and services being delivered.
Volume flexibility	The total output which the company can achieve for a given product and service mix.	The time taken to change the total level of output.
Delivery flexibility	The extent to which delivery dates can be changed.	The time taken to reorganize the delivery system for the new delivery date.

In general, the benefit of flexibility from the customer's point of view is that it speeds up response by being able to adapt to customer needs. The ability of the internal operation to react to changes will also help maintain the dependability objective.

CASE STUDY 2.2

Gecko Head Gear

Jeff Sacré turned his small, struggling, surfboard business into one of Europe's leading specialist helmet manufacturers on the basis of a casual conversation. His business was extremely seasonal and so he was looking to find a way of diversifying his products. Speaking to a lifeboatman, he found the RNLI needed a lighter, more suitable helmet for use on the seas. It happened that he had been working on a helmet for surfers and so was well placed to supply the RNLI. After eventually securing the contract with RNLI, the question for Sacré was where to take the business next.

Some potential markets sprang to mind immediately: specialist helmets could be usefully worn by river police, coastguard and customs officers – and a recent model has been designed specifically for helicopter winchmen. But, as the craze for new, extreme sports blossomed throughout the 1990s, a much wider market suddenly presented itself. Skateboarders, snowboarders, mountain bikers and powerboat racers all needed protection.

Prototype headgear was produced, tested and modified for each discipline, and users were encouraged to respond with comments and suggested improvements. Gecko soon discovered that producing low-volume, handmade products was a distinct advantage when it comes to satisfying the niche markets of extreme sports. It involved less financial risk and allowed for the continual, minor improvements that customers wanted. "We decided not to go down the automated production route," says Sacré "and it seems to have paid off. Making everything by hand gives us the crucial advantage of flexibility, so we can add altimeters and video cameras, torches and two-way radio systems – pretty well anything a customer asks for."

Source: The Department of Trade and Industry, www.dti.gov.uk
Crown copyright material is reproduced with the permission of HMSO and the Queen's Printer for Scotland

1   How has Gecko used flexibility to compete?

**Case Study 2.2
Question**

Cost

Cost is considered to be the finance required to obtain the inputs (i.e., transforming and transformed resources) and manage the transformation process which produces finished goods and services. If an organization is competing on price then it is essential that it keeps its cost base lower than the competition. Then it will either make more profit than rivals, if price is equal, or gain market share, if price is lower. Cost is also important for a strategy of providing a product or service to a market niche, which competitors cannot provide. Thus, cost proximity (i.e., to ensure costs are close to the market average) is important to maximize profits and deter competitors from entering the market.

> **COST:**
> the finance required to obtain the inputs and manage the transformation process which produces finished goods and services.

The major categories of cost are staff, facilities (including overheads) and material. The proportion of these costs will differ between operations but averages are staff 15%, facilities 30% and material 55%. Thus, it can be seen that the greatest scope for reducing cost lies with a reduction in the cost of materials. A relatively small proportion of costs are usually assigned to direct labour.

The level and mix of these costs will be dependent on the volume and variety of output and the variation in demand. Increased volume means that the cost per unit will decrease as resources can be dedicated to the production or delivery of a particular service. However, diseconomies of scale (Chapter 5) can still occur due to increased organizational complexity which can lead to poor communication. Increases in volume may be achieved with current resources or require significant investment in equipment and labour. The cost implications of increases in volume must therefore be considered carefully. Variety of output will increase complexity and, thus, costs. However, this complexity can be reduced by using such techniques as design simplification and standardization, increasing mix flexibility in moving from one product to another.

Finally, cost is dependent on the other performance objectives. It was noted earlier that increased flexibility can lead to a decrease in the cost of the product or service design. In fact, improvements in all the performance objectives can lead to a reduction in cost.

The Performance Objectives from an Internal and External Perspective

We can categorize the benefits of excelling at the performance objectives from an internal and external perspective (Table 2.2). This is useful because, even though a performance objective may have little relevance in achieving performance that external stakeholders, such as customers, value, it may bring benefits in improving the capability of operations from an internal perspective. When we look at approaches to strategy in the next section we find that competitiveness is not just a matter of simply improving performance along specific external competitive dimensions, but incorporates the development of internal capabilities that provide specific operating advantages.

You may have noticed in Table 2.2 that the internal benefit of low cost derives from improving performance of the other performance objectives. Figure 2.3 shows how this is determined and, thus, provides an indication of how operations can combine the performance criteria of low cost with criteria such as high

Table 2.2   Internal and external benefits of the performance objectives

Performance objective	Internal (operations) benefits	External (market) benefits
Quality	Reduces costs and increases dependability	Providing error-free products
Speed	Reduces queues and inventories	Get products to customers fast
Dependability	Saves money, time and minimises disruption	Meeting delivery commitments
Flexibility	Able to absorb some of the problems caused by changing demand	Cope with changing demands
Cost	The effects of high quality, speed, dependability and flexibility are generally to reduce costs within the operation	Being able to offer the product to the market at a price it will bear, while still achieving a return for the business

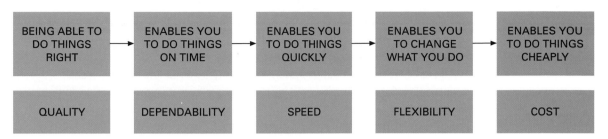

Figure 2.3 All of the performance objectives affect cost

quality and flexibility. It also shows that strategies that rely on immediate cost cutting (and, thus, risk damage to the operations capability) could be replaced by strategies that aim to improve performance on the other performance objectives which will then lead to a reduction in cost. It has been suggested that an improvement strategy should tackle the performance objectives in the order of quality, dependability, speed, flexibility and finally cost (Slack *et al.*, 2004).

CASE STUDY 2.3

Operations Strategy in Action

Almost every company seems to be restructuring itself to face the downturn, be it through financial engineering, or by retrenching to core activities. So, they sell off foreign subsidiaries (Aviva), recent diversifications (ABB), or in desperate cases almost anything that's worth something and isn't nailed to the floor (Vivendi and Marconi). Oddly, few firms make a thing about going back to the real basics, which is manufacturing or, more accurately, operations. Odd, because competing operationally – making and selling things better and more cheaply than the opposition – is the simplest and best strategy of all. In tough times like these, most other 'strategies' look like sorry substitutes for failing to get the basics right in the first place.

Consider the PC industry, where the undisputed leader, Dell, is an operations story par excellence. By managing boring old logistics and distribution – building to order and selling direct to consumers – supremely well, Dell has streamlined operations and costs so effectively that it can cut prices aggressively to gain market share while rivals HP/ Compaq, IBM and Gateway struggle to keep up. Dell has profitably pushed up its market share from 5 to 15% in the past 5 years, while other technology companies retrench and retreat. It is also launching enthusiastically into printers and other peripherals – a strategic move, to be sure, but hardly one that took rocket science to figure out. If Dell can make and sell attractive computers more cheaply than its rivals, it's a fair bet it can do the same for printers and the rest as well.

Schefenacker Vision Systems (formerly part of Britax) is a maker of car wing mirrors. Schefenacker has been improving its mirrors for more than 10 years. It can now satisfy the most demanding customers – for example, from its plant near Portsmouth it delivers a possible 420 permutations of mirrors daily direct to Jaguar's assembly line in the Midlands to match each car that comes down the assembly line.

The ability to do this cost-effectively is an entry ticket to lots of international business. Less obviously, the company's virtuosity allows it to design and build better, more sophisticated parts – for instance, with lighting or electronics built in. That allows it to go upmarket, where margins are wider. At the same time, as with Dell, it also gives it the possibility of expanding up and down the value chain. Thanks to relentless emphasis on doing more with less, over the past year Schefenacker has freed up space on the factory floor for five new production cells. It uses these to manufacture simple parts which it had previously outsourced to others. Strategic result: Schefenacker no longer pays the other guy's profit margin, spreads overheads across a larger base and can suck waste out of a larger section of the supply chain. Manufacturing director Mickey Love says: "Lean production gives you an opportunity to make things that you can sell to customers you didn't have before."

Of all the advantages of operations excellence as a strategy, its impact on people is the most momentous. In firms that take this route, improvement of every aspect of design, manufacture, distribution, delivery and service is by definition strategic. Better product quality or a day sliced off delivery lead time is a strategic, not tactical, move. That means improvement is part of the day job for every individual; which also means 100% participation, with no choice.

The secret is that operating excellence makes strategy easy. As Richard Schonberger, one of the original proselytizers for lean manufacturing, said: "What makes a great team is the basics. Then almost anything the coach chooses to do makes the coach look like a shrewd strategist."

Source: Excerpt from 'Business: The basics that beat the world: Making things better and cheaper is the best strategy of all' by Simon Caulkin, *The Observer*, 3 November 2002
Reproduced by permission of Simon Caulkin

Case Study 2.3 Questions

1   Read the article and discuss how operations can provide strategic advantage.

2   Discuss the performance of the company in terms of the five performance objectives.

Operations Strategy Approaches

The nature of the development of approaches to operations strategy has changed over time. For most of the 20th century market conditions were characterized by a mass production era with an emphasis on high volume and low cost production. Operations strategy was characterized by improving efficiency through aspects such as achieving a high utilization of equipment and having a closely supervised workforce undertaking standardized operations. This perspective was challenged by a new approach from Japan of lean operations (Chapter 13). Here, the emphasis was not on low cost and high volume, but on operations providing capabilities in areas such as reliability, speed and flexibility. This was achieved through such aspects as training staff in problem solving, using general purpose equipment for flexibility and eliminating waste in all its forms. Neither of the approaches of 'mass' or 'lean' can be seen as strategies in themselves in that to be successful an operations strategy should support the competitive advantage being pursued by the business strategy. This means that the aim of the organization's operations strategy will be to seek a fit between the way it competes in the market and how operations is designed and managed. This 'fit' can be achieved in many ways and will in part be dependent on the operations current capabilities.

Market-based Approach to Operations Strategy

Figure 2.4 shows the main elements of the **market-based approach to operations strategy**.

Using this approach an organization makes a decision regarding the markets and the customers within those markets that it intends to target. Along with meeting customer needs within a market the position the organization takes in that market will in part depend on the actions of its competitors. Thus, the organization's market position is one in which its performance enables it to attract customers to its products or services in a more successful manner than its competitors. The next step is to translate the market position into a list of criteria or objectives which define what kind of performance is required in order to successfully compete in the markets chosen. Different authors use different terms for these measures – e.g., 'performance criteria' (Hill, 2005) and 'competitive priorities' (Gaither, 2002) – but the term 'competitive factors' will be used here. 'Competitive factor' is the term used to describe the dimension on which a product or service wins orders in the Hill methodology for Operations Strategy formulation described

MARKET-BASED APPROACH TO OPERATIONS STRATEGY: based on decisions regarding the markets and the customers within those markets that the organization intends to target.

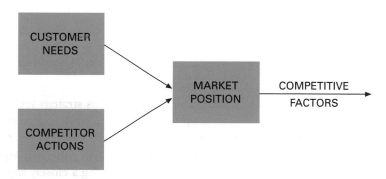

Figure 2.4   Market-based approach to operations strategy

later in this chapter. Some examples of competitive factors are terms such as fast delivery, a wide range of services or a low price.

Resource-based Approach to Operations Strategy

RESOURCE-BASED APPROACH TO OPERATIONS STRATEGY: based on an assessment of the operations resources and processes.

A **resource-based view of operations strategy** works from the inside-out of the firm, rather than the outside-in perspective of the market-based approach. Here, an assessment of the operations resources and processes leads to a view of the operations capability (Figure 2.5).

The operations resources are categorized in Chapter 1 into transforming and transformed resources. Transforming resources are the facilities and staff that do the work on the transformed resources that delivers the goods or services to the customer. The transformed resources can be classified into materials, customers and information. However, even more important to the capability of an organization may be its intangible resources such as brand loyalty, supplier relationships, technological skills, design skills and a detailed understanding of customer markets. What is important to consider regarding an organization's intangible resources is that their value may not be recognized (they may not necessarily be included on the firm's balance sheet) and they are most likely to have been developed over time through experience and a process of learning. This second attribute makes them less easy to copy by competitors than tangible assets that can be bought in relatively rapidly. Processes are the way in which the firm operates its resources. Processes may follow formal rules laid down in company documentation, but informal processes are likely to form a large part of the way in which the organization operates. Informal processes are undertaken in a way that is dependent on factors such as the knowledge accumulated by staff, the relationships between staff members and the shared values and understandings of members of the organization. The nature and complexity of formal and informal processes and tangible and intangible resources is central to the resource-based

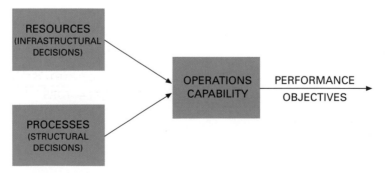

Figure 2.5   Resource-based approach to operations strategy

view of strategy that the externally unobservable (within firm) factors are at least as important as observable industry market (between firm) factors in determining competitive advantage. The area of organizational learning (Chapter 18) is relevant to a resource-based view of operations strategy in terms of managing and developing capabilities.

Reconciling the Market-based and Resource-based Strategy Approaches

It has been found that not all companies pursue strategy in accordance with a pure market-based approach and it has been found that competitiveness is not just a matter of simply improving performance along specific competitive dimensions, but incorporates the development of capabilities that provide specific operating advantages. Thus, the resource-based view of strategy is that operations takes a more active role in providing long-term competitive advantage. Thus, resource and process decisions are concerned, not only with implementing a chosen competitive strategy, but are required to provide the platform for the development of new capabilities that are difficult for competitors to replicate. Thus, the idea is that a resource-based view is not a substitute for a market position developed under a market-based view of strategy, but operation capabilities can allow a company to take up an attractive market position and can protect it from competitive threat (Figure 2.6).

What makes the development of operations strategy particularly challenging is that not only should the market-based and resource-based views of strategy need to be considered at a point in time, but the changing characteristics of markets and the need to develop operations capabilities over time means a dynamic as well as a static view of strategy is required. For example, dynamic capabilities (Slack, 1991) are built not only from the firm's resources and processes mediated by

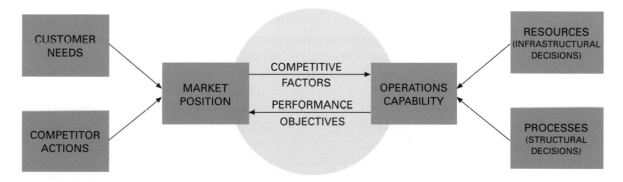

Figure 2.6   Reconciling the market-based and resource-based approaches to operations strategy

external market influences, but also driven by how managers make judgements about the firm and its future.

CASE STUDY 2.4

Texon

Sales of Texon jeans label material T484 continues to grow across the globe. Texon T484 cellulose material is available in eight different colour options, offering a distinct advantage over competitors who offer a very limited choice. Its product gauges run from 0.55 mm to 0.80 mm thick, and the material is available in rolls or sheets. Texon T484 was first introduced in 1991 when over 50 tons were sold. By 2003, the volume had increased to nearly 800 tons. From this quantity of almost 2 million square metres of material, labels can be produced for around 460 million pairs of jeans. 2004 is expected to see a significant growth with sales going into 34 countries around the world. According to statistics, the world production of jeans is estimated at around 3 billion pairs, of which approximately 1.5 to 1.7 billion pairs feature a label made from cellulose material. In other words, one-third of the world's production of jeans has a Texon jeans label. Texon continues to build on its shoemaking and innovative materials expertise to apply skills beyond footwear to other industries requiring high-quality, high-performance non-woven and cellulose products in apparel, automotive, furniture, luggage and filtration.

Source: 'Texon T484 "jeans label" success continues', www.texon.com
Reproduced by permission of Texon International

Case Study 2.4 Question

1 Relate market-based and resource-based strategy approaches to Texon.

Operations Strategy Formulation

The following approach to operations strategy provides useful guidance in dealing with the issue of aligning operations to competitive needs. The emphasis within the Hill methodology (Hill, 2005) is that strategic decisions cannot be made based on information regarding customer and marketing opportunities addressed solely from a marketing function's perspective, but the operations capability must also be taken into account. Hill proposes that the issue of the degree of 'fit' between the proposed marketing strategy and the operations ability to support it is resolved at the business level in terms of meeting corporate (i.e., strategic) objectives. Thus, Hill provides an iterative framework that links together the corporate objectives; which provide the organizational direction, the marketing strategy; which defines how the organization will compete in its chosen markets, and the operations strategy; which provides capability to compete in those markets. The framework consists of five steps:

1 define corporate objectives;
2 determine marketing strategies to meet these objectives;
3 assess how different products win orders against competitors;
4 establish the most appropriate mode to deliver these sets of products;
5 provide the infrastructure required to support operations.

In traditional strategy formulation, the outcome of Step 3 is 'passed on' to Steps 4 and 5 and no further feedback occurs between steps in the process. The Hill methodology requires iteration between all five steps in order to link operations capability into decisions at a corporate level. This model is shown graphically in Table 2.3.

The steps in the Hill methodology are now described in more detail.

Table 2.3 Framework for reflecting operations strategy issues in corporate decisions

		Operations strategy		
1 Corporate objectives	2 Marketing strategy	3 How do you qualify and win orders in the market place?	4 Delivery system choice	5 Infrastructure choice

• Growth
• Survival
• Profit
• Return on investment
• Other financial measures
• Environmental targets
	• Product/service markets and segments
	• Range
	• Mix
	• Volumes
	• Standardization versus customization
	• Level of innovation
	• Leader versus follower alternatives
		• Price
		• Quality conformance
		• Delivery:
		  speed
		  reliability
		• Demand increases
		• Colour range
		• Product/service range
		• Design leadership
		• Technical support supplied
		• Brand name
		• New products and services – time to market
			• Choice of various delivery systems
			• Trade-offs embodied in these choices
			• Make-or-buy decisions
			• Capacity:
			  size
			  timing
			  location
			• Role of inventory in the delivery system
				• Function support
				• Operations planning and control systems
				• Quality assurance and control
				• Systems engineering
				• Clerical procedures
				• Payment systems
				• Work structuring
				• Organizational structure

Source: T. Hill, *Operations Management* (2000), p. 39.
Reproduced with permission of Palgrave Macmillan.

Step 1   Corporate Objectives

Step 1 involves establishing corporate objectives that provide a direction for the organization and performance indicators that allow progress in achieving those objectives to be measured. The objectives will be dependent on the needs of external and internal stakeholders and so will include financial measures such as profit and growth rates as well as employee practices such as skills development and appropriate environmental policies.

Step 2   Marketing Strategy

Step 2 involves developing a marketing strategy to meet the corporate objectives defined in Step 1. This involves identifying target markets and deciding how to compete in these markets. This will require the utilization of product/service characteristics such as range, mix and volume that the operations activity will be required to provide. Other issues considered will be the level of innovation and product development and the choice of 'leader' or 'follower' strategies in the chosen markets.

Step 3   How Do Products Win Orders in the Market Place?

COMPETITIVE FACTORS:

a range of factors such as price, quality and delivery speed, derived from the marketing strategy, on which the product or service wins orders.

This is the crucial stage in Hill's methodology where any mismatches between the requirements of the organization's strategy and the operations capability are revealed. This step provides the link between corporate marketing proposals and the operations processes and infrastructure necessary to support them. This is achieved by translating the marketing strategy into a range of **competitive factors** (e.g., price, quality, delivery speed) on which the product or service wins orders. These external competitive factors provide the most important indicator as to the relative importance of the internal operations performance objectives discussed earlier in this chapter. Figure 2.7 provides examples of how different (external) competitive factors will require a focus on the corresponding (internal) performance objectives.

Figure 2.7 does not imply a one-to-one relationship between competitive factor and performance objectives. This is because of the interrelationships between the performance objectives (e.g., speed will be partly dependent on other performance objectives such as cost and dependability). Thus, the figure shows that a particular external competitive factor will provide an indication of the relative importance of the internal performance objective.

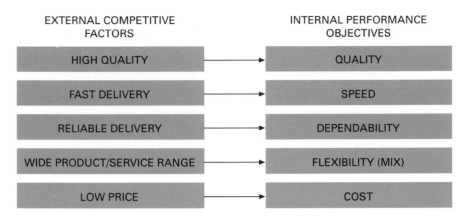

Figure 2.7   The relationship between competitive factors and performance objectives

At this stage, it is necessary to clarify the nature of the markets that operations will serve by identifying the relative importance of the range of competitive factors on which the product or service wins orders. Two measurements systems are described which do this.

Measuring the Relative Importance of the Competitive Factors – Hill

Hill distinguishes between the following types of competitive factors which relate to securing customer orders in the market place:

■ *Order-winning factors* – these are factors which contribute to winning business from customers. They are key reasons for customers purchasing the goods or services, and raising the performance of the order-winning factor may secure more business.
■ *Qualifying factors* – these are factors which are required in order to be considered for business from customers. Performance of qualifying factors must be at a certain level to gain business from customers, but performance above this level will not necessarily gain further competitive advantage.

From the descriptions above it can be seen that it is, therefore, essential to meet both qualifying and order-winning criteria in order to be considered and then win customer orders.

Measuring the Relative Importance of the Competitive Factors – Slack

An alternative to the order-winning and qualifying competitive factors used by Hill is to use two dimensions – importance and performance – to help operations

horizontal movement (i.e., changing customer perceptions of the relative importance of competitive factors) should be considered. The position of the performance objectives on the matrix will change, without any actions from the organization, as customer preferences change and competitor performance improves. Thus, improvement strategies should take the dynamic nature of the variables onto account.

Influences on the Relative Importance of the Competitive Factors

The measures above have considered the influence of customers (Hill) and customers and competitors (Slack) on the relative importance of the competitive factors. These influences are now considered in more detail.

Customers

Customers will value a range of competitive factors for any particular product/service; thus, it is necessary to identify the relative importance of a range of factors. The concept of 'order-winning' and 'qualifying factors' of Hill helps distinguish between those factors that directly contribute to winning business and those that are necessary to qualify for the customer's consideration between a range of products/services. The importance of this is that while it may be necessary to raise performance on some factors to a certain level in order to be considered by the customer, a further rise in the level of performance may not achieve an increase in competitiveness. Instead, competitiveness may then depend on raising the level of performance of different 'order-winning' factors. It may also be the case that the order-winning and qualifying factors will differ for different customer groups that the organization may be serving. One strategy for dealing with divergent customer demands is to use the idea of the focused factory and to break the plant into units allocated on the basis of 'order-winner' and 'order-qualifying' criteria.

Competitors

Competitor actions will also influence the basis on which competition is based and may require a change in priorities of the competitive factors used by the organization. For example, if an organization is competing on price and a competitor enters the market and takes market share by competing on faster delivery, the organization may need to consider that as a new competitive factor. The significance of this influence is that the initiative for change had been provided by a competitor, not the customer.

The Product/service Life Cycle

The Product/service Life Cycle (PLC) provides one way of generalizing customer and competitor behaviour over time. The PLC is an attempt to describe the

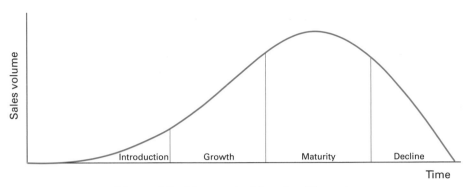

Figure 2.9   The product/service life cycle

change in sales volume for a particular product or service from being introduced into a market until its withdrawal. The model shows sales volume passing through the four stages of introduction, growth, maturity and decline (Figure 2.9). The model is useful in that each stage in the life cycle requires a different approach from the operations function and, thus, emphasizes the need for a range of capabilities from the operations function. The drawback of the approach is that it may be difficult to predict when the product/service will enter the next stage of the cycle or even determine what stage of the cycle the product/service is currently in! The main stages of the PLC can be described as follows:

- *Introduction* – on introduction the product/service specification may frequently be changed as feedback is received from customers. Operations will need to maintain flexibility in terms of design changes and response to changes in demand levels. Quality levels need to be maintained, despite frequent design changes, in order to ensure customer acceptance.
- *Growth* – if the introduction of the product/service has been successful then a period of sales growth occurs. Competitors may also enter the market. The main concern of operations will be to meet what may be a rapid increase in demand whilst maintaining quality levels.
- *Maturity* – after a period of growth, customer demand will be largely satisfied and demand will level off. The market may be dominated by a few organizations offering a standard product/service. Competition on price will be important and so the main issues for operations will be minimizing costs and maintaining a dependable supply.
- *Decline* – after a certain time the need for a product/service will be satisfied, or a new product/service will be introduced undertaking the tasks of the original. At this point, sales will decline, competitors will drop out of the market and remaining competition will be focused on price, indicating a need for operations to minimize costs.

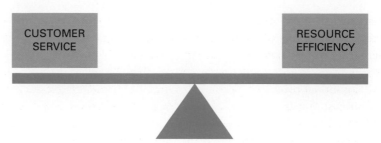

Figure 2.10   Trade-off relationship between customer service and resource efficiency

dependability and flexibility) and resource efficiency (which can be considered as determining the remaining performance objective of cost) is shown in Figure 2.10.

In order to analyse this trade-off it is necessary to understand that the resource efficiency of a system determines the cost of producing a product while customer service will influence selling price. Profitability is a function of both total production cost and sales revenue.

The trade-off relationship means that to gain an improvement on one side of the profitability model, there will be a consequent penalty to be paid on the other. An example of this relationship is a trade-off between delivery performance and the cost of holding high stocks of materials. The better delivery performance is in a trade-off with the cost of material stocks. Alternatively, the improvement and penalty may both lie on the same side of the model. An example of this is between overhead and material costs. Machine overheads can be reduced by increasing their utilization and building stocks of materials; conversely, reducing material stocks adversely effects utilization and increases overheads.

There are two basic approaches to managing trade-offs.

The first approach is to manage the trade-off factors within the constraints of the operations system. This involves ensuring that an operations relative achievement in each dimension of performance should be driven by the requirements of the market. This is not a straightforward process as there may be costs and risks involved in changing relative performance levels and the complexity of trade-off relationships can mean other trade-offs are affected. Although this approach is characterized by an acceptance of the constraints of the operations system, it can in itself lead to an improvement in overall performance.

The second approach is to follow an improvement approach and loosen the constraints on the operations system. This involves improving the capability of operations to enable improvement in both dimensions of performance or improvement in one dimension while preventing or limiting any deterioration in the other. This again is not a straightforward process and requires costs and risks in improving performance levels. Chapter 18 covers improvement approaches.

A characteristic of trade-offs is that if the operation is working well within its capability then one aspect of performance may be improved without a decrease in performance in its trade-off relationship. In effect, the capabilities of the operation exceed the requirements of the markets, and excess capability is being unused. Also, the nature of the trade-off relationship will most likely be complex and step changes may occur within the trade-off relationship. For example, the effect of adding an additional product to a product range may suddenly have a large trade-off effect on cost. Finally, the whole nature of the trade-off relationship can be changed by how resources are deployed and processes organized with the operations system. One such change is the implementation of the idea of focus which is considered in the next section.

Focus

The concept of **focus** (Skinner, 1974) is to align particular market demands with individual facilities to reduce the level of complexity generated when attempting to service a number of different market segments from an individual organization. This is because it is difficult and probably inadvisable for operations to try to offer superior performance over competitors across all of the performance objectives. Usually, organizations succeed when they organize their resources and compete across one or two performance objectives. Also, the capabilities of the organization will usually mean that it can do some things better than others and a strategy that uses inherent strengths will be more likely to offer a competitive advantage. This does not mean that capabilities cannot be changed over time, but it is likely that at any one time there are certain things that an organization can do well and certain things that it cannot do satisfactorily, if at all.

> **FOCUS:**
> aligns particular market demands with individual facilities to reduce the level of complexity generated when attempting to service a number of different market segments from an individual organization.

The idea of focus has been used by many firms to break up large and complex organizations into more simple and focused operations. Although many managers argue that the breakup of organizations leads to higher costs in terms of duplication of equipment, floor-space and overheads, many companies have found that focusing has led to a decrease in operating and overhead costs (Hayes *et al.*, 2005). Many of the advantages of focus can be obtained without the subdivision of the organization through methods such as:

■ *Simplification* – through elimination of products or services that are seldom requested by customers.
■ *Operation-within-an-Operation* – this involves dividing a facility into separated work areas, with the advantage of reducing the considerable expense of setting up independent operations (see JIT and focused factory section).
■ *Cell layout* – dedicated to a small group of people and equipment to a subset of products or services (Chapter 4).
■ *Process design* – using business process management to provide an integrated design for the processing steps involved in the manufacture of a product or delivery of a service (Chapter 8).

Part 2 ▪ Introduction

8 Agile operations aims to respond quickly to changing market demand in order to retain current markets and gain new market share by developing the capability of its resources.

Exercises

1. Evaluate strategy development at the corporate, business and functional levels of an organization.
2. Indicate how a major investment decision could be analysed in terms of its effect on the capability of the operations function.
3. How can the relative significance of the five performance objectives be determined in the formulation of the organization's strategic direction?
4. Discuss the main types of flexibility
5. Explain the significance for management of linking operations strategy, marketing strategy and corporate objectives.
6. Evaluate the strategic role of the operations function.
7. Evaluate the potential advantages and disadvantages of focused manufacturing.
8. Compare and contrast the concepts of trade-offs and agile operations.

References

Gaither, N. and Frazier, G. (2002), *Operations Management*, 9th Edition, South-Western College Publishing.

Hayes, R.H. and Wheelwright, S.C. (1988), *Restoring Our Competitive Edge: Competing through Manufacturing*, John Wiley & Sons.

Hayes, R., Pisano, G., Upton, D. and Wheelwright, S. (2005), *Operations, Strategy, and Technology: Pursuing the Competitive Edge*, John Wiley & Sons.

Hill, T. (2005), *Operations Management*, 2nd Edition, Palgrave Macmillan.

Johnson, G., Scholes, K. and Whittington, R. (2005), *Exploring Corporate Strategy: Text and Cases*, 7th Edition, FT Prentice Hall.

Mintzberg, H. and Waters, J.A. (1995), Of strategies: Deliberate and emergent, *Strategic Management Journal*, July/September.

Skinner, W. (1974), The focused factory, *Harvard Business Review*, May/June, 113–121.

Skinner, W. (1985), *Manufacturing: The Formidable Competitive Weapon*, John Wiley & Sons.

Slack, N. (1991), *Manufacturing Advantage: Achieving Competitive Manufacturing Operations*, Mercury.

Slack, N. and Lewis, M. (2002), *Operations Strategy*, Pearson Education Ltd.

Slack, N., Chambers, S. and Johnston, R. (2004), *Operations Management*, 4th Edition, Pearson Education Ltd.

Teece, D.J. and Pisano, G. (1994), The dynamic capabilities of firms: An introduction, *Industrial and Corporate Change*, 3(3).

Further Reading

Brown, S., Lamming, R., Bessant, J. and Jones, P. (2005), *Strategic Operations Management*, 2nd Edition, Elsevier Butterworth-Heinemann.

Web Links

www.softwareceo.com Many articles available on operations strategy.

www.aom.pace.edu/bps/bps.html The business policy and strategy division of the Academy of Management (US). Contains links to organizations and consultancies in the area of strategic management.

www.clarahost.clara.net/www.geckoheadgear.co.uk/index.html Gecko headgear site.

Chapter 3
Process Types

■ Manufacturing Process Types
   ● Project
   ● Jobbing
   ● Batch
   ● Mass
   ● Continuous
■ Service Process Types
   ● Professional Service
   ● Service Shop
   ● Mass Service
   ● Alternative Service Process-type definitions
■ Matching Process Type with Volume and Variety
■ Choosing a Process Type

Learning Objectives

After reading this chapter, you should be able to:

1 Describe the main manufacturing process types.

2 Describe the main service process types.

3 Discuss alternative service process-type definition.

4 Explain the relationship between process type and the operations volume and variety of output.

5 Discuss the process-type decision.

Introduction

In operations the design of the process is categorized into types for manufacturing and services. The choice of process design is most dependent on the volume and variety of the product or service that the organization offers. Generally, manufacturing and services providers serve their customers on a continuum between a combination of low-variety and high-volume products and services to a combination of high-variety and low-volume products and services. The chapter provides categories for process designs, called 'process types', for different volume and variety combinations. The reasons for matching a particular volume and variety combination with a particular process type is then discussed.

Manufacturing Process Types

In manufacturing, process types can be considered under five categories of project, jobbing, batch, mass and continuous (Figure 3.1). A description of each process type is followed by some examples of where each process type might be used.

Project

Processes that produce products of high variety and low volume are termed 'projects'. **Project processes** are used to make a one-off product to a customer specification. A feature of a project process is that the location of the product is stationary. This means that transforming resources, such as staff and equipment that make the product, must move or be moved to the location of the product. Other characteristics of projects are that they may require the coordination of many individuals and activities, demand a problem-solving approach to ensure they are completed on time and have a comparatively long duration of manufacture. The timescale of the completion of the project is an important performance measure. Because each project is unique it is likely that transforming resources will comprise general purpose equipment which can be used on a number of

PROJECT PROCESS: used to make a one-off product to a customer specification. A feature of a project process is that the location of the product is stationary.

product itself. Examples of a continuous process include an oil refinery, electricity production and steel making.

Service Process Types

The classification of service process types are more recent and less standardized than the manufacturing process types outlined above. In this text three service process types, professional service, service shop and mass service, are categorized in terms of their ability to cope with different volume and variety characteristics (Figure 3.2).

Professional Service

Professional service processes operate with high variety and low volume. They are characterized by high levels of customization, in that each service delivery will be tailored to meet individual customer needs. This customization requires communication between the service provider and customer and so professional services are characterized by high levels of customer contact and a relatively high proportion of staff supplying the service in relation to customers. The emphasis in a professional service is on delivering a process rather than a tangible product

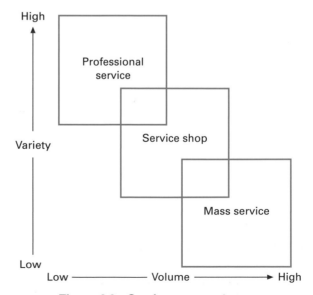

Figure 3.2   Service process types

associated with a process. An example of this is a management consultancy where the client is paying for the expertise and problem-solving skills of the consultants. The physical report that is generated at the end of the consultancy assignment is a documentation of the process, but it is the success of the process itself which is of interest to the client. Examples of a professional services include management consultancy, doctors and health and safety inspectors.

Service Shop

Service shop processes operate with a medium amount of variety and volume. There will be a certain amount of customization of the service, but not as extensive as in professional services. There will be, therefore, a mix of staff and equipment used to deliver the service. There is an emphasis both on the service delivery process itself and any tangible items that are associated with the service. For example, the success of a restaurant is dependent on the level of service attained in terms of achieving an appropriate ambience, but also the quality of the food itself. The variety of food offered provides a compromise between a personal chef who can cook meals to order (professional service) and a standard food item such as a hamburger (mass service). Examples of service shops include banks, shops, restaurants and travel agencies.

SERVICE SHOP PROCESS: operates with a medium amount of variety and volume. There will be, therefore, a mix of staff and equipment used to deliver the service.

Mass Service

Mass service processes operate with a low variety and high volume. There will be little customization of the service to individual customer needs and limited contact between the customer and people providing the service. Because the service is standardized it is likely that equipment will be used to improve the efficiency of the service delivery process. The emphasis in a mass service is on the tangible item that is associated with the service delivery. For example, supermarkets have certain differences in terms of layout and ambience but the major emphasis is on the provision of food items of the required price and quality. Examples of mass service providers are supermarkets, rail services and airports.

MASS SERVICE PROCESS: operates with a low variety and high volume. There will be little customization of the service to individual customer needs and limited contact between the customer and people providing the service.

Alternative Service Process-type Definitions

As mentioned earlier, the process-type definitions for services are not standardized and, in particular, the definition of service shops may be subdivided into those that lie on the professional service boundary relating to those professional services that have grown in volume and standardized their service and organizations that

this particular volume and variety position a batch process provides what is termed the 'lowest cost' position.

If a jobbing process type was used in this position then operations would have too much flexibility for the amount of variety required. Thus, they would have higher costs than another producer supplying the same market using a batch process type. This is due to the efficiencies made by moving from general purpose equipment and setting up for each individual item to the use of more specialized equipment and the need only to set up for a whole group or batch of products at a time. If a mass process type was used in this position then the operation would have too little flexibility for the amount of variety required. Thus, they would have higher costs than another producer supplying the same market using a batch process type. This is due to the high changeover costs they would incur in moving from one product to another in order to meet the required variety of output required by the market. This concept can also be related to matching the volume and variety of service processes using Figure 3.2.

Choosing a Process Type

A choice of process type must meet both market needs in terms of the volume and variety requirements of customers and also the technical needs in terms of the configuration of resources to deliver a service or product. Process-type choice is strategic because it can represent a large amount of capital investment in terms of equipment and work force and so sets a constraint around which the company can compete. The difficulty of the procedure of process-type choice is that process decisions can take a relatively large amount of time and money to implement whereas market needs in a competitive environment can change rapidly.

Although the process-type descriptions are quite distinct, in reality many operations blur these definitions; so, for example, there may be elements of batch processing in jobbing-dominated processes and batching in mass processes. In practice, process types within an organization will lie on a continuum across the process types, with processes within a particular process-type category showing different characteristics.

Companies may also use a combination of process types (e.g., jobbing and batch) for different product lines within a manufacturing plant. In services there may also be a mix of process types, with front-office customer-facing activities undertaken as a professional service, whilst back-office operations are organized as a service shop. See Chapter 1 for more details on front-office and back-office service operations.

The choice of process type for a process may also change over time. This may occur either at the level of the organization or at an individual product or service level.

At the level of the organization the company may be following a growth strategy, which involves standardization of its product or services or a strategy for increasing the range of products and services to avoid competing on price alone.

A strategy for manufacturing companies who are successful and wish to grow is to standardize products and enter higher volume markets over time as they acquire more financial backing. This growth may take place gradually, however, and so the point at which increased volumes necessitates a change in process type to match the volume/variety characteristics of the market may not be apparent. The choice of process type in these cases may be made using a breakeven analysis that calculates profit at different volume levels (Russell and Taylor, 2002). One consequence of process choice is that for increasing volume, the level of investment in equipment required to ensure a cost-efficient operation increases. This requirement for capital investment can be a barrier for new companies entering a market and so many small companies with limited finances provide a customized service to a niche market, in which labour skills are more important than supporting infrastructure.

Many service companies operate in a niche market and the Web has provided a platform for many of them to market their services effectively. However, many service companies wish to grow and so may need to standardize their service. Thus, in order to provide a consistent service level at higher volumes it may be necessary to 'package' the service the company provides to enable a lower skill base to deliver the service and to ensure consistent service quality. However, low volume, professional-type services rely on the capability of the individuals working for them who provide tailored solutions for their clients. Thus, a key factor in managing growth is that it may involve both a loss of autonomy of these existing staff and a need for training of additional staff to deliver the 'packaged' service.

At the level of the individual product or service, there may be a repositioning of that product or service in the market place at a new volume/variety mix. Also, within the portfolio of products and services that an organization delivers, an individual product or service will progress through a life cycle in terms of sales from introduction to maturity to decline, the process that best suits the needs of the firm will need to change to match the volume and variety of the output (Noori and Radford, 1995).

Two concepts that should be considered when designing an operations process are the following. The idea of 'focus' in manufacturing and services is used to help reduce the level of complexity involved when attempting to service a number of market segments and is covered in Chapter 2. The concept of mass customization, which attempts to provide the capability to produce both a high volume and high variety of products and services through the use of flexibility, is covered in Chapter 7.

Chapter 4
Layout Design

■ Layout Design

- ● Fixed Position Layout
- ● Process Layout
- ● Cell Layout
- ● Product Layout
- ● Characteristics of Layout Types

■ Detailed Layout Design

- ● Production Flow Analysis
- ● Line Balancing

Learning Objectives

After reading this chapter, you should be able to:

1 Describe the basic layout types.

2 Evaluate the appropriateness of a layout type for a manufacturing or service process type.

3 Explain the concept of group technology.

4 Understand the concept of production flow analysis.

5 Understand the line-balancing technique.

Introduction

Layout design concerns the physical placement of resources such as equipment and storage facilities. The layout is designed to facilitate the efficient flow of customers or materials thorough the manufacturing or service system. Layout design is important because it can have a significant effect on the cost and efficiency of an operation and can entail substantial investment in time and money. In many operations the installation of a new layout, or redesign of an existing layout, can be difficult to alter once implemented due to the significant investment required on items such as equipment. This chapter describes the main categories of layout and techniques for detailed layout design.

Layout Design

Following the selection of the operations process type (see Chapter 3) it is necessary to select the **layout** (arrangement of facilities) of the operation. Figure 4.1 shows the relationship between manufacturing and service process types and layout types.

LAYOUT DESIGN: the arrangement of facilities in a service or manufacturing operation.

As can be seen from Figure 4.1, there are four basic layout types of fixed position, process, cell and product layout. As stated, the choice of layout type will follow from the process design choice. However, as can be seen from Figure 4.1, there is often a choice of layout types for a particular process type (such as a process layout or cell layout for batch process types). In this case the choice will depend on the characteristics of the layout type that are particularly relevant for the product or service that is to be delivered. An analysis may also be made using the trade-off between unit cost of production and variety of output that was used to determine process type in Chapter 3. For example, a cell layout is more likely to be relevant for relatively high-volume batch systems where the cost of dedicated resources can be met by the lower unit cost of a high volume of product or service flowing through the cell.

The characteristics of each of the layout types will now be considered.

each group of resources in turn, based on their individual requirements. Because of their flexibility, process layouts are widely used. One advantage is that in service systems they allow a wide variety of routes that may be chosen by customers depending on their needs. Another advantage is that the product or service range may be extended and as long as no new resources are required may be accommodated within the current layout.

An important issue with process layouts is the management of the flow of products or services between the resource groups. One problem is that transportation between process groups can be a significant factor in terms of transportation time and handling costs. Another problem is that the number of products or services involved and the fact that each product/service can follow an individual route between the process groups, makes it difficult to predict when a particular product will be delivered or a service completed. This is because at certain times the number of customers or products arriving at a particular process group exceeds its capacity and so a queue forms until resources are available. This queuing time may take up a significant part of the time that the product or customer is in the process. This behaviour can lead to long throughput times (i.e., the time taken for a product or customer to progress through the layout). In a manufacturing organization a significant amount of time may be spent 'progress chasing' to give certain products priority to ensure they are delivered to customers on time. In a service system the customers may feel they are queuing in the system longer than they perceive is necessary for the service they require. However, in services there may be flexibility to add or remove staff to match the current arrival rate of customers to the service delivery point.

From Figure 4.1 process types associated with a process layout are jobbing and batch process types in manufacturing and service shops in services. Examples of process layouts include supermarkets, hospitals, department stores and component manufacturers.

Cell Layout

CELL LAYOUT:
cells are created from placing together resources which service a subset of the total range of products or services.

GROUP TECHNOLOGY:
the process of grouping products for manufacture or services for delivery.

A **cell layout** attempts to combine the efficiency of a product layout with the flexibility of a process layout. Cells are created from placing together resources which service a subset of the total range of products or services. Figure 4.4 shows how a process layout with similar resources in departments has been redesigned as a series of three cells. Note how the routing of products is simplified using the cell layout format. The products are now processed in a single cell and need not be transported between departments.

When grouping products or services together in this way the grouping is termed a family. The process of grouping the products or services to create a family is termed **group technology**.

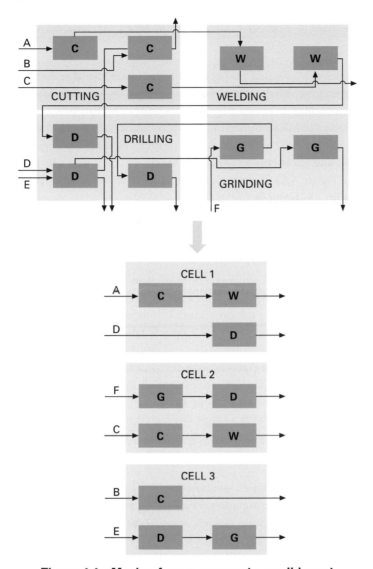

Figure 4.4   Moving from a process to a cell layout

Group technology has three aspects:

1   Grouping Parts into Families

Grouping parts or customers into families has the objective of reducing the changeover time between batches, allowing smaller batch sizes, and thus improving flexibility. Family formation is based on the idea of grouping parts or customers together according to factors such as processing similarity.

2 Group Physical Facilities into Cells to Reduce Transportation Time between Processes

Physical facilities are grouped into cells with the intention of reducing material or customer movements. Whereas a process layout involves extensive movement of materials or customers between departments with common processes, a cell comprises all the facilities required to manufacture a family of components or deliver a service. Material and customer movement is, therefore, restricted to within the cell and throughput times are, therefore, reduced. Cells can be U-shaped (see Figure 4.6) to allow workers to work at more than one process whilst minimizing movement.

3 Creating Groups of Multi-skilled Workers

Creating groups of multi-skilled workers enables increased autonomy and flexibility on the part of operators. This enables easier changeovers from one part to another and increases the job enrichment of members of the group. This, in turn, can improve motivation and have a beneficial effect on quality.

Creating cells with dedicated resources can significantly reduce the time it takes for products and services to pass through the process by reducing queuing time. It also offers the opportunity for automation due to the close proximity of the process stages. Thus, process technology can be used to replace a number of general purpose resources with a single dedicated multi-functional system such as a Flexible Manufacturing System (see Chapter 6). A disadvantage of cell layouts can be the extra expenditure due to the extra resources required in moving to a cell layout.

From Figure 4.1 process types associated with a cell layout are batch and mass process types in manufacturing and service shops and mass services in services. Examples of cell layouts include custom manufacture, maternity unit in a hospital, cafeteria with multiple serving areas. In services a cell layout could involve an insurance organization organized by type of claim (e.g., car, home, travel).

Product Layout

PRODUCT LAYOUT:
a layout with the resources required for a product or service arranged around the needs of that product or service.

Product layouts, also termed 'line layouts', arrange the resources required for a product or service around the needs of that product or service. Figure 4.5 shows a configuration of a product layout. Here, the material flows through four stages. The line may be automated or people may be assigned to one or more stages.

In manufacturing applications such as assembly lines with a high volume of a standard product the products will move in a flow from one processing station to the next. In contrast to the process layout in which products move to the

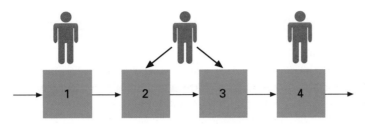

Figure 4.5   Product layout

resources, here the resources are arranged and dedicated to a particular product or service. The term 'product layout' refers to the arrangement of the resources around the product or service. In services the requirements of a specific group of customers are identified and resources set up sequentially so the customers flow through the system, moving from one stage to another until the service is complete.

A key issue in product layouts is that the stages in the assembly line or flow line must be 'balanced'. This means that the time spent by components or customers should be approximately the same for each stage, otherwise queues will occur at the slowest stage. The topic of line balancing is considered later in this chapter.

The product or line layout is an efficient delivery system in that the use of dedicated equipment in a balanced line will allow a much faster throughput time than in a process layout. The major disadvantage of the approach is that it lacks the flexibility of a process layout and only produces a standard product or service. Another issue is that if any stage of the line fails, then, in effect, the output from the whole line is lost and so it lacks the robustness to loss of resources (e.g., equipment failure or staff illness) that the process layout can provide.

An alternative to the straight line configuration shown in Figure 4.5 is to adopt a 'U-shape' design as in Figure 4.6. Here, material flows through eight stages of

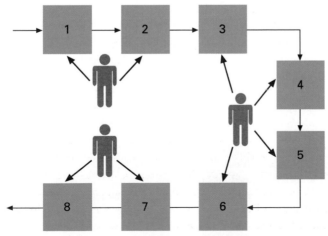

Figure 4.6   'U-shape' product layout

production or assembly which are assigned to three people. An advantage of the U-shape is that it may allow people (or equipment) to be assigned to multiple stages and, thus, help balance the line.

From Figure 4.1 process types associated with a product layout are mass and continuous process types in manufacturing and mass services in services. Examples of product layouts include car assembly, self-service cafes and car valeting.

Characteristics of Layout Types

Table 4.1 summarizes the main characteristics of operations systems using each of the four main layout types.

Although the main layout types can be adapted to meet the needs of a particular manufacturing or service system, it may be the case that a mix of layout types is required within a single operation. For example, hospitals are basically a process

Table 4.1 Characteristics of operations for each layout type	
Layout type	*Characteristics of operations that use layout type*
Fixed position	Very high product and mix flexibility, but very high unit cost
	The product or customer does not move, the resources are arranged around them
	There can be a high variety of tasks for staff
	A major issue for operations is the scheduling and coordination of activities over time
Process	High product and mix flexibility
	Complex flow can lead to high levels of work-in-progress and high throughput times
	Low utilization of resources
	Flexible in terms of handling additions to the product/service mix
	Robust in that non-availability of resources do not stop delivery of product/service if other group resources remain
Cell	Can provide flexibility of process layout and efficiency of product layout
	Resources can be matched to product or service demand so work-in-progress and, thus, throughput times are much lower than process layout
	Variety of tasks offers opportunity for automation and more variation in duties for personnel
	Can be costly to move and purchase additional plant necessary to rearrange existing layout
Product/Line	Standard product or service in high volumes at low unit cost
	Can specialize equipment to product or service needs
	Allows relatively little variety in product or service
	Line configuration leads to danger of failure of one process stage, effectively stopping output from the whole line
	Work can be repetitive if personnel are always based at one process stage

layout with people with similar needs (e.g., intensive care) grouped together. However, the layout also shows characteristics of a fixed position layout in that staff, medicines and equipment are brought to the location of the customer.

Detailed Layout Design

Once the layout type has been chosen, its detailed configuration must be designed to meet the needs of a particular implementation.

In a fixed position layout there will be a relatively low number of elements and there are no widely used techniques to help locate resources.

The relative positioning of equipment and departments in a process layout can be analysed in terms of minimizing transportation costs or distances using an activity matrix. When a number of factors need to be taken into account, including qualitative aspects, relationship charts may be used. Process maps (described in Chapter 8) can also be used to show the flow of materials, customers and staff through the layout. In some instances, such as retail layout design, software is available that takes into consideration both financial aspects of layout design and customer requirements such as aesthetics and lighting (Hope and Mühlemann, 1997).

In this chapter the techniques of production flow analysis for cell layouts and line balancing for product layouts will be covered.

Production Flow Analysis

A cell layout uses the concept of group technology to group resources into cells to process families of parts or customers. **Production Flow Analysis (PFA)** (Burbidge, 1989) is a group technology technique that can be used to identify families of parts with similar processing requirements. To show how PFA works Figure 4.7 shows an example of a process layout.

PRODUCTION FLOW ANALYSIS (PFA): a group technology technique that can be used to identify families of parts with similar processing requirements.

Five parts (A, B, C, D, E) are produced in a process layout consisting of a drill department with three drills (D), a lathe department with two lathes (L), a milling department with one mill (M) and a heat treatment department with one heat treatment machine (HT).

The routings taken by the parts is shown in Table 4.2.

In order to identify families of parts the first step in PFA is to draw a grid of parts against machines and mark which parts are processed on which machine (Table 4.3).

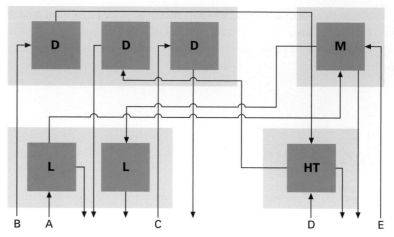

Figure 4.7   Example process layout

Table 4.2 Part routing sequences for machine shop	
Part	*Routing sequence*
A	Lathe, mill
B	Drill, heat treatment
C	Drill
D	Heat treatment, drill
E	Mill, lathe

	Lathe	*Mill*	*Heat treat*	*Drill*
A	✓	✓		
B			✓	✓
C				✓
D			✓	✓
E	✓	✓		

Table 4.3   PFA routing matrix

The next step is to observe which machines have parts in common. In this case it can be seen that lathe and heat treatment could form one cell and drill and mill could form another cell. Redraw the grid, rearranging the rows and columns to place parts using the machines in the adjacent cells. There can be two or more cells formed (Table 4.4).

Table 4.4	Rearranged PFA routing matrix			
	Lathe	*Mill*	*Heat treat*	*Drill*
A	✓	✓		
E	✓	✓		
C				✓
D			✓	✓
B			✓	✓
	CELL 1		CELL 2	

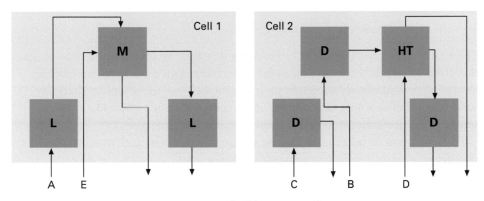

Figure 4.8   Cell layout routing

The cell layout can now be drawn, using the cells defined using the PFA analysis and referring back to the routing sequences in Table 4.2.

Figure 4.8 shows the cell layout routing. What is immediately apparent is that the routing of parts is much clearer and routing distances are smaller than in the process layout (Figure 4.7).

Line Balancing

A product layout consists of a number of processes arranged one after another in a 'line' to produce a standard product or service in a relatively high volume. These systems which have a characteristic flow (product) layout use specialized equipment or staff dedicated to achieving an optimal flow of work through the system. This is important because all items follow virtually the same sequence of operations. A major aim of flow systems is to ensure that each stage of production is able to maintain production at an equal rate. The technique of **line balancing** is used to ensure that the output of each production stage is equal and maximum efficiency is attained.

LINE BALANCING:
used to ensure that the output of each production stage in a line layout is equal and maximum efficiency is attained.

Line balancing involves ensuring that the stages of production are coordinated and bottlenecks are avoided. Because of the line flow configuration the tasks in the line must be undertaken in order (precedence) and the output of the whole line will be determined by the slowest or bottleneck process. The actual design of the line is thus guided by the order of the tasks which are involved in producing the product or delivering the service and the required output rate required to meet demand. This provides information which determines the number of stages and the output rate of each stage.

The steps in line balancing are as follows.

1 Draw a Precedence Diagram

The first step in line balancing is to identify the tasks involved in the process and the order in which these tasks must be undertaken. Once the tasks have been identified, it is necessary to define their relationship to one another. There are some tasks that can only begin when other tasks have been completed. This is termed a serial relationship and is shown graphically in Figure 4.9.

The execution of other tasks may be totally independent and, thus, they have a parallel relationship shown graphically in Figure 4.10.

Precedence diagrams are used to show the tasks undertaken in a line process and the dependencies between these tasks. Thus, it is easy to see that Task C, for example, can only take place when Tasks A and B have completed (see Figure 4.11).

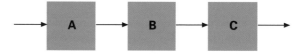

Figure 4.9   Serial relationship of tasks

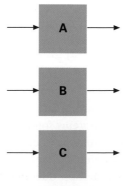

Figure 4.10   Parallel relationship of tasks

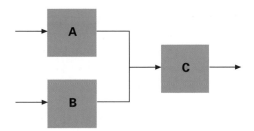

Figure 4.11   Precedence diagram

2   Determine the Cycle Time for the Line

For a particular line process we will wish to reach a desired rate of output for the line to meet projected demand. This is usually expressed in work items per time period (e.g., 30 parts per hour). Another way of expressing this output rate is that 30 parts per hour means that a part must leave the system every 2 minutes (60 minutes/30 parts). This measure, termed the 'cycle time', represents the longest time any part is allowed to spend at each task.

Thus:

$$\text{Cycle time} = \text{Available time/Desired output}$$

Taking into consideration the discussion of bottleneck processes above, the cycle time for the line process is thus determined by the task with the highest cycle time or lowest output level.

3   Assign Tasks to Workstations

Once the cycle time for the line has been calculated, we have the cycle time for each stage or workstation in the line process. We can now allocate tasks to each workstation based on their task times. As a rule of thumb, it is more efficient to allocate eligible tasks to a workstation in the order of longest task times first. When the total task time would exceed the cycle time for a workstation then it is necessary to start a new workstation and repeat the allocation of tasks as before. If a task time is longer than the workstation cycle time then it is necessary either to allocate multiple tasks in parallel in order to meet the target time or to break the task down into smaller elements.

4   Calculate the Efficiency of the Line

When tasks are assigned to workstations it is very unlikely that their total tasks times at each workstation will match the cycle time exactly. A measure of how close these two values do meet for the whole line, is called the line efficiency.

To calculate the line efficiency:

$$\text{Line efficiency } \% = \frac{\text{Sum of the task times}}{\text{Number of workstations} * \text{Desired cycle time}} * 100$$

It should be noted that the issue of line balancing will be complicated by constraints such as factory layout, material handling between stages and availability of worker skills. Other factors in designing product layouts include.

Variability in Task Times

A major factor in achieving a proper line balance is to gather accurate estimates of task times in the line flow process. If timings are just based on an average of observations then there is a danger that the effect of variations on task times will not be considered. This can be limited somewhat by keeping a number of job elements in a task which reduces variability and increases flexibility. Simulation modelling (Chapter 8) can be used to investigate these variations as well as the effect of random variations such as machine breakdown.

Mixed Model Lines

The use of a multi-model line (Chapter 13) to process a range of products, rather than a single product type, also increases the complexity of the line balancing process.

Shape of the Line

Although the sequence of workstations in a product layout is linear, the actual shape of the line need not be a straight line. The actual shape of the line can be an S shape, U shape, O shape or L shape. Factors which are used when deciding on a suitable shape include the ability of people to communicate, the ability of robots and people to reach parts and transportation distances between workstations.

Job Enlargement

After taking into consideration the constraints imposed by precedence and cycle time, a decision must be made regarding the level at which a task is broken down and how the elements of the task are allocated to personnel. For instance, motivation can be improved by allocating the whole process to a single person instead of allocating smaller tasks to a number of people in a line.

Line Balancing in a Manufacturing Plant

This study concerns a former division of a major UK-based manufacturer of railway rolling stock and equipment. The plant manufactures a range of bogies which are the supporting frame and wheel sets for rail vehicles. The company has a history of supplying the passenger train market in the UK but over a period of time low demand and increased competition had led it to enter new markets including European inner-city transport and the supply of freight bogies to Far East countries. The need to compete on a global basis led the company to re-evaluate its manufacturing facility with particular emphasis on the need to increase output, reduce lead times and increase flexibility. To meet these demands management had identified areas where substantial investment was required.

The Production Process

The facility layout is on a product line basis with the manufacturing process consisting of six main stages of fabrication, welding, frame machining, paint, fitting and quality audit. Each stage must be completed in order before the next stage can begin. The stages are now briefly described:

Fabrication — the fabrication stage prepares the bogie frame sections from sheet steel and bought-in castings. A custom template is designed from which the parts required are cut from sheet steel to standard batch sizes. Parts not needed immediately are held in storage. Processed parts and castings are brought together to form a bogie 'kit' which is assembled on a jig and taken to the subsequent welding stage.

Welding — a bogie sub-assembly is manually welded on a jig at a workstation to form a main bogie frame.

Frame machining — The main bogie frame is then transferred to equipment for the machining of any holes or bores needed for the fixing of sub-assemblies such as the braking and suspension systems. Bogies are fixed to a table and the machine processes the frame according to a preset operation sequence.

Paint — the frame is then manually painted while being suspended from an overhead moving circular track.

Fitting — manufactured sub-assemblies and bought-in components such as motors are then assembled on the bogie frame. The frames are placed on supports and are moved along a line at different stages of assembly with overhead cranes.

Quality audit — final inspection is carried out to ensure all bogies meet the required specification. It was usual that a certain amount of paint touch-up work is required at this stage due to damage caused to the paint finish during the fitting stage.

The Line Balancing Study

The focus of the study was on product layout design with the main objective being to ensure that the performance of the whole manufacturing system would meet required

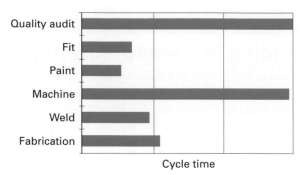

Figure 4.12   Cycle time of manufacturing stages

output levels. The output level was converted into a target cycle time (i.e., time between manufacture of products or output rate). As stated, the product layout consists of six main stages with the product passing through each stage in turn. This means that the effective cycle time for the whole system is determined by the stage with the longest cycle time. The study objective was to obtain a balanced line (i.e., all cycle times equal) which would enable a smooth parts flow through the production stages facilitating the introduction of a pull-type Just-In-Time (JIT) production control system.

A simulation model (Chapter 8) was used to estimate the cycle time at the main manufacturing stages. The graph (Figure 4.12) shows clearly where management effort needed to be directed to achieve the target cycle time.

The quality audit stage was set at a nominal amount by management. Significant problems had occurred at this stage with the spray finish on the bogie frames being damaged during the sub-assembly fitting stage. This had to be rectified by a manual touch-up process which could take longer than the original spray time. The paint area would also need to be reconfigured due to new environmental controls. The problems had been recognized by management and an investment in an epoxy paint plant producing a hard-wearing finish was planned.

The bogie frame machining centre had previously been recognized by management as a bottleneck process. The bogie frame went through a number of pre-programmed steps on the machine and the cycle time was dependent on the capability of the machining centre itself. Consequently, a major part of the planned investment was a new machining centre with a quoted cycle time below the target. An investigation of the fabrication processes revealed that although the cycle times were above target, the majority of this time was used for machine setup. Figure 4.13 shows the effect on cycle time of a reduction in setup time of 10% to 90%.

From Figure 4.13 it is clear that to achieve the target cycle time a setup reduction of 50% is required. A team was assembled to achieve this target and it was met by the use of magnetic tables to hold parts ready for processing. The simulation was rerun and the results (Figure 4.14) show the system achieving the required performance. It can be

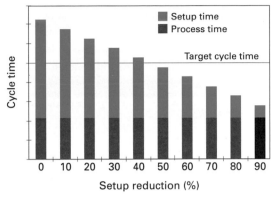

Figure 4.13 Setup reduction

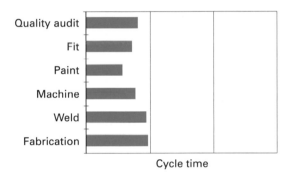

Figure 4.14 Cycle time of manufacturing stages

seen that a further reduction in fabrication setup times and a reconfiguration of the welding line would reduce the overall cycle time further, producing a more balanced line and increasing capacity utilisation.

By implementing the changes outlined in the study the simulation was able to predict the following improvements in performance (Table 4.5). In the table,

$$\text{Cycle efficiency} = 100\% - \% \text{ idle time}$$

where % idle time = Idle time per cycle/Total cycle time.

Table 4.5 Line balancing study results

Performance measure	Change (%)
Cycle time	−65
Lead time	−19
Output per week	+220
Cycle efficiency	+29

These are substantial improvements in performance and meet the output targets set by management. However the results shown in Figure 4.18 show that further reductions in the cycle times for the fabrication and weld stages would lead to a further increase in cycle efficiency, reflecting a more balanced line, and thus a further increase in output.

Source: from Greasley (2004) *Journal of Manufacturing Technology Management*
© **MCB UP Ltd (www.emeraldinsight.com/jmtm.htm)**

**Case Study 4.1
Questions**

1   What are the reasons given for the need to balance the line?

2   What strategies are used to balance the line?

3   Identify alternative strategies to balance the line.

Summary

1 There are four basic layout types of fixed position, process, cell and product.

2 A fixed position layout is used when the product or service cannot be moved. A process layout is one in which resources which have similar processes or functions are grouped together. A cell layout is created by placing together resources which serve a subset of the total range of products or services. A product layout arranges the resources required for a product or service around the needs of that product or service.

3 Group technology has three aspects of grouping parts into families, grouping physical facilities into cells and creating multi-skilled workers.

4 Production flow analysis is a group technology technique that can be used to identify families of parts with similar processing requirements.

5 The technique of line balancing is used to ensure that the output of each stage in a product line layout is equal and maximum utilization is attained.

Exercises

1. For the assembly of a TV what type of layout would you use? What are the reasons for this choice?

2. What are the advantages that a cell layout attempts to achieve compared with the other layout types?

3. What are the benefits of the group technology technique?

4. The following parts are produced in a factory with a process layout comprising separate departments for each of the four operations: lathe, grind, drill and machining.

Part No.	Routing sequence
24	Grind
12	Lathe, drill
67	Grind, machine
45	Lathe, drill
32	Lathe, drill
76	Grind, machine

Use Production Flow Analysis (PFA) to show how the plant could be organized into cells employng Group Technology to identify families of parts.

5. A company is currently organized with machines grouped into departments based on their function. The sequence of operations taken for each component is:

Part No.	Routing sequence
487	Lathe, mill, grind, drill
723	Shear, punch press, grind, deburr
245	Mill, drill, grind
29	Shear, punch press, punch press, deburr

a. Draw a diagram of the plant and trace the routing sequence for each component.
b. Use PFA to analyse the routings and identify similarities between the components.
c. Group the components into families.
d. On the basis of the families identified in (c) specify cells for producing the components and trace the flow of work through the reorganized plant.
e. If the company currently has one of each machine, how many additional machines are required?

6. Use PFA to indicate how the following plant could be reorganized into cells. Currently, the process layout consists of a lathe department with two lathes, a grinder department with two grinders, with all other departments having a single machine each:

Part No.	Routing sequence
A1	Press, lathe
B2	Drill, mill, deburr
C3	Lathe, grinder, press
D4	Grinder, lathe
E5	Lathe, mill, drill
F6	Drill, grinder, deburr

7. Explain the need for line balancing.
8. What are the main techniques in determining capacity for a product layout and a process layout?

References

Burbidge, J.L. (1989), *Production Flow Analysis for Planning Group Technology*, Oxford University Press.

Greasley, A. (2004), The case for the organizational use of simulation, *Journal of Manufacturing Technology Management*, **15**(7), 560–566.

Hope, C. and Mühlemann, A. (1997) *Service Operations Management: Strategy, Design and Delivery*, Prentice Hall.

Further Reading

Chase, R.B., Aquilano, N.J. and Jacobs, F.R. (2003), *Operations Management for Competitive Advantage*, 10th Edition, McGraw-Hill.

Slack, N., Chambers, S. and Johnston, R. (2004), *Operations Management*, 4th Edition, Pearson Education.

Stevenson, W.J. (2005), *Operations Management*, 8th Edition, McGraw-Hill/Irwin.

Web Links

www.manufacturingadvice.org.uk/categories/Manage/Production/ cs_horstmann_1.jsp DTI Manufacturing Advice Service. Case study of redesign and line balancing in a cell layout.

www.webtek.biz/gormanjones/casestudy1.asp Gorman Jones. Short case study showing the use of production flow analysis and line balancing by a consultancy organization.

www.protech-ie.com/flb.htm Production Technology. Software for line balancing applications

www.proplanner.com/Product/Details/LineBalancing.aspx ProPlanner. Software for single and mixed model line-balancing applications.

www.sixsigmainstitute.com/training/plb_training.shtml Lean Sigma Institute. Training in line balancing

Chapter 5

Facility Design and Location

■ Supply Network Design

■ Long-term Capacity Planning
  ● Capacity Volume
  ● Capacity Timing

■ Facility Location
  ● Supply-side Influences
  ● Demand-side Influences

■ Location Selection Techniques
  ● Weighted Scoring
  ● The Centre of Gravity Method
  ● Locational Cost–Volume Analysis

Learning Objectives

After reading this chapter, you should be able to:

1 Discuss the issue of supply network design.

2 Discuss the concept of economies of scale.

3 Discuss the concept of economies of scope.

4 Describe the approaches of lead capacity, match capacity and lag capacity.

5 Consider the facility location decision in terms of supply-side influences and demand-side influences.

6 Undertake the location selection techniques of weighted scoring, the centre of gravity method and locational cost–volume analysis.

Introduction

The location decision is one of the key strategic decisions facing an organization and involves business strategy (e.g., growth), marketing (entering new market segments) and operations (providing capability to meet customer needs) as well as other functions such as finance. The location decision may also involve a long-term commitment in terms of the purchase or lease of a building and a significant financial investment. For many service organizations, such as retail outlets, the location of the facility must be convenient for the potential customer base and is, thus, an important factor in the success of the organization.

In this book, facility design is taken in a broad sense to mean the decisions surrounding how capacity will be supplied by the organization to meet market demand. This may be achieved internally by the organization by the construction of facilities or externally by agreement with suppliers. There are three main issues involved in decisions regarding this area.

1   How Will the Capacity Be Supplied? (Supply Network Design)

This will address the topic of the design of the organization's supply network. This includes decisions on the configurations of the organization's relationship with its suppliers and the choice about what activities the organization should undertake internally and what should be subcontracted to other agencies.

2   How Much Capacity Should Be Supplied? (Long-term Capacity Planning)

This covers the question of how much long-term capacity should be supplied by the organization.

3   Where Will the Capacity Be Located? (Facility Location)

This covers the question of the geographical location of capacity supplied by the organization.

Supply Network Design

Every operation, as well as supplying capacity to the market in terms of goods and services, will require capacity in the form of inputs to the manufacturing and services process, such as materials, people and equipment. Thus, when designing an operations facility consideration must be made regarding the relationship of the organization with its suppliers of the capacity required in order to provide the goods and services the facility is producing. Two aspects of this relationship with suppliers are considered. The configuration of all the suppliers, termed the 'supply network', and the choice regarding what the organization should do itself and what it should contract others to do.

For some organizations, decisions may often be taken in the context of the integrated global strategy of an organization. A global firm is organized into a network which means that operations at several locations can perform tasks for a given customer group and/or a single facility can perform a task for several downstream (customer) groups. Networks can improve delivery and cost performance relative to fixed supply facilities because the network can pool demand and increase volume to reduce cost and choose different facilities to provide products for a given customer under different conditions. The use of a network should lead to a more robust system that avoids capacity bottlenecks through the use of close coordination facilitated by utilizing communications technology.

The **global organization** attempts to extend and coordinate internal operations to create new value through a consolidation of manufacturing, reduced delivery costs and economies of scale. The aim is to create an international network of operations which will sell the same products in several countries, increase overall sales thereby reducing the cost per unit of development, coordinate the work of subsidiaries to provide a product/service to the global customer and shift production in response to exchange rate fluctuations. An international network also requires an improvement of global supply chain performance which coordinates the location and capacity of plants as well as the purchasing function. The improvements will aim to secure economies of scale and scope by using a global supply chain to reduce unit costs through lower transportation expenses.

The issue of the design of the supply network is considered in Chapter 15 on supply chain management. In particular, the issues of supply chain integration and the use of e-commerce are directly related to supply network decisions.

SUPPLY NETWORK DESIGN: the configuration of the organization's relationship with its suppliers and the choice about what activities the organization should undertake internally and what should be subcontracted to other agencies.

GLOBAL ORGANIZATION: extends and coordinates internal operations to create new value through a consolidation of manufacturing, reduced delivery costs and economies of scale.

CASE STUDY 5.1

The Supply Network and Corporate Responsibility

In today's global economy no company can operate in isolation. Every organization becomes part of a complex supply network where goods and services are bought from chosen sources and suppliers, and then sold on to a customer or distributor. Between 30% and 80% of an organization's output comes from bought-in goods and services. The figures will only get larger as business continues to embrace outsourcing. A focus on cost, flexibility and efficiency remains paramount in managing the supply chain. But the Chartered Institute of Purchasing and Supply (CIPS) has discovered that one of the biggest challenges facing any organization is the ability to manage not only its own code of corporate responsibility but also those of its suppliers, ensuring they adopt the same environmental and ethical principles. The risks to corporate reputation are enormous if, for example, a supplier is caught making components from illegally logged wood, or is using child labour. The risks in this area are growing as more and more organizations are working across the world. The onus is on companies to seek assurances that there is nothing untoward in their extended supplier networks. Out of sight, out of mind, is not an acceptable way to do business and is a sure-fire recipe for disaster.

Source: excerpt from 'Suppliers can be the weakest link' by Ken James (chief executive of the Chartered Institute of Purchasing and Supply), *The Evening Standard* (London), 29 March 2004

Case Study 5.1 Question

1   Discuss the impact of corporate responsibility in managing the supply network.

LONG-TERM CAPACITY PLANNING:

covers the question of how much long-term capacity should be supplied by the organization. This decision needs to be made within a long-term plan which provides a fit with the operations strategy of the organization.

Long-term Capacity Planning

The level at which management sets the level of capacity is a key determinant of the competitiveness of the organization. This decision needs to be made within a long-term plan which provides a fit with the operations strategy of the organization. The operations strategy should define the nature of the markets in which the organization intends to compete in terms of characteristics such as product mix, volume and geographic spread which will impact on the amount and type of capacity required. Thus, it is not simply a matter of attaining a sufficient amount of capacity to meet the expected demand, but the capacity must be available at the time needed and in the current format to ensure that targets are met. For example, if it is required to meet sudden changes of demand in an overseas market, the transportation time for the capacity supplied in a local location may mean it cannot supply the market within the time required. There will also be constraints on overall capacity caused by a scarcity of certain types of capacity (such as employee skills). Thus, the availability of different type of capacity must be considered in order to avoid bottlenecks occurring. This section will consider long-term capacity issues in terms of the volume of capacity required and the timing of when that capacity should be acquired. Short- and medium-term capacity planning issues in terms of meeting customer demand are covered in Chapter 11.

Capacity Volume

Economies of Scale

In determining the optimum capacity level for a facility the concept of **economies of scale** is considered. Economies of scale relate to the capital costs of building a new facility and the fixed costs of operating a facility.

The capital costs of building a facility do not increase proportionally as its capacity increases, so, for example, a facility with twice the capacity of another facility will not have capital costs twice as high. This may suggest that the use of a single large facility that supplies all capacity needs is the most appropriate strategy. However, at a certain capacity level for a particular location, diseconomies of scale may set in. These may include the transportation costs incurred in supplying a large geographical area from a single location, the speed of delivery from a single location to the customer becomes too slow and the added complexity of a large organization may cause communication and coordination problems.

As a facility is expanded and fixed costs remain the same the average cost of producing each unit will fall until the best operating level of the facility is reached and the lowest average unit cost met. Past a certain point, however, diseconomies of scale occur and average unit costs rise. This is due to the required capacity output of the facility being higher than what it has been designed for. Operating at this level can cause loss of efficiency from factors such as poor decision making due to management layers, congestion of materials and staff, complexity of combining many products and services, extensive use of (relatively expensive) shift working and overtime and reduced morale of staff due to working conditions. The relationship between average unit of cost of output and volume for different facility sizes is shown in **Figure 5.1**.

The decision regarding the volume of capacity is complex, because it is unlikely that the amount of capacity required from a facility will be fixed over the long term. Therefore, there is a choice to be made between building a facility which provides more capacity than is currently needed, but will provide sufficient capacity for planned growth in output or to match the facility design to current

ECONOMIES OF SCALE:
as a facility is expanded and fixed costs remain the same, the average cost of producing each unit will fall until the best operating level of the facility is reached and the lowest average unit cost met.

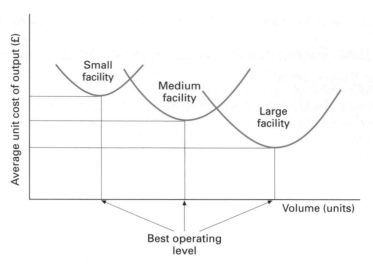

Figure 5.1   Best operating level for facility size

capacity requirements, achieve maximum economies of scale, and then incur the cost of expansion to meet any future increase in capacity requirements. The expansion route is less risky, particularly when the forecast of future demand is uncertain, as it requires less finance to be tied up in the facility infrastructure. However, construction costs can be considerably decreased if the complete facility is built in one phase. The decision will be based on the strategy of the firm and, in particular, the likely growth rate of the products or services the facility will supply.

When considering economies of scale benefits it is important to understand that the rationalization of a number of facilities into a single large facility will achieve economies of scale only if the multiple facilities are doing the same type of work. Simply putting the work of a number of facilities doing different activities within one building is unlikely to achieve economy of scale benefits.

ECONOMIES OF SCOPE:

are created by the ability to produce many products in one highly flexible production facility more cheaply than in separate facilities.

Economies of Scope

Traditionally, significant investment in process technology, such as automation, has only been justified for high-volume products where economies of scale provide a lowest average cost per unit. However, modern process technology, such as Flexible Manufacturing Systems (FMSs), described in Chapter 6, provide flexibility and allow a range of products to be produced quickly and efficiently. Thus, **economies of scope** are created by the ability to produce many products in one highly flexible production facility more cheaply than in separate facilities.

CASE STUDY 5.2

Positive Evidence for Gas and Power Convergence

What are the quantifiable benefits of power/gas convergence? Three different answers were given by panel members at UBS Warburg's utility conference in June, but the basic message was the same – it's worth it. TXU Europe's finance director Paul Marsh said that for the retailer, a dual gas/power customer was 50–75% more valuable than a single-product customer, yielding a profit of GBP40 against around GBP25. There was further value in the fact that a dual customer was less likely to switch again.

Belgian utility Tractebel's chief executive Jean-Pierre Hansen focused on the benefits higher up the value chain. Switching gas from power generation to sell into a gas market peak was worth EUR25–30m/yr to Tractebel if globalized across the group (i.e., including its Dutch generator Epon). Any shortfall in power could be made up by imports from France or Switzerland, or by switching to a back-up generation fuel, Hansen concluded. From the US, Keith Meyer, an executive director at CMS Energy, said arbitrage added 3 percentage points to profit margins in the combined gas/power business. There were clear, measurable benefits then, flowing from what CMS calls "the growing technical and commercial interaction between power and gas."

Meyer made the point that, while horizontal mergers brought economies of scale, horizontal gas/power convergence brought 'economies of scope'; diversity but between complementary products – heat, energy management services, and risk management. "Getting behind the customer's meter and looking after energy management at, say, GM cars, gets us more 'bang for buck' – it's more profitable – than just selling energy." He expected convergence to continue "a long way" before it provoked any regulatory response.

Source: FT.com site, 13 June 2000 © The Financial Times Ltd

1   Discuss the use of the term 'economies of scope' in the case study.

Case Study 5.2 Question

Balancing Capacity

In calculating capacity volume another factor to take into account is that the total capacity of any system is dependent on the process with the smallest capacity, called the 'bottleneck'. Thus, in order for the system to operate at its most efficient it is necessary to equalize the capacity between processes. The capacity of sequential processes can be visualized as a series of pipes of varying capacity, with the smallest pipe limiting the capacity of the whole system (**Figure 5.2**).

In Figure 5.2 the total capacity of the system is limited by the capacity at Process 3. Thus, Process 3 is the bottleneck process.

BALANCING CAPACITY:

equalizing the capacity of a number of sequential processes.

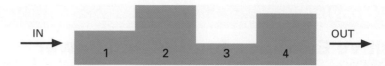

Figure 5.2   Diagram of the capacity of four sequential processes

One measure that can be used to assess the balance of the system is the cycle efficiency where:

$$\text{Cycle efficiency} = 100\% - \% \text{ Idle time}$$

where % Idle time = Idle time per cycle/Total cycle time.

The cycle time is a measure of the time between output of each unit, and is related to output as follows:

$$\text{Cycle time} = \frac{1}{\text{Output rate}}$$

Thus, for an output rate of 30 products an hour the cycle time is 2 minutes (i.e., a unit is produced or a service delivered every 2 minutes).

See Chapter 4 for details of the line-balancing technique for equalizing cycle times for sequential processes.

SUBCONTRACTING NETWORKS:
long-term contractual arrangements made with suppliers to supply goods and services.

Subcontracting Networks

An alternative to obtaining capacity volume within the organization is to develop subcontractor and supplier networks. Here, long-term contractual arrangements are made with suppliers to supply goods and services which means less capacity is required by the subcontracting organization. An advantage of this approach is that less capital is required for production and delivery facilities. There is also the flexibility to decrease capacity supplied to meet falling market demand without incurring the costs of under-utilization of resources or to increase capacity without the expense of additional resources. A disadvantage is the risk that subcontractors may not be able to meet changing capacity requirements. There is also a risk of the loss of skills inherent in outsourcing activities. Different forms of organizational relationships are covered in the supply chain integration section of Chapter 15.

Capacity Timing

An organization can adopt three main approaches to ensuring the correct amount of capacity is available at the right time to meet future plans. Three approaches of lead capacity, match capacity and lag capacity are outlined.

Lead Capacity

The first option is to obtain extra capacity above forecast demand (**lead capacity**) and so maintain a capacity 'cushion' to try to ensure capacity is sufficient if demand increases above forecast. This has the advantage of helping to maintain high levels of customer service and responding quickly to increases in customer demand, but has the disadvantage of the cost of maintaining the capacity cushion for all the different types of capacity (people, equipment, locations) required over time. An advantage of using a capacity cushion is that the cushion can be allocated to different products and services over time as the nature of demand fluctuates, although this is limited by specialization of resource (e.g., only certain trained people can do certain tasks).

A number of factors will impact on deciding the nature of the capacity cushion in a lead capacity strategy. The size of the cushion will be a trade-off between the costs of too much capacity in terms of unused resources against the costs of too little capacity in terms of using options such as overtime and outsourcing to meet customer demands, or losing customer orders through an inability to supply them quickly enough. The capacity cushion decision should also take into consideration the strategic context. For example, a new product or service in its growth phase may require a large capacity cushion to maximize customers, while for a product or service in the mature or decline stage of its life cycle a smaller cushion may be more appropriate.

> **LEAD CAPACITY:**
> to obtain extra capacity above forecast demand and so maintain a capacity 'cushion' to try to ensure capacity is sufficient if demand increases above forecast.

Match Capacity

The second option is to simply obtain capacity to match forecasted demand. The advantage of this option is that it avoids the costs of a capacity cushion and the use of strategies such as outsourcing may be used to quickly fill capacity shortfalls. The disadvantage is the problem outlined earlier in terms of loss of performance due to variability in demand.

> **MATCH CAPACITY:**
> the capacity to match forecast demand.

Lag Capacity

The third option is to only add capacity when extra demand is present which would utilize the additional resources (**lag capacity**). This has the advantage of ensuring a high utilization of capacity acquired, but may mean customers are lost as they move to competitor products and services before the additional capacity has been acquired.

> **LAG CAPACITY:**
> addition of capacity when extra demand is present which would utilize the additional resources.

Using Inventory to Smooth Capacity

In manufacturing organizations, capacity can be maximized by producing inventory when demand is lower than supply in order that inventory can be used to supplement capacity when demand exceeds supply. This, in effect, smoothes demand fluctuations and ensures speed of delivery response. It has, however, the disadvantage of the costs of holding inventory and even of inventory becoming obsolete. It is also not applicable to front line services which cannot be held as inventory (see Chapter 11 for more information on using inventory for capacity management).

Timing the Capacity Increments

When undertaking a lead capacity or match capacity approach it is unlikely that the capacity cushion can be adjusted or the capacity matched smoothly, but adjustments will be made in increments (e.g., the purchase of new equipment or hiring of new staff). Thus, there is a need to determine the timing of capacity increments.

In a lag capacity strategy the acquisition of new capacity is triggered by an increase in demand. One aspect of this strategy is that competitors, also following a lag strategy, will increase their capacity simultaneously which may lead to an increase in the cost of capacity. This behaviour may also lead to over-capacity in the market, increasing competitive pressures. Organizations following a lead or match capacity strategy may avoid these problems by adding capacity when demand is low (i.e., at the low point of the business cycle). This strategy can reduce costs but carries the obvious risk that the demand planned for may not materialize.

An alternative approach is to build capacity, not simply for relatively short-term fluctuations in demand, but to a strategy of increasing market share over the long term. Again this approach is risky in the sense that it is not following a forecast demand pattern. In order to reduce risk some organizations use the fact that their performance in the market is relative to the performance of their competitors. Thus, capacity is added in response to the capacity expansion of the market leader. Whether it transpires that the capacity is needed or not, the relative position of the organization in respect to its competitors remains the same. These approaches have the disadvantage of being essentially reactive (either to demand or competitors) and do not take into account how capacity expansion can be used in a proactive manner as part of an operations strategy.

A number of companies have grown rapidly (e.g., Wal-Mart, easyJet) by continually adding new capacity and lowering costs in an attempt to freeze competitors out of the market. Retailing is an industry where quick expansion into geographical locations can freeze competitors out of those geographical locations that can only support a single retail outlet of a certain type. In some cases, it may form part of the business strategy to build over-capacity to secure a locational presence or provide a higher level of performance of a performance objective such as delivery speed.

Facility Location

There are three main reasons why a location decision is required. The first reason is that a new business has been created and requires facilities in order to manufacture its product or service its customers. The second reason is that there is a decision to relocate an existing business due to factors such as the need for larger premises or to be nearer a customer base. The third reason is to expand into new premises as part of a growth strategy. For each of these scenarios the **facility location** decision can be considered in terms of its effect on costs and the size of the facility.

A company's competitiveness will be affected by its location, as the choice of location will impact on costs for elements such as transportation and labour. In terms of cost a location decision is costly and time consuming to change. The costs include the purchase of land and construction of buildings. An organization may be located inappropriately due to a previous poor location decision and an unwillingness to face the costs of a subsequent relocation. A change in input costs, such as materials or labour, may also lead to a need to change location. The cost of establishing a new service facility is relatively low compared with a manufacturing plant with its associated equipment. Also, service facilities generally need to be in close contact with their customers. This has led to multiple service outlets being established in locations which serve a target market. Whereas manufacturing sites will often be located to minimize costs, services will be located to maximize income from customers.

In order to meet the long-term demand forecast for the product or service it is necessary to consider the size of the facility. Within a medium-term planning cycle the size of the facility will impose an upper limit on the organization's capacity. Purchasing additional components from suppliers or subcontracting work can increase this level. However, these strategies may lead to higher costs and, thus, a loss of competitiveness.

The location decision can be considered in terms of factors that vary in such a way as to influence cost as location varies (supply-side factors) and factors that vary in such a way as to influence customer service as location varies (demand-side factors). The location decision can be seen as a trade-off between these factors. In service organizations a need for customer contact may mean that demand-side influences will dominate while in a manufacturing company labour and distribution costs may mean supply-side influences dominate.

> **FACILITY LOCATION:** the geographical location of capacity supplied by the organization.

Supply-side Influences

Distribution Costs

Distribution and transportation costs can be considerable, especially for a manufacturing organization that deals in tangible products. The sheer volume of the raw material involved in operations such as steel production means that a location decision will tend to favour areas near to raw materials. A manufacturer and seller of custom-built furniture, however, will need to be near potential customers. For service companies such as supermarkets and restaurants the need to be in market-oriented locations means that the cost of transportation of goods will not be a major factor in the location decision. However, many service organizations require distribution of stock from warehouses whose location should be considered carefully (Chapter 15).

Distribution across country borders means that a whole series of additional costs and delays must be taken into account, including import duties and delays in moving freight between different transportation methods (e.g., air, rail, truck, sea). A site near to an airport or a rail link to an airport may be an important factor if delivery speed is important.

Labour Costs

Labour costs have generally become less important as the proportion of direct labour cost in high-volume manufacturing has fallen. What is becoming more important is the skills and flexibility of the labour force to adapt to new working methods and to engage in continuous improvement efforts. The wage rate of labour can be a factor in location decisions, especially when the service can be provided easily in alternative locations. Information technology companies involved in data entry can locate in alternative countries without the customer being aware.

Energy Costs

Some manufacturing companies use large amounts of power to operate production processes. Thus, energy costs and the availability of enough energy to meet forecast demand can be important factors in the location decision.

Site and Construction Costs

Both the cost of the land and the cost of purchasing materials and building a facility are directly related to the location decision. These costs should be considered together as relatively low-cost land may require substantial preparation to make it suitable for building development.

Intangible Factors

There are also a number of factors that are not financial but may have an effect on the location decision. These include the potential for objections to development on environmental grounds, to local regulations regarding business developments and to the necessary quality of life in the area needed to attract skilled employees.

Demand-side Influences

Labour Skills

The need for a pool of skilled labour is becoming increasingly important. However, it may be possible in some instances to use skilled labour from a remote location (e.g., the use of computer programmers in India for American software companies).

DEMAND-SIDE INFLUENCES: when the location decision is considered in terms of factors that vary in such a way as to influence customer service as location varies.

Location Image

Retail outlets, in particular, will wish to locate in an area which 'fits' with the image they are trying to project. Often, shopping districts will be associated with a particular type of retail outlet (e.g., designer clothing).

Customer Convenience

For many service organizations, in particular, the location of the facility must be convenient for the potential customer. This can range from restaurants where customers may be prepared to travel a short distance, to hospitals where the speed of response is vital to the service. The physical link between customer and service provider can be in either direction. For example, household goods such as gas ovens and central heating boilers will be serviced by staff at the customer's home.

CASE STUDY 5.3

Moving Textile Manufacturing Overseas

Due to global competitive pressures, many garment manufacturers have scaled down or closed their operations in the UK and moved overseas. Due to lower labour costs, in what is a labour-intensive industry, production has increased in such areas as Asia. A textile manufacturer based in Leicester, UK produces a range of cotton and lycra textile mixes which are used for garments such as T-shirts and women's tights. It has decided to supplement its UK operations and locate a textile production facility in Sri Lanka.

The move will permit the design of a more efficient layout in a purpose-built factory, as opposed to the current facilities which are placed across a number of locations and buildings within the UK. An important part of the layout planning activity is the estimation of the quantity of work-in-progress inventory within the proposed facility. The estimation of inventory levels is critical because the relative bulk of inventory means the amount of floor-space required could be considerable. The need to sink drainage channels for effluent from the knit and dye machines and the size and weight of the machinery involved, means that it would be expensive and time consuming to change the factory layout after construction.

Case Study 5.3 Questions

1 Discuss the supply-side and demand-side influences on the facility location decision described in the case study.

2 Describe how the technique of business process simulation (Chapter 8) could help in the design of the new factory layout.

Location Selection Techniques

The location selection process consists of identifying a suitable region/country, identifying an appropriate area within that region and finally comparing and selecting a suitable site from that area. A number of techniques for location selection are now described.

Weighted Scoring

WEIGHTED SCORING: consists of determining a list of factors that are relevant to the location decision. Each factor is then given a weighting that indicates its relative importance compared with the other factors. Each location is then scored on each factor and this score is multiplied by the factor value. The alternative with the highest score is then chosen.

In most situations cost will not be the only criteria for a location decision. **Weighted scoring** attempts to take a range of considerations into account. Weighted scoring, also referred to as 'factor rating' or 'point rating', provides a rational basis for evaluation of alternative locations by establishing a composite value for each alternative. The ratings include factors based on qualitative as well as quantitative factors. The procedure consists of determining a list of factors that are relevant to the location decision. This may include convenience to customers, labour skills, transportation facilities, etc. Each factor is then given a weighting that indicates its relative importance compared with the other factors. Each location is then scored on each factor and this score is multiplied by the factor value. The alternative with the highest score is then chosen. The usefulness of the method is dependent on identifying the appropriate location factors and devising a suitable weighting for each. One approach is to use the method to assess the intangible factors (e.g., quality of life) only and then determine if the difference between the intangible scores is worth the cost of the difference in tangible costs between the locations.

Worked Example 5.1

Weighted Scoring

New Technologies Ltd is an organization that specializes in simulation modelling consultancy. They have identified three sites on the West Coast of the USA which have approximately equal initial and operating costs. The sites have been evaluated on a score of 1 to 10 (10 being best) against the following criteria and weighting assigned by management.

		City		
	Weight	Los Angeles	Portland	Seattle
Pool of skilled system modellers	0.5	6	4	5
University research in modelling	0.3	3	5	3
Recreational and cultural activities	0.2	5	3	4

Rank the three cities in order of their total weighted points score.

Solution

$$\text{Los Angeles} = (6 \times 0.5) + (3 \times 0.3) + (5 \times 0.2) = 4.9$$
$$\text{Seattle} \quad = (5 \times 0.5) + (3 \times 0.3) + (4 \times 0.2) = 4.2$$
$$\text{Portland} \quad = (4 \times 0.5) + (5 \times 0.3) + (3 \times 0.2) = 4.1$$

The Centre of Gravity Method

The **Centre of Gravity method** can be used to determine the location of a distribution centre by minimizing distribution costs. In services, when locating a retail outlet, the gravity method can be used to maximize profit (Fitzsimmons and Fitzsimmons, 1998). The method assumes distribution costs change in a linear fashion with the distance and the quantity transported. The method also assumes the quantity transported is fixed for the duration of the journey. The relative coordinates of the distribution points are placed on a map and the location of the distribution point should be at the centre of gravity of the coordinates. To find this point the average of the x-coordinates and y-coordinates are found using the following equations:

$$\bar{x} = \frac{\sum x_i Q_i}{\sum Q_i}$$

$$\bar{y} = \frac{\sum y_i Q_i}{\sum Q_i}$$

THE CENTRE OF GRAVITY METHOD: can be used to determine the location of a distribution centre by minimizing distribution costs. The relative coordinates of the distribution points are placed on a map and the location of the distribution point should be at the centre of gravity of the coordinates.

where Q_i = Quantity to be transported to destination i
x_i = x-coordinate of destination i
y_i = y-coordinate of destination i
$\bar{x}$ = x-coordinate of centre of gravity
$\bar{y}$ = y-coordinate of centre of gravity

Worked Example 5.2

Centre of Gravity Method

A manufacturing organization wishes to build a centralized warehouse system which will serve a number of production facilities in Germany. The expected demand and relative grid references for the facility are given below.

Location	Demand (units/year)	Relative grid reference
Hamburg	40 000	(3, 7)
Cologne	20 000	(1, 4)
Stuttgart	35 000	(3, 2)
Munich	70 000	(4, 1)
Dresden	45 000	(6, 5)
Berlin	110 000	(5, 6)

At what location, in terms of grid reference, should the warehouse be situated?

Solution

$$\bar{x} = \frac{(3 \times 40\,000) + (1 \times 20\,000) + (3 \times 35\,000) + (4 \times 70\,000) + (6 \times 45\,000) + (5 \times 110\,000)}{40\,000 + 20\,000 + 35\,000 + 70\,000 + 45\,000 + 110\,000}$$

$$\bar{y} = \frac{(7 \times 40\,000) + (4 \times 20\,000) + (2 \times 35\,000) + (1 \times 70\,000) + (5 \times 45\,000) + (6 \times 110\,000)}{40\,000 + 20\,000 + 35\,000 + 70\,000 + 45\,000 + 110\,000}$$

$\bar{x} = 4.2$

$\bar{y} = 4.3$

Locational Cost–Volume Analysis

LOCATIONAL COST–VOLUME ANALYSIS: indicate when a particular location is superior for a particular volume level by analysing the mix of fixed and variable costs

Locational cost–volume analysis will indicate when a particular location is superior for a particular volume level by analysing the mix of fixed and variable costs. Some costs such as the costs of building the facility will be fixed, while others such as the level of demand will vary with the location. The relationship between both of these factors will vary for each location being considered. The procedure for graphical cost–volume analysis is as follows:

1 Determine the fixed and variable costs for each location.
2 Plot the total cost (i.e., fixed + variable) lines for the location alternatives on the graph.
3 Choose the location with the lowest total cost line at the expected volume level.

The equation for expressing costs in terms of location is:

$$TC = VC \cdot X + FC$$

where TC = Total cost
  VC = Variable cost per unit
  X = Number of units produced
  FC = Fixed costs

Worked Example 5.3

Locational Cost–Volume Analysis

A manufacturing organization is considering the following locations for its plant.

	Barcelona	Madrid
Variable costs	£1.60/unit	£1.25/unit
Annual fixed costs	200 000	180 000
Initial fixed costs	1 400 000	1 600 000

a Draw a cost–volume graph for both locations over a 5-year period at a volume of 200 000 units per year.
b Which location has the lowest cost?
c At what volume do the locations have equal costs?

Solution

a Cost at year 0:

$$Barcelona = 1\,400\,000$$

$$Madrid \quad = 1\,600\,000$$

Cost at year 5:

$$Barcelona = 1\,400\,000 + (5 \times 200\,000) + (5 \times 200\,000 \times 1.75)$$

$$= £4\,150\,000$$

$$Madrid \quad = 1\,600\,000 + (5 \times 180\,000) + (5 \times 200\,000 \times 1.25)$$

$$= £3\,750\,000$$

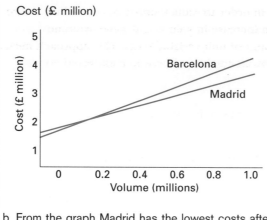

b From the graph Madrid has the lowest costs after 5 years.

c If X equals the number of years until costs are equal.

Using subscript B for Barcelona and M for Madrid:

$$TC_B = TC_M$$

$$1\,400\,000 + 200\,000X + (200\,000 \times 1.75)X$$
$$= 1\,600\,000 + 180\,000X + (200\,000 \times 1.25)X$$

$$1\,600\,000 - 1\,400\,000 + 180\,000X - 200\,000X + 250\,000X - 350\,000X = 0$$

$$200\,000 - 120\,000X = 0$$

$$X = \frac{200\,000}{120\,000} = 1.6 \text{ years}$$

This method has assumed that fixed costs are constant for the volume range when, in fact, step changes may occur in fixed cost expenditure to meet certain volume levels. Also, variable costs are assumed to have a linear (straight-line) relationship with volume, when this may not be so. Some cost–volume models may incorporate a non-linear (curved) relationship. Another assumption is that output of the facility has also been aggregated into one product that may not reflect the complexity of how a mix of products affects costs over a range of volumes.

If the analysis includes the economics of the logistics activity for a range of volumes then it is possible to review make-or-buy issues and, thus, the mix between in-house and the subcontracting of components. Again, the decision will concern the relationship between fixed and variable costs through the product life cycle. The relationship between fixed and total costs, termed the 'operational gearing', is important in determining if production should be initiated and when it should cease. The operation with low fixed costs and, thus, low operational gearing will have more flexibility in responding to changes in market demand over time. In other words, if fixed costs are low the company does not require high volumes to break even and can, thus, decrease output to match demand more easily. A high-volume producer, however, invests in specialized equipment and, thus, increases operational gearing in order to reduce unit costs and, thus, create greater profit potential. Thereby, an increase in volume for a high-volume producer will only add a small amount of unit variable costs. This approach means the high-volume producer will prefer to operate as close to capacity limits as possible to maximize profit.

Summary

1 Supply Network Design concerns the relationship of the organization with its suppliers of capacity.

2 Economies of scale refer to the characteristic that as a facility is expanded and fixed costs remain the same, the average cost of producing each unit will fall.

3 Economies of scope are created by the ability to produce many products in one highly flexible facility more cheaply than in separate facilities.

4 A lead capacity strategy maintains a capacity cushion (extra capacity above forecast demand) in order to ensure sufficient capacity if demand increases. A match capacity strategy aims to obtain capacity to match forecast demand. A lag capacity strategy is to acquire additional capacity when extra demand is present.

5 Facility location factors can be considered as influencing cost as location varies (supply-side factors) and influencing customer service as location varies (demand-side factors).

6 Location selection techniques include the weighted scoring method which attempts to take a range of considerations into account when choosing a location. The centre of gravity method determines location by minimizing distribution costs (or maximizing profits for a retail outlet). Locational cost–volume analysis indicates which location is suitable for a particular volume level by analysing the mix of fixed and variable costs.

Exercises

1. Outline how a strategy of globalization will impact on a policy of pursuing economies of scale advantages.
2. Evaluate the strategies of lead capacity, match capacity and lag capacity for a retail outlet.
3. For an organization with which you are familiar discuss the location decision in terms of supply-side influences and demand-side influences.
4. A manufacturing organization is looking at the following two locations:

	Birmingham	Manchester
Variable costs	£14/unit	£16/unit
Annual fixed costs	£12 000 000	£15 000 000
Initial fixed costs	£165 000 000	£145 000 000

a. Draw a cost–volume graph for both locations over a 10-year period at a volume of 750 000 units per year.

b. Which location has the lowest cost at the end of the 10-year period?

c. At what volume do these locations have equal costs?

5. The following table lists the weightings representing the relative importance of factors for the location of a retail site. Four potential sites have been given a score out of 100 for each factor:

		Site			
Factor	Weight	A	B	C	D
Construction cost	0.1	90	60	80	70
Operating cost	0.1	90	80	90	85
Population density	0.4	70	90	80	75
Convenient access	0.2	75	80	90	90
Parking area	0.2	60	70	85	75

Rank the four sites in order of their total weighted points score for suitability for the proposed location.

6. A retail chain has four major stores in the East Midlands area which have the following monthly demands rates:

Store location	Monthly demand (units)
Derby	2000
Nottingham	1000
Leicester	1000
Sheffield	2000

The following map shows the relative coordinates of the four outlets:

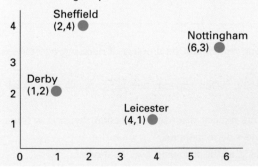

The organization has decided to find a 'central' location in which to build a warehouse. Find the coordinates of the centre that will minimize distribution costs.

7. A company has decided to relocate from three separate facilities – Plant A, Plant B and Plant C – to a new facility, Plant D. Using the centre of gravity method determine the best location for Plant D to serve its customers using the facility locations and yearly demand shown below.

Facility	Location coordinates	Demand (per year)
A	(175, 280)	6000
B	(50, 200)	8200
C	(150, 75)	7000

8. The following diagram shows a line process:

$$ \boxed{A} \rightarrow \boxed{B} \rightarrow \boxed{C} \rightarrow \boxed{D} $$

Stage	Capacity (units/hr)
A	120
B	140
C	110
D	150

a. What is the total system capacity?
b. Which stage is the bottleneck?
c. What is the level that system capacity can be increased to by increasing the bottleneck capacity only?
d. Calculate the current cycle efficiency.
e. Calculate the cycle efficiency when the bottleneck capacity is increased as in (c).

References

Fitzsimmons, J.A. and Fitzsimmons, M.J. (1998), *Service Management: Operations, Strategy and Information Technology*, 2nd Edition, McGraw-Hill.

Further Reading

Egelhoff, W.G. (1993), Great strategy or great strategy implementation: Two ways of competing in global markets, *Sloan Management Review*, Winter, 37–50.

Flaherty, M.T. (1996), *Global Operations Management*, McGraw-Hill.

Lei, D. and Slocum, J.W. (1992), Global strategy, competence building and strategic alliances, *California Management Review*, Fall, 81–97.

Mair, A. (1994), *Honda's Global Local Corporation*, Macmillan.

Schroeder, R.G. and Flynn, B.B. (2001), *High Performance Manufacturing: Global Perspectives*, John Wiley & Sons.

Web Links

www.bizhelp24.com/small_business/economies_of_scale.shtml BizHelp24. Outline of use of economies of scale for small business.

www.ofcom.org.uk/static/archive/oftel/publications/about_oftel/2002/smpg0802.htm Oftel's market review guidelines. Criteria for the assessment of significant market power. Contains definitions of economies of scope, economies of scale and vertical integration.

www.bbc.co.uk/coventry/features/stories/2002/10/centre-of-england.shtml BBC. How the BBC found the location of the centre of England using the centre of gravity method!

Chapter 6
Process Technology

■ Process Technology for Materials

- ● Software Systems
- ● Hardware Technologies
- ● Computer-Integrated Manufacture (CIM)

■ Process Technology for Information

- ● Operational Information Systems
- ● Management Information Systems
- ● E-business
- ● E-commerce
- ● M-business
- ● Customer Relationship Management (CRM)

■ Process Technology for Customers

Learning Objectives

After reading this chapter, you should be able to:

1 Explain the role of process technologies for materials processing.

2 Explain the role of information technology in the accumulation, organization and distribution of information.

3 Outline the distinguishing features of operational information systems and management information systems.

4 Define the terms 'e-business' and 'e-commerce'.

5 Discuss how technology can be used for customer processing in operations systems.

Introduction

In Chapter 1 we defined the objective of an operations system as converting transformed resources from inputs into outputs in the form of goods and services. Transformed resources can be in the form of material, information and customers and this section will show the use of technology in the transformation of these resource categories. Technology is an important aspect of operations as it has led to a large growth in productivity in both manufacturing where the emphasis is on technology for material and information transformation and services where the emphasis is on technology for information and customer transformations. In addition to the technologies described in this chapter, technologies relevant to operations are discussed throughout this text, including ERP (Chapter 14) and project management software (Chapter 16).

Process Technology for Materials

COMPUTER-AIDED DESIGN (CAD): allows the designer to create drawings on a computer screen to assist in the visual design of a product or service.

There are many technological advances which are specific to a certain industrial sector (e.g., new material technologies used for construction). This section will describe some of the software systems and hardware technologies which have had a widespread impact on manufacturing firms in many industries.

Software Systems

COMPUTER-AIDED PROCESS PLANNING (CAPP): transmits a process plan of how parts will be manufactured to a machine tool. It can also sequence parts through a number of process steps.

Computer-Aided Design (CAD) is one of the most widespread technologies, used in even relatively small firms. A CAD system allows the designer to create drawings on a computer screen to assist in the visual design of a product or service. The drawings can be viewed from any angle and there is a facility to zoom in to allow inspection of a design in detail (Figure 6.1). Drawings are held in a database for future use and dissemination between designers and engineers across the company.

　Computer-Aided Process Planning (CAPP) extends CAD by transmitting a process plan of how parts will be manufactured to the machine tool (e.g., by

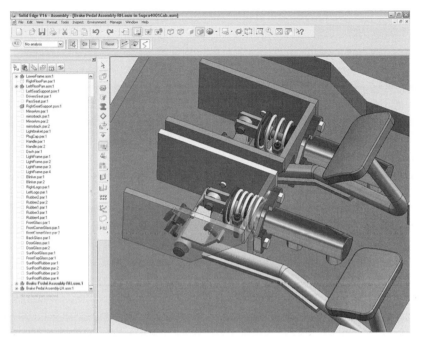

Figure 6.1 Image showing two different sub-assemblies that contain the exact same spring; however, because the distance between the faces in the sub-assembly is defining the variable spring length, it can be represented in different states of 'compression'.

Source: www.cad-portal.com/eWeekly/product_reviews/SolidEdgeV16_WebGallery/pages/Image11.php3
Reproduced by permission of TechniCom Inc.

deciding on how individual pieces are to be cut from a sheet of metal). CAPP systems can also sequence parts through a number of process steps. **Computer-Aided Engineering (CAE)** takes the drawings in a CAD system and subjects the designs to simulated tests. For example, the behaviour of an engineering design for elements of a bridge can be observed under various amounts of stress. This allows various designs options to be tested quickly and cheaply.

COMPUTER-AIDED ENGINEERING (CAE): takes the drawings in a CAD system and subjects the designs to simulated tests.

CASE STUDY 6.1

Spencer Davies Engineering

Thanks to a carefully planned e-business strategy, Spencer Davies Engineering has dramatically improved the efficiency of its production process and expanded the breadth of its offer.

Spencer Davies has introduced technology across the company, from a website and customer database to CAD/CAM, an intranet and production control on the shop floor.

Its strategy has been to balance bigger, structural investments in core functions – such as in CAD/CAM – with smaller applications that reduce employees' administrative burdens. The result of this approach is that each successive investment brings specific and cumulative benefits. For example, the original CAD/CAM investment improved the quality, speed and breadth of offer. When combined with email, which now accounts for 60% of client communications, designs can come directly from clients and go immediately to the shop floor, saving up to a week on every job. Handling the processes electronically makes then easier to review and the company can now hold less stock, ordering online from suppliers to secure the best deals.

The company intranet includes a research library, company documentation, job descriptions and a contact database of customers and suppliers. This has been integral in maintaining internal communications, giving staff the tools they need, and improving customer service. Offsite engineers, meanwhile, are equipped with laptops, digital cameras and mobile phones so work can be budgeted, completed and approved on the spot. The company is also looking at integrating other aspects of its supply chain: it uses online procurement for office supplies and puts outsourcing enquiries on the Internet via engineering bulletin boards.

Spencer Davies' e-business strategy has allowed it to expand while continuing to streamline its business. Its ICT investments have also produced greater auditing and management reporting facilities, giving the company the ability to evaluate future investments before committing financial resources. "We've been able to quantify the benefits thanks to technology," says Owain Davies, Managing Director.

The time taken from design stage to the finished product has been dramatically reduced. Today, if the information is sent electronically by customers, the job can reach the production stage within 30 seconds. The company is now better equipped to tackle more complex engineering projects and consequently appeals to more potential customers. "Our investment in technology has allowed us to develop the business and look at new markets," explains Owain.

The improvement in communications with suppliers has been due in large part to enthusiasm from Spencer Davies Engineering. "Most of our suppliers are not eager to work electronically and that's a barrier," admits Owain. "What I'm trying to do is show the benefits of technology and persuade them to come on board. Once they see the business benefits, we can usually win them over."

In addition to the direct benefits of the company's investment in ICT, Owain has noticed some equally important, but unexpected results. Spencer Davies' positive, forward-thinking attitude is producing a competitive advantage. "We are getting some valuable customer referrals," explains Owain. "Our use of technology gives them the confidence to recommend our services. Technology has definitely allowed us to get more for our money. It's now easier for us to sell because of the information that we have."

Source: Department of Trade and Industry, www.dti.gov.uk
Crown copyright material is reproduced with the permission of HMSO and the Queen's Printer for Scotland

1   What impact does the use of technology have on the competitive performance of Spencer Davies?

Case Study 6.1 Question

Hardware Technologies

Computer Numerically Controlled (CNC) machines are machine tools that can be controlled by computer. Machining Centres (MCs) involve more complex technology and incorporate features such as the ability to carry tools that can be automatically changed depending on the requirements of the operation being undertaken.

A **robot** is a programmable machine that can undertake tasks that may be dangerous, dirty or dull for people to carry out. A robot may have an arm and end effector that is used to pick, hold and place items. Robots can generally undertake tasks quicker and more consistently than humans.

Automated Material Handling (AMH) systems are designed to improve efficiency in the movement, storage and retrieval of materials. Types of systems include Automated Guided Vehicle (AGV) systems that transport material on driverless vehicles to various locations in the plant. Automated Storage and Retrieval Systems (AS/RS) handle the storage and retrieval of materials using computers to direct automatic loaders to pick and place items in a storage facility.

Flexible Manufacturing Cell (FMC) systems integrate individual items of automation described above to form an automated manufacturing system that can consist of two or more CNC machining centres, a robot and a cell computer which coordinates the various operations in the cell. The robot can be used to handle the parts that are being processed and also to perform tool changing

COMPUTER NUMERICALLY CONTROLLED MACHINES (CNC): tools that can be controlled by computer.

ROBOT: a programmable machine that can undertake tasks that may be dangerous, dirty or dull for people to carry out.

AUTOMATED MATERIAL HANDLING (AMH) SYSTEMS: improve efficiency in the movement, storage and retrieval of materials.

FLEXIBLE MANUFACTURING CELL (FMC): integrates individual items of automation to form an automated manufacturing system.

The high-speed tray system offers a unique and cost-effective solution for rapid transit between concourses or terminal buildings or remote screening facilities. It operates at speeds up to 12 metres per second, or 2300 feet per minute, and can handle up to 3000 bags per hour.

Figure 6.2   A high-speed baggage transport system
Source: www.rco.com/services/materialhandling.htm

operations. The tool is the element of the CNC machine (e.g., the drill bit) that is used to process the part. The robot, under the direction of the cell computer, can sense when a tool needs changing either for processing requirements or if the tool is worn and needs replacing.

Flexible Manufacturing Systems (FMS) extend the facilities of an FMC by incorporating automatic parts loading and unloading facilities and an automated guided vehicle system for parts movement, in addition to several CNC MCs and robots.

The system configuration shown in Figure 6.3 is made up of the following components:

> **FLEXIBLE MANUFACTURING SYSTEMS (FMS):** extend the facilities of an FMC by incorporating automatic parts loading and unloading facilities and an automated guided vehicle system for parts movement.

■ DC-4AS high-speed milling machines (3 units);
■ HF-4M multi-centre with a swivelling head (1 unit);
■ MM2500 3-D coordinate measuring machine (1 unit);
■ transfer system;
■ setup station;
■ pallet stocker;
■ manipulator;
■ system control.

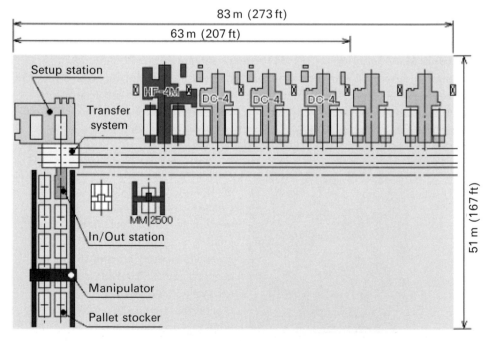

Figure 6.3 Diagram of a flexible manufacturing system layout

Source: www.snkc.co.jp/english/fms/index/fmseng1.htm

FMS systems held out the possibility of factories without people, where the robots and computers would perform all the material handling and processing tasks necessary. However, due to the complexities involved in producing a wide product range fully automated plants have proved to be impractical.

Flexibility (the production of a range of products at low cost that can be delivered quickly to customers) is a key strategic aim for operations. In terms of manufacturing this translates into the ability to perform rapid low-cost switching from one product line to another. An FMS is designed to provide fast, low-cost changes from one part to another, lower direct labour costs due to automation and achieve consistent and better quality due to automated control. However, the FMS machines may have a limited ability to adapt to changes in the product specification, a substantial amount of pre-planning is necessary before an FMS can be operated and the systems are very expensive in terms of capital investment. Due to these factors FMCs are often used as an alternative, due to their lower complexity and lower cost. FMSs are most relevant to the production of items such as small batches of machined goods. Another option to achieve flexibility is to use the Just-In-Time (JIT) philosophy of a flexible work force and small simple machines.

Computer-Integrated Manufacture (CIM)

When the above technologies are integrated using a computer network and database system the resulting automated system is termed **Computer-Integrated Manufacture (CIM)**. Whereas an FMS system is generally concerned with automation directly related to the transformation process, CIM is an automation of the product and process design, planning and control and manufacture of the product. In a fully integrated system the areas of design, testing, fabrication, assembly, inspection and material handling are automated and integrated using technology. For example, **Computer-Aided Manufacturing (CAM)** extends the use of CAD by transmitting the design held in the CAD system electronically to computer-controlled machine tools. Systems that combine these two functions are often referred to as CADCAM. CADCAM systems represent a major tool for operations in linking the design and manufacturing processes.

> **COMPUTER-INTEGRATED MANUFACTURE (CIM):** automation of the product and process design, planning and control and manufacture of the product.

> **COMPUTER-AIDED MANUFACTURING (CAM):** extends the use of CAD by transmitting the design held in the CAD system electronically to computer-controlled machine tools.

Process Technology for Information

Most organizations use some form of computer-based technology to accumulate, organize and distribute information. Most computers are now connected together in some form of network. A Local Area Network (LAN) is usually limited to a company occupying a single building or even several buildings across a large company site. A small-scale network such as this allows people to share information, communicate via systems such as email and share facilities such as printing and software applications. A Wide Area Network (WAN) may connect people across a city, country or between different countries. If the WAN enables communication across the whole company, it is referred to as the 'enterprise network' or 'enterprise-wide' network. To minimize the size of investment in wide area communications a company can use a Value-Added Network (VAN) which is a network rented out by a service provider.

In the 1960s the use of **Electronic Data Interchange (EDI)** became established (Chapter 15). This allows the exchange of structured information, such as orders, invoices, delivery advices and payment instructions, over a network allowing, for example, the automatic reordering and payment for stock from a supplier without human intervention. The automated transfer of money between organizations is referred to as Electronic Funds Transfer (EFT). The most common platform for networked IT is the Internet which is a global network of millions of connected networks that uses a transmission method called the 'Transmission Control Protocol over Internet Protocol' (TCP/IP) to communicate with one another. There is no global control over transmissions using this method, these are governed by the requester and sender of the information.

The majority of Internet services are available to any business or consumer who has access to the Internet. However, if information is limited to those within the organization it is termed an 'intranet'. If access is extended to some others, but not everyone beyond the organization, this is an 'extranet'. The World Wide Web (WWW) provides a standard method for exchanging and publishing information on the Internet. It provides a graphical environment with hyperlinks which allow users to readily move from one document or web site to another by selecting an image or text highlighted by underlining and/or a different colour.

In order to understand how the information technology is applied, it is useful to outline some of the types of information systems that use information technology in manufacturing and service organizations. Operational Information Systems are generally concerned with process control, transaction-processing communications and productivity. Management Information Systems are concerned with assisting decision-making activities. Other types of information systems considered are e-business systems, m-business systems and customer relationship management systems.

ELECTRONIC DATA INTERCHANGE (EDI):
the exchange of structured information, such as orders, invoices, delivery advices and payment instructions, over a network.

Operational Information Systems

Operational systems are used for the tasks involved in the daily running of a business. Their performance is often vital to an organization and they are sometimes described as mission-critical or strategic information systems. We consider three types of operational systems:

- *Transaction Processing Systems (TPSs)* – these systems involve recording and processing data that result from an organization's business transactions. Applications include real time (online) processing of balance enquiries in a cash-point system and batch processing of customer bills for utilities. TPSs are generally for frequent and routine transactions at an operational level in the organization.
- *Office Automation Systems (OASs)* – OASs are used to manage the administrative functions in an office environment and are often critical to service-based industries. They include groupware which assists teams of people working together through facilities such as email and teleconferencing within or between companies.
- *Workflow Management Systems (WFMSs)* – automate a business process by providing a structured framework to support the process. They can assign tasks to people, allow collaboration between people sharing tasks, retrieve information needed to complete a task (e.g., customer details). They can also provide an overview of the status of each task which can be used in conjunction with Document Image Processing (DIP) to provide automated routing of documents across a computer network. Figure 6.4 shows an example of a screen display of a workflow system of a requisition-approval process.
- *Process control systems* – these include systems such as CAD, CAM and FMS which are important in manufacturing industries for controlling the manufacture of goods. These systems have been covered earlier in this chapter.

Management Information Systems

Management information systems can be defined as systems used to support tactical and strategic decision making. Three types of management information systems are:

- *Decision Support Systems (DSSs)* – these provide information and models in a form to facilitate tactical and strategic decision making. Types of DSS include Expert Systems (ESs) to represent the knowledge and decision-making skills of specialists and neural networks which learn problem-solving skills by exposure to a wide range of problems.
- *Information Reporting Systems (IRSs)* – these provide pre-specified reports for day-to-day decision making. Reports include periodic reports such as weekly sales summary and exception reports triggered by events such as production levels falling below normal.

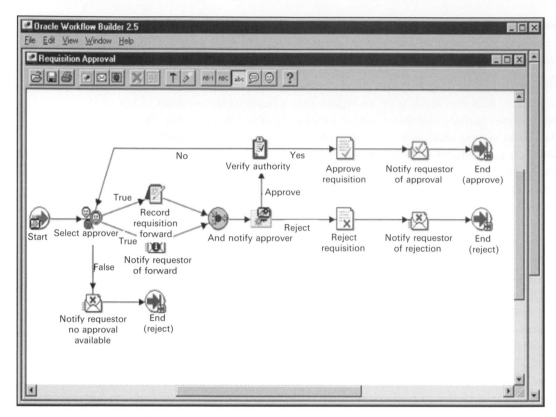

Figure 6.4 Screen display of a workflow system

Source: www.oracle.com/appsnet/products/procurement/collateral/ds_workflow.html
Copyright © 2000, Oracle. All rights reserved.

■ *Executive Information Systems (EISs)* – these provide senior managers with a system to analyse, compare and highlight trends to help govern the strategic direction of a company. Data warehouses are large database systems containing detailed company data on sales transactions which are analysed to assist in improving the marketing and financial performance of companies. They have to a large extent displaced EIS in software purchases for strategic and tactical decision making. Data marts are small-scale data warehouses which hold departmental information. The term 'data mining of data warehouses' is used to refer to an attempt to identify relationships between variables in order to assist decision making.

E-business

E-BUSINESS:

the transformation of business processes through the use of Internet technologies.

E-business can be seen as the transformation of business processes through the use of Internet technologies. The definition by IBM (www.ibm.com/e-business) is as follows:

e-business (e' biz' nis): The process of using Web technology to help businesses streamline processes, improve productivity and increase efficiencies. Enables companies to easily communicate with partners, vendors and customers, connect back-end data systems and transact commerce in a secure manner.

From this definition it can be seen that e-business includes e-commerce (see next section) but is broader in scope in that it also refers to the use of Internet technology to support internal processes. E-business opportunities can be classified in terms of whether an organization is using the Internet to transact with consumers, called **Business-to-Consumer (B2C)** or other businesses, called **Business-to-Business (B2B)**. B2B transactions predominate over the Internet, in terms of value, if not frequency. This is explained by the fact that there are many more opportunities for B2B transactions than B2C, both between an organization and its suppliers, together with intermediaries, and through distributors such as agents and wholesalers with customers. Additionally, there is a higher level of access to the Internet among businesses than among consumers, and a greater propensity to use it for purchasing. There are also two additional types of transaction: that where consumers transact directly with consumers (C2C) and that where they initiate trading with business (C2B). Note that the terms C2C and C2B are less widely used but they do highlight significant differences between Internet-based commerce and earlier forms of commerce. C2C interactions were relatively rare, but are now very common in the form of online auctions and communities. As well as the models described, it has been suggested that employees should be considered as a separate type of interaction through the use of intranets (internal Internet-based networks) – this is sometimes referred to as 'Employee-to-Employee' (E2E). The benefit to business of adopting e-business is a mix of cost reduction achieved through lower costs of information transfer and processing and the potential for increased revenue arising from increased reach to a larger audience. The benefits of e-business for operations relate to areas such as supply chain integration using B2B and B2C interactions as well as the increased efficiency and effectiveness of internal business processes using E2E interactions. For an example of an e-business system see the description of e-procurement described in Chapter 15.

BUSINESS-TO-CONSUMER (B2C): Web-based commercial transactions between an organization and consumers.

BUSINESS-TO-BUSINESS (B2B): Web-based commercial transactions between an organization and other organizations.

CASE STUDY 6.2

Amazon Aims to Be King of Online Retail Jungle

When Jeff Bezos launched Amazon.com in 1995, he wanted it to be 'earth's largest bookstore'. Now it has an even grander sounding ambition: to be 'earth's most customer-centric organization'. Amazon is no longer just an online book and music retailer, but has transformed into a virtual 'mall' selling golf balls to plasma screen TVs. Many are sold through its site by other retailers such as Gap, the fashion chain, Nordstrom, the department store retailer, or Target, the discounter. That strategy, launched with a partnership with Toys R Us in August 2000, has accelerated in the past year. Click on Amazon's US web site today and find a clothing store with partners ranging from Eddie Bauer to Urban Outfitters, and its sporting goods store, launched last month, with more than 3000 brands covering 50 sports.

Unlike its books business, Amazon does not hold these products in its warehouses and fulfil customers' orders: its partners do that. Amazon takes the orders and rakes off a commission. Roger Blackwell, professor of marketing at the Fisher College of Business at Ohio State University, says Amazon has shifted from a business-to-consumer operator to more of a business-to-business operator. Amazon calls it going from retailer to 'retail platform'. The market approves. From a low of $5.97 2 years ago, when investors fretted it might run out of money, Amazon's shares have mushroomed to almost $60, reaching valuations last seen during the Internet boom. Investors have bet it will be one of the few Internet pioneers to reach long-term profitability.

Tuesday's third-quarter earnings, after the market close, may provide more evidence. Quarterly revenues are expected to be up more than 30% to $1.12bn, according to Reuters Estimates, with pro forma earnings – which exclude various costs, but are the figures analysts forecast – of 10 cents per share, against breakeven a year ago. "Amazon could not survive unless it evolved to a business-to-business service provider model," says Mr Blackwell. "There's certainly more money to be made from selling [services] to Target and Nordstrom than selling books to consumers."

Its retail partnerships take several forms. First is the so-called 'merchants@' programme, including its clothing, sporting goods and toy stores, where Amazon earns fees or commissions for taking orders. This also includes its Marketplace area, where small businesses and individuals can sell new and used goods. Transactions here account for about 20% of Amazon's unit sales.

Second is 'merchants.com'. Here Amazon operates websites for other retailers under their names, using its e-commerce expertise, again earning fees or commissions. Third are co-branded 'syndicated' stores, where Amazon sells its products through someone else's site. Consumers clicking on Borders.com, website for one of the biggest US bricks-and-mortar book stores, for example, find themselves at a site styled 'Borders teamed with Amazon.com'. A similar arrangement applies at Waterstones, the UK bookseller.

Amazon claims to be indifferent to whether customers buy goods new or used from its own business, from partners or individuals. It makes money from each transaction, it says, aiming simply to be a "place where people can find, discover, and buy anything they want to buy online." That makes it potentially the dominant Internet shopping destination. Respective margins on its own and third-party transactions are not disclosed. But analysts suggest it can earn bigger margins on selling partners' goods, without storage and distribution costs. Heath Terry of CSFB estimated in a recent research report that operating margins on third-party business could top 30%. The strategy has risks. Amazon has worked hard to build up its customer base by shifting to a lower priced strategy, offering free shipping and price discounts. It has no control, however, over partners' pricing while some manufacturers such as Nike have attempted to keep their products off a site they see as an inappropriate sales channel for their brand.

The strategy also brings Amazon into closer competition with another Internet pioneer: eBay. eBay's 'Buy it now' function increasingly allows consumers to purchase at fixed prices rather than at auction, and it also has partnerships with other retailers. And there is still the matter of paying off Amazon's $2bn debt. "Amazon has no price/ earnings ratio, because it has no earnings," says Mr Blackwell. "This is a company built on faith in the future."

Source: FT.com site, Neil Buckley, 20 October 2003
© The Financial Times Ltd

1   Discuss how Amazon is moving from B2C to B2B Internet transactions.

**Case Study 6.2
Question**

E-commerce

Electronic commerce (e-commerce) is often thought to simply refer to buying and selling using the Internet: people immediately think of consumer retail purchases from companies such as Amazon. But, e-commerce involves much more than electronically mediated financial transactions between organizations and customers. Many commentators refer to e-commerce as all electronically mediated transactions between an organization and any third party it deals with. By this definition, non-financial transactions such as customer requests for further information would also be considered to be part of e-commerce. When evaluating the impact of e-commerce on an organization, it is instructive to identify opportunities for buy-side and sell-side e-commerce transactions as depicted in **Figure 6.5**, since business information systems with different functionality will need to be created to accommodate transactions with buyers and suppliers. **Buy-side e-commerce** refers to transactions to procure resources needed by an organization from its suppliers. **Sell-side e-commerce** refers to transactions involved with selling products to an organization's customers.

In addition to buy-side and sell-side transactions, Figure 6.5 also shows the internal (or inside) processes that are part of e-business. They include transactions related to the buy side such as procurement and sell-side-related transactions such as dealing with customer enquiries as well as basic administrative functions related to employee leave and pay.

ELECTRONIC COMMERCE (E-COMMERCE): electronically mediated information exchanges between an organization and its external stakeholders.

BUY-SIDE E-COMMERCE: transactions between a purchasing organization and its suppliers.

SELL-SIDE E-COMMERCE: transactions between a supplier organization and its customers.

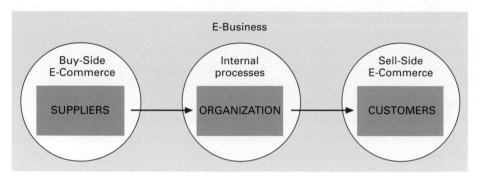

Figure 6.5   Buy-side and sell-side e-commerce

M-business

M-business can be defined as the integration of Internet and wireless communications technology. It is a result of mobile communications facilitated by broadband (high bandwidth) Internet connections and wireless technology (e.g., mobile phones using radio waves). Mobile computing allows people choice in how they communicate by offering multiple devices, applications and tools from which to select and it permits people to control the time and frequency with which they obtain information. Some of the applications for m-business include:

■ *Procurement* – the extension of e-procurement applications to enable orders to be taken using handheld devices (e.g., barcode readers).
■ *Order fulfilment and delivery management* – delivery information is input using a tablet and the customer can track their order immediately over the Internet.
■ *Asset tracking* – the monitoring of materials internally will extend to the monitoring of highly mobile geographically dispersed assets.
■ *Service management* – service requests can be automatically dispatched to field personnel to ensure timely response and efficient scheduling.

CASE STUDY 6.3

Kennedys

With three international offices, seven associate offices and six different locations throughout the UK, supporting the mobility of key staff was an important consideration for Kennedys, a UK litigation firm.

Kennedys wanted to provide its employees with a way to access their work systems (e.g., their calendars, contacts and email inboxes) while on the move. The company decided a system whereby staff had remote access to its network would improve efficiency throughout the company and enable flexible working, vital in a business where staff are constantly 'in the field' and not necessarily working to strict office hours. The high-pressure world of litigation means that lawyers need regular access to their work systems to stay on top of their diaries and to manage 'time management' issues while outside the office.

Following a consultation on the company's communications services, Kennedys invested in BlackBerry devices – handheld devices for sending and receiving emails and accessing office features, like contacts and the corporate calendar, on the move. BlackBerry is a more advanced step from traditional PDAs and also allows full access to the Internet and all data sent and received are fully encrypted. The device is made available to any employees that want to use it – to date, 70 Kennedys partners have taken up the initiative, while the company claims to be one of the first businesses to take up this new technology.

Kennedys now has plans to roll out the device to a total of up to 200 employees. Kennedys' Carolyn Lees says BlackBerry has provided fast Internet access on the move, the ability to set up 'virtual private networks', which allow out-of-office access, making working practices far more efficient. Lees says: "We can quantify the improvements only in terms of how much more productivity we see and the great accessibility to our work systems that we all now have." She adds that the 'immediacy' of electronic communications is a key benefit of the new system, while accessibility to programmes across the Web has been improved greatly.

Key issues at Kennedys have been with educating users about the new systems. The speed of change, says Lees, means that users often get left behind and it is, thus, vital to train employees and other users such as suppliers effectively so that the new technologies can be exploited effectively. Initial increased complexity presents problems, but the new technologies are designed to reduce complexity in terms of working practices. Training, she says, is the key. She says: "People skills are still the key to success." Also, Lees says, it is vital to build in contingency plans to cope with problems that may arise, adding that she has used IT publications and online forums on the Web to keep herself updated on the latest ICTs, while Kennedys relies on consultancy help on new technology projects.

While Kennedys looks to enable more and more of its employees with the new BlackBerry devices, it continues to develop an ICT strategy "geared towards retaining and acquiring new clients." Overall, Lees says it intends "to continue to remain competitive with our ICTs and to improve business efficiencies."

Source: Department of Trade and Industry, www.gov.dti.uk
Crown copyright material is reproduced with the permission of HMSO and the Queen's Printer for Scotland

1   How does the use of the BlackBerry device help the effectiveness of the service Kennedys provides?

Case Study 6.3
Question

Customer Relationship Management (CRM)

Customer Relationship Management (CRM) covers the whole process by which relationships with customers are built and maintained. CRM systems are designed to integrate the range of information systems that contain information regarding the customer. These include applications such as customer details and preference databases, sales order-processing applications and sales force automation. The idea is to acquire customers, retain customers and increase customer involvement with the organization.

CRM systems are built around a database and when this database is accessed by employees and customers, using a web site, the technology is often referred to as e-CRM. Common applications which would be integrated in a CRM system include:

■ *Customer Data Collection* – this can include personal details such as age, sex and contact address. Also, a record of purchase transactions undertaken in terms of factors such as location, date, time, quantity and price. This information can be used by call centre staff to improve and tailor their services to individual customers.
■ *Customer Data Analysis* – the captured data allows the categorization and targeting of customers according to criteria set by the firm. This information can be used to improve the effectiveness of marketing campaigns.
■ *Sales Force Automation* – the entire sales cycle from lead generation to close of sale and after sales service can be facilitated using CRM.

The technology must support all of these applications through whatever communications channel the customer and employee use. Communication channels include face-to-face, mail, phone, email as well as Web-based interaction. As with other technologies, the implementation of CRM is a choice between attempting to integrate a number of legacy (existing) systems such as sales order processing or choosing a single-vendor supplier such as for ERP. Single-vendor systems from suppliers such as SAP and Oracle are able to provide better integration and, thus, potentially better customer service. However, they are relatively expensive to install and one firm is unlikely to supply the best-in-class applications in all aspects of the CRM implementation.

CASE STUDY 6.4

The Everyman Theatre

The Everyman Theatre developed a CRM system to maximize the marketing potential of the customer information it was receiving through its online ticketing system. It built a Web service programme that runs constantly, interrogating new bookings to retrieve specific information such as the person's email address, whether the tickets were bought as a result of a specific promotion, etc. This information is moved over to the marketing database, which continues to grow as more relevant information is added. The programme also builds a list of everyone who visited a show the previous evening. These customers are automatically emailed, thanked for their visit and invited to click on a link that takes them to the website to fill in a survey on their experience at the Theatre.

Source: www.dti.gov.uk/bestpractice
Crown copyright material is reproduced with the permission of HMSO and the Queen's Printer for Scotland

1   What benefits does the Everyman Theatre gain from the use of their CRM system?

**Case Study 6.4
Question**

CASE STUDY 6.5

How to Click with Your Customers

In the past 10 years, customer relationship management, or CRM as it is known, has attained near mythical status within organizations. Some of the most successful companies in the world have built their operations around the notion that an ability to understand and deal directly with their customers helps to reduce costs and improve sales, but, most importantly in an age of radical competition, actually increases loyalty and profitability by providing a more personalized and responsive service. The model on which this virtuous circle relies is the notion that every transaction with an organization should improve your next experience. The world's greatest retailers, like Tesco and Amazon, view every shopping basket as not just a sale but as another opportunity to understand. These companies religiously study every interaction in the service of delivering better specification to their supplier and improved value to their customers.

This is not an easy job; in fact, applying this model of continuous improvement is fiendishly difficult and relies not just on a complete devotion to the principle of putting the customer at the centre of how your organization thinks, but, most importantly, it stands and falls on the follow-through of the policies, processes and technologies used to support this vision. The notion of customer focus has so permeated organizational culture that even the public sector has embraced the concept that one size does not necessarily fit all. This wasn't always the case; in fact, it wasn't more than 10 years ago that databases were still a novel part of most organizations. So, the idea of pulling together a single real time view of a customer's history from information gleaned from both within (and sometimes beyond) their organization was still in the realm of science fiction.

The nirvana which the CRM travellers seek is a company where the extremities are perfectly attuned to the needs and realities of the customer. This is the world where all customer-facing employees have all the information they need at their fingertips, so when they interact with you they can appear as if they've known you forever, understand your issues and suggest solutions that at best will make you spend more and at worst will make sure you don't defect to the competition. Chasing nirvana has always been a frustrating and expensive business. IDC predicts that $11.4bn will be spent worldwide on CRM applications by 2008. But the bills don't stop with the software. The real money is being made by businesses like Accenture and IBM in services like CRM training and outsourcing which are expected by IDC to be worth $93bn in 2005.

However, the history of most CRM implementations has been nothing short of disastrous. Gartner reports that most businesses underestimate costs by as much as 75%. Large businesses will typically spend between $30m and $90m over a 3-year period in technology, staff, consulting services and training related to CRM but Gartner suggests that over 50% of these implementations are considered a failure by the customers.

Source: excerpt from 'How to click with your customers' by Saul Klein, *The Guardian*, 6 September 2004
© Guardian Newspapers Ltd 2004

Case Study 6.5
Questions

1   How does the concept of CRM fit within a culture of continuous improvement?
2   Why do so many CRM implementations fail?

Process Technology for Customers

One distinguishing feature of services is that the customer is often present while the service is being delivered. In fact, the contact between the customer and service provider is often the service itself, such as a visit to the dentist. In order to provide a consistent level of quality of service, it is, therefore, important that the service providers are well trained and motivated. One approach to improving service delivery is to encourage the participation of the customer in the service delivery process itself. Thus, instead of passively waiting for a service, the customer can be enabled by technology to avail themselves of the service at a time of their choosing and to make choices regarding that service. From a service provider viewpoint, this has the advantage of reducing staffing requirements and empowering customers by giving them a greater sense of control over the type of service they require.

However, customers have different preferences and many facilities may well need both customer-driven and traditional people-based service delivery systems. For example, it is common to see a customer using an Automatic Teller Machine (ATM) at a bank while another customer prefers to enter the bank and queue to see a clerk for exactly the same service. While ATM technology has allowed banks to significantly reduce their number of branches and staffing requirement, there is still a need to provide customer contact for some services and some customers. The ATM is an example of a wider use of technology to provide self-service facilities for services such as meals and drinks. Again, a choice between self-service and a full-service option is often provided.

Summary

1 Process technologies for material processing cover a wide range of facilities such as design, engineering and manufacture.

2 Information technology such as computer network systems can be used to accumulate, organize and distribute information.

3 Operational information systems are used for tasks involved in the daily running of the business. Management information systems are used to support tactical and strategic decision making.

4 E-business can be seen as the transformation of business processes through the use of Internet technologies. E-commerce can be seen as electronically mediated transactions between an organization and any third party it deals with.

5 Technology such as automated teller machines can be used to provide assistance when the customer is present in the service delivery process.

Exercises

1. What are the advantages of using CAD technology?
2. Describe the major elements of FMS and evaluate the concept.
3. Discuss how CIM could provide strategic advantage.
4. What is the relevance of process technology to service organizations.
5. Identify process technology that may be found in a large retail organization.
6. Describe the categories of operational information systems and management information systems and provide business examples of their use for each category.
7. Describe the purpose of workflow management systems throughout the organization.
8. Explain the relationship between the concepts of e-commerce and e-business.
9. What are the potential advantages of CRM?

Further Reading

Bocij, P., Chaffey, D., Greasley, A. and Hickie, S. (2006), *Business Information Systems: Technology, Development and Management for the E-business*, 3rd Edition, Pearson Education.

Hayes, R., Pisano, G., Upton, D. and Wheelwright, S. (2005), *Operations, Strategy, and Technology: Pursuing the Competitive Edge*, John Wiley & Sons.

Web Links

www.abb.com ABB. Supplier of many automation devices, such as robotic systems.

www.denford.co.uk/cim.html Denford UK. Suppliers of CIM systems.

www.autodesk.co.uk AutoDesk Inc. AutoCAD software for product design.

www.graphisoft.com Graphisoft Inc. ArchiCAD software for product design.

www.proviasoftware.com Provia Software Inc. Suppliers of Automated Storage and Retrieval Systems (AS/RS).

www.e-consultancy.com Online digest of consultant and analyst reports in e-business.

www.wfmc.org Workflow Management Coalition. Contains introductory papers on the purpose and components of workflow systems.

www.gsmworld.com/index.shtml GSM Association. Global trade association for GSM mobile operators.

www.cornwell.co.uk/crm.htm Cornwell Management Consultants. An example of a definition of CRM provided by a consultancy organization.

www.wired.com/news/ebiz *Wired Magazine*. News and articles on e-business topics.

Chapter 7
Product and Service Design

- ■ Service Design
- ■ The Design Process
  - ● Idea Generation
  - ● Feasibility Study
  - ● Preliminary Design
  - ● Final Design
- ■ Improving Design
  - ● Concurrent Design
  - ● Design For Manufacture (DFM)
  - ● Mass Customization
  - ● Quality Functional Deployment (QFD)
  - ● Taguchi Methods

Learning Objectives

After reading this chapter, you should be able to:

1 Understand issues involved in the design of services.

2 Describe the main steps in the design process.

3 Discuss the use of concurrent design.

4 Understand the term 'mass customization'.

5 Describe the role of DFM, QFD and Taguchi methods in improving design.

Introduction

Good design of products and services is an essential element in satisfying customer needs and, therefore, ensuring the long-term success of the organization. The success of the design process is primarily dependent on the relationship between the marketing, design and operations functions of the organization. These functions need to cooperate in order to identify customer needs and produce a cost-effective and quality design that meets these needs. The marketing function will undertake tasks such as conducting market research to evaluate consumer needs and provide a forecast of demand in the market place taking into account competitive pressures and the external environment. The design function will undertake the design of the product or service and the design of the process that will produce the product or deliver the service. It is operations' role to efficiently produce the product or deliver the service as designed using the specified process.

In addition, the role of suppliers is becoming increasingly important in product design due to the practice of outsourcing or contracting to another company part of the design or production of the product itself. Finance will also be involved in providing capital for development costs and facilities. It will need to evaluate the success of any products introduced into the market place and provide estimates of when the investment made to bring the product to market will be paid back. Calculations will need to include factors such as overhead costs as well as costs directly attributable to the product. Communication between all of these functions can be facilitated by the use of accounting and information systems that allow up-to-date and accurate information to be available across the organization.

The chapter will first discuss some of the attributes of service design before outlining the steps involved in the design of a product or service. There is then a discussion of some of the techniques that may be used to improve the results of the design process. Many of the techniques are concerned with ensuring that final quality is high by taking appropriate action at the design stage.

Service Design

In service design the overall set of expected benefits that the customer is buying is termed the 'service concept'. The service will usually consist of a combination of goods and services and is termed the **service package**. Fitzsimmons and Fitzsimmons (1994) define the service package as a bundle of goods and services consisting of the following four features:

1 *Supporting Facility* – the physical resources that must be in place before a service can be offered.
2 *Facilitating Goods* – the material purchased or consumed by the buyer or items provided by the customer.
3 *Explicit Services* – the benefits that are readily observable by the senses and consist of the essential or intrinsic features of the service.
4 *Implicit Services* – psychological benefits that the customer may sense only vaguely or extrinsic features of the service.

The point is that the providers of the service may only focus on the delivery of the explicit service and neglect the other components of the service package. It is important to recognize the effect on the level of service that all the elements of the service package have.

A service is an experience, not simply the receiving of a good, and so the customer will be in contact with the service as it is delivered. This means the service design must take into account how the individual customer will react to the service as it is delivered. This is not easy as all customers are different and have different expectations of what the service will provide. This requires close cooperation between operations and marketing to identify a target customer market and ensure that the service design is meeting their needs.

Another feature of service design is that because the service is intangible it is often difficult to test quality levels before the service is provided. From the customer's point of view quality may only be assessed when the service is provided or perhaps an indication of service quality may be gained by seeking the views of others who have experience of the service required. Quality can be designed into the service by taking the design features and implementing a quality system to maintain conformance to design requirements. The techniques of QFD and Taguchi discussed later in this chapter are relevant in ensuring service design quality.

Finally, it should be remembered that most products are accompanied by some sort of service (e.g., a 1-year warranty for a washing machine) and most services are accompanied by some sort of product (e.g., a consultancy report presented at the end of a consultancy project); so, generally, product and service design will be considered together as part of the whole design concept.

CASE STUDY 7.1

Benugo

Taking its name from co-founders Ben and Hugo Warner, Benugo cafes opened for business in 1998. They offered customers a new style of cafe with 'pizzazz', in an environment where people could relax and enjoy their food. With 11 cafe shops in and around London, 150 staff employed throughout the business and annual revenues of over £6m, Benugo has proved to be a big hit with customers. "At Benugo we know that the customer always has a choice," says Tim Parfitt, Finance Director. "We want Benugo to be that choice as often as possible."

But, in today's market margins are low and competition is fierce. Business survival depends on sustaining profitability and maintaining customer satisfaction. This is why Tim was intrigued by the proposition from technology solutions provider, Broadscape. The proposal was to provide Benugo's customers with high-speed Internet access over a Wireless Local Area Network (WLAN) with a WiFi access point. This would effectively mean that a customer could come into a Benugo's cafe, open up their laptop and have instant access to the Internet without having to plug in any cables. Benugo trialled the idea in two of their cafes. They offered wireless Internet connections free of charge as long as customers spent £2 or over on food or coffee for every 30 minutes of use. A short flyer tells customers how to set up the WiFi access on their laptop and within minutes they're online. Broadscape's installation also included Bluetooth which allowed compatible PDAs to connect to the Internet as well. The innovative aspect of the system is that customers are not charged directly for Internet access, which, in turn, means that there are no billing issues and nothing complicated to consider with billing updates.

Source: Department of Trade and Industry, www.dti.gov.uk
Crown copyright material is reproduced with the permission of HMSO and the Queen's Printer for Scotland

Case Study 7.1 Question

1   How does the concept of the service package relate to the facilities offered by Benugo?

The Design Process

The design process involves the following steps (shown in Figure 7.1).

Traditionally, the design process is undertaken as a number of sequential steps, shown in Figure 7.1, with work undertaken within functional areas (such as marketing, design and engineering). The problem with the traditional approach is the cost and time involved in bringing the product to market. In some business sectors (e.g., IT) shrinking product life cycles have meant that new products or improvements to existing products are required in an ever shorter timescale.

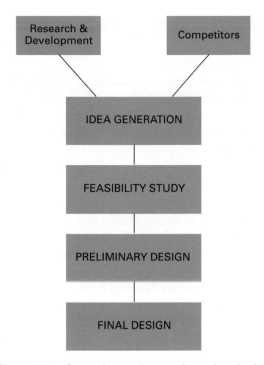

Figure 7.1   Steps in product and service design

Another problem with the traditional approach to design is the lack of communication between functional specialists involved in the different stages of design. This can lead to an attitude of passing the design to the next department without any consideration of problems that may be encountered at later design stages. An example of this is decisions made at the preliminary design stage that adversely affect choices at the product build stage. This can cause the design to be repeatedly passed between departments to satisfy everyone's needs, increasing time and costs.

Alternative approaches to design called 'concurrent design' or 'simultaneous engineering' are where contributors to the stages of the design effort provide their expertise together throughout the design process as a team. Concurrent design reduces the time wasted when each stage in the design process waits for the previous stage to finish completely before it can commence. By facilitating communication through the establishment of a project team, the problem of a lack of communication between functions can be reduced. Concurrent design is discussed in more detail later in this chapter. The steps involved in the design process are now outlined in detail.

Idea Generation

Ideas for new products and services can come from a variety of sources, including the organization's Research and Development (R&D) department, suggestions from customers, market research data, salespeople, competitor actions or developments in new technology. The major source of new ideas or innovations will be dependent largely on the organization's strategy.

The Research and Development Function

For an organization that has a strategy of being first to the market with a new product or service, ideas will be devised principally from the organization's own R&D department. For an organization with a similar product to their competitors, innovation may be primarily in the design and manufacture stages to attain lower production costs. Successful product innovation comes from understanding the customer and identifying their needs. Various data collection methods such as questionnaires, focus groups and interviews should be used to gain sufficient understanding of customer requirements.

R&D can take on the following forms:

- *Pure Research* – knowledge-oriented research to develop new ideas with no specific product in mind.
- *Applied Research* – problem-oriented research to discover new ideas with specific commercial applications.
- *Development* – product-oriented research concerned with turning research ideas into products.

Pure research is often based in universities and funded by government agencies and so it is necessary for organizations to maintain close contact with the relevant institutions. Applied research will be undertaken by most organizations. The cost of undertaking R&D is high and there will be many failed projects, but the payoff from the small number of successes may be vital to the organization's continued profitability.

CASE STUDY 7.2

R&D at Toyota

Toyota utilizes a multi-phase development process. Synergy between these phases helps assure Toyota can consistently bring forward-thinking, high-quality, attractive products quickly to its customers.

1   Basic Research and Development

This phase defines the basic direction of development. It entails developing basic parts, the building blocks of a vehicle.

2   Advanced Engineering Development

This phase is where breakthroughs in technology occur. In order to keep one step ahead of its competitors, this phase focuses on new components and systems research.

3   Product Development

This phase centres around developing new vehicle models.

Source: www.toyota.co.uk
Reproduced by permission of Toyota (GB) PLC

1 What do you consider are the benefits of the multi-phase approach adopted by Toyota?	**Case Study 7.2 Question**

Competitors

Competitors can provide a good source of ideas and it is important that the organization analyses any new products or services as they are introduced to the market and make an appropriate response. **Reverse Engineering** is a systematic approach to dismantling and inspecting a competitor's product to look for aspects of design that could be incorporated into the organization's own product. This is especially prevalent when the product is a complex assembly such as a car, where design choices are myriad.

Benchmarking compares a product or service against what is considered the best in that market segment and then making recommendations on how the product or service can be improved to meet that standard. Although a reactive strategy, benchmarking can be useful to organizations who have lost ground to innovative competitors. More details on benchmarking are given in Chapter 18.

> **REVERSE ENGINEERING:** a systematic approach to dismantling and inspecting a competitor's product to look for aspects of design that could be incorporated into the organization's own product.

Feasibility Study

The marketing function will take the ideas created in the idea generation stage and form a series of alternative concepts on which a feasibility study is undertaken. The concept refers not to the physical product or specification of the service that the person is buying but the overall set of expected benefits that a customer is receiving. For instance, a restaurant meal consists not only of the meal itself, but the level of attention and the general surroundings. Thus, the concept is referring to the combination of physical product and service, called the 'package', which

> **BENCHMARKING:** compares a product or service against what is considered the best in that market segment and makes recommendations on how the product or service can be improved to meet that standard.

delivers a set of expected benefits to the customer. Once a concept has been formulated, it must then be submitted to a market, economic and technical analysis in order to assess its feasibility.

Market Analysis

MARKET ANALYSIS: evaluates the design concept with potential customers through interviews, focus groups and other data collection methods.

A **market analysis** consists of evaluating the design concept with potential customers through interviews, focus groups and other data collection methods. A physical product may be tested by supplying a sample for customer evaluation. The market analysis should identify whether sufficient demand for the proposed product or service exists and its fit with the existing marketing strategy.

At a strategic level the organization can use the Product Life Cycle (PLC) to determine the likely cost and volume characteristics of the product or service. The life cycle describes the volume over sales over time in four phases of introduction, growth, maturity and decline (more details on stages in the PLC are given in Chapter 2).

By relating the PLC to the design process in the *introduction* phase, production costs are high and design changes may be frequent. However, there may be little or no competition for the new product or service and so it may be possible to charge a premium price to customers. The *growth* phase sees a rapid increase in volume and the possibility of competitors entering the market. At this stage it is important to establish the product or service in the market as firmly as possible in order to secure future sales. Costs should be declining as process improvements and standardization take place. In the *mature* phase, competitive pressures will increase and it is important that sales are secured through a brand image to differentiate it from competitors. There should be a continued effort at design improvement to both the product or service itself and the process that delivers it. Some products, such as consumer durables, may stay in the mature phase almost indefinitely, and techniques such as advertising are used to maintain interest and market share. Many services can be improved by the exploitation of technological developments such as Internet banking. In the *decline* phase, before the product or service is discontinued or modified to meet customer needs, the focus should be on optimizing profits while minimizing new investment.

The PLC is a useful tool in developing a portfolio of products and services to different stages of the life cycle, although it can be difficult to identify when they will enter the next stage of the life cycle or even what stage of the life cycle they are now in.

ECONOMIC ANALYSIS: develops estimates of production and delivery costs and compares them with estimates of demand.

Economic Analysis

Economic analysis consists of developing estimates of production and delivery costs and comparing them with estimates of demand. In order to perform the analysis an accurate estimate of demand is required, possibly derived from statistical forecasts of industry sales and estimates of market share in the sector the product or service is competing in. These estimates will be based on a predicted price range for the product or service which is compatible with its position in the market. In order to assess the feasibility of the product or service, estimates of costs in terms of such factors as staffing, materials and equipment must be obtained. Techniques such as cost/benefit analysis, decision theory and accounting measures such as Net Present Value (NPV) and Internal Rate of Return (IRR) may be used to calculate the profitability of a product. Another tool that can be used is the Cost–Volume–Profit (CVP) model.

The Cost–Volume–Profit Model

The CVP model, which was used in Chapter 5 for location decisions (see Figure 5.3), can also be used to provide an estimate of the profit level generated by a product at a certain product volume. The model assumes a linear relationship of cost and revenue to volume.

If revenue is given by the following formula:

$$TR = SP \times X_S$$

where TR = Total revenue
SP = Selling price
X_S = Units sold.

And cost is given by the following formula:

$$TC = FC + VC \times X_P$$

where TC = Total cost
FC = Fixed cost
VC = Variable cost per unit
X_P = Number of units produced.

Then profit can be given by the following formula:

$$P = TR - TC$$

where P = Profit
TR = Total revenue
TC = Total cost.

Assuming $X_S = X_P$ (i.e., all products made are sold), then the volume for a certain profit can be given by the following formula:

$$X = \frac{P + FC}{SP - VC}$$

where X = Volume (units)
P = Profit
FC = Fixed costs
SP = Selling price
VC = Variable costs

When Profit = 0 (i.e., Selling costs = Production costs), called the 'breakeven point', volume can be calculated by the following formula:

$$X = \frac{FC}{SP - VC}$$

Worked Example 7.1

Cost–Volume–Profit Model

A manufacturer produces a product with the following parameters:

$$\text{Selling price } (SP) = £7/\text{unit}$$
$$\text{Variable cost } (VC) = £4/\text{unit}$$
$$\text{Fixed costs } (FC) = £15\,000/\text{week}$$

a What is the breakeven point?

b How many do they need to sell to make £15 000 profit a week.

Solution

a At breakeven point, $P = 0$:

$$X = \frac{FC}{SP - VC}$$
$$= \frac{15\,000}{7 - 4}$$
$$= 5\,000 \text{ units/week}$$

b At $P = 15\,000$:

$$X = \frac{P + FC}{SP - VC}$$
$$= \frac{15\,000 + 15\,000}{7 - 4}$$
$$= 10\,000 \text{ units/week}$$

Using the CVP Model for Multiple Products

If a firm produces more than one product using the same fixed costs the total profit can be calculated. The weighted contribution (Selling price – Variable cost) is calculated as follows:

$$WC = \sum_{i=1}^{n} M_i(SP_i - VC_i)$$

where WC = Weighted contribution

M_i = Product mix as a percentage of the total sales for product i
(where $i = 1$ to n, n = Number of products)

SP_i = Selling price for product i

VC_i = Variable cost for product i.

The volume for a certain profit level is given by the following formula:

$$X = \frac{P + FC}{WC}$$

where X = Volume (units)
  P = Profit
  FC = Fixed costs
  WC = Weighted contribution.

Worked Example 7.2

CVP Model for Multiple Products

The following product mix is planned.

	Pliers	Saws
Product mix	0.75	0.25
Selling price/unit	£1.50	£3.20
Variable cost	£1.20	£1.80

Annual fixed cost = £20 000

What is the Breakeven point?

Solution

$$WC = \sum_{i=1}^{n} M_i(SP_i - VC_i)$$

$$= 0.75 \times (1.50 - 1.20) + 0.25 \times (3.2 - 1.8)$$

$$= 0.75 \times 0.3 + 0.25 \times 1.4$$

$$= 0.575$$

At Profit = 0:

$$X = \frac{FC}{WC}$$

$$= 20\,000/0.575$$

$$= 34\,783 \text{ units}$$

Technical Analysis

Technical analysis consists of determining whether the technical capability to manufacture the product or deliver the service exists. This covers such issues as ensuring materials are available to make the product to the specification required, ensuring the appropriate machinery and skills are available to work with these materials and securing staff skills necessary to deliver a service. The technical analysis must take into account the target market and so designers have to consider the costs of reaching the customer with the product or service in order to ensure it can be sold at a competitive price.

Preliminary Design

Design concepts that pass the feasibility stage enter preliminary design. The specification of the concept – what a product or service should do to satisfy customer needs – is translated into a technical specification of the components of the package (the product and service components that satisfy the customer needs defined in the concept) and the process by which the package is created. The specification of the components of the package requires a product and service structure which describes the relationship between the components and a Bill Of Materials (BOM) or list of component quantities derived from the product structure. The process by which the package is created is considered under process design (Chapter 8).

Final Design

The final design stage involves refining the preliminary design through the use of a prototype until a viable final design can be made. Computer-Aided Design (CAD) and Simulation Modelling can be used at this stage to build a computer-based prototype and refine the product and process design. The final design will be assessed in three main areas of Functional Design, Form Design and Production Design.

FUNCTIONAL DESIGN:
ensures the design meets the performance characteristics that are specified in the product concept.

Functional Design

Functional design is used to ensure the design meets the performance characteristics that are specified in the product concept. Two aspects of functional design are reliability and maintainability.

RELIABILITY:
the probability that a product or service will perform its intended function for a specified period of time under normal conditions of use.

Reliability
Reliability is an important performance characteristic and measures the probability that a product or service will perform its intended function for a specified period of time under normal conditions of use. The reliability of each part of the product or service must be determined by reference to the criteria of 'failure' and 'normal' service. These criteria are determined by reference to customer expectations and cost levels. Reliability can be determined by either the

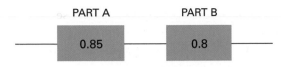

Figure 7.2   Product reliability (serial)

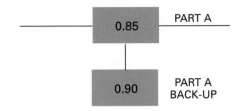

Figure 7.3   Product reliability (back-up)

probability of failure during a given test or the probability of failure during a given time. Strategies for improving product or service reliability include simplified design (e.g., fewer parts in a product), improved reliability of individual elements of the product or service and the adoption of back-up product or service elements.

The probability of failure during a given test is a function of the reliability of component parts and the relationship of those parts. For a product of two component parts the reliability is the product of the probabilities (Figure 7.2):

$$\text{Reliability} = 0.85 \times 0.8 = 0.68$$

Note that the product reliability (0.68) is much smaller than the component parts and will continue to decline as the number of parts increases. For a product with back-up components the following applies (Figure 7.3):

$$\text{Reliability} = 0.9 + 0.85 * (1 - 0.9) = 0.985$$

Note that the product reliability (0.985) is much higher than the component parts, but the cost of providing a back-up makes its use relevant in only critical components.

The probability of failure during a given time is expressed as a distribution pattern of failures over time. Failure rates tend to follow the pattern shown in Figure 7.4 where defective parts fail early and then the failure rate rises again towards the end of a product's life. There are a small number of random failures between these points.

The reciprocal of the actual failure rate, found by product testing, is called the Mean Time Between Failures (MTBF) and if it is found to follow a negative exponential distribution the reliability (probability that the product will not fail before time T) can be found as follows:

$$P(\text{no failure before } T) = e^{-T/MTBF}$$

where $e = 2.7183$
        $T = $ Time period
    $MTBF = $ Mean time between failures.

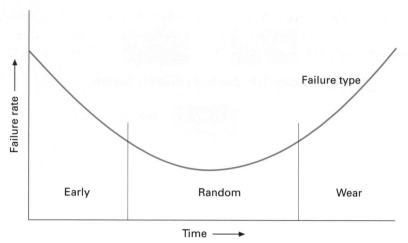

Figure 7.4 Failure pattern over time

Worked Example 7.3

Mean Time Between Failure (MTBF)

If the life of a product follows a negative exponential distribution and the average lifespan $= 10$ years, what is the probability that the product will fail after 5 years?

Solution

$$MTBF = 10$$
$$T = 5$$
$$P(\ ) = e^{-5/10}$$
$$= 0.61$$

Thus, there is a 61% chance of lasting 5 years. Conversely, there is a 39% chance of failure during this time period.

Maintainability

MAINTAINABILITY:
considers the cost of
servicing the product or
service when it is in use.

Maintainability considers the cost of servicing the product or service when it is in use. This may include such issues as the ability of the customer to maintain a product or the need for trained personnel to undertake maintenance or repair activities. Maintainability is connected to issues such as the cost of the product (it may be cheaper to throw away rather than to repair the product) and its reliability (very high reliability will reduce the importance of maintainability).

Product maintainability can be expressed as the Mean Time To Repair (MTTR). Thus, the availability of a product can be calculated by combining the MTBF measure, along with the time taken to repair these failures (MTTR):

$$\text{Availability} = \frac{MTBF}{MTBF + MTTR}$$

Maintainability can be improved by modular design to enable whole modules to be replaced rather than the lengthy investigation of faults. Maintenance schedules should also be specified to help prevent problems from occurring. An improved ability to perform under adverse conditions (termed the 'design robustness') will improve maintainability.

Form Design

Form design refers to the product aesthetics such as look, feel and sound if applicable. This is particularly important for consumer durables but even industrial appliances should at least project an image of quality. In services the design of the supporting facility, such as the room décor, lighting and music in a restaurant provide an important element of the service design.

> **FORM DESIGN:**
> product aesthetics such as look, feel and sound if applicable.

Production Design

Production design involves ensuring that the design takes into consideration the ease and cost of manufacture of a product. Good design will take into consideration the present manufacturing capabilities in terms of material supplies, equipment and personnel skills available. The cost of production can be reduced by the following methods:

> **PRODUCTION DESIGN:**
> ensures the design takes into consideration the ease and cost of manufacture of a product.

- *simplification* – reducing the number of assemblies;
- *standardization* – enabling the use of components for different products and modules;
- *modularization* – combining standardized building blocks in different ways to create a range of products.

CASE STUDY 7.3

Product Development at Fracino

By getting designers, engineers and marketers to work closely together, Fracino has been able to establish itself in an incredibly competitive market. Close collaboration means Fracino's coffee machines meet its customers' requirements exactly. The business decided to create project teams of designers, engineers and marketers who could work together at all stages of the process to assure the quality of the final project.

Now, a three- or four-strong team sees each project from original concept, through prototyping and testing, to component supply and assembly. This creates real dedication and focus and means that modifications can be made quickly and seamlessly. Fracino also involves key customers in the prototyping phase to make sure the final product meets customers' needs.

Source: www.dti.gov.uk/bestpractice
Crown copyright material is reproduced with the permission of HMSO and the Queen's Printer for Scotland

**Case Study 7.3
Question**

1 Explain the advantages of the collaborative approach to product development adopted by Francino.

Improving Design

This chapter will now explore a number of techniques that have been developed in an attempt to improve the design process. Although they have a greater applicability to product design than to service design, they do have some relevance to service design.

Concurrent Design

**CONCURRENT
DESIGN:**

when contributors to the stages of the design effort provide their expertise together throughout the design process as a team.

Concurrent design, also known as 'simultaneous development', is when contributors to the stages of the design effort provide their expertise together throughout the design process as a team. This contrasts with the traditional sequential design process when work is undertaken within functional departments. The problem with the traditional approach is the cost and time involved in bringing the product to market. In some business sectors (e.g., consumer electronics) shrinking product life cycles have meant that new products or improvements to existing products are required in an ever shorter timescale. Concurrent design reduces the time wasted when each stage in the design process waits for the previous stage to finish completely before it can commence. For example, critical equipment, some of which may take an extended time to purchase and install, is identified and procured early in the design process in order to reduce the overall development time.

Another problem of the traditional approach to design is the lack of communication between functional specialists involved in the different stages of design. This can lead to an attitude of throwing the design over the wall without any consideration of problems that may be encountered by later stages. An example of this is decisions made at the preliminary design stage that adversely effect choices at the product build stage. This can cause the design to be repeatedly passed between departments to satisfy everyone's needs, increasing time and costs. By facilitating communication through the establishment of a project team, problems of this type can be reduced.

Design For Manufacture (DFM)

An important aspect of good design is that the product designed can be produced easily and at low cost. **Design For Manufacture (DFM)** is a concept which views product design as the first step in the manufacture of that product. DFM not only incorporates guidelines on such aspects as simplification, standardization and modularization but also techniques such as Failure Mode and Effect Analysis (FMEA) and Value Engineering (VE).

> **DESIGN FOR MANUFACTURE (DFM):**
> a concept which views product design as the first step in the manufacture of that product.

Failure Mode and Effect Analysis (FMEA)

Failure Mode and Effect Analysis (FMEA) is a systematic approach to identifying the cause and effect of product failures. The approach involves the following:

■ list the function of the component parts of the product;
■ define the failure modes (e.g., leakage, fatigue) for all parts;
■ rank the failures in order of likelihood and seriousness;
■ address each failure in rank order, making design changes where necessary.

> **FAILURE MODE AND EFFECT ANALYSIS (FMEA):**
> a systematic approach to identifying the cause and effect of product failures. The idea of FMEA is to anticipate failures and deal with them at the design stage.

The idea of FMEA is to anticipate failures and deal with them at the design stage. The term Failure Mode, Effect and Criticality Analysis (FMECA) is used when a criticality factor is used to rank the failures. The critical factor is the product of the following three values on a scale of 1 to 10:

P = Probability of failure occurring

S = Criticality of failure

D = Difficulty of detection before use by the consumer

Thus, the critical factor = $P \times S \times D$.

Value Engineering (VE)

Value Engineering (VE) aims to eliminate unnecessary features and functions that do not contribute to the value or performance of the product. It is derived from the idea of Value Analysis (VA) which was developed to improve the actual design, particularly taking into account the use of new technology. The technique uses a team approach and follows a formal procedure which has the following core activities:

> **VALUE ENGINEERING (VE):**
> eliminates unnecessary features and functions that do not contribute to the value or performance of the product.

■ *Define function* – this involves defining each function of the product and its cost.

■ *Gather alternatives* – a team will brainstorm new ways to accomplish the functions.

■ *Evaluate alternatives* – each idea generated is evaluated for feasibility and cost.

The technique can be used during design or as a continuous improvement tool during production when a flexible design specification is needed to accommodate suggestions at the production stage.

Mass Customization

MASS CUSTOMIZATION: combines high-variety and high-volume output in order to provide the customer with customized products at a relatively low price.

Mass customization (Fetzinger and Hau, 1997) is an attempt to combine high-variety and high-volume output in order to provide the customer with customized products at a relatively low price. The expansion of options available in motor vehicles (e.g., engine size, engine type, body style) is an example of this approach. The ability to combine high volume and high variety can be achieved by excelling at the flexibility performance objective (Chapter 2) in order to provide high variety, without the costs usually involved in achieving this. One way of doing this is to incorporate the ideas, related to design for manufacture, of simplification, standardization and modularization at the design stage. Vonderembse and White (2004) describe three levels of customization:

■ *Customer contact customization* – where the product or service is tailored to individual needs. For example, a haircut or bicycle can be designed and delivered to meet the specification provided by an individual customer.

■ *Adaptive customization* – where a standard product or service can be customized to meet individual needs. For example, a car can be customized by the customer by ordering from a list of options such as metallic paint and air conditioning. Here, customization starts at the production rather than design stage.

■ *Presentation customization* – where standard products are presented differently to different customers. This can be achieved through differences in elements such as packaging, delivery channel, terms and conditions of purchase and stated use. Here, the level of customization occurs after the product is produced.

QUALITY FUNCTIONAL DEPLOYMENT: translates the voice of the customer (what the customer needs) into technical design requirements (how these needs are met).

Quality Functional Deployment (QFD)

Quality Functional Deployment (QFD) is a structured process that translates the voice of the customer (what the customer needs) into technical design requirements (how these needs are met). It is particularly relevant to the concept of concurrent design as it complements the use of teams in attempting to coordinate design objectives. The technique consists of a series of tables which translate requirements at successive design stages as follows:

■ *The House of Quality*

> Customer requirements → Product characteristics

■ *Parts Deployment*

> Product characteristics → Part characteristics

■ *Process Planning*

> Part characteristics → Process characteristics

■ *Operating Requirements*

> Process characteristics → Operations

The most used matrix is the House of Quality that converts customer requirements into product characteristics. The House of Quality matrix is shown in Figure 7.5.

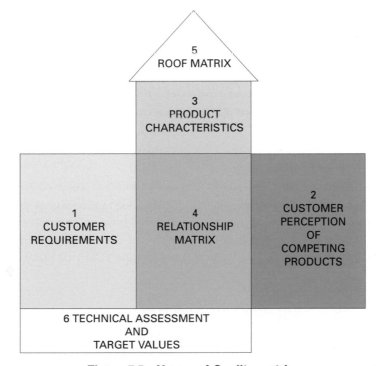

Figure 7.5   House of Quality matrix

The elements of the House of Quality are described below:

1 *Customer requirements* – this links the attributes of the product that are important to the customer along with their relative importance.
2 *Customer perceptions of competitive products* – this compares customer perceptions of the organization and competitors' performance for each of the customer requirements. It provides information on relative performance and also identifies where competitive advantage can be attained by improving relative performance on a highly ranked customer requirement.
3 *Product characteristics* – this lists the product characteristics, expressed in engineering terms and grouped where appropriate.
4 *Relationship matrix* – this correlates the attributes of customer requirements with product characteristics. The relationship may be a positive or negative one and assists in identifying design changes to product characteristics to meet customer requirements.
5 *Roof matrix* – this explores the interaction between product characteristics. This assists identification of an adverse change in a product characteristic as a consequence of a change in another characteristic.
6 *Technical assessments and design targets* – this section includes performance measures to compare the product with competitors. It also contains chosen critical design factors such as cost and importance.

Any change in product characteristic as a result of analysis of customer requirements is then carried forward to the parts deployment matrix and then converted to the process planning and, finally, operating requirements matrix. In this way QFD enables the full consequences of any design change to be assessed and operationalized. The technology provides a method of communicating the effect of change quickly amongst all the members of the design team.

Taguchi Methods

Genichi Taguchi suggests that product failure is mainly a function of design. Taguchi argues that quality must be designed into a product and that it cannot be inspected in later if the design is not good. Three of the techniques for imposing design quality are robust design, Quality Loss Function (QLF) and DOE.

Robust Design

The robustness of a product is defined by its ability to withstand variations in environmental and operating conditions. **Robust design** is the process of designing-in the ability of the product to perform under a variety of conditions

ROBUST DESIGN:
the process of designing-in the ability of the product to perform under a variety of conditions and so reducing the chance of product failure.

and so reducing the chance of product failure. In order to achieve this Taguchi suggests a focus on consistency of parts rather than just requiring manufacture within a tolerance. The tolerance arbitrarily defines a cut-off point between poor quality and good quality which may not be recognized by the customer. Taguchi has formalized the effect on customer dissatisfaction as the actual value deviates from the target value (i.e., the distance from the tolerance limit) called the Quality Loss Function (QLF). Taguchi argues that consistency is especially important in assembled products where parts at either end of their tolerance limit can result in a poor-quality product. Thus, the ability to produce a part to a consistent specification through design is important.

Quality Loss Function (QLF)

The **Quality Loss Function (QLF)** is a simple cost estimate which shows how customer preferences are oriented towards consistently meeting quality expectations and that a customer's dissatisfaction (i.e., quality loss) increases geometrically as the actual value deviates from the target value (Figure 7.6).

The QLF can be expressed mathematically:

$$L = k * d^2$$

where L — Quality loss
      $k =$ Cost coefficient $=$ Consumer loss/(Functional tolerance)^2
      $d =$ Deviation from target value $= x_1 - T$
      $x_1 =$ Measure of item i
      $T =$ Target value.

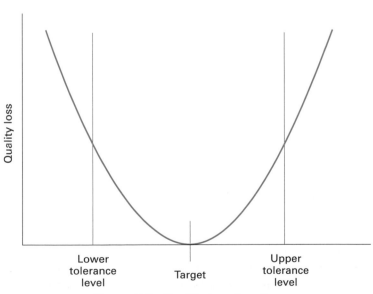

Figure 7.6   Quality loss function

Consumer loss consists of factors such as the cost of repair, the cost of correcting the results of a failure and the cost of not being able to use the product while it is being repaired. Functional tolerance is the deviation from a target value at which most customers will demand a repair or replacement.

Design Of Experiments (DOE)

DESIGN OF EXPERIMENTS (DOE):

identifies factors which affect a product's performance by providing a way of testing a number of design options under various operating and environmental conditions.

Design Of Experiments (DOE) aims to identify factors which affect a product's performance by providing a way of testing a number of design options under various operating and environmental conditions. In other words, DOE provides a method of achieving robust design. The conditions that cause a poor product performance are separated into controllable and uncontrollable factors. In a design situation, controllable factors are design parameters such as material type or dimensions. Uncontrollable factors derive from the wear of the product, such as the length of use or settings, or are environmental such as heat and humidity. A good design will have variables that act in a robust fashion to the possible occurrence of uncontrollable factors.

Summary

1 Service design relates to the combination of goods and service elements termed the 'service package'.

2 The steps in the design process are idea generation, feasibility study, preliminary design and final design. Ideas for new products can come from the organization's R&D function, customers, market research data, competitors or technological development. The feasibility study consists of a market, economic and technical analysis. Preliminary design consists of forming a technical specification of the components of the package. The final design will be assessed in the three main areas of functional design, form design and production design.

3 Concurrent design can reduce the time and cost involved in the product design process.

4 Mass customization is an attempt to combine high variety and high volume of output in order to provide the customer with customized products at a relatively low price.

5 Design for manufacture aims to ensure a product design can be produced easily and at low cost through guidelines on such aspects as simplification, standardization and modularization. QFD is a structured process that translates customer needs into technical design requirements. Taguchi methods for imposing design quality include Robust Design, QLF and DOE.

Exercises

1. A manufacturer produces a product with the following specifications:

Selling price = £15.00/unit

Variable cost = £10.00/unit

Fixed costs = £10 000/week

   a. What is the breakeven point?
   b. How many do they need to sell to make £20 000 profit a week?
2. The following product mix is planned:

	Knives	Forks	Spoons
Product mix	0.4	0.4	0.2
Selling price (£/unit)	0.07	0.08	0.05
Variable cost (£/unit)	0.05	0.06	0.03

Annual fixed cost = £1000

   a. What is the breakeven point?
   b. At what volume will Profit = £5000, given the current product mix?
   c. If the price of a spoon is reduced by £0.01, what volume is required to make a
      profit of £5000?
3. An assembly is made up of four components arranged as follows:

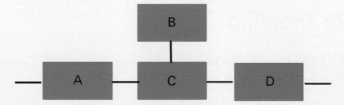

   The components can be purchased for three different suppliers with the following
   reliability ratings:

	Supplier		
Component	1	2	3
A	0.94	0.95	0.92
B	0.86	0.80	0.90
C	0.90	0.93	0.95
D	0.93	0.95	0.95

   a. If only one supplier is chosen to supply all four components, which should be
      selected?

b. What supplier should be selected for the following configuration?

4. Discuss the objectives of functional design, form design and production design.
5. Explain the role of standardization, simplification and modularization in design.
6. Outline the objectives of FMEA.
7. What is the purpose of QFD?
8. How would you implement a concurrent design programme?

References

Fetzinger, E. and Hau, L.L. (1997), Mass customization at Hewlett Packard: The power of postponement, *Harvard Business Review*, **75**(1), 116–121.

Fitzsimmons, J.A. and Fitzsimmons, M.J. (1994), *Service Management for Competitive Advantage*, McGraw-Hill.

Vonderembse, M.A. and White, G.P. (2004), *Core Concepts of Operations Management*, John Wiley & Sons.

Further Reading

Berman, B. (2002) Should your firm adopt a mass customization strategy?, *Business Horizons*, July/August, 51–60.

Hope, C. and Mühlemann, A. (1997), *Service Operations Management: Strategy, Design and Delivery*, Prentice Hall.

Pine, B., Best, V. and Boynton, A. (1993), Making mass customization work, *Harvard Business Review*, September/October, 108–119.

Taguchi, G. and Clausing, D. (1990), Robust quality, *Harvard Business Review*, January/February, 65–75.

Web Links

www.design-council.org.uk Design Council. Wide-ranging site including information on all aspects of design.

www.roundtable.com A variety of resources for product and technology development.

www.autocad.com AutoCAD. One of the most popular software packages for designing new products.

www.design-iv.com Design IV. Consultancy specializing in Design For Manufacture and Assembly (DFMA). Site has information on conferences, software and training.

Chapter 8
Process Design

■ Business Process Management (BPM)

■ Steps in Process Design

- 1   Identifying and Documenting Process Activities
- 2   Identifying Processes for Improvement
- 3   Evaluating Process Design Alternatives

■ Tools for Process Design

- Process Activity Charts
- Process Mapping
- Service Blueprinting
- Business Process Simulation

Learning Objectives

After reading this chapter, you should be able to:

1 Understand the role of business process management.

2 Describe the steps in process design.

3 Evaluate the use of process design techniques such as process activity charts, process mapping and service blueprinting.

4 Describe the relevance of using business process simulation to study manufacturing and service processes.

Introduction

One of the roles of operations management can be seen as putting into practice at an operational level the strategy of the organization. One of the ways it does this is in the design of the processes that deliver the goods and services to customers. Chapter 3 covers the issue of choosing a process type which provides a match to the volume and variety needs of the market. Once the process type has been chosen, the actual processes that deliver the goods and services must be designed. Chapter 7 covers design of the physical product and the elements that go to make up a service.

This chapter covers the area of how we design the flow of people and products through manufacturing and service processes (once a process type and layout has been chosen). The concept of Business Process Management (BPM) is introduced to show the scope of the field. The design of processes is complex and so the use of tools to assist this task is usually required. Some of the tools associated with the design of processes are, thus, covered.

Business Process Management (BPM)

Business Process Management (BPM) (also called 'Business Process Improvement' (BPI)) is the term used to refer to the analysis and improvement of business processes. A process is a set of activities designed to produce a desired output from a specified input. The process orientation matches the idea of the main objectives of the operations function as the management of the transformation process of inputs (resources) into outputs (goods and services) covered in Chapter 1. Although BPM is usually used in the broad sense it is also used more narrowly to refer to software technologies for automating the management of specific processes. In its widest sense, however, BPM brings together aspects such as:

■ assessment models such as ISO9000 (Chapter 17);
■ modelling techniques such as business process simulation (Chapter 8);

> **BUSINESS PROCESS MANAGEMENT (BPM):**
> the analysis and improvement of business processes.

- improvement approaches such as Business Process Reengineering (BPR) (Chapter 17);
- implementation of information technologies such as workflow systems (Chapter 6).

BPM has been developed by authors such as Rummler and Brache (1995) who provide a method of undertaking the technique using organizational analysis and process analysis and design. BPM is concerned with the following:

- linking corporate strategy and business processes;
- providing measurement of process performance at a strategic level;
- design and management of the processes that deliver the organization's goods and services;
- implementation of process change, both manually by employees and by the use of IT systems.

For implementation of processes that are performed by employees, consideration is made of such factors as job descriptions, motivations systems, supervision, training and evaluation of performance. A Six Sigma approach (Chapter 17) may be used in this area.

For the implementation of processes automated by IT systems, consideration is made of such factors as software development and maintenance. Use is made of software tools such as work flow (Chapter 6), business process simulation (Chapter 8) and packaged enterprise applications such as ERP (Chapter 14).

CASE STUDY 8.1

How Dell Keeps Going in Europe

Dell's Irish factory is the sort of plant you might think would have been closed down long ago, and its functions shifted to a lower cost location in Asia. At first glance, it resembles the much derided screwdriver-type assembly operation, with little evidence of automation, and lots of youthful-looking workers on the factory floor doing what seem to be relatively simple tasks. But Dell's Limerick plant, the US company's sole manufacturing centre in Europe, is unique – the only plant controlled by any of the main multi-national electronics makers that is still producing personal computers in Europe. International Business Machines' Scottish facility has long since relocated to Asia and the Irish manufacturing operations of Apple and Gateway have done likewise.

Dell's survival is the result of a set of management systems that seek to create continuing improvements in the way the business operates, through cost reduction, cutting back on waste and increasing the quality and speed of the processes. The factory not only has to produce more efficiently than those of rival companies, but it is also benchmarking its performance daily in its effort to stay ahead of Dell's own operations in China and Malaysia.

"If you're looking at labour rates in Europe and labour rates in Asia, clearly we will never compete on an hourly cost. But you have to have an efficient model so that the element of labour in the model is significantly reduced. You're making the model efficient end to end," says Nicky Hartery, who runs the factory and is responsible for a direct labour force of about 3000, as well as another 1200–1400 in support industries in the region. His title is vice-president, manufacturing and business operations for Europe, the Middle East and Africa, an area where, in the year to March 31, Dell reported sales worth $8.5bn of PC products, from laptops to notebooks to various computer peripherals.

Dell will this year make savings of $200m in its European operations, through the application of its lean manufacturing guidelines, and what it calls 'Business Process Improvement (BPI).

"We're at all times looking for better, faster ways of doing things. Our staff are aligned not just to making PCs, which I would call sustaining engineering, but there's a development engineering function – developing better tools, better techniques, improved tools, improved techniques – so that our throughput is significantly better and the quality of what we do is significantly better," he says. Dell estimates that it is able to improve productivity – the value of output per employee per hour – by 3–4% every quarter. Is it sustainable? Mr Hartery's answer is simple: "The esprit de corps around here is we know we have to get better to be around tomorrow."

He explains: "Let's assume our output of PCs is X. Our output tomorrow will be $2X$. But they'll still be made in the same space. We just won't add more lines to make them. We create an engineering capability for further velocity in the line." He cites the way the company handles components and other inputs arriving at the factory. As a result of better management of its supply chain, it only has to carry enough material for two hours of production. The bulk of the components now come straight off the container truck into the assembly line. The volume of parts that are kept in storage by suppliers has been reduced by 40% in the past year alone. To maintain the momentum, a team of between 50 and 80 people are assigned full time to the job of identifying ways to improve the process.

"We don't just work on productivity within the four walls of the our factory. I don't think we'd survive doing that. We have to make sure its the right model, end to end, from our vendor base, our sub-tier vendor base, all the way to our customer," says Mr Hartery, who, although originally from Waterford, has worked for two decades in the US information technology industry. Dell's attitude to sales is less that of a traditional manufacturing facility than a store. "We will not do anything here if the customer doesn't ask us to. We don't build inventory. If we had no orders to fill tomorrow, with 3000 people on site, then we wouldn't do anything for the day." This so-called direct sales method means it never has more than 2 days of inventory, against several weeks for its competitors that have to ship product from Asian locations.

Dell argues that this approach allows it to make rapid use of the latest components. "If Intel launches a new processor, we will be first to market with it. Why? Because we don't have weeks of inventory to work through. If they're launching next Monday, on Tuesday we can be shipping that product," Mr Hartery explains. He argues that the productivity gains the plant is making are not obvious to the outside observer because they are based more on human intelligence than on the deployment of high-technology equipment. "When you go on the floor of the factory you are not going to see a lot of automation. The process does not lend itself to automation. There is a lot of intelligence involved," says Mr Hartery.

It is different from the way traditional manufacturing processes were organized, where individual workers execute repetitive tasks to produce a finished product. This is sometimes referred to as progressive assembly. Dell adopts what it calls 'a single person build', where one worker will assemble a whole unit from outer casing to the internal electronics. It might be slower, but it increases quality, and encourages workers to look for ways to make improvements. The system is based on clear rewards. The company runs a system of coloured belts to denote skill levels, and there are monthly 'town halls' where individuals are acclaimed for their performance, often by a group of their workmates.

"The traditional manufacturing method was to train people to do X and then ask them to do X plus 1, and it would cost you more. That is not the electronics industry or the PC industry, where change is dynamic. Ten years ago it was very different. But if we are doing the same thing a year from now, then I worry."

Source: John Murray Brown, FT.com site; 31 May 2004
© **The Financial Times Ltd**

Case Study 8.1 Question

1   Contrast the use of the approach of process improvement used at Dell and the use of automation to increase efficiency.

Steps in Process Design

The task of designing processes should be undertaken in a structured manner and the steps involved can be described as:

1   Identifying and documenting the process activities.
2   Identifying processes for improvement.
3   Evaluating process design alternatives.

1   Identifying and Documenting Process Activities

The identification of activities in a current process design is a data collection exercise using methods such as examination of current documentation, interviews and observation.

For the design of new processes, techniques such as functional analysis exist. This technique for mapping service processes starts by defining a high-level description of the service and then successively breaks down that description into a number of functions. Processes are then created by arranging the functions in the sequence in which the activities defined by the functions are performed.

In service processes it is useful to have a customer at the start and end of the process in order to evaluate the impact of the quality of the process on the customer. Another aspect of service process design is the important role that customers play in the delivery of the service. In order to incorporate the interactions between the customer and the service provider during service, processes can be classified into operational activities, which are the steps needed to deliver the service to the customer and customer service activities, which are the customer and service provider interactions.

Customer service activities tend to get overlooked in process design because they are measured by attributes such as responsiveness and friendliness which are attributes of people and, thus, more difficult to measure. The key here is to design procedures around this customer and service provider interactions that maximize the reliability of the quality of service.

In order to provide a framework for the design and improvement of service processes the techniques of process mapping and service blueprinting can be utilized and are described later in this chapter.

2   Identifying Processes for Improvement

Once the process mapping has been completed it is necessary to prioritize the process elements which will be allocated resources for improvement.

The identification of the relevant business processes for improvement can be undertaken using a scoring system such as the performance/importance matrix (Martilla and James, 1977) on which processes can be plotted in terms of how well the organization performs them and how important they are.

Slack and Lewis (2002) outline a model in which prioritization is governed by importance to customers and performance against competitors.

Greasley (2004a) presents a scoring system developed in conjunction with a public sector organization in which it is necessary to take into consideration a number of stakeholder views. The system consists of a two-dimensional marking guide based on the impact of the process on the critical success factors determined in a balanced scorecard review and an assessment of the scope for innovation (i.e., the amount of improvement possible) to the current process design. Processes which are strategically important and offer the largest scope for improvement are prioritized under this model.

3 Evaluating Process Design Alternatives

There are many ways in which a process can be designed to meet particular objectives and so it is necessary to generate a range of innovative solutions for evaluation. Three approaches which can be used to generate new ideas are:

- *Generating new designs through brainstorming* – this approach offers the greatest scope for radical improvements to the process design but represents a risk in the implementation of a totally new approach. A deep understanding of the process is required in order that the design will be feasible.
- *Modifying existing designs* – this approach is less risky than a blue skies approach but may mean the opportunity for a radical improvement in process design is missed.
- *Using an established 'benchmark' design* – this approach applies the idea of identifying the best-in-class performer for the particular process in question and adopting that design. Disadvantages with this approach may be that the process design of the best-in-class performer may not be available or the context of the best-in-class performer may not match the context for the new design.

The process map or service blueprint provides an overall view of the current or expected process design and this should be used in order that an overall view is taken when process design options are generated. This helps to ensure that design solutions proposed in a specific area do not have a detrimental effect in other areas of the process and, thus, affect overall process performance.

The design of service processes, in particular, is a key factor in meeting the needs of the customer. In services the process incorporates employees, customers and facilitating goods in a dynamic event which may be undertaken in a different manner each time, according to the demands of the individual customer. The interaction between the customer and service provider can be analysed using the service blueprint diagrams described in this chapter.

In designing services Shostack (1987) categorizes services by their complexity, the number and interdependency of process elements and divergency – how many different ways they can be performed. Once a service has been documented it can be analysed for opportunities either to increase or decrease one or both of these variables.

Peppard and Rowland (1995) provide a number of areas for the potential design of processes under the headings of Eliminate, Simplify, Integrate and Automate (ESIA) (Table 8.1).

It will be necessary to reduce the number of design alternatives generated and this can be achieved by a rating scheme that scores each design solution against key performance dimensions such as response time and cost of operation. The outcome of this analysis will be a reduced number of design solutions which can then be subjected to more detailed analysis.

Table 8.1	ESIA areas for potential redesign		
Eliminate	*Simplify*	*Integrate*	*Automate*
Over-production	Forms	Jobs	Dirty
Waiting time	Procedures	Teams	Difficult
Transport	Communication	Customers	Dangerous
Processing	Technology	Suppliers	Boring
Inventory	Problem areas		Data capture
Defects/failures	Flows		Data transfer
Duplication	Processes		Data analysis
Reformatting			
Inspection			
Reconciling			

Source: Peppard and Rowland (1995)

This analysis is often undertaken using mathematical models such as queuing theory (Chapter 11) and techniques such as Business Process Simulation (BPS) (Chapter 8). The BPS technique allows the predicted variability in a process design to be incorporated in a computer model and, thus, the robustness of the design over time can be assessed.

Tools for Process Design

A number of tools are available to assist in the task of redesigning processes. These tools can help in all stages of the design process including documentation of processes, identification of processes for redesign and for evaluating design alternatives.

Process Activity Charts

A **process activity chart** (also called a 'process chart') is often used to analyse the steps of a job or how a set of jobs fit together into the overall flow of a process (e.g., the steps involved in processing a customer order received by telephone). There are five main symbols in a process activity chart as shown in Figure 8.1.

An example process chart for a generic administration process is shown in Figure 8.2.

The process activity chart performs a number of functions including identifying the task sequence, task relationships, task delays (by including average task times), task movements and worker assignment to tasks. The charts can be used in

PROCESS ACTIVITY CHART:

a charting device which is often used to analyse the steps of a job or how a set of jobs fit together into the overall flow of a process.

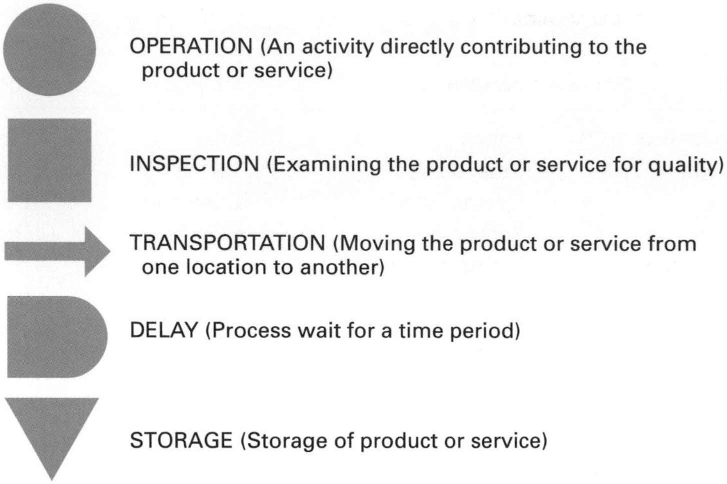

OPERATION (An activity directly contributing to the product or service)

INSPECTION (Examining the product or service for quality)

TRANSPORTATION (Moving the product or service from one location to another)

DELAY (Process wait for a time period)

STORAGE (Storage of product or service)

Figure 8.1   Symbols for a process activity chart

conjunction with a written job description to form a detailed outline of a job. The charts can also be useful in the first stage of a job improvement scheme. There are, however, a number of limitations to the charts. Processes with decision points and parallel processes cannot be shown on a process activity chart. Process mapping can be used to incorporate these aspects. Also, only average task times are used to calculate the process time, and variability in task times is not taken into account. BPS can be used to incorporate variability.

Process Mapping

PROCESS MAPPING:
the use of a flowchart to document the process, incorporating process activities and decision points.

Documenting the process can be undertaken by the construction of a **process map**, also called a 'flowchart'. This is a useful way of understanding any business process and showing the interrelationships between activities in a process. For larger projects it may be necessary to represent a given process at several levels of detail. Thus, a single activity may be shown as a series of sub-activities on a separate diagram. Figure 8.3 shows the representations used in a simple process-mapping diagram.

Figure 8.4 shows a process map of activities undertaken by traffic police in response to a Road Traffic Accident (RTA) incident. The process map shows that following the notification of a RTA incident to the police by the public, a decision is made to attend the scene of the incident. If it is necessary to attend the RTA scene the officer travels to the location of the incident. After an assessment is made of the incident, the officer returns to the station to complete and submit the appropriate paperwork. If a court case is scheduled and a not guilty plea has been entered then the officer will be required to attend the court proceedings in person. Otherwise, this is the end of the involvement of the officer.

Process description   **Process symbol**

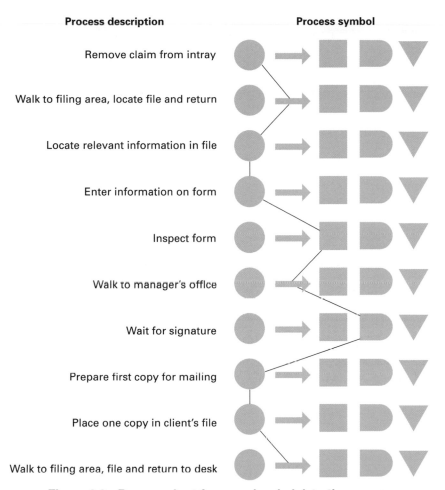

Remove claim from intray

Walk to filing area, locate file and return

Locate relevant information in file

Enter information on form

Inspect form

Walk to manager's offIce

Wait for signature

Prepare first copy for mailing

Place one copy in client's file

Walk to filing area, file and return to desk

Figure 8.2   Process chart for generic administration process

Meaning	Symbol
Process/Activity	
Decision point	
Start/End point	
Direction of flow	

Figure 8.3   Symbols used for a process map

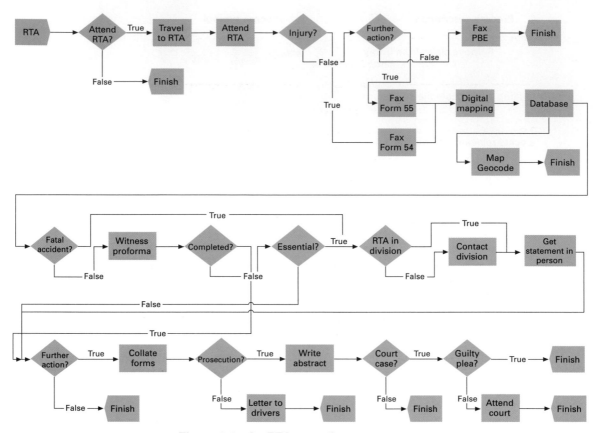

Figure 8.4 An RTA reporting process map

Process maps are useful in a number of ways. For example, the actual procedure of building a process map helps people define roles and see who else does what. This can be particularly relevant to public sector organizations in which modelling existing processes can be used to build consensus on what currently happens. The process map can also serve as a first step in using BPS as it identifies the processes and decision points required to build the model.

Service Blueprinting

As discussed in the section on identifying process activities, it is important in service processes to document the interaction between the customer and the service provider. Process maps can be extended to show how a business interacts with customers. One system is called Service System Mapping (SSM) (Laguna and Markland, 2005). Shostack (1984) has developed a flowchart (termed a 'blueprint') which structures the process activities either side of a customer line of visibility

Customer

Front stage ——————— *line of interaction* ———————

Service provider

————————— *line of visibility* —————————

Set-up functions

Back stage ————— *line of internal interaction* —————

Support functions

————————— *line of implementation* —————————

Management functions

Figure 8.5   Service blueprint template

(Figure 8.5). The activities above the line are visible to the customer and those below the line are operations that the customer does not see. Activities above the line of visibility are subdivided into two fields separated by the line of interaction, this divides activities undertaken by the customer and the service provider. Below the line of visibility a line of internal interaction separates the activities of front line personnel who carry out setting up actions prior to service provision (not in view of the customer) and support personnel who contribute materials or services required for the provision of the service. Finally, the line of implementation separates support activities from management activities such as planning, controlling and decision making.

Figure 8.6 shows an example service blueprint for a restaurant.

The objective of the **service blueprint** is that it not only charts the service process flow (from left to right) as does a process map, but also shows the structure of the service organization on the vertical axis, showing relationships between, for example, internal customers, support staff and front line providers. In particular, the diagram aims to highlight the interactions between the customer and process where customer services can be affected. The diagrams can also be used as a design tool to determine staffing levels, job descriptions and selection of equipment and as a control tool to identify gaps in service provision through the analysis of fail points. Fail points are potential service system shortfalls between what the service delivers and what the targeted customers have been led to expect.

> **SERVICE BLUEPRINTING:** a charting device for processes which documents the interaction between the customer and the service provider.

Business Process Simulation

Defining Business Process Simulation

The use of a simulation model on a computer to mimic the operation of a business means that the performance of the business over an extended time period can be

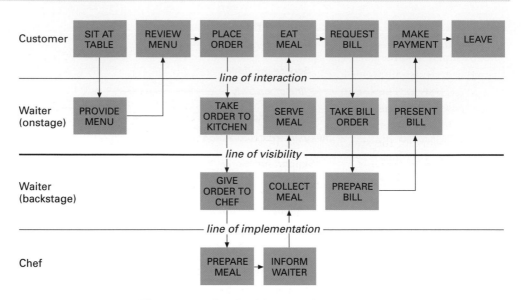

Figure 8.6   Service blueprint for restaurant

observed quickly and under a number of different scenarios. Simulation, in general, covers a large area of interest and so a short explanation is given of common terms used. Simulation can refer to a range of model types from spreadsheet models, system dynamic simulations and discrete event simulation. BPS is usually implemented using discrete event simulation systems which move through time in (discrete) steps. Most simulation modelling software is now implemented using graphical user interfaces employing objects or icons that are placed on the screen to produce a model. These are often referred to as Visual Interactive Modelling (VIM) systems. When a discrete event simulation system using a visual interactive modelling interface is used in the context of a process-based change method it is commonly referred to as a **Business Process Simulation (BPS)**.

BUSINESS PROCESS SIMULATION: the use of computer software, in the context of a process-based change, that allows operation of a business to be simulated.

Why Use Business Process Simulation?

The ease of use and usefulness of process design techniques such as process mapping has meant their use is widespread. BPS requires a significant investment in time and skills but it is able to provide a more realistic assessment of the behaviour of manufacturing and service processes than most other process design tools. This is due to its ability to incorporate the dynamic (i.e., time-dependent) behaviour of operations systems. There are two aspects of dynamic systems which need to be addressed.

Variability

Most business systems contain variability in both the demand on the system (e.g., customer arrivals) and the durations (e.g., customer service times) of activities within the system. The use of fixed (e.g., average) values will provide some indication of performance, but simulation permits the incorporation of statistical distributions and, thus, provides an indication of both the range and variability of the performance of the system. This is important in customer-based systems when not only is the average performance relevant, but also performance should not drop below a certain level (e.g., customer service time) or customers will be lost. In service systems, two widely used performance measures are an estimate of the maximum queuing time for customers and the utilization (i.e., percentage time occupied) of the staff serving the customer.

Interdependence

Most systems contain a number of decision points that affect the overall performance of the system. The simulation technique can incorporate statistical distributions to model the likely decision options taken. Also the 'knock-on' effect of many interdependent decisions over time can be assessed using the simulation's ability to show system behaviour over a time period.

Worked Example 8.1

Variability in Service Systems

A manager of a small shop wishes to predict how long customers wait for service during a typical day. The owner has identified two types of customer, who have different amounts of shopping and so take different amounts of time to serve. Type A customers account for 70% of custom and take on average 10 minutes to serve. Type B customers account for 30% of custom and take on average 5 minutes to serve. The owner has estimated that during an 8-hour day, on average the shop will serve 40 customers.

Solution 1

The owner calculates the serve time during a particular day:

$$\text{Customer A} = 0.7 \times 40 \times 10 \text{ minutes} = 280 \text{ minutes}$$

$$\text{Customer B} = 0.3 \times 40 \times 5 \text{ minutes} = 60 \text{ minutes}$$

Therefore, the Total service time = 340 minutes and gives a utilization of the shop till of $340/480 \times 100 = 71\%$.

Thus, the owner is confident all customers can be served promptly during a typical day.

A simulation model was constructed of this system to estimate the service time for customers. Using a fixed time between customer arrivals of 480/40 = 12 minutes and with a 70% probability of a 10-minute service time and a 30% probability of a 5-minute service time, the overall service time for customers has a range of between 5 to 10 minutes and no queues are present in this system.

Service time for customer (minutes)

Average	8.5
Minimum	5
Maximum	10

Solution 2

In reality, customers will not arrive equally spaced at 12-minute intervals, but will arrive randomly with an average interval of 12 minutes. A simulation is used to simulate a time between arrivals of customers which follows an exponential distribution (the exponential distribution is often used to mimic the behaviour of customer arrivals) with a mean of 12 minutes. The owner was surprised by the simulation results:

Service time for customer (minutes)

Average	17
Minimum	5
Maximum	46

The average service time for a customer had doubled to 17 minutes, with a maximum of 46 minutes!

Worked Example 8.1 demonstrates how the performance of even simple systems can be affected by randomness. Variability would also be present in this system in other areas such as customer service times and the mix of customer types over time. The simulation method is able to incorporate all of these sources of variability to provide a more realistic picture of system performance.

Using Business Process Simulation for Business Process Management

In order to undertake a successful simulation study a number of steps must be followed. The main steps in developing a simulation model (Greasley, 2004b) are:

Define the Study Objectives

A number of specific study objectives should be derived which will provide a guide to the data needs of the model, set the boundaries of the study (scope), the level of modelling detail and define the experimentation analysis required. It is necessary to refine the study objectives until specific scenarios defined by input variables and measures that can be defined by output variables can be specified. General improvement areas for a process design project include aspects such as the following:

■ *changes in process logic* – changes to routing, decision points and layout;
■ *changes in resource availability* – shift patterns, equipment failure;
■ *changes in demand* – forecast pattern of demand on the process.

Many projects will study a combination of the above, but it is important to study each area in turn to establish potential subjects for investigation at the project proposal stage.

Data Collection and Process Mapping

Once the simulation project objectives have been defined, and the scope and level of detail set, the modeller should prepare a specification of the data required for the model build. It is useful at this stage to identify the source of the information, its form (e.g., documentation, observation, interview) and any personnel responsible for supplying the relevant information. A process map specification should define what processes will be mapped. The process map should provide a medium for obtaining information from a variety of viewpoints regarding the system being organized. In particular, issues of system boundaries (i.e., what to include and what to omit from the analysis) can be addressed.

Modelling Input Data

A specification of the type of statistical analysis used for modelling input variables and process durations should be made. A trace-driven model will require no statistical analysis of input data, but a forecasting model may require that the data is fitted to a suitable probability distribution. The level of data analysis will depend on the study objectives, time constraints and the amount of raw data available.

Building the Model

A number of vendors offer business process simulation software packages. An example of a BPS is the ARENA system shown in Figure 8.7. The simulation is represented by symbols which closely relate to the standard process mapping symbols. The simulation is constructed by dragging the appropriate symbol from the window at the left-hand side of the screen and placing it on the main view window. The symbols are then connected together to represent the process flow. Each symbol is then double-clicked with the mouse to reveal a menu which allows

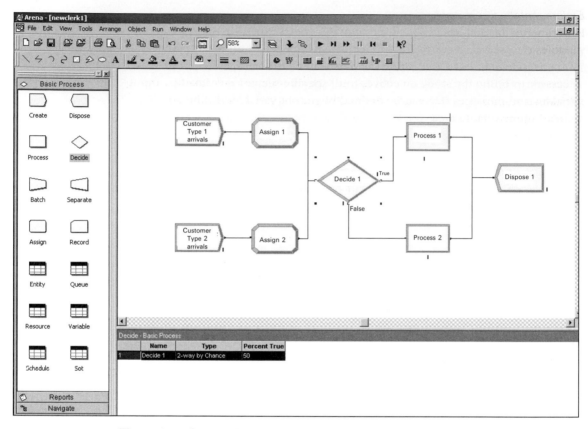

Figure 8.7   Screen display of a Business Process Simulation

ARENA simulation software screen dump (see www.arenasimulation.com)
Reproduced by permission of Rockwell Simulations

entry of parameters such as process times. When all the simulation data are entered the 'run' button is clicked and the simulation moves through time. Animation features can be added as required and reports provide information on performance measures such as resource utilizations and queuing times.

Validation and Verification

Verification or debugging time can be difficult to predict but some estimation of verification time can be made from the estimated complexity and size of the proposed model. Validation will require the analyst to spend time with people who are familiar with the model being studied to ensure model behaviour is appropriate. A number of meetings may be necessary to ensure that the simulation model has sufficient credibility with potential users. Sensitivity analysis may be required to validate a model of a system that does not currently exist. The type of sensitivity analysis envisaged should be defined in the project proposal.

Experimentation and Analysis

Experimentation and analysis aims to study the effects which changes in input variables (i.e., scenarios defined in the objectives) have on output variables (i.e., performance measures defined in the objectives) in the model. The number of experiments should be clearly defined as each experiment may take a substantial amount of analysis time. For each experiment the statistical analysis required should be defined.

Implementation

The results of the simulation study must be presented in report form which should include full model documentation, study results and recommendations for further studies. An implementation plan may also be specified. The report can be supplemented by a presentation to interested parties. The duration and cost of both of these activities should be estimated. Further allocation of time and money may be required for aspects such as user training, run-time software licence and telephone support from an external consultant.

In terms of the process design steps outlined at the start of this chapter, BPS is particularly relevant to the evaluation of process design alternatives. It should also be noted that the process mapping technique, often used to identify and document process activities, represents the basis for the simulation model design. After the use of the process map a decision can be made if the more in-depth analysis provided by the BPS is required. The following case study provides an example of the use of BPS in a process-centred change project.

CASE STUDY 8.2

Designing a Custody of Prisoner Process at a Police Force

The custody process under investigation includes the arrest process, from actual apprehension of a suspect, to processing through a custody suite (which contains booking-in, interview and detention facilities) to a possible court appearance. A number of different police roles are involved in the custody process including arrests by a Police Constable (PC), taking of personal details by a Custody Officer and supervision of persons in detention by a Jailer. The first objective of the study was to identify staff costs involved in arresting a person for a particular offence under the current design. The second objective of the study was to predict the change in utilization of staff as a result of redesigning the allocation of staff to activities within the custody process. The main stages of the investigation are now outlined.

Identify and Document the Process Activities

A process map (Figure 8.8) was constructed after discussions with police staff involved in the custody process. As this process was legally bound, documentation on the order of processes and certain requirements such as meals, visits and booking-in details was collated. The main activities in the arrest process are shown in the process map. Each decision point (diamond shape) will have a probability for a yes/no option. The first decision point in the arrest process is whether to conduct a search of the location of the arrest. For all decisions during the arrest process an independent probability distribution is used for each type of arrest (e.g., theft, violence, drugs) at each decision point. The staffing rank required for each process is indicated above the process box. Personnel involved in the arrest process include the PC, Custody Officer, Jailer and Inspector. The role of each rank is indicated on the process map for each activity.

To model the variability in process times a number of estimated times were collected from a number of custody officers. In addition, videotapes of the booking-in and interview procedures were viewed and timings taken.

The demand level of each arrival type is estimated from which a statistical distribution for the 'time between arrivals' is usually determined. In this case data were gathered on the timing of arrests over a period of time from information contained within booking-in sheets. From these data the demand pattern was analysed for a typical police station during a day and for each day in a week. As expected, demand fluctuated

CUSTODY OF PRISONER PROCESS MAP

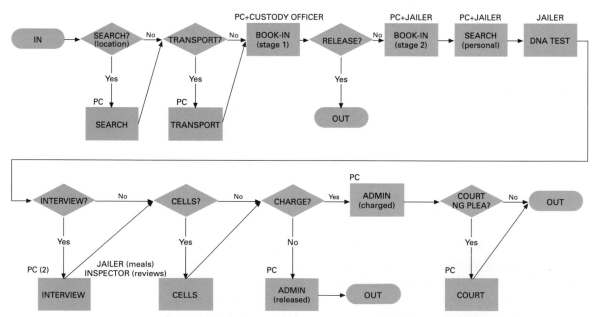

Figure 8.8   Process map of the custody of prisoner process

both during the day and differed between days in the week. It was decided to use historical data to drive the model due to the nature of the demand, with a number of arrests occasionally occurring simultaneously – as a result of a late-night brawl, for example! – which would be difficult to reflect using an arrival distribution. Additionally, the use of actual data would assist in model validation as model performance could be compared with actual performance over the period simulated. This approach was feasible because the focus of the study was on the investigation of the comparative performance between different configurations of custody operation rather than for use as a forecasting tool.

Most processes will consume resource time, which may be of a machine or person, and these resources need to be identified and their availability defined. If the resource is not available at any time, then the process will not commence until the resource becomes available. In this case the main resources are PC, Custody Officer and Jailer.

Evaluating Process Design Alternatives

In order to measure and analyse process performance, a BPS was constructed using the ARENA simulation system. This system uses icons (representing processes) that are placed on a screen area. The icons are connected by links to represent the logic of the process. Process duration and resource allocation to processes is made by double-clicking a process icon and entering data in the pop-up menu dialog box. An animated display is constructed by using an in-built graphics package, which permits the construction of background (static) elements such as the process layout schematic and animated (dynamic) elements which move across the screen. Figure 8.9 shows the custody display that consists of representations of the main custody area facilities (i.e., booking-in desk, interview rooms and cells) and the dynamic elements (i.e., arrested persons and police staff) that move between the custody facilities.

Before the model results are recorded, model behaviour must be checked to ensure that the model is providing valid results. Verification is analogous to the practice of 'debugging' a computer program. This is accomplished by techniques such as a structured walkthrough of the model code, test runs and checking of the animation display. Validation is about ensuring that model behaviour is close enough to the real world system for the purposes of the simulation study. To achieve this, the model builder should discuss and obtain information from people familiar with the real world system including operating personnel, industrial engineers, management, vendors and documentation. Also, the technique of sensitivity analysis, to test the behaviour of the model under various scenarios and compare results with real world behaviour, can be used.

Once the model had been validated, it was run over a set time period and results collected. At this stage the model is simply reproducing the behaviour of the current process. This 'as-is' model provided a visual representation of the whole process, which was important to provide a consensus that the model provides a convincing representation of the process. Demonstration of the model between interested parties

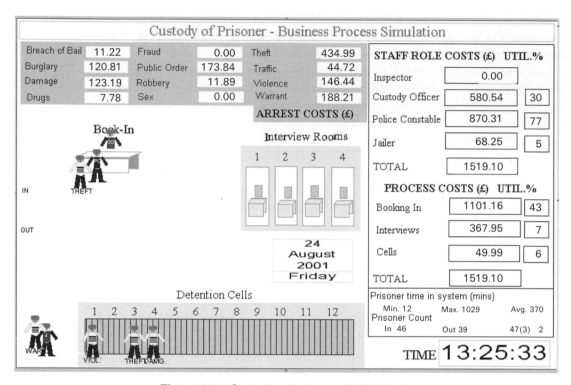

Figure 8.9   Custody of prisoner BPS display

provided a forum for communication of model behaviour and helped identify any anomalies.

In this study the aim of the model was to identify the main sources of cost in the system and, thus, provide strategies which would enable cost to be reduced. At present a budget-based approach meant that costs were not allocated to activities within the process. Each time a process was activated in the model by an arrested person being processed through the custody system, a cost was calculated by multiplying the activity duration by the cost per time unit for the resource allocated to that process. The initial analysis aimed to identify the cost incurred for each type of arrest incorporated in the model. The cost for each arrest type is a function not only of the number of arrests but the likelihood of an arrest leading to interview, detention and court procedures. In this case relatively trivial theft offences (usually involving children shoplifting) are causing a heavy workload and, thus, a high cost. Thus, a driving factor behind the overall cost structure has been identified. A possible way of reducing cost could be to decrease the theft activity through crime prevention activities, for example.

In this case the 'to-be' model was used to explore the reduction of staffing cost by reallocating staff roles to processes. By estimating resource costs, in this case staff wages, it was possible to estimate the effects and feasibility of proposals to reallocate and civilianize staffing duties within the custody process.

Once a future process design has been decided, the simulation helps to implement this change in a number of ways. The graphical display provides an excellent tool with which to communicate the process to stakeholders such as management, customers and the work force. The 'before' and 'after' graphic displays can be used to show how the changes will affect the process in practice. Also, the display of the new process design can be utilized to train staff in the new operation and provide them with an overview of process behaviour which enables them to see the relationship between a particular process activity and the overall process behaviour.

The graphics are complemented by performance measures to quantify before and after performance and, thus, demonstrate potential improvement. In the custody of prisoner case, measures of staff utilization were important in demonstrating the feasibility of the reallocation of tasks between staff. The figures also quantify potential savings in the utilization of police staff time, enabling plans to be made for the reallocation of staff time to other duties. In the analysis of workload in terms of arrest types, cost was used as a measure of the aggregated staff resource allocated to each arrest type that is serviced by the police. The simulation analysis could take account, not only of the number of arrests of each type, but the variable number of processes (e.g., interview, court appearances by PCs) that each arrest triggered. The modelling of the complexity of interdependencies between arrest processes and the variability of arrest demand allowed an accurate picture of where cost/effort was being spent. These figures provided an impetus to focus expenditure on programmes, such as crime prevention, which could have a substantial effect on cost/effort and could free resources to provide an improved overall performance.

Source: from Greasley (2003) *Business Process Management Journal*
© MCB UP Ltd (www.emeraldinsight.com/bpmj.htm)

1   What benefits does the case study demonstrate can be gained from using BPS for process design?

2   Can you identify any disadvantages of using BPS?

Summary

1 BPM provides a method of undertaking the analysis and improvement of business processes.

2 The steps in process design are identify and document process activities, identify processes for improvement and evaluate process design alternatives.

3 A process activity chart can be used to analyse the steps of a job. A process map can be used to show the interrelationships between activities in a process. A service blueprint is a flowchart which documents the interaction between the customer and the service provider.

4 Business process simulation is a technique that can be used to measure the performance of processes over time by taking into consideration variability and interdependence factors.

Exercises

1. Draw a process activity chart for the processing of a book order from an Internet site.
2. Draw a process map for a potential property buyer making a telephone enquiry to a residential housing estate agency.
3. Draw a service blueprint for servicing a car. Include in your diagram the customer, the supervisor who takes the bookings and schedules them, the mechanics and the car parts suppliers.
4. Past proceedings of the Winter Simulation Conference can be found at www.informs-cs.org/wscpapers.html. Browse the Web and find case studies, noting the number of simulation applications by industry sector.
5. Describe how variability and interdependence affect the operation of a railway system.

References

Greasley, A. (2003), Using business process simulation within a Business Process Reengineering approach, *Business Process Management Journal*, 9(4), 408–420.

Greasley, A. (2004a), Process improvement within an HR division at a UK police force, *International Journal of Operations and Production Management*, 24(2/3), 230–240.

Greasley, A. (2004b), *Simulation Modelling for Business*, Ashgate Publishing.

Laguna, M. and Markland, M. (2005), *Business Process Modeling, Simulation and Design*, Pearson Education.

Martilla, J.A. and James, J.C. (1977), Importance–performance analysis, *Journal of Marketing*, January.

Peppard, J. and Rowland, P. (1995), *The Essence of Business Process Re-engineering*, Prentice Hall.

Rummler, G.A. and Brache, A.P. (1995), *Improving Performance: How to Manage the White Space on the Organization Chart*, Jossey Bass/John Wiley & Sons.

Shostack, L.G. (1984), Designing services that deliver, *Harvard Business Review*, **62**(1), 133–139.

Shostack, L.G. (1987), Service positioning through structural change, *Journal of Marketing*, **51**, 34–43.

Slack, N. and Lewis, M. (2002), *Operations Strategy*, Pearson Education.

Further Reading

Anupindi, R., Chopra, S., Deshmukh, S.D., Van Mieghem, J.A. and Zemel, E. (1999), *Managing Business Process Flows*, Prentice Hall.

Kalakota, R. and Robinson, M. (2003), *Services Blueprint: Roadmap for Execution*, Addison-Wesley.

Kelton, W.D., Sadowski, R.P. and Sadowski, D.A. (2002), *Simulation with Arena*, 2nd Edition, McGraw-Hill.

Ramaswamy, R. (1996), *Design and Management of Service Processes*, Addison-Wesley.

Smith, H. and Fingar, P. (2003), *Business Process Management: The Third Wave*, Meghan-Kiffer Press.

Web Links

www.bptrends.com Business Process Trends. Excellent portal with numerous resources regarding BPM.

Simulation Organizations

www.informs-cs.org Institute for Operations Research and Management Science: Simulation Society. Contains links to conferences and conference papers.

www.scs.org The Society for Modeling and Simulation International. Conference details and links to journal and publications.

www.scs-europe.net/ The Society for Modeling and Simulation: European Council. European conference details and links to journals and publications.

www.iasted.org/index.htm The International Association of Science and Technology for Development. Contains links to simulation conferences and journal.

Simulation Software Vendors

www.arenasimulation.com/ Rockwell Software (ARENA)

www.simul8.com Simul8 Corporation (SIMUL8)

www.maad.com Micro Analysis and Design (Micro Saint)

www.promodel.com Promodel Corporation (Promodel)

www.lanner.com Lanner Group Inc. (WITNESS)

Chapter 9
Job and Work Design

■ Behavioural Aspects of Job Design
- The Job Characteristics Model
- Empowerment
- Sociotechnical Systems

■ Physical Aspects of Job Design
- Physical Design
- Environmental Design

■ Work Study
- Method Study
- Work Measurement

■ Technology for Job Design: Human Capital Management Systems (HCMSs)

Learning Objectives

After reading this chapter, you should be able to:

1 Describe the elements of the job characteristics model.

2 Discuss the role of empowerment.

3 Describe the sociotechnical systems approach.

4 Describe the use of ergonomics in terms of physical and environmental design.

5 Understand work study techniques.

6 Describe an example of the use of technology for job design.

Introduction

Operations management deals with the management of personnel that create or deliver an organization's goods and services. Job and work design consists of the formal specifications and informal expectations of an employee's work-related activities and should try to meet the needs of both the jobholder and the organization. The main elements of job and work design are behavioural aspects which impact on employee motivation and the physical effects of work. Work Study represents an attempt to measure the performance of work and thus lead to better designed jobs. At an organizational level, software such as Human Capital Management Systems (HCMSs) can be used to manage the activities of employees.

Behavioural Aspects of Job Design

In Chapter 1 it was explained that one of the key differences between manufacturing and services was the fact that in services it is likely that the producer of the service will come into contact with the customer. The customer may indeed be, to a greater or lesser extent, involved in the actual delivery of the service. This means service employees and customers frequently work together and, thus, the behaviour of employees is likely to have a major effect on the customer's perceived level of service quality. The level of satisfaction of service employees in turn has been found to have an impact on the quality of the service delivered (Schneider and Bowen, 1993).

The implication is that employees that are not motivated (due to factors such as low wages, boring tasks and inadequate training) will be dissatisfied and this will lead to a poor perception of service quality by customers. Technology is often used as a way of 'controlling' employee behaviour in these circumstances, but in services, in particular, it is difficult to replace the element of human interaction completely. The reasons why organizations have dissatisfied employees may be partly due to external factors such as an under-investment in education and training by government, but also by a short-term focus on minimizing easily quantifiable costs such as for training. The long-term benefits of employee satisfaction leading to customer satisfaction are much harder to quantify and will achieve a payback over a relatively long time period.

Three theories which have had a significant impact on the behavioural aspects of job design are the job characteristics model, empowerment and sociotechnical systems.

The Job Characteristics Model

The Hackman and Oldman (1980) job characteristics model is useful in providing suggestions of how to structure jobs to include more motivators. The model links job characteristics with the desired psychological state of the individual and the outcomes in terms of motivation and job performance. The model takes into account individual differences and provides a structure for analysing motivational problems at work and to predict the effects of change on people's jobs and to help plan new work systems. The model proposes five desirable characteristics for a job:

> **JOB CHARACTERISTICS MODEL:** links job characteristics with the desired psychological state of the individual and the outcomes in terms of motivation and job performance.

- *Skill Variety (SV)* – the extent to which a job makes use of different skills and abilities.
- *Task Identity (TI)* – the extent to which a job involves completing a whole identifiable piece of work rather than simply a part.
- *Task Significance (TS)* – the extent to which a job has an impact on other people, both inside or outside the organization.
- *Autonomy (AU)* – the extent to which the job allows the jobholder to exercise choice and discretion in their work.
- *Feedback (FB)* – the extent to which the job itself (as opposed to other people) provides the jobholder with information on their performance.

The model proposes that the presence of these characteristics will lead to desirable mental states in terms of meaningful work (CV, TI, TS), responsibility for outcomes of work (AU) and knowledge of the results of work (FB). These mental states will in turn lead to higher motivation and quality of work performance. The effects predicted by the model are moderated by factors such as the importance an individual attaches to challenge and personal development.

The five core job characteristics can be combined to provide a Motivating Potential Score (MPS) using the following formula:

$$\text{MPS} = \frac{SV + TI + TS}{3} \times AU \times FB$$

The formula shows that the addition of skill variety (SV), task identity (TI) and task significance (TS) means that a low score on one of these variables can be compensated by a high score on another. The formula also shows that the combined effect of these three variables (which are divided by 3) are only equal to the other two job characteristics (autonomy AU and feedback FB) on their own.

The following are examples of approaches to job design that have been used in an attempt to bring these desirable job characteristics to people's work leading to an improved mental state and, thus, increased performance.

Job Rotation

Job rotation involves a worker changing job roles with another worker on a periodic basis. If successfully implemented, this can help increase task identity, skill variety and autonomy through involvement in a wider range of work tasks, with discretion about when these mixes of tasks can be undertaken. However, this method does not actually improve the design of jobs and it can mean that people gravitate to jobs that suit them and are not interested in initiating rotation with colleagues. At worst it can mean rotation between a number of boring jobs with no acquisition of new skills.

Job Enlargement

Job enlargement involves the horizontal integration of tasks to expand the range of tasks involved in a particular job. If successfully implemented, this can increase task identity, task significance and skill variety by involving the worker in the whole work task either individually or within the context of a group.

Job Enrichment

Job enrichment involves the vertical integration of tasks and the integration of responsibility and decision making. If successfully implemented, this can increase all five of the desirable job characteristics by involving the worker in a wider range of tasks and providing responsibility for the successful execution of these tasks. This technique does require feedback so that the success of the work can be judged. The managerial and staff responsibilities potentially given to an employee through enrichment can be seen as a form of empowerment. This should, in turn, lead to improved productivity and product quality.

There are a number of factors which account for the fact that job rotation, job enlargement and job enrichment are not more widely implemented.

First, the scope for using different forms of work organization will be dependent to a large extent on the type of operation in which the work is organized. Job shop manufacturing will require skilled workers who will be involved in a variety of tasks and will have some discretion in how they undertake these tasks. Sales personnel may also have a high level of discretion in how they undertake their job duties. The amount of variety in a batch manufacturing environment will to a large extent depend on the length of the production runs used. Firms producing large batches of a single item will obviously have less scope for job enrichment than firms producing in small batches on a make-to-order basis. One method for providing job enlargement is to use a cellular manufacturing system, which can permit a worker to undertake a range of tasks on a part. When combined with responsibility for cell performance, this can lead to job enrichment. Jobs in mass production industries may be more difficult to enlarge. Car plants must work at a certain rate in order to meet production targets and on a moving line it is only viable for each worker to spend a few minutes on a task before the next worker on the line must take over. A way of overcoming this problem is to use teams. Here, tasks are exchanged between team members and performance measurements are supplied for the team as a whole. This provides workers with greater variety and feedback, but also some autonomy and participation in the decisions of the team.

Second, financial factors may be a constraint on further use. These may include the performance of individuals who actually prefer simple jobs, higher wage rates paid for the higher skills of employees increasing average wage costs and the capital costs of introducing the approaches. The problem is that many of the benefits associated with the technique, such as an increase in creativity, may be difficult to measure financially.

Finally, the political aspects of job design changes have little effect on organizational structures and the role of management. Although job enrichment may affect supervisory levels of management (e.g., by replacement of a supervisor with a team leader), the power structure which is used to justify management decisions for personal objectives remains intact.

CASE STUDY 9.1

The Case for Job Enrichment

Psychologists have carried out a mass of research to find out what makes us work hard, yet managers stubbornly ignore the findings. Instead, they stick to two discredited theories of motivation – the carrot and the stick.

The carrot method is based on a deeply dark view of human character which basically contends that we only do things because of the pay cheque. But, in reality, all that happens when money is the motivation is that people demand more and more cash to do less and less. Increasingly, they concentrate on tasks which can make them the most money – which is not the same as those which are the most helpful to each other or to the organization as a whole. Meanwhile, other employees who are less well paid become envious and resentful and may seek to settle the score by stealing covertly from the organization or fiddling the books.

The other well-tried motivational method is the stick, which involves being threatened with punishment, humiliation, lost wages or the sack if you don't produce the goods at the rate your boss would like. This approach merely leads to most employees investing huge efforts in avoiding being caught slacking, which means working at the minimum level required to avoid a kicking. But the big problem with both the carrot and the stick is that they ignore the obvious fact that some of the most motivated human behaviour occurs in areas where no financial reward or punishment is involved (e.g., the motivation of a mother to care for her child, or a husband to please his wife, or a golfer to improve his swing). So what does motivate us to work hard? To find out, researchers asked people a basic question: What do you find most rewarding about work? The answers are all psychological and have little to do with money or fear. What the workers wanted was a sense of achievement, recognition from colleagues of their good work, a sense of responsibility, a sense of career advancement and, finally, a feeling of personal growth. The problem is that few work environments are designed to produce any of the rewards on this list.

To improve things, people need to be given more freedom to do the job the way they want to do it, rather than as dictated by 'policy', guidelines or managers. This will give them a sense of personal responsibility and ownership over their work. Workers also need to be given a clear idea of what counts as doing a good job – yet too often managers and workers don't actually agree on the key goals of the organization. And employees should be given 'natural' units of work which they can find rewarding. For example, as the NHS becomes increasingly specialized, no individual doctor or nurse takes overall responsibility for a patient – and so none of them feels the glow of a job well done as the patient recovers.

What is needed is a strategy known as 'job enrichment'. At its very heart is the understanding that the most motivated people work extremely hard without much direct financial reward and without constant check-ups. So the key to job enrichment is the notion of workers understanding themselves better, or the manager developing a better sense of individual workers and helping them form a deeper connection with their work. The problem with job enrichment is not that it's the most effective way psychology knows to improve motivation – it definitely is – but that it requires us to devote the necessary time to think more deeply about why we go to work and what we get out of it on a personal level. It is this time which is often in scarce supply, and which we are reluctant to devote to our working lives because we are trapped in a cycle of extreme busyness but busy doing things which de-motivate us in the long run.

At first, job enrichment feels strange as a way of thinking about work, because it requires us to focus on the positive aspects of work and ourselves, rather than to focus on problems and devote all our energies to fixing those. So the truth about job enrichment is that it is based on the radical and disturbing idea that actually most people want to do a good job: they just find that turning up for work is usually a real turnoff.

Source: 'There must be a better way to get us working' by Raj Persaud, *The Evening Standard*, 29 March 2004

Case Study 9.1
Question

1   What issues would you address in order to achieve job enrichment for employees?

Empowerment

The ideas of job enrichment have led to the concept of **empowerment**. Empowerment is characterized by an organization in which employees are given more autonomy, discretion and responsibility in decision making. Autonomy can be defined as the degree to which people can and do make decisions on their own within their working context (Van Looy *et al.*, 2003).

EMPOWERMENT: characterized by an organization in which employees are given more autonomy, discretion and responsibility in decision making.

Empowerment is especially relevant to service operations as customers and employees interact in the service delivery process. Because the customer is involved in the service delivery process and may require a response to individual requests, the process may differ each time it is performed. This implies that the employee will require a certain level of autonomy in order to satisfy customer needs. This level of autonomy, however, will differ between operations and Bowen and Lawler (1992) describe a continuum of service operations from a 'production line' approach characterized by the simplification of tasks, use of equipment and little discretion in decision making to an 'empowered' approach characterized by more discretion and autonomy and less emphasis on the systems surrounding service employees. The reason for this continuum is that the benefits of empowerment in terms of employee and customer satisfaction need to be weighed against the costs of selection and training and potential poor decisions made by empowered workers. However, it could be argued that all workers need empowerment to some extent, even in 'production line'-type environments, as it is easy to under-estimate the autonomy that can be exercised even in what may seem simple tasks.

In terms of implementing empowerment at the level of an individual employee, the approach is that providing more autonomy to employees will increase their motivation and, thus, satisfy customer needs. However, individual motivation will be dependent on a combination of autonomy and other dimensions which relate to the individual and task in hand. These dimensions are as follows (Van Looy *et al.*, 2003):

■ *Meaning* – which can be seen as the value of a work goal, as perceived by the individual in relations to his or her own ideals and standards.
■ *Competence* – the individual's belief that he or she is able to perform the required activities adequately.
■ *Self-determination* – the individual's sense of having a say in initiatives and regulating work actions.
■ *Strategic Autonomy* – which refers to the extent to which people can influence the content of the job.
■ *Impact* – the degree to which an employee can influence outcomes of their direct work environment.

Figure 9.1   Empowerment as a pyramid

From Van Looy *et al.* (2003)
Source: *Services Management*, ed. B. Van Looy, P. Gemmel and R. Van Dierdonck
Reproduced by permission of Pearson Educaton Ltd. © 2003

Figure 9.1 outlines the relationship between the five dimensions described above. The figure shows that the Meaning and Competence dimensions seem to be necessary for the dimensions of Self-determination, Impact and Strategic Autonomy. The implication of this is that when attempting to implement empowerment, in addition to examining the degree of autonomy present, a degree of meaningfulness and competence should be present. Empowerment can be seen as a process which starts with the creation of meaning and feelings of competence and evolves towards levels of self-determination, impact and even strategic autonomy.

CASE STUDY 9.2

Innocent

Set up in 1998, fruit smoothies company Innocent (www.innocentdrinks.co.uk) sells its drinks in 3000 outlets throughout the UK, Ireland and Paris. The company attributes its success to allowing each member of staff to work in the way that suits them best. Because the company believes that individuals work optimally in different ways, it allows them to design their own work–life balance. In practice, this means that people who like getting up at the crack of dawn get in early and leave early, whilst others choose to come in a bit later and stay later, without any need for a formal flexitime system.

Staff are encouraged to work from home on days when they need some peace and quiet. And they are also able to pursue other interests, which means that Innocent retains skilled people rather than losing them. For example, the company's youngest employee works 4 days a week to allow him to do a college design course on Fridays.

Another employee wanted to go travelling, so Innocent gave him 6 weeks off in order to fulfil his ambition. People are also given time off for hobbies, and the company offers a hobby fund, workplace yoga and free fruit in the office. The company has won several awards including the Shell Live Wire Award for Best London Entrepreneurs and the National Business Award for Best Investor in People from SMEs 2002, and is the fastest growing food and drinks company in the UK. "The success of Innocent is down to the performance of each individual within the company," Richard Reed, Managing Director.

Source: Department of Trade and Industry, www.dti.gov.uk
Crown copyright material is reproduced with the permission of HMSO and the Queen's Printer for Scotland

1   How do the policies at Innocent relate to the concept of Empowerment?

**Case Study 9.2
Question**

Sociotechnical Systems

The **sociotechnical systems** approach originated in the UK during the 1950s and distinguishes between the social and technical sub-systems within the organization. The idea is that these two aspects should be designed in parallel to achieve an overall optimum system. The approach is focused on group or team work and proposes the use of **autonomous work groups** which would be able to decide on their own methods of working and should be responsible for handling problems as they arise. This focus on the redesign of work at the group level is the major way in which autonomous workgroups can be distinguished from job enrichment. Typically, an autonomous work group will be responsible for the whole delivery of a product or service and are often associated with the use of cell layouts (Chapter 5). An early high-profile adopter of the autonomous work group approach, based on sociotechnical systems theory, is the car manufacturer Volvo.

SOCIOTECHNICAL SYSTEMS:
a job design approach that suggests that the social and technical sub-systems within the organization should be designed in parallel to achieve an overall optimum system.

AUTONOMOUS WORK GROUPS:
groups of people who decide on their own methods of working and take responsibility for handling problems as they arise. They will, typically, be responsible for the whole delivery of a product or service.

Physical Aspects of Job Design

In addition to behavioural factors, job design should consider the physical effects of work. The term **ergonomics** is used to describe the collection of information about human characteristics and behaviour to understand the effect of design, methods and environment. Two areas of major concern are the interaction with physical devices, such as computer terminals, and with the environment, such as the office.

ERGONOMICS:
collection of information about human characteristics and behaviour to understand the effect of design, methods and environment.

Physical Design

When required to operate a physical device a worker must be able to reach the controls and apply the necessary force to them. Although the average person is capable of a variety of tasks, the speed and accuracy of any actions can be affected by the location of a device. Because the human part of this system obviously cannot be designed, considerable thought must be placed into the location of the device taking into account human capabilities.

Anthropometric Data

ANTHROPOMETRIC DATA:

information concerning factors related to the physical attributes of a human being, such as the size, weight and strength of various parts of the human body.

Anthropometric data is information concerning factors related to the physical attributes of a human being, such as the size, weight and strength of various parts of the human body. From this information it is possible to gather data on the range of motion, sitting height, strength, working height and other variables. The data can then be used to ensure that the vast majority, say 95% of the population, has the capability to use the device efficiently. For instance, the reach required to operate equipment should be no greater than the shortest reach of all the persons required to operate it. In some cases, equipment may need adjustment devices built in to cater for different needs. The adjustable car seat is an example of this. Other designs are more subtle. For instance, the arrangement of a number of dials so they all point in the same direction during normal operation enables much speedier checking by an operative.

Environmental Design

This involves the immediate environment in which the job takes place. Some environmental variables to consider include:

Noise

Excessive noise levels can not only be distracting but can lead to damage to the worker's hearing. Noise is measured in decibels (dB) on a logarithmic scale that means that a 10-dB increase in noise equates to a 10-fold increase in noise intensity. Extended periods of exposure above 90 dB have been judged to be permanently damaging to hearing. Higher sound intensities may be permitted for short exposures but no sound as high as 130 dB should be experienced.

Illumination

The level of illumination depends on the level of work being performed. Jobs requiring precise movements will generally require a higher level of illumination. Other lighting factors such as contrast, glare and shadows are also important.

Temperature and Humidity

Although humans can perform under various combinations of temperature, humidity and air movement, performance will suffer outside an individual 'comfort zone'. Obviously, the nature of the task will affect the temperature range under which work can be undertaken.

CASE STUDY 9.3

Rare

The first seeds of the company that would one day become the internationally renowned Rare were sown way back in the late 1970s, amidst a clutter of arcade boards in a terraced house in Ashby de la Zouch, Leicestershire. Momentum was building for the first great home-gaming boom of the early 1980s, and Tim and Chris Stamper were determined to be ready for it. Thus was 'Ultimate – Play The Game' born. Ultimate was to attain a near-legendary status in the European 8-bit world during its relatively brief existence, kicking off with the launch of Jetpac on its platform of choice, the Sinclair Spectrum, in the summer of 1983. But as the mid-1980s drifted by, the home computer market began to wane and the Stampers became keenly aware that the future of the industry lay elsewhere – in the emerging breed of international consoles. Ultimate finally ground to a halt, and from its ashes rose the phoenix of Rare, based now in a farmhouse in the nearby village of Twycross, set up primarily to study and develop for the Nintendo Entertainment System (NES). Rare went on to produce a total of around 60 games for the NES and Game Boy (with occasional dabblings in the Mega Drive/ Genesis and Game Gear markets) over the next few years, from Slalom to Marble Madness, RC Pro-Am to Battletoads. But, it was Donkey Kong Country (DKC) on the SNES, released in late 1994, which was to suddenly hurl Rare back into the limelight. One of the biggest selling videogames of all time, DKC was the beginning of a multi-platform franchise which has seen sales of well over 30 million copies to date. During 1999 Rare underwent another massive change, finally making the move from its long-time headquarters of a converted farmhouse to a custom-built centre of operations more suited to the business of creating cutting edge videogames. The multi-million pound development at Manor Park, just down the road from Twycross, was designed and constructed over the course of 5 years to strict guidelines that ensured the preservation of the area's rural charm. Featuring fully landscaped grounds, a state-of-the-art internal climate management system and, vitally, much more free space to house the ever-increasing body of staff, this new HQ offered the perfect environment for Rare's production teams to go on creating the highly regarded titles for which they'd become known. If nature is not your thing, then there is also an outside five-a-side football pitch, basketball hoop and golfing nets. Further still, if sport is not your niche, there are meeting rooms for gaming and a football table resides in the canteen. On top of a competitive starting salary, Rare offer an annual bonus, private healthcare for employees and their families, life assurance, critical illness cover, use of the employee assistance programme and discounted Microsoft products from the company store for all new employees.

Source: www.rare.co.uk

Case Study 9.3 Question

1   Discuss the appropriateness of the work environment offered by Rare for its employees.

Work Study

WORK STUDY:
measures the performance of jobs and consists of two elements: method study and work measurement.

Work study, which has been developed to measure the performance of jobs, consists of two elements: method study and work measurement. To use this approach work should be sufficiently routine and repetitive to make it feasible to derive an average time from a sample of operators and operations. It must also be possible for the worker to vary their rate of work voluntarily in a measurable way. Therefore, it can be applied quite readily to routine manual or clerical work but lends itself less well to indirect work such as maintenance or non-repetitive work such as professional and managerial duties.

Method Study

METHOD STUDY:
divides and analyses a job in order to reduce waste, time and effort.

Dividing and analysing a job is called **method study** and was pioneered by Gilbreth (1911). The method takes a systematic approach to reducing waste, time and effort. The approach can be analysed in a six-step procedure:

1   *Select* – tasks most suitable will probably be repetitive, require extensive labour input and be critical to overall performance.

2   *Record* – this involves observation and documentation of the correct method of performing the selected tasks. Process charts are often used to represent a sequence of events graphically. They are intended to highlight unnecessary material movements and unnecessary delay periods.

3 *Examine* – this involves examination of the current method, looking for ways in which tasks can be eliminated, combined, rearranged and simplified. This can be achieved by looking at the process chart and redesigning the sequence of tasks necessary to perform the activity.

4 *Develop* – developing the best method and obtaining approval for this method. This means choosing the best alternative, taking into account the constraints of the system such as the performance of the firm's equipment. The new method will require adequate documentation in order that procedures can be followed. Specifications may include tooling, operator skill level and working conditions.

5 *Install* – implement the new method. Changes such as installation of new equipment and operator training will need to be undertaken.

6 *Maintain*   routinely verify that the new method is being followed correctly.

New methods may not be followed due to inadequate training or support. On the other hand, people may find ways to gradually improve the method over time. Learning curves can be used to analyse these effects.

Motion Study

Motion study is the study of the individual human motions that are used in a job task. The purpose of motion study is to try to ensure that the job does not include any unnecessary motion or movement by the worker and to select the sequence of motions that ensure that the job is being carried out in the most efficient manner possible. The technique was originated by Gilbreth (1911) who studied many workers at their jobs and from among them picked the best way to perform each activity. He then combined these elements to form the best way to perform a task.

For even more detail, videotapes can be used to study individual work motions in slow motion and analyse them to find improvement – a technique termed 'micromotion analysis'. Gilbreth's motion study research and analysis has evolved into a set of widely adopted principles of motion study, which are used by organizations as general guidelines for the efficient design of work. The principles are generally categorized according to the efficient use of the human body, efficient arrangement of the workplace and the efficient use of equipment and machinery. Table 9.1 summarizes these principles into general guidelines.

Motion study is seen as one of the fundamental aspects of scientific management and, indeed, it was effective in the design of repetitive, simplified jobs with the task specialization which was a feature of the mass production system. The use of motion study has declined as there has been a movement towards greater job responsibility and a wider range of tasks within a job. However, the technique is still a useful analysis tool and, particularly in the service industries, can help improve process performance.

> **MOTION STUDY:**
> the study of the individual human motions that are used in a job task with the purpose of trying to ensure that the job does not include any unnecessary motion or movement by the worker.

Table 9.1   Summary of guidelines of motion study

Efficient use of the human body
- Work should be rhythmic, symmetrical and simplified
- The full capabilities of the human body should be employed
- Energy should be conserved by letting machines perform tasks when possible

Efficient arrangement of the workplace
- Tools, materials and controls should have a defined place and be located to minimize the motions needed to get to them
- The workplace should be comfortable and healthy

Efficient use of equipment
- Equipment and mechanized tools enhance worker abilities
- Controls and foot-operated devices that can relieve the hand/arms of work should be maximized
- Equipment should be constructed and arranged to fit worker use

---

Work Measurement

WORK MEASUREMENT:
this determines the length of time it will take to undertake a particular task.

The second element of work study is **work measurement** which determines the length of time it will take to undertake a particular task. This is important not only to determine pay rates but also to ensure that each stage in a production line system is of an equal duration (i.e., 'balanced', see Chapter 4), thus ensuring maximum output. Usually, the method study and work measurement activities are undertaken together to develop time as well as method standards. Setting time standards in a structured manner permits the use of benchmarks against which to measure a range of variables such as cost of the product and share of work between team members. However, the work measurement technique has been criticized for being misused by management in determining worker compensation. The time needed to perform each work element can be determined by the use of historical data, work sampling or, most usually, time study.

Time Study

TIME STUDY:
the use of statistical techniques to arrive at a standard time for performing one cycle of a repetitive job.

The purpose of **time study** is to use statistical techniques to determine a standard time for performing one cycle of a repetitive job. This is arrived at by observing a task a number of times. The standard time refers to the time allowed for the job under specific circumstances, taking into account allowances for rest and relaxation. The basic steps in a time study are indicated below:

1 *Establish the standard job method* – it is essential that the best method of undertaking the job is determined using method study before a time study is undertaken. If a better method for the job is found then the time study analysis will need to be repeated.

2 *Break down the job into elements* – the job should be broken down into a number of easily measurable tasks. This will permit a more accurate calculation of standard time as varying proficiencies at different parts of the whole job can be taken into account.

3 *Study the job* – this has traditionally been undertaken with a stopwatch, or electronic timer, by observation of the task. Each time element is recorded on an observation sheet. A videocamera can be used for observation, which permits study away from the workplace, and in slow motion which permits a higher degree of accuracy of measurement.

4 *Rate the worker's performance* – as the time study is being conducted a rating of the worker's performance is also taken in order to achieve a true time rating for the task. Rating factors are usually between 80% and 120% of normal. This is an important but subjective element in the procedure and is best done if the observer is familiar with the job itself.

5 *Compute the average time* – once a sufficient sample of job cycles have been undertaken an average is taken of the observed times called the 'cycle time'. The sample size can be determined statistically, but is often around five to fifteen due to cost restrictions.

6 *Compute the normal time* – adjust the cycle time for the efficiency and speed of the worker who was observed. The normal time is calculated by multiplying the cycle time by the performance rating factors:

$$\text{Normal time } (NT) = \text{Cycle time } (CT) \times \text{Rating factor } (RF)$$

7 *Compute the standard time* – the standard time is computed by adjusting the normal time by an allowance factor to take account of unavoidable delays such as machine breakdown and rest periods. The standard time is calculated as follows:

$$\text{Standard time } (ST) = \text{Normal time } (NT) \times \text{Allowance}$$

Worked Example 9.1

Time Study

PCB Ltd wants to determine the standard time for a manual solder operation on one of their new circuit boards. From the following task times observed during a time study exercise calculate the standard time for the job. Assume the worker who has been observed is 10% slower than average at this task. Assume an allowance factor of 20%.

Sample No.	1	2	3	4	5	6	7	8	9	10
Time (sec)	6.7	7.1	7.3	7.0	7.1	6.8	6.9	6.8	7.1	7.0

Solution

Cycle time (CT) = Average of samples = 69.8/10 = 6.98

Normal time (NT) = $CT \times RT$ = 6.98 × 0.9 = 6.282

Standard time (ST) = NT × Allowance = 6.282 × 1.2 = 7.54 seconds

---

Predetermined Motion Times

One problem with time studies is that workers will not always cooperate with their use, especially if they know the results will be used to set wage rates. Combined with the costs of undertaking a time study, a company may use historical data in the form of time files to construct a new standard job time from a previous job element. This has the disadvantage, however, of the reliability and applicability of old data.

PREDETERMINED MOTION TIMES:

provide generic times for standard micromotions such as reach, move and release which are common to many jobs.

Another method for calculating standard times without a time study is to use the **Predetermined Motion Time** System (PMTS) which provides generic times for standard micromotions such as reach, move and release which are common to many jobs. The standard item for the job is then constructed by breaking down the job into a series of micromotions that can then be assigned a time from the motion time database. The standard time for the job is the sum of these micromotion times. Factors such as load weight for move operations are included in the time motion database.

The advantages of this approach are that standard times can be developed for jobs before they are introduced to the workplace without causing disruption and needing worker compliance. Also, performance ratings are factored into the motion times and so the subjective part of the study is eliminated. The timings should also be much more consistent than historical data, for instance. Disadvantages include the fact that these times ignore the context of the job in which they are undertaken (i.e., the timings are provided for the micromotion in isolation and are not part of a range of movements). The sample is from a broad range of workers in different industries with different skill levels, which may lead to an unrepresentative time. Also, the timings are only available for simple repetitive work which is becoming less common in industry.

WORK SAMPLING:

a method for determining the proportion of time a worker or machine spends on various activities and, as such, can be very useful in job redesign and estimating levels of worker output.

Work Sampling

Work Sampling is useful for analysing the increasing proportion of non-repetitive tasks that are performed in most jobs. It is a method for determining the proportion of time a worker or machine spends on various activities and, as such, can be very useful in job redesign and estimating levels of worker output. The basic steps in work sampling are indicated below:

1 *Define the job activities* – all possible activities must be categorized for a particular job (e.g., worker idle and worker busy states could be used to define all possible activities).

2 *Determine the number of observations in the work sample* – the accuracy of the proportion of time the worker is in a particular state is determined by the observation sample size. Assuming the sample is approximately normally distributed the sample size can be estimated using the following formula:

$$n = (z/e)^2 * p(1-p)$$

where $n =$ Sample size

$z =$ Number of standard deviations from the mean for the desired level of confidence

$e =$ The degree of allowable error in the sample estimate

$p =$ The estimated proportion of time spent on a work activity.

The accuracy of the estimated proportion p is usually expressed in terms of an allowable degree of error e (e.g., for a 2% degree of error, $e = 0.02$). The degree of confidence would normally be 95% (giving a z value of 1.96) or 99% (giving a z value of 2.58).

3 *Determine the length of the sampling period* – there must be sufficient time in order for a random sample of the number of observations given by the equation in Step 2 to be collected. A random number generator can be used to generate the time between observations in order to achieve a random sample.

4 *Conduct the work sampling study and record the observations* – calculate the sample and calculate the proportion (*p*) by dividing the number of observations for a particular activity by the total number of observations.

5 *Periodically recompute the sample size required* – it may be that the actual proportion for an activity is different from the proportion used to calculate the sample size in Step 2. Therefore, as sampling progresses it is useful to recompute the sample size based on the proportions actually observed.

Worked Example 9.2

Work Sampling

The FastCabs Company has a complement of 25 cabs on duty at any one time. The manager of the company wishes to determine the amount of time a cab driver is sitting idle which he estimates at 35%. The cabs were called over a period of a week at random to determine their status. If the manager wants the estimate to be within ±5% of the actual proportion with a confidence level of 95%, estimate the sample size required.

Solution

$$n = (z/e)^2 * p(1 - p)$$

where $z = 1.96$ (at 95% confidence, from normal table)

$e = 0.05$

$p = 0.35$

thus:

$$n = \left(\frac{1.96}{0.05}\right)^2 * 0.35(1 - 0.35)$$

$$= 350$$

Therefore, 350 samples are required.

Learning Curves

LEARNING CURVES: provide an organization with the ability to predict the improvement in productivity that can occur as experience is gained of a process.

Organizations have often used **learning curves** to predict the improvement in productivity that can occur as experience is gained of a process. Thus, learning curves can give an organization a method of measuring continuous improvement activities. If a firm can estimate the rate at which an operation time will decrease then it can predict the impact on cost and increase in effective capacity over time.

The learning curve is based on the concept of when productivity doubles, the decrease in time per unit is the rate of the learning curve. Thus, if the learning curve is at a rate of 85%, the second unit takes 85% of the time of the first unit, the fourth unit takes 85% of the second unit and the eighth unit takes 85% of the fourth and so on.

Mathematically, the learning curve is represented by the function:

$$y = ax^{-b}$$

where $x =$ Number of units produced

$a =$ Hours required to produce the first unit

$y =$ Time to produce the xth unit

$$b = \text{constant equal to } \frac{-(\ln p)}{(\ln 2)}$$

where $\ln = \log_{10}$

$p =$ Learning rate (e.g., 80% = 0.8).

Thus, for an 80% learning curve:

$$b = \frac{-(\ln 0.8)}{\ln(2)} = \frac{-(-0.233)}{(0.693)} = 0.322$$

Worked Example 9.3

Learning Curves

A company is introducing a new product and has determined that an 80% learning curve is applicable. Estimates of demand for the first 4 years of production are 100, 150, 175 and 200. The time to produce the first unit is estimated at 100 hours. Estimate the cumulative labour hours required for each of the first 4 years of production.

Solution

$$y = ax^{-b}$$

where $b = -(\ln p)/(\ln 2)$
  $a = 100$
  $p = 0.8$
  $b = -\ln 0.8/\ln 2 = 0.322$

Thus for year 1:

$$x = 100$$

$$y = 100 \times 100^{0.322}$$

$$= 440 \text{ hours}$$

The results for the first 4 years of production are shown in the table below.

Year	Equation	Cumulative labour hours
1	$100(100)^{0.322}$	440
2	$100(250)^{0.322}$	592
3	$100(425)^{0.322}$	702
4	$100(625)^{0.322}$	795

Learning curves are usually applied to individual operators, but the concept can also be applied in a more aggregate sense, termed an 'experience' or 'improvement curve', and applied to such areas as manufacturing system performance or cost estimating. Industrial sectors can also be shown to have different rates of learning.

It should be noted that improvements along a learning curve do not just happen and the theory is most applicable to new product or process development where scope for improvement is greatest. In addition, step changes can occur which can alter the rate of learning, such as organizational change, changes in technology or quality improvement programmes. To ensure learning occurs the organization must invest in factors such as research and development, advanced technology, people and continuous improvement efforts (Chapter 17).

Technology and Job Design: Human Capital Management Systems (HCMSs)

As in other areas of operations management, technology is used widely to implement programmes. In the area of job design, one recent development has been the introduction of a software application called **Human Capital Management Systems (HCMSs)**. This application provides an enterprise-wide platform that manages everything from payroll and benefits to recruiting and staff deployment. The software is designed to provide an integrated Web-based solution across the organization, similar to the concept of Enterprise Resource Planning (ERP) (Chapter 14) and is offered by ERP vendors such as Oracle. The following case study discussed some of the issues relevant to the implementation of HCMS.

> **HUMAN CAPITAL MANAGEMENT SYSTEM (HCMS):** a Web-based software application that manages human resource functions such as payroll, recruitment and staff deployment across the organization.

CASE STUDY 9.4

A shift in working practices

How do you annoy busy operations managers in charge of banks of staff working complex shift patterns, in one easy move? Reintroduce the concept of automated work force management systems and watch the air turn blue. Computerized work force management systems are back, albeit with a new, more touchy–feely friendly Web face, reflected in their new description: Human Capital Management (HCM) systems. Nearly every old and new software vendor specializing in Human Resources (HR) and Enterprise Resource Planning (ERP) systems, are shifting their systems online and lobbying chief executives with their new 'carbon unit-friendly' solutions. Accordingly, operations managers will be ready with all the reasons why the last lot of work force management systems largely bombed big time.

The old systems were individual software packages designed to replace time-consuming paper-based procedures. They were typically based on time and motion studies and took the form of time and attendance-style systems. Their intention was to make it easier and quicker for local managers to roster staff so as to address business needs more effectively, and save managers' time and businesses' money while ensuring that all union rights, workplace legislation and company policies were properly adhered to.

But, in practice, most of the systems were too complicated and time consuming to learn, too scientific and inflexible in their approach to interpret real life and individual business needs, and of greater benefit to the HR department than to operations managers since they recorded items such as weekly pay and outstanding holiday entitlements. In addition, they ignored the individual skills and work pattern preferences of shop and factory floor staff, and took no account of customer service levels. And they failed to acknowledge the local expertise of operations managers who are well versed in the peculiar vagaries of their work.

But by far the biggest indignity was that the systems rode roughshod over operations managers' sensibilities. They smacked of Big Brother interfering from head office – some anonymous senior executive with no knowledge of the local work force dictating how shift workers should be managed in a one-size-fits-all approach. An 'us and them' situation quickly arose. The result? Operations managers simply switched the systems off and continued using their tried-and-tested paper-based work force management methods. So much for progress.

And yet, there is no doubt the theory behind automating work force management procedures was sound. Even today, operations managers in shift-intensive sectors, such as manufacturing and retail, are estimated to spend more than 4 to 6 hours a week planning staff schedules on paper. They often work with little supporting information other than their own local knowledge and experience: the skills, staff preferences and local business pressures. This is one reason why today's software vendors are having another stab at reintroducing work force management systems, and the key weapon in their armoury to overcome yesterday's hostile reception of such systems is the Web.

The new breed of the Web-based HCM system is, by and large, more user friendly, requiring only basic training since access is via customizable Web browsers which are familiar to most, if not all managers these days. They are also more flexible in their approach, placing the managers in control of creating their own preferred computerized method of working, one that acknowledges his or her knowledge of local business and staff needs. In addition, some can help managers simultaneously and quickly juggle all manner of priorities, including business expectations and forecasts in line with seasonal fluctuations, budgets and costs, staff skills, availability and preferences, equity and fairness in allocating unattractive jobs, customer service levels and expectations, administration, and compliance with policy, employment and health and safety legislation and union agreements.

Many systems also integrate with others (e.g., customer relationship management and point of sale systems). This means that key managers in the business, from the chief executive downwards, can tap into real time work force information and plan future business resourcing based on a myriad of employee data (e.g., individual staff skills and preferences for working hours). These are the main HCM vendors' sales arguments, but there are also independent statistics that support their claims. A report by Chorleywood Consulting estimates that the time spent using old methods of work force management could be cut by 50–80% using the new Web-based HCM software. Aberdeen Research predicts that the HCM market, currently worth at least £120m, will grow to be worth £10bn by 2003 as companies recognize that effectively managed 'people assets' have the potential to increase shareholder value among larger companies by as much as 30%.

With today's volatile economic climate playing havoc with supply and demand, making production, planning and staffing schedules harder to predict, and, increasingly, complex employment and workplace legislation flowing out of Brussels, not to mention shift workers across all sectors starting to demand more flexible working patterns as they search for a happier work/life balance, the job of the operations manager is not getting any easier.

Web-based HCM systems could be the answer, but businesses need to involve operations managers in choosing such systems to ensure they genuinely address the right needs – too many of the big software vendors are simply tweaking their HR and ERP systems to fit the new HCM buzzword. Smaller fry HCM vendors, including Blue Pumpkin, Kronos Systems, Open Text, Rostima and TempoSoft, are trying harder. Some of these are already well known to operations managers, while others were deliberately set up to address the problems of the work force management tools of the past.

It is early days yet for HCM systems, but they just may deliver on their promises. The question is: Who is brave enough to find out?

Source: 'A shift in working practices' by Lindsey Nicolle, *The Times*, 31 January 2002

Case Study 9.4 Question

1   What are the potential advantages and disadvantages of HCM systems for the Operations Manager?

Summary

1 The job characteristics model links job characteristics to performance through an intervening variable: motivation. Approaches to job design that have attempted to increase motivation (and thus performance) are job rotation, job enlargement and job enrichment.

2 Empowerment has been developed in response to an individual need for challenging and meaningful work and the expectations of employers in a market place characterized by rapid change and new technologies.

3 Sociotechnical systems theory distinguishes between the social and technical sub-systems within the organization and states that these two aspects should be designed in parallel to achieve an overall optimum system.

4 Ergonomics uses information about human characteristics and behaviour to understand the effect of physical and environmental design.

5 Work study consists of two elements: method study and work measurement. Method study consists of dividing and analysing a task in a systematic manner in order to improve the method of carrying out that task. Work measurement consists of determining the length of time it will take to undertake a task in order to establish a benchmark against which performance can be measured.

6 Web-based HCMSs provide an integrated Web-based platform for the design of jobs.

Exercises

1. Evaluate the job design approaches of job rotation, job enlargement and job enrichment.
2. Compare the job characteristics model with the concept of empowerment.
3. What is the difference between empowerment and autonomy?
4. Discuss the relevance of empowerment to successful operations management.
5. The following cycle times have been observed for a job consisting of five elements. A performance rating factor has been calculated for each element. Assume an allowance factor of 15%.

Element	Cycle time	Ratings factor
1	3.6	1.05
2	4.8	0.9
3	2.9	1.0
4	4.9	1.1
5	1.7	0.95

   a. Determine the normal time (NT) for each element.
   b. Determine the overall normal time.
   c. Determine the standard time.
6. Calculate the sample size required to estimate the time a supervisor spends in a maintenance department. Management believe that 50% of the supervisor's time is spent in maintenance. They require an estimate to be within ±5% of the actual proportion with a 95% degree of confidence.
7. An electrical goods manufacturer is producing an electronic component for a washing machine. It is estimated that it will take 150 hours to produce the first unit. The standard learning curve for this type of component is 90%. What are the cumulative labour hours required for 500 units produced?
8. Discuss the major approaches to job design as they relate to the operations function.

References

Bowen, D. and Lawler, E. (1992), The empowerment of service workers: What, why, how and when, *Sloan Management Review*, Spring, 31–39.

Gilbreth, F. (1911), *Motion Study*, Van Nostrand.

Hackman, R.J. and Oldman, G. (1980), *Work Redesign*, Addison-Wesley.

Schneider, B. and Bowen, D.E. (1993), The service organization: Human resources management is crucial, *Organizational Dynamics*, **21**(4), 39–52.

Van Looy, B., Gemmel, P. and Van Dierdonck, R. (eds) (2003), *Services Management: An Integrated Approach*, 2nd Edition, Pearson Education.

Further Reading

Bailey, J. (1993), *Managing People and Technological Change*, Financial Times/ Prentice Hall.

Bessant, J. (2003), *High Involvement Innovation: Building and Sustaining Competitive Advantage through Continuous Change*, John Wiley & Sons.

Daft, R.L. (2003), *Organization Theory and Design*, 8th Edition, South-Western College Publishing.

Mullins, L.J. (2004), *Management and Organizational Behaviour*, 7th Edition, Pitman.

Mundel, M.E. and Danner, D.L. (1994), *Motion and Time Study: Improving Productivity*, 7th Edition, Prentice Hall.

Parker, S. and Wall, T. (1998), *Job and Work Design: Organizing Work to Promote Well-Being and Effectiveness*, Sage Publications.

Web Links

www.ergonomics.org.uk The Ergonomics Society. News, information and conferences concerning ergonomics and human factors.

www.eee.bham.ac.uk/eiac Ergonomics Information Analysis Centre. Contains over 170 000 abstracts in the area of ergonomics.

www.acsco.com/tseng.htm Applied Computer Services Inc. Software for time and motion studies.

www.peoplesoft.co.uk/corp/en/products/ent/hcm/index.jsp Oracle Human Capital Management systems.

www.blue-pumpkin.com/ Blue Pumpkin website.

www.rostima.com/ Rostima website.

Part 3
Management

CHAPTER 13 **Lean Operations and JIT**
The Philosophy of JIT and Lean Operations
JIT and Lean Techniques
JIT in Service Systems
Implementing JIT and Lean Operations

CHAPTER 14 **Enterprise Resource Planning**
Resource Planning
Materials Requirements Planning
Manufacturing Resource Planning (MRP II)
Distribution Requirements Planning (DRP)
Enterprise Resource Planning (ERP) Systems

CHAPTER 15 **Supply Chain Management**
Supply Chain Design
Activities in the Supply Chain

CHAPTER 16 **Project Management**
Project Management Activities
Projects and Organizational Structure
The Role of the Project Manager
Network Analysis

CHAPTER 17 **Quality**
Defining Quality
Total Quality Management (TQM)
Six Sigma Quality
Statistical Process Control (SPC)
Acceptance Sampling

CHAPTER 18 **Improvement**
Continuous Improvement
The Learning Organization
Business Process Reengineering (BPR)
Systems Thinking
Balanced Scorecard
Activity-Based Costing (ABC)
Benchmarking

Chapter 10

Planning and Control

■ Operations Planning

- P : D Ratios

■ Operations Control

- Loading

- Sequencing

- Scheduling

■ Optimized Production Technology (OPT)

Learning Objectives

After reading this chapter, you should be able to:

1 Evaluate resource-to-order, make-to-order and make-to-stock planning policies.

2 Describe the principal approaches to the operations control task of loading.

3 Describe the use of priority rules for the operations control task of sequencing.

4 Discuss the operations control task of scheduling.

5 Identify techniques for scheduling in manufacturing and service operations.

6 Describe the operations control system of Optimized Production Technology (OPT).

Introduction

Planning and control is about matching customer demand to the operations capacity. In the long term, this can be considered as a design issue and is covered in Chapter 5 of this text. This chapter is concerned with short-term planning and control in order to meet estimated demand. This task is made challenging because of the unstable nature of market demand which works against the execution of an efficient and effective operations system.

One way of dealing with unstable demand is to produce the product or service (or elements of the product or service) in advance. The first part of this chapter evaluates the use of make-to-stock, make-to-order and resource-to-order planning policies.

The second part of this chapter examines the activities that form operations control tasks. These generally consist of loading (determining capacity and volumes), sequencing (deciding on the order of execution of work) and scheduling (allocating a start and finish time to a customer order). A number of techniques for operations control are then described and the OPT operations control system is described. Further operations control systems that are discussed in this text include Just-In-Time (JIT) and lean operations (Chapter 13), Enterprise Resource Planning (ERP) (Chapter 14), supply chain management (Chapter 15) and project management (Chapter 16).

Operations Planning

The predictability of demand for goods and services can range from a situation of what is essentially dependent demand (i.e., demand can be predicted) to a high level of unpredictability (independent demand). Planning policies to meet this continuum are shown in Table 10.1.

Thus, in a dependent demand-type situation it is not necessary to activate a planning system and acquire resources until a delivery date for an order is received. Both transforming (e.g., staff, machinery) and transformed (e.g., bricks for a house) resources may be acquired at the appropriate time for delivery. This

Table 10.1   Planning policies for demand types

Demand type	Planning policy	Resources required in stock
Dependent	Resource-to-order	None
Independent (low variability)	Make-to-order	Transforming
Independent (high variability)	Make-to-stock	Transforming Transformed

RESOURCE-TO-ORDER:
when it is not necessary to activate a planning system and acquire resources until a delivery date for an order is received.

MAKE-TO-ORDER:
a planning policy which acquires the raw material which is used to construct the product on the receipt of a customer order.

MAKE-TO-STOCK:
a planning policy which produces a forecast of demand for the product.

P:D RATIO:
compares the demand time D (from customer request to receipt of goods/services) with the total throughput time P of the purchase, make and delivery stages.

is termed a **resource-to-order** planning policy. In an independent demand situation when demand is relatively predictable, the transforming resources such as staff and machinery may be in place on a permanent basis. However, the transformed resources (i.e., the raw material which is used to construct the product) may be acquired on the receipt of a customer order. This is termed a **make-to-order** planning policy. Finally, if demand is unpredictable, the organization will use a **make-to-stock** planning policy which produces a forecast of demand for the product.

Two implications arise from the planning policy utilized by the organization. In a make-to-stock system each order must be small compared with total capacity, otherwise the risk of making to stock, and not finding a customer for the order, will be too high. Also, a resource-to-order system implies each order is large compared with total system capacity to make the organization of resources worthwhile. The other implication is that of customer delivery time performance. Whilst the customer will only 'see' the delivery time from stock in a make-to-stock system, in a make-to-order system the delivery cycle will include the purchase, make and delivery stages. This effect is examined using P:D ratios.

P:D Ratios

The **P:D ratio** is a concept derived by Shingo (1981) and compares the demand time D (from customer request to receipt of goods/services) to the total throughput time P of the purchase, make and delivery stages. The purchase stage involves acquiring necessary resources from internal and external suppliers, the make stage includes the processing of resources through the operations system, and the deliver stage involves packing and distribution of the finished good to the customer.

The relationship between the planning and control systems and the P:D ratio is shown in Figure 10.1.

Thus, in a resource-to-order system the demand time and throughput time are essentially the same. The purchase–make–deliver cycle is not triggered until a

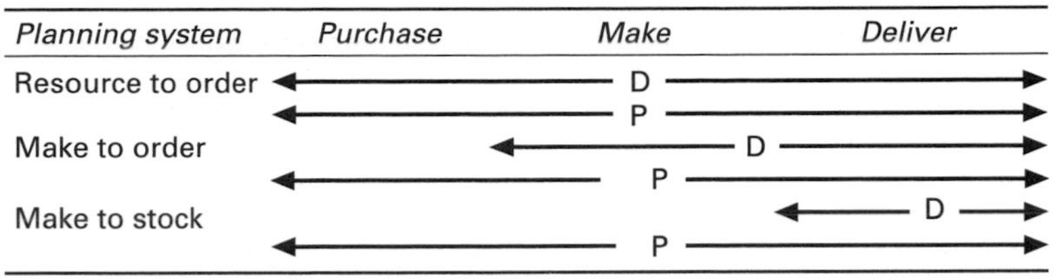

Planning system	Purchase	Make	Deliver

Figure 10.1   The relationship between the P : D ratio and the planning policy

customer order is received. In a make-to-stock system the demand time is essentially the time of delivery from stock to the customer.

The P : D ratio makes the implications for the delivery time to the customer explicit. In a resource-to-order system the purchase, make and deliver stages all affect delivery performance. In a make-to-stock system, however, the customer only 'sees' the delivery time. However, although delivery performance is improved in a make-to-stock system, the item is being produced to a forecast demand which is subject to error. The risk of producing to this forecast increases with the ratio of P to D, as an increase in throughput times means that the item must be produced to a demand further into the future. Thus, reducing the P : D ratio will reduce the risk inherent in the planning policy.

Operations Control

This section examines the activities that form operations control tasks. These generally consist of loading (determining capacity and volumes), sequencing (deciding on the order of execution of work) and scheduling (allocating start and finish time to a customer order).

Loading

Loading involves determining the available capacity for each stage in a process and allocating a work task to that stage. The calculation of available capacity must take account of both planned factors such as machine maintenance and unplanned factors such as machine breakdowns and worker absenteeism. These issues are dealt in more detail in Chapter 11. There are two principle approaches to loading.

LOADING:
involves determining the available capacity for each stage in a process and allocating a work task to that stage.

Finite Loading

Finite loading allocates work up to an agreed fixed (finite) upper limit. This may be because:

■ the upper limit of capacity is fixed (e.g., seats on an aircraft, although this does not rule out the policy of overbooking to ensure that all capacity is actually utilized!);
■ the upper limit can be fixed through a policy such as using an appointment system;
■ there is a policy of limiting availability to the market (e.g., a limited edition of an expensive watch may enhance demand).

Infinite Loading

Infinite loading does not place a limit on the work loaded onto a stage. This may be because:

■ it is not possible to limit demand (e.g., emergency hospital treatment should not be refused);
■ it is acceptable to have a drop in performance. In manufacturing or services if demand exceeds capacity a queue will form. This may be acceptable in some instances (e.g., shopping outlets) when the customer understands the cost of always providing instant service is too high.

Sequencing

SEQUENCING:
the sequential
assignment of tasks or
jobs to individual
processes.

Sequencing (also known as 'dispatching') is the sequential assignment of tasks or jobs to individual processes. In order to attempt to control the progress of a job through a process a job priority system is used. The priority of jobs queuing at a process determines the order in which they are processed. The difficulty lies in determining an appropriate priority rule to obtain the best performance. Priority rules include:

■ *DDS (Customer Due-Date)* – job with nearest customer due-date to the current date.
■ *FCFS (First Come, First Served)* – job arriving first at a process (i.e., in order of arrival).
■ *SPT/SOT (Shortest Process Time/Shortest Operating Time)* – job with shortest process/operating time among waiting jobs.
■ *LPT (Longest Process Time)* – job with longest process time among waiting jobs.

All the rules have different advantages and disadvantages. The SPT rule ensures that jobs with the shortest process time progress rapidly, thus the number of jobs processed should be high, and this rule will generally give the best performance. However, a disadvantage of the SPT rule is that when the demand on the process is high this may mean a job with a longer process time may have an unacceptably long wait and is always at the end of the queue.

Rules can also use a combination of factors to determine the sequence, such as the Critical Ratio (*CR*) which is the ratio of the time left until the job's due-date to the expected elapsed time for the job to be processed through the remaining processes to its completion:

$$\text{Critical Ratio } (CR) = \frac{\text{Due date} - \text{Current date}}{\text{Days required to complete job}}$$

If the ratio is less than 1 the job is behind schedule and should receive priority.

Gantt charts (Chapter 16) can be employed to show the effect of different job-sequencing strategies on the performance of the process.

Worked Example 10.1

Sequencing

A copyshop offers a photocopying service to customers. Currently, it uses an FCFS system because this seems the fairest way of working for the customers. However, the manager of the shop suspects that an alternative sequencing rule may improve performance. Using the data collected below, try the FCFS, DDS and SPT sequences and state which rule provides the best performance using the measure of average lateness.

Job arrival sequence	Processing time (days)	Customer due-date (days)
A	5	7
B	4	6
C	2	5
D	2	6
E	1	3

Trying the FCFS Rule

Job arrival sequence	Processing time (days)	Customer due-date (days)	Process time (FCFS) (days)	Lateness (days)
A	5	7	$0+5=5$	0
B	4	6	$5+4=9$	3
C	2	5	$9+2=11$	6
D	2	6	$11+2=13$	7
E	1	3	$13+1=14$	11

$$\text{Average lateness} = \frac{0+3+6+7+11}{5} = \frac{27}{5} = 5.4 \text{ days}$$

Trying the DDS Rule

Job arrival sequence	Processing time (days)	Customer due-date (days)	Process time (DDS) (days)	Lateness (days)
A	5	7	$9+5=14$	7
B	4	6	$3+4=7$	1
C	2	5	$1+2-3$	0
D	2	6	$7+2=9$	3
E	1	3	$0+1=1$	0

$$\text{Average lateness} = \frac{7+1+0+3+0}{5} = \frac{11}{5} = 2.2 \text{ days}$$

Trying the SPT Rule

Job arrival sequence	Processing time (days)	Customer due-date (days)	Process time (SPT) (days)	Lateness (days)
A	5	7	$9+5=14$	7
B	4	6	$5+4=9$	3
C	2	5	$3+2=5$	0
D	2	6	$1+2=3$	0
E	1	3	$0+1=1$	0

$$\text{Average lateness} = \frac{7+3+0+0+0}{5} = \frac{10}{5} = 2.0 \text{ days}$$

Of the three rules the SPT rule provides the best performance with an average job lateness of 2 days.

Johnson's Rule

An optimal solution to the job-sequencing problem has been found for the special case in which all jobs flow through two work centres or processes in the same order. Johnson's (1954) rule minimizes the overall lead time (start of first job to end of last job) in this case, assuming other costs (such as machine setup costs moving from one product to another) are not dependent on the job sequence chosen. Setup times are included in job process times.

The following steps should be followed:

1 List the processing time for all jobs for both stages of production.
2 For unscheduled jobs select the job with the shortest time in either stage.
3 If the shortest time is for the first processing stage:

> *Put the job as early as possible in the job sequence.*

If the shortest time is for the second processing stage:

> *Put the job as late as possible in the job sequence.*

If the time on the first stage for one job equals the time on the second stage for some other job:

> *Fill the earliest slot with the job having this amount of time for the first stage and fill the latest slot with the job having this amount of time for the second stage.*

If both jobs have the same time for both stages:

> *Place them at either end of the sequence.*

4 Delete the job selected and repeat the steps until all jobs have been sequenced.

Worked Example 10.2

Johnson's Rule

A manufacturing department has five jobs which must be processed on the sand process and then on the varnish process. Determine the sequence that will allow the set of five jobs to be completed in the minimum time.

| Job | Process time (minutes) | |
	Sand	Varnish
A	6	3
B	4	5
C	2	3
D	6	6
E	3	7

Solution

1   Shortest time is 2 for C in the sand stage; therefore, put as early as possible in the job sequence:

2   Next shortest time is 3 for A in the varnish stage and 3 for E in the sand stage; therefore, put E as early as possible in the job sequence and A as late as possible in the job sequence:

3   Next shortest is 4 for B in the sand stage; therefore, put B as early as possible in the job sequence:

4   The only job remaining is job D; therefore, the final sequence is as follows:

To find the completion time a Gantt chart is used to total up the job completion time.

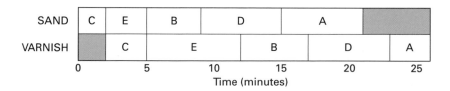

Thus, the total completion time is 26 minutes.

It should be emphasized that the rule is only applicable to a flow through two work centres in the same order and does not consider individual job due-dates in constructing the schedule.

Scheduling

Scheduling is the allocation of a start and finish time to each order while taking into account the loading and sequencing policies employed. The scheduling process is usually driven by the need to manage a number of jobs or customers in the system and ensure they are completed or receive their order by a target due-date. Scheduling in services and manufacturing is discussed before a number of scheduling techniques are described.

SCHEDULING:
the allocation of a start and finish time to each order while taking into account the loading and sequencing policies employed.

Scheduling in Services

What makes scheduling particularly challenging in service systems is that services are generally produced and delivered by people, whose performance may be less predictable and more variable, than manufacturing processes. A major factor in scheduling in services is varying the size of the workforce to meet variations in demand. This area is covered in the workforce scheduling technique section later in this chapter. Another issue in service scheduling is the fact the services are not only delivered by people but are also consumed by people. In fact, the customer may be part of the service itself or require the service on request. The combination of the difficulty in predicting when demand will occur (e.g., when will people arrive at a bank) and the short lead time between requesting the service and requiring its delivery (e.g., a few minutes for bank service) brings a challenge to scheduling in services. In practice, a trade-off is made between providing enough capacity (staff) to provide customer satisfaction (no wait for service) and the cost of providing that capacity when it is not needed.

Scheduling in Manufacturing

In manufacturing systems the issue of scheduling is about ensuring that the capacity available is directed towards activities that will ensure that performance targets for delivery and lead times are met. The approach to scheduling in manufacturing is largely dependent on the volume and variety mix of the manufacturing system itself and so scheduling approaches will be considered under the headings of line, batch and jobbing process types (see Chapter 3 for an explanation of these process types).

Mass Process-type Scheduling
Mass process-type systems produce a standard product in a relatively high volume. These systems which have a characteristic flow (product) layout use specialized equipment dedicated to achieving an optimal flow of work through the system. This is important because all items follow virtually the same sequence of

operations. A major aim of flow systems is to ensure that each stage of production is able to maintain production at an equal rate. The technique of line balancing is used to ensure that the output of each production stage is equal and maximum utilization is attained.

Batch Process-type Scheduling

Batch systems process a range of product types in batches (groups), thus combining some of the economics of repetitive production with the variety of a jobshop. Scheduling in these configurations is a matter of ensuring that the batch of work introduced to the process will be completed to meet customer due-dates. Two issues which affect the job completion time and, thus, the ability to meet due-dates are the transfer batch size and the job sequence. The transfer batch size refers to the size of the batch of parts that is processed at a workstation before progressing to the next workstation. The actual order size may be greater than this, but is divided into a number of transfer batches to decrease the time the jobs take to pass through the production process. The job sequence is the order in which jobs are entered on to the production process. This will not, however, be the order they are completed as different jobs will pass through different workstations and will have different process times.

The Materials Requirements Planning (MRP) approach (Chapter 14) is often used to determine the batch size and timing (job sequence) of jobs to meet a projected demand expressed in the form of a Master Production Schedule (MPS) that is developed from customer orders and demand forecasts. A closed-loop MRP system will check the feasibility of any schedule against the capacity available over the planning period. An OPT system (see later in this chapter) will focus on ensuring that the bottleneck processes are kept busy as they determine the output of the whole process.

A problem with batch production control is the tendency for managers to try to keep all workstations busy at all times which leads to Work-In-Progress (WIP) queues at heavily loaded workstations. Excessive WIP can seriously impede the ability to schedule batch systems successfully by creating long lead times and by making it difficult to determine the correct job priority for new work entering the system. An aim of the JIT system (Chapter 13) is to eliminate this inventory and make the production control process more transparent. MRP systems use a technique called 'production activity control' to try to ensure that the production system is working to plan. The technique consists of two main components of Input/Output Control and Priority Control which are covered later in this chapter.

Jobbing Process-type Scheduling

A jobbing system deals with a number of low-volume, high-variety products. Each product is customized to a customer order and so the production planning and control system must deal with a changing mix of jobs. Because the job may not have been produced before, it may be difficult to estimate the elements of lead time for each job. Because each product has a unique routing and component structure it is also difficult to use systems such as MRP for production planning and control. The pattern of flow through a jobshop consists of a number of workstations with queues of work in front of them and what approaches to a random flow path connecting the workstations. The technique of job sequencing is used to schedule in jobbing-type systems.

Workforce Scheduling

Workforce scheduling aims to ensure that available staff are deployed to maximize the quality of service delivery to the customer. The amount of staff available will have been determined by long-term and more strategic decisions taken on the amount of staff required, often termed 'manpower planning policies'. For day-to-day operations, however, the problem is how to deploy the staff available to best effect. This may be done with the use of a **workforce schedule** which determines the daily workload for each member of staff. This daily workload may cover a normal 8-hour day or two- or three-shift working for certain service providers such as hospitals and police. The allocation of staff available must take into consideration a number of factors such as the number of staff available (taking into account absentees), the skills the individual staff possess, the demand over time for the services the staff supply and the working preferences of the staff themselves.

> **WORKFORCE SCHEDULE:** determines the daily workload for each member of staff.

As mentioned earlier, the need to provide a service for immediate consumption by the customer and the inability to store a service delivery as inventory means that the capacity provided in the schedule needs to meet customer demand closely. If sufficient capacity is not provided, this can lead to overworked staff and delays in service provision, both leading to a fall in the quality of service. The flexibility to undertake a number of tasks can be used to provide a strategy for responding to short-term fluctuation in demand. For example, you have probably witnessed the reallocation of staff from replenishing goods in a supermarket to working on a till in response to a sudden increase in customers checking out.

Workforce scheduling can be undertaken by estimating the demand for the operation and then scheduling staff to meet this demand. The use of Gantt charts (Chapter 16) or specialized computer software (e.g., project management software such as Microsoft Project) can be used to facilitate this process.

CASE STUDY 10.1

Car Mechanics Ltd

Car Mechanics Ltd currently offer an express service for car exhaust repair and replacement. It is envisaged to widen the range of services offered to the customer by also performing a tyre change service. Many of the current customers tend to wait until the exhaust has failed and, thus, arrive at the premises requiring a new exhaust immediately! They also usually wait at the premises while the repair takes place and don't, in general, like to have to wait for more than 30 minutes for the service to be completed.

Case Study 10.1 Question

1   What steps could you take to ensure customer satisfaction with the exhaust service is not affected by adding the new tyre change service?

Line Balancing

LINE BALANCING: ensures that the stages of a line process are coordinated and bottlenecks are avoided.

The issue of **line balancing** is important in a line flow process in a service or manufacturing operation which is broken down into a number of stages. Line balancing involves ensuring that the stages of the process are coordinated and bottlenecks are avoided. Because of the line flow configuration the output of the whole line is determined by the slowest or bottleneck stage. This means a reduction in process time at a non-bottleneck will have no effect on the overall output rate. The actual design of the line is guided by the tasks which are involved in producing the product or delivering the service and the required output rate required to meet demand. This provides information which determines the number of stages and the output rate of each stage. The output rate is usually expressed in terms of the **cycle time** which is the time taken to produce or deliver one unit of output:

CYCLE TIME: time taken to produce or deliver one unit of output.

$$\text{Cycle time} = \frac{1}{\text{Output rate}}$$

Thus, an output rate of 30 units/hour gives a cycle time of $1/30/60 = 2$ minutes. Thus, a unit of output is delivered every 2 minutes. This means each stage of the line process must be able to undertake its process within 2 minutes. If the process time is greater than 2 minutes, then it must be reduced by either splitting the stage into multiple stages or assigning more resources (e.g., assigning two people or running two machines in parallel) to reach the desired output rate. Note that the stage will be idle if its process time is less than the target cycle time of 2 minutes. Thus, in order to achieve maximum efficiency each stage must match the target cycle time as closely as possible.

Once the target cycle is calculated (derived from the output rate), it is necessary to decide on the number of workstations and allocate tasks to them. This can be achieved by using computer software, but heuristic or rule-of-thumb methods can usually give good results. The heuristic methods involve allocating tasks, in process order, to each process stage until the stage process time reaches the target cycle time. Remaining tasks are allocated to further stages. In general, if there is a choice of tasks to allocate to a stage then the task with the longest process time is allocated first to provide more flexibility in providing a balanced line.

A major factor in achieving a proper line balance is to gather accurate estimates of task times in the line flow process. If timings are just based on an average of observations then there is a danger that the effect of variations on task times will not be considered. This can be limited somewhat by keeping a number of job elements in a task which reduces variability and increases flexibility. Simulation modelling (Chapter 8) can be used to investigate these variations as well as the effect of random variations such as machine breakdown. It should also be noted that the issue of line balancing will be complicated by constraints such as layout design, material handling between stages and availability of people skills. The use of a line to produce a range of products or services, rather than a single product or service type, also increases the complexity of the line-balancing process. Further details of line balancing are given in Chapter 4.

Input/Output Control

Input/Output Control helps to control the length of queues in front of processes and, thus, the process lead time (Process time + Queue time). The queue time is the most variable and usually the largest factor in determining process lead time. Typical values for the breakdown of process lead times in small batch manufacturing are:

INPUT/OUTPUT CONTROL: controls the size of the queues at processes in order that queue times are more consistent and predictable.

Transportation time:	20%
Setup time:	10%
Process time:	15%
Queue time:	55%

Queue time can, in fact, be as high as 80–95% of the total lead time in some instances. Each one of the above factors can be reduced. Setup time can be reduced by a setup reduction programme which involves separating internal and external operations (Chapter 13). Process time can be reduced through the use of process technology (Chapter 16) or learning curve effects (Chapter 9). Transportation time can be reduced by improved layout (Chapter 4) or increased use of material handling equipment such as conveyors (Chapter 6). However, lead time is most affected by queue time. It is not just the length of the queuing time but the variability which affects the ability to successfully undertake planning and control activities. If the queue time is not known then the lead time cannot be estimated and so it is not known whether the item will meet its scheduled completion.

Input/Output control attempts to control the size of the queues at processes in order that queue times are more consistent and predictable. The method measures the actual flow of work into a work centre and the actual flow of work from that workstation. The difference is the amount of WIP at that process. By monitoring these figures using input/output reports, capacity is adjusted in order to ensure queues do not become too large and average actual lead time equals planned lead time as closely as possible. It is particularly important to provide control at each process in manufacturing assembly operations as a delay of a component at one process may affect the progress of a whole assembly at a subsequent process.

Priority Control

Priority control also takes an overall view of the production process so that if an assembly is waiting for one delayed part this part will get priority over jobs arriving earlier at that workstation. The priority rule is implemented at each workstation by issuing a dispatch list (schedule) for that workstation, listing jobs for that operation in order of completion date. Thus, jobs further over the completion date will get priority. Each time a component leaves a workstation it will be added to the dispatch list for the next workstation.

Optimized Production Technology (OPT)

OPTIMIZED PRODUCTION TECHNOLOGY (OPT): operations control system that is based on the identification of bottlenecks within the production process.

Optimized Production Technology (OPT) is an operations control system that is based on the identification of bottlenecks within the production process. Goldratt and Cox (1997) define these bottlenecks as any resource whose capacity is less than or equal to the demand placed on it. This approach attempts to avoid much of the complexity of scheduling by focusing on bottlenecks. The idea is that system output is determined by bottlenecks so it is essential to schedule non-bottleneck resources to ensure maximum use of the bottleneck resources themselves.

In identifying bottlenecks, OPT views the production process as a whole with respect to the market and the business within which it operates. OPT makes the assumption that all manufacturers have the aim of making money as their overriding objective. This goal is defined in terms of three performance measures (Goldratt and Cox, 1997):

■ throughput;
■ inventory;
■ operational expense.

Throughput is the rate at which the production system generates money through sales. Throughput, however, does not equal manufacturing output as any output not sold is seen as waste in the long run. OPT, therefore, does not consider 'finished goods' stocks as assets. Inventory is defined as all the money that the system has invested in goods that it intends to sell. OPT excludes labour costs and indirect expenses from inventory valuation. Operational Expense is that which the system spends in order to turn inventory into throughput. This includes all expenses, both direct and indirect. Goldratt and Cox (1997) use these performance criteria to restate the goal of a manufacturing organization as:

> *To reduce operational expense and reduce inventory whilst simultaneously increasing throughput.*

To understand why OPT focuses on bottlenecks it is necessary to understand how OPT differs from traditional approaches to production planning. The traditional approach is to balance (i.e., make equal) capacity at all the workstations in response to anticipated demand from the master production schedule. However, there are two reasons why a production facility cannot be balanced to the demands of production. These are non-determinance and interdependence and relate to the issues of variability and interdependence covered in Chapter 8.

Non-determinance simply refers to the fact that the information used to derive the production schedule may not be of a fixed nature. For example, the process time for an activity will vary each time it is performed. The rate usually quoted will be the average of these times. However, it can be shown that statistical fluctuations around the average can have a significant bearing on plant performance. Interdependence refers to the fact that most stages in production are connected in some way to other stages. For example, Stage A cannot start until Stage B has finished, which cannot start until Stages C and D have finished, etc. The effect of interdependence is to accumulate the fluctuations caused by non-determinance from stage to stage downstream of the production process. This is because the ability to go faster than average depends on the ability of all others in front of the process while there is no limit to go slower. Therefore, fluctuations don't average out but accumulate and the end of the line has to make up for the accumulation of all the slowness. This behaviour has led Goldratt (1981) to suggest the following recommendation for dealing with an unbalanced plant:

■ Bottlenecks must be identified, and since they determine the rate of throughput for the whole plant, must be carefully protected from disturbances and potential delays to assure full utilization.

■ The resources must be organized so the bottleneck resource is used primarily at one of the earliest stages of production.

■ Instead of trying to eliminate at random over-capacity of non-bottlenecks, we must strive to arrange some resources such that one has sufficient over-capacity to fully support the bottleneck. Ideally, this would involve a gradual increase of over-capacity as we go downstream.

These recommendations move away from trying to match capacity with demand to managing the whole system to the pace set by the bottlenecks. The principles underlying this approach are as follows:

1   *Balance the flow, not capacity* – by trying to maintain flow in a balanced capacity plant means that all stages are expected to work to full capacity. In a non-balanced system (i.e., all systems) inventory will accumulate at bottleneck resources. Thus, capacity should be used only when necessary, as in JIT control systems (Chapter 13).

2   *Constraints determine non-bottleneck utilization* – bottlenecks should pace production and determine the level of utilization for non-bottleneck resources. The only machine to be working at 100% capacity is the bottleneck.

3   *Activation is not always equal to utilization* – to activate a resource not needed at the bottleneck is a waste.

4   *An hour lost at a bottleneck is an hour lost for the entire system* – in effect, an hour lost at the bottleneck is an hour lost of factory output, as it can never be made up.

5   *An hour saved at a non-bottleneck is a mirage* – an hour saved at a non-bottleneck will not actually increase output of the whole system.

6   *Bottlenecks govern throughput and inventory* – inventory will accumulate at the bottleneck. There is no point in inventory after this stage because throughput is determined by the rate of production at the bottleneck.

7   *The transfer batch size should not always equal a process batch size* – at non-bottlenecks, transfer batches can be small to speed up the flow of WIP, as an increase in total setup time is not critical. At bottleneck resources these transfer batches then accumulate into larger process batches to save setups and maximize output.

8   *Process batches should be variable, not fixed* – the process batch should not be determined by some fixed lot-sizing rule, for instance, but should be varied to balance the flow of the manufacturing cycle.

9   *Set the schedule by examining all the constraints simultaneously* – Manufacturing Resource Planning (MRP II) systems predetermine batch size, lead times and set schedules accordingly. OPT suggests that all the constraints of a complex network are considered simultaneously using the simulation capabilities of the OPT software.

The OPT planning and control approach uses the terminology of the Drum, Buffer and Rope:

■ *The Drum* – determines the rate of production. In MRP and JIT control systems the rate of production is determined primarily from market demand but with OPT the bottleneck resources are used to develop the schedule ensuring that bottleneck capacity is not exceeded. Other non-bottleneck resources are scheduled to serve the bottlenecks by varying process batch and transfer batch sizes. Thus, the bottleneck resource sets the drumbeat for the entire process.

■ *The Buffer* – placed at certain locations to prevent unforeseen events disrupting output of finished goods. There are two types of inventory buffer. Time buffers are determined by the amount of output the system could produce during the period of time it takes to correct a disruption. They are generally placed before bottleneck resources. Stock buffers are inventories of finished goods determined by forecasts of possible demand fluctuations.

■ *The Rope* – the rate of the operation of processes which come after the bottleneck are determined by the rate of output from the bottleneck machine. To control the rate of processes before the bottleneck there is a linkage between the bottleneck and the processes that feed it termed the 'rope'. The rope can take the form of a planned production schedule or an informal discussion between employees at the bottleneck and employees at other workstations.

Figure 10.2 shows the use of the drum, buffer and rope control system. It shows a flow of material from Process A to Process E, with a bottleneck resource being Process C. Normally, without any control mechanism, excess inventory will build up in front of the bottleneck Process C. What is required is an inventory buffer in front of C, so that, as the bottleneck resource, it is always busy (despite variations in supply), but does not allow the build-up of too much inventory. This is achieved by the use of a communication link (the rope) between Process C and the upstream Process A. This communication could be in the form of a schedule or an informal discussion between personnel. The buffer in front of Process C is called a 'time buffer' and ensures work is always present for Process C, no matter what the schedule.

Although OPT can be relatively quickly implemented it needs expertise for correct implementation which may not be available for small organizations. The OPT software may also be expensive for some organizations. OPT could also be criticized for not containing continuous improvement activities of JIT although these could be incorporated and the two approaches could be used in combination to form a continuous improvement effort.

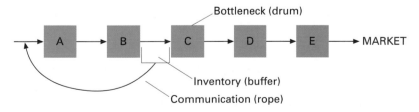

Figure 10.2 Drum, Buffer and Rope in an OPT control system

Summary

1 In a make-to-stock system each order must be small compared with total capacity or the risk of making to stock and not finding a customer for the order will be too high. A resource-to-order system means that each order is large compared with total system capacity to make the organization of resources worthwhile. Whilst the customer will only 'see' the delivery time from stock in a make-to-stock system, in a make-to-order system the delivery cycle will include the purchase, make and delivery stages.

2 Loading involves determining the available capacity for each stage in a process and allocating a task to that stage. The two principle approaches to loading are finite loading which allocates work up to a fixed limit and infinite loading which does not place a limit on the work loaded onto a stage.

3 Sequencing is the sequential assignment of tasks or jobs to individual processes. Sequencing can be undertaken using priority rules such as DDS, FCFS and SPT.

4 In services, scheduling involves varying the size of the workforce to meet variations in demand. The approach to scheduling in manufacturing is largely dependent on the volume and variety mix of the manufacturing system.

5 Techniques for scheduling include workforce scheduling, line balancing, input/output control and priority control.

6 OPT is based on the identification of bottlenecks within the production process. The OPT planning and control approach uses the terminology of Drum, Buffer and Rope.

Exercises

1. What are the implications of the P:D ratio for a manufacturing organization?
2. A jobshop has five jobs which must be processed on Machine 1 and then on Machine 2 (times in minutes). Determine the sequence that will allow the set of five jobs to be completed in the minimum time. State the total job completion time.

Job	Machine 1	Machine 2
A	8	3
B	4	5
C	7	6
D	5	10
E	9	3

3. The following six jobs are to be scheduled on a piece of equipment.

Job	1	2	3	4	5	6
Duration (days)	6	4	2	8	1	5
Due-date	6	20	22	24	2	10

   a. Prepare a Gantt chart that will provide a schedule showing when jobs are to be undertaken on the machine. Use the FCFS rule.
   b. Using FCFS how long will it take to complete all the jobs?
   c. Given the due-dates shown calculate the average job lateness when FCFS is used.
   d. Given the due-dates shown calculate the average job lateness when SPT is used.
   e. What disadvantage is SPT likely to exhibit in a heavily loaded jobshop?
4. Evaluate the use of the SPT/SOT in a retail and a manufacturing environment.
5. A small manufacturer produces custom parts that first require a shearing operation and then a punch operation. There are five jobs to be processed and the processing times (minutes) are estimated as the following:

Job	Shear	Punch
1	4	5
2	4	1
3	10	4
4	6	10
5	2	3

   Use Johnson's algorithm to identify the processing sequence that will give the lowest overall throughput time. Use a Gantt chart to illustrate the sequence and state the total job completion time.
6. What are the main issues in the scheduling of jobbing, batch and line systems?
7. Discuss the advantages and disadvantages of the OPT approach to production planning.
8. Define the terms 'drum', 'buffer' and 'rope' as used in OPT terminology.

References

Goldratt, E.M. (1981), The unbalanced plant, *APICS 1981 International Conference Proceedings*, pp. 195–199.

Goldratt, E.M. and Cox, J. (1997), *The Goal: A Process of Ongoing Improvement*, 2nd Edition, Gower.

Johnson, S.M. (1954), Optimal two- and three-stage production with setup times included, *Naval Research Quarterly*, **1**, 61–68.

Shingo, S. (1981), *Study of Toyota Production System*, Japan Management Association.

Further Reading

Chase, R.B., Aquilano, N.J. and Jacobs, F.R. (2003), *Operations Management for Competitive Advantage*, 10th Edition, McGraw-Hill.

Goldratt, E.M. (1994), *It's Not Luck*, Gower.

Goldratt, E.M. and Fox, R. (1986), *The Race*, North River Press.

Srikanth, M.L. and Cavallaro, H.E. (1993), *Regaining Competitiveness: Putting the Goal to Work*, 2nd Revised Edition, North River Press.

Web Links

http://www.goldratt.com/ The Goldratt Institute home page.

http://www.sytsma.com/htm/theorypages.htm Web site containing links to Theory of Constraints resources.

www.toyota.co.uk Web site containing detailed information on world car production.

www.stg.co.uk Site containing details of OPT software.

www.production-scheduling.com Advice on scheduling using spreadsheets.

Chapter 11

Capacity Management

■ Measuring Demand

■ Measuring Capacity

- Product Mix
- Design, Effective and Actual Capacity

■ Reconciling Capacity and Demand

- Level Capacity
- Chase Demand
- Demand Management
- Yield Management

■ Evaluating Alternatives and Making a Choice

- Cumulative Representations
- Queuing Theory
- The Psychology of Queues

■ Appendix: Forecasting

- Introduction
- Forecasting Techniques
- Qualitative Forecasting Methods
- Quantitative Forecasting Methods

Learning Objectives

After reading this chapter, you should be able to:

1 Describe the elements in medium-term capacity planning.

2 Understand the effects of product mix on capacity.

3 Evaluate the three pure strategies for reconciling capacity and demand.

4 Understand approaches to demand management in services.

5 Understand the use of cumulative representatives to evaluate a level capacity planning approach.

6 Discuss the use of queuing theory to explore the trade-off between the amount of capacity and level of demand.

7 Discuss the relevance of propositions about the psychology of customer waiting time.

8 Understand qualitative and quantitative techniques for forecasting.

Introduction

In operations management a definition of capacity should take into account both the volume and the time over which capacity is available. Thus, capacity management is not just about providing customers with services or goods in the amount requested, but at the time they are requested too.

Capacity issues can be considered as long term and form part of the operations strategy. For example, a strategy of capacity expansion may be used to provide a presence in geographical locations before competitors can gain access to a market. These long-term capacity issues are considered in Chapter 5. In this chapter short-to medium-term capacity issues are considered. These are mainly concerned with ensuring sufficient capacity of the right type is available at the right time to meet demand for the planning period.

The setting of capacity to meet the demands of the organization is termed 'capacity planning and control'. The capacity planning and control activity should be undertaken using a systematic approach employing the following steps:

■ measuring demand;
■ measuring capacity;
■ reconciling capacity and demand;
■ evaluating alternatives and making a choice.

The measuring demand step requires that future demand be estimated, the measuring step requires the measurement of present capacity, reconciling capacity and demand requires analysis of capacity planning approaches and the final step requires a method of choosing a suitable capacity planning approach. This chapter is structured around these steps in capacity planning and control.

Measuring Demand

For a long-term estimate of demand the strategic planning process will define the markets in which the organization will compete and such factors as the range and volume of products and services in these market segments. The marketing strategy will be evaluated in terms of corporate objectives. Corporate objectives are usually expressed in terms of financial measures such as growth or profitability. The role of marketing strategy and operations strategy in meeting corporate objectives is discussed in Chapter 2.

Based on the marketing strategy and forecasts of demand (see chapter appendix) the organization can formulate a long-range business plan that will include capital budgets for expanding facilities and major equipment investment. Because of the relatively long lead time of acquiring these facilities they are considered in the short- to medium-term planning horizon to represent the effective capacity limit of the organization. Thus, long-range demand factors are covered in the design section of this book in Chapter 5 under the heading of Long-term Capacity Planning.

In the medium term (approximately 2–18 months) planning is undertaken by various functions (manufacturing, marketing, finance, etc.) in order to coordinate efforts to achieve the business plan within the constraints made by the long-term decisions made in that plan. The planning process can be described as working in cycles, with each cycle confirming detailed plans for the next time period and sketching more tentative plans for the following period. At the next planning meeting these tentative plans are now considered in more detail and the cycle repeats. This process means that the organization can build on previous plans instead of attempting to devise new plans at each planning cycle. This reduces planning time and leads to more continuity in decision making. The aggregate planning process will evaluate the production plan in order to ensure sufficient capacity is available to undertake the output targets.

The production plan (or operations plan in a service organization) states the amount of output which will be delivered from the operations function over the medium-term business plan. The output can be expressed in terms of volume, currency or units. For example, a retail outlet may commit to sales of clothes in terms of sales value or units sold during the next 12-month period. The production plan provides an overall guide to the level of output from the manufacturing/operations department that will be coordinated with other functions such as marketing and finance.

It is necessary to break the production plan down into a level of detail required for procurement and operational purposes. This means that the demand for each individual product and, thus, the materials, components and work tasks required to produce it, must be specified. The Master Production Schedule (MPS) states the volume and timing of all products that have a significant demand on manufacturing resources. Further details of the MPS in relation to a materials requirements planning system are provided in Chapter 14.

Measuring Capacity

Measuring capacity may at first seem straightforward, especially when compared with the uncertainty inherent in estimating demand. However, capacity is not fixed but is a variable that is dependent on a number of factors. Capacity takes many different forms such as storage space, employee skills availability, equipment numbers and transportation facilities. Any of these types of capacity may be the limiting factor or bottleneck on the capacity of a process. The actual bottleneck, and thus capacity, may also change over time. Working practices such as hours worked and holiday entitlement can also affect capacity calculations and may change over time. For example, a change in company policy may decrease the number of hours worked a week by employees and, thus, reduce capacity. The amount of capacity required to deliver a particular process at a particular level may change over time due to the experience gained and improvements made to process design. Capacity available in multiple locations may not be simply totalled as transportation time and costs may make available capacity in a particular location unsuitable. Capacity is time based and so capacity under-utilized due to a drop in demand cannot be used later when demand increases. Thus, the actual capacity available will be less the more demand fluctuates.

Measuring capacity in services is a particular challenge. Generally, services need to be more custom designed and involve more personal contact in order to meet specific customer needs. Thus, customer contact has a number of impacts on the way the service can be run. Customer involvement tends to provide an opportunity for special requests and instructions to be issued by the customer, which tends to disrupt routine procedures and, thus, efficiency. Capacity may be lost in providing conversation to the customer in addition to delivering the actual service. Quality is closely related to the customer's perception of satisfactory service. Operations employees employed where high levels of customer contact occur must be skilled in interpreting what the customer really wants. Thus, the level of customer/client contact can have a direct effect on the efficiency and, thus, capacity availability that an operation can achieve.

There are a variety of methods to achieve efficiency and still provide the customer with good service. One way to limit the disruption from unusual requests is to standardize the service (e.g., a fast food restaurant). A common strategy to improve the overall efficiency of the operation is to keep separate those parts of the operation that do not require direct customer contact. Operations are divided into front office where interaction with the customer takes place and back office where directions are primarily taken from managers, not customers (see Chapter 1).

Two further issues to consider when measuring capacity are product mix and the definitions of design and effective capacity.

Product Mix

Only when a narrow product (or service) range is involved can capacity be measured reasonably accurately and in this case be quoted in terms of output volume. The effect of product mix on capacity is shown in Worked Example 11.1.

Worked Example 11.1

The Effect of Product Mix on Capacity

The following assembly times are given for three models of a washing machine:

	Assembly time (minutes)
Washer (basic)	50
Washer (deluxe)	150
Washer (dryer)	250

The target weekly output is given as 100 units. Calculate the total output for a product ratio of $4:2:1$ for washer (basic), washer (deluxe) and washer (dryer) and total output for a product ratio of $3:2:2$.

Solution

For a product mix ratio of $4:2:1$ the total output is as follows:

$$\text{Ratio} = 4:2:1$$

$$\text{Assembly time for 7 units} = (4 \times 50) + (2 \times 150) + (1 \times 250) = 750 \text{ minutes}$$

$$\text{Assembly minutes available} = 9000$$

Therefore:

$$\text{Weekly output} = \frac{9000}{750} \times 7 = 84 \text{ units}$$

For a product mix ratio of $3:2:2$ the output is as follows:

$$\text{Ratio} = 3:2:2$$

$$\text{Assembly time for 7 units} = (3 \times 50) + (2 \times 150) + (2 \times 250) = 950 \text{ minutes}$$

$$\text{Assembly minutes available} = 9000$$

Therefore:

$$\text{Weekly output} = \frac{9000}{950} \times 7 = 66 \text{ units}$$

Thus, a change in product mix from $4:2:1$ to $3:2:2$ alters the weekly capacity output from 84 to 66 units.

With a changing product mix, therefore, it may be more useful to measure capacity in terms of input measures, which provides some indication of the potential output. Also, for planning purposes when demand is stated in output terms it is necessary to convert input measures to an estimated output measure. For example, in hospitals which undertake a range of activities, capacity is often measured in terms of beds available, an input measure. An output measure such as number of patients treated per week will be highly dependent on the mix of activities the hospital performs. Estimates of capacity based on output can also be misleading as part of this output may be accounted for by either inventory (e.g., patients) part way through the process or the use of additional resources (e.g., overtime, equipment rental, contracting out) that could not normally be treated as part of the organization's capacity.

Design, Effective and Actual Capacity

The design capacity of an operation represents the theoretical output of a process as it was designed. However, this level of capacity is rarely met due to occurrences that prevent the operation producing its full output. These occurrences are termed 'planned' and 'unplanned factors' (Figure 11.1).

Planned factors are activities whose timing can be determined in advance. They include such items as maintenance, training and machine setup time. During these activities the output from the operation is lost. One of the ways to reduce this loss of output for manufacturing processes is to use the technique of setup reduction (Chapter 13) which attempts to undertake as much of the setup process as possible while the operation is still in use. In services, training of personnel may take place during the year when seasonal demand is low.

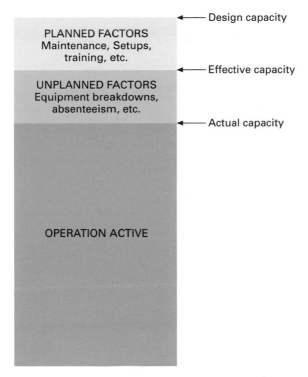

Figure 11.1 Design, effective and actual capacity

The capacity remaining after loss of output due to planned factors is termed the effective capacity of the process. However, this will also be above the level of capacity which is available due to unplanned occurrences such as machine breakdowns and worker absenteeism. These are more difficult to deal with than planned factors, because by definition their timing cannot be predicted. In order to minimize these disturbances, action should be taken such as preventative maintenance (Chapter 13). This involves undertaking planned maintenance activities, if possible when demand is low. These activities can include replacing equipment parts before they fail, in order to reduce unplanned breakdowns. Worker absenteeism could be reduced by improving motivation. This could be achieved by changing the job design using the ideas of the job characteristics model described in Chapter 9.

After taking both planned and unplanned factors into account there remains the capacity available for processing, termed the actual capacity of the operation.

Two measures which you often see used in relation to these capacity measures are utilization and efficiency. Utilization gives the proportion of time a process is in actual use compared with its design capacity and efficiency gives the proportion of time a process is in use compared with its effective capacity.

EFFECTIVE CAPACITY:
the capacity remaining after loss of output due to planned factors such as maintenance and training.

ACTUAL CAPACITY:
the capacity remaining after loss of output due to both planned factors and unplanned factors. Unplanned factors include equipment breakdown and absenteeism.

UTILIZATION:
the proportion of time a process is in actual use compared with its design capacity.

EFFICIENCY:
the proportion of time a process is in use compared with its effective capacity.

Thus:

$$Utilization = \frac{Actual\ capacity}{Design\ capacity}$$

$$Efficiency = \frac{Actual\ capacity}{Effective\ capacity}$$

Both measures are usually given in terms of percentages. A utilization of 60% means that a process was producing output for 60% of a time period. An efficiency rating of 60% denotes that a process was producing output for 60% of a time period in which it was available to produce output (i.e., it was not being used for maintenance or other planned activities).

Reconciling Capacity and Demand

Methods for reconciling capacity and demand can be classified into three 'pure' strategies of level capacity, chase demand and demand management. Due to the complexity of capacity management and the need to optimize a range of performance objectives it is usually necessary to combine the three pure strategies described and form a mixed capacity planning strategy. The three strategies are now described.

Level Capacity

LEVEL CAPACITY: sets processing capacity at a uniform level throughout the planning period regardless of fluctuations in forecast demand. This means production is set at a fixed rate, usually to meet average demand and inventory is used to absorb variations in demand. For a service organization, output cannot be stored as inventory so a level capacity plan involves running at a uniformly high level of capacity.

Level capacity sets the processing capacity at a uniform level throughout the planning period regardless of fluctuations in forecast demand. This means output is set at a fixed rate, usually to meet average demand, and inventory is used to absorb variations in demand. During periods of low demand any over-production can be transferred to finished goods inventory in anticipation of sales at a later time period (Figure 11.2). The disadvantage of this strategy is the cost of holding inventory and the cost of perishable items that may have to be discarded. To avoid producing obsolete items, firms will try to create inventory for products which are relatively certain to be sold. This strategy is also of limited value for perishable goods.

For a service organization, output cannot be stored as inventory so a level capacity plan involves running at a uniformly high level of capacity (Figure 11.3). The drawback of the approach is the cost of maintaining this high level of capacity, although it could be useful when the cost of lost sales is particularly high. In order to overcome this problem the concept of 'partitioning demand' is used which involves keeping capacity in the customer contact area consistently high, so customers are not kept waiting, and keeping capacity in the non-contact areas at a

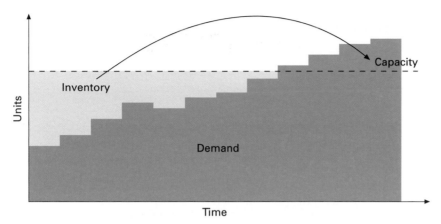

Figure 11.2   Level capacity plan

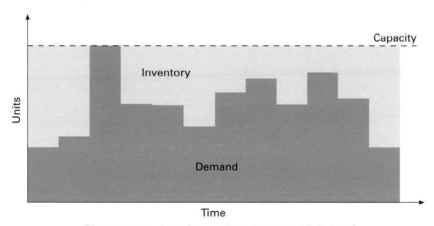

Figure 11.3   Level capacity plan at a high level

more uniform level. Another strategy is for services to 'store' their output by performing part of their work in anticipation of demand. An example is purchasing and displaying goods before actual customer demand occurs.

Chase Demand

Chase demand seeks to match output to the demand pattern over time. Capacity is altered by such policies as changing the amount of part-time staff, changing the amount of staff availability through overtime working, changing equipment levels and subcontracting. The chase demand strategy is costly in terms of the costs of activities such as changing staffing levels and overtime payments. The costs may be particularly high in industries in which skills are scarce. Disadvantages of subcontracting include reduced profit margin lost to the subcontractor, loss of

CHASE DEMAND:
matches output to the demand pattern over time. Capacity is altered by such policies as changing the number of part-time staff, changing the amount of staff availability through overtime working, changing equipment levels and subcontracting.

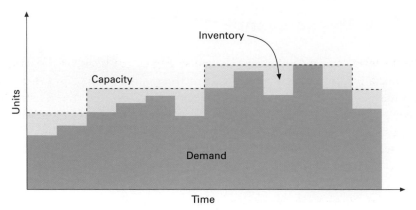

Figure 11.4 Chase demand plan

control, potentially longer lead times and the risk that the subcontractor may decide to enter the same market. For these reasons a pure chase demand strategy is more usually adopted by service operations which cannot store their output and so make a level capacity plan less attractive. A graphical representation of a chase demand plan is shown in Figure 11.4.

In services when the operation cannot usually match the demand rate with its capacity level, its objective becomes one of developing a capacity profile that matches its demand profile, to the extent that this is feasible and economically viable. Strategies for achieving this include:

■ *Staggered workshift schedules* – scheduling the availability of capacity to cover demand involves constructing work shifts so that the number of operators available at any one time matches the demand profile (e.g., a fast food restaurant).

■ *Part-time staff* – more flexibility to schedule and smooth the work demand is often available for those parts of a service where the customer is not present and the service is provided by working with some surrogate for the customer. A strategy of using part-time staff needs to trade off the cost of not doing some work with the extra cost of employing the staff.

■ *Subcontractors* – if there is not enough capacity, additional capacity can be obtained from outside sources (e.g., surgeries employing contract doctor services to cover weekends).

■ *Multi-skilled floating staff* – having multi-skilled staff increases flexibility in capacity decisions. For example, in the case of a hospital it might be desirable to have some floating capacity that can be shifted from one department to another if the number of patients or the amount of nursing attention required in each department varies.

■ *Customer self-service* – with this option, the service capacity arrives when the demand does. Customers at supermarkets and many department stores select most of their own merchandise.

Demand Management

While the level capacity and chase demand strategies aim to adjust capacity to match demand, the **demand management** strategy attempts to adjust demand to meet available capacity. There are many ways this can be done, but most will involve altering the marketing mix (e.g., price, promotion, etc.) and will require coordination with the marketing function. A graphical representation of a demand management plan is shown in Figure 11.5.

Demand management strategies include:

■ *Varying the price* – during periods of low demand, price discounts can be used to stimulate the demand level. Conversely, when demand is higher than the capacity limit, price could be increased.

■ *Advertising* – advertising and other marketing activities can be used to increase sales during low-demand periods.

■ *Alternative products* – this is the use of existing processes to make or sell alternative products during low-demand periods. An example is the way many garden centres use their premises to sell Christmas decorations during the winter months when gardening activity is low.

■ *Maintenance of a fixed schedule* – some services can schedule the times at which the service is available (e.g., airlines and rail services). Demand occurs as people purchase tickets to use some of the previously scheduled transportation capacity.

■ *Use of an appointment system* – the pattern of demand variations over the longer term can also have a significant influence on the planning of efficient service operations. The ideal would be to achieve uniform utilization of service capacity, but this is unlikely unless an appointment-only policy is operated. Some services are provided by appointment (e.g., a dentist). Use of an

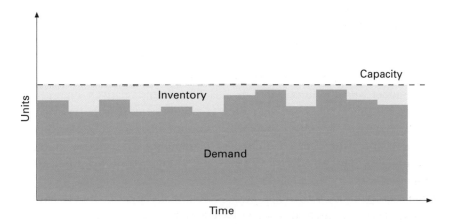

Figure 11.5 Demand management plan

appointment system permits demand to be moved into available time. The delay between a request for an appointment and the time of the appointment may depend on the backlog or queue of waiting work.

■ *Delayed delivery* – delaying jobs until capacity is available serves to make the workload more uniform (e.g., a bank teller). In addition, routine work may be set aside to make capacity available for rush jobs.

■ *Providing economic incentives for off-peak demand* – some operations have a high capital investment in the capacity they have to provide their services. The unit cost of capacity that is used only occasionally for peak demand is very high. These operations try to keep demand as uniform as possible by the use of economic inducements (e.g., off-peak electricity and off-peak telephone calls).

Yield Management

YIELD MANAGEMENT: the use of demand management strategies aimed at maximizing customer revenue in service organizations. It is particularly appropriate when the organization is operating with relatively fixed capacity and when it is possible to segment the market into different types of customers.

The use of demand management strategies are often particularly developed in service industries where capacity cannot be stored (output cannot be held as stock and used later) and demand is stochastic (there is variability in when customers request the service and how long it takes to service them). **Yield management** aims to maximize customer revenue in these service organizations and is particularly appropriate when the organization is operating with relatively fixed capacity and when it is possible to segment the market into different types of customers.

The airline industry provides an example of the use of yield management. It has well-developed policies for ensuring as many seats as possible are occupied on their flights. Once a flight route has been scheduled and an aircraft allocated to that route, the costs of operating the aircraft, including staffing, maintenance and fuel costs are fixed and the variable cost in accommodating each additional passenger on a flight are very low. In addition, capacity is lost once the flight takes place and cannot be stored for later use. The airline, thus, will want to fill as many seats as possible whilst maximizing the overall price the customers pay. One business model which airlines use to do this is to charge relatively high prices in advance to customers when the guarantee of a flight is more important than the price (e.g., business customers) and then discount fares close to the flight time to maximize revenue (through such outlets as e-commerce sites such as www.lastminute.com). An alternative strategy is to start prices low to ensure a proportion of capacity is sold and then increase the price as capacity becomes scarce as the flight fills. If the flight is not reaching its target for booked seats, discounts may be offered to customers to increase sales – budget airlines such as easyJet (www.easyjet.com) and Bmibaby (www.bmibaby.com) use this model.

Yield Management

When Megabus, the nationwide discount bus service, launched last month, it stated that it was following the example of the no frills airlines such as easyJet by running its business off the back of an online ticketing system. In fact, it showed its total commitment to the model by becoming the first UK travel operator to sell tickets exclusively over the Web. After 4 weeks of operation, Megabus has 20 000 hits per day on its site and a quarter of a million tickets have been sold for its 18 destinations. The company says that being Web based has enabled its owners, Stagecoach, to go from initial idea to launch in only 6 months and to deliver a completely ticketless operation.

Online ticketing has been a dramatic success. easyJet founder Stelios Haji-Ioannou initially said the Internet was "just for geeks" but later he did a U-turn, launching the first UK online booking for an airline in April 1998. A year later, the site was selling 15% of all tickets online, and today the figure is 98%. easyJet's call centre now only takes bookings for flights less than 2 weeks ahead. The simplicity of online booking is partly responsible for its success. However, the way it integrates what are known as yield management systems (or revenue management systems) is the secret of how it is transforming the travel industry.

Yield management software, first devised by academics in the 1980s for American Airlines, allows operators to segment seats into scores of different price brackets, like steps on an escalator, with prices that change in relation to demand, the time remaining and the flight date (which triggers seasonal differences). Such software has grown in sophistication to the extent that it is now commonplace for prices to be modified in real time and respond to subtle changes in buying patterns or sudden events that impact on demand. In essence, pricing is set by predicting demand from the previous year's travel patterns, and modified whenever the operator believes that prices need to be shifted up or down.

Ian Tunnacliffe, an analyst with Meta Group, says that such software is transforming the travel industry: "Traditionally, it was a massive investment: now it can be bought off the shelf for around £100 000 from a handful of suppliers. And the major airlines are taking it to the next level with systems that look at their whole network of routes and assign 'bid prices' to each leg to gain the maximum revenue across the whole network. The systems are also finely honed to try to ensure that customers willing to pay at one level do not get tempted into paying less – it's about creating conditions to prevent them taking advantage of lower fares on the system."

easyJet, which recently took over rival Go, now sells 149 seats every 20 seconds and handles 20m passengers a year. easyJet Web manager Simon Pritchard says the aim is still about driving a higher level of Web sales: "We look at what people do on a phone call and try to offer that online." Last year, easyJet added the ability to look up booking details and make changes to a booking, succeeding in shifting 70% of such transactions online. Four staff run the Web operations, while 100 are needed in the call centre, which shows the cost savings of pushing activities online.

In a *Guardian* interview last year, Haji-Ioannou described how easyJet's yield management system works: "We start with a low headline price that grabs attention, then raise it according to demand. But we won't tell you how high it will go, or how quickly." Lack of visibility of the pricing model appears to be part of the secret of running such systems. So how do buyers behave on the Web? "People do all kinds of weird and wonderful things," says Pritchard, "for example, many buyers trawl the site repeatedly to try and figure out pricing and get the best deal." So why not make pricing more transparent? He says easyJet is looking at a range of options for improving the site but that its message is simple: "book early for the best deals."

easyJet and the other no frills airlines have the benefit of running simpler yield management systems than the larger airlines they threaten to engulf. They sell all or most of the tickets themselves, which makes it simpler for the systems to manage minute-to-minute changes. Large airlines sell direct, and through huge worldwide reservation systems (Amadeus, Galileo, Sabre) that provide online services for a global network of travel agents and online travel agents such as eBookers, Lastminute.com, Expedia and Travelocity. The larger airlines usually allocate a set number of seats for online sales to ensure a spread across different distribution channels.

A further channel has been created by airlines banding together to form their own online agent sites such as Opodo and Orbitz. They also sometimes sell what are known as 'opaque tickets' on sites like Lastminute.com. These are offered cheaply to offload what might be called 'distressed stock'. The catch is that the customer must agree to buy the ticket before being told which airline they are flying. "This allows airlines to offload seats without sending out a message to buyers that a particular flight is going cheap," said an industry insider.

Amadeus, which also provides online ticketing systems for airlines, says that when buyers surf the Web, only 1 in 300 visits to booking sites results in a sale. "We call it the Look-to-Book ratio," says Ian Wheeler, managing director of Amadeus e-Travel. "Most people look at four or five sites online before they buy. This is a sea change for the industry, and the result is that operators with legacy systems experience crashes [PC] due to increased traffic when offers and promotions are available."

"A few years ago, buyers would call two to four travel agents and get a maximum of 12 quotes; now they go online and in the same time get about 600 quotes. A call centre just can't do that." Meta Group's Tunnacliffe says the large airlines are now facing a fork in the road: "They either think revenue management has gone too far and should be simplified or they are investing heavily in making it even more sophisticated. We advocate the latter. Only a handful of airlines have really implemented ticketing that takes account of the whole network they run because it involves structural change for the airline, because the system will override local pricing and sales incentives that may be in place. But the real revolution takes place when you tie these systems into the computers that organize scheduling. That is the long-term challenge."

With hotel and car hire following the online sales trend, most observers believe that booking services in the travel industry will increasingly be Web based, leading to a radical shake-up of distribution channels and the role of travel agents. Haji-Ioannou's ability to make a U-turn – and his faith in yield management systems – looks like paying off many times over.

Source: 'Inside IT: Just the Ticket' by Ken Young, *The Guardian*, 8 April 2004.

1   What is the impact of the Internet on yield management systems?

2   What general capacity issues are evident within the case?

Case Study 11.1
Questions

Evaluating Alternatives and Making a Choice

Capacity planning involves evaluating the capacity requirements and determining the best way to meet these using a capacity planning approach which is feasible and low cost. The term 'aggregate planning' is sometimes used to describe the process of aggregating (i.e., grouping) capacity requirements over a medium-term planning horizon to provide the best way to meet these requirements. In order to choose a capacity plan which meets the above criteria it is necessary to try to predict the consequences of that plan. This can be done with varying levels of accuracy and cost using the following methods:

■ cumulative representations;
■ queuing theory;
■ the psychology of queuing.

Cumulative Representations

One method of evaluating a level capacity planning approach is to simply plot the cumulative demand and cumulative capacity for a product over the planning time period. As discussed earlier, capacity is required in the right volume, at the right time. When pursuing a level capacity plan, even though over time inventory levels may be sufficient to meet demand, this does not mean that inventory levels will be sufficient to meet demand at a particular point in time. Thus, a running total or cumulative count of inventory, which should always meet or exceed cumulative demand, is used to ensure no stock-outs occur. An example of the use of **cumulative representations** is shown in Figure 11.6.

CUMULATIVE REPRESENTATION: a running total or cumulative count of inventory, which should always meet or exceed cumulative demand. It is used to ensure no stock-outs occur when using a level capacity plan.

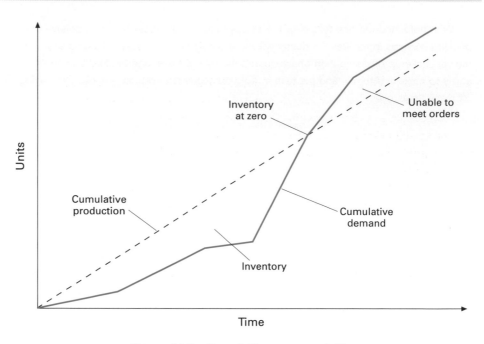

Figure 11.6   Cumulative representations

Figure 11.6 shows the relationship between capacity and demand over time and, thus, enables an assessment of the capacity plan. When the cumulative demand line is below the cumulative capacity, the distance between the lines is the level of inventory at that time. If the demand line lies above the capacity line then this represents a shortage of capacity at that time. Because the graph shows the cumulation of capacity and demand, it takes into account the usage of any surplus inventory in periods when demand exceeds supply (i.e., when the graphs meet, inventory is zero). The cumulative representation graph can show if the capacity plan is meeting demand. This occurs when the capacity line is always along or above the demand line over the planning period.

To assess the effect of capacity planning approaches on the capacity plan involves adjusting the gradient of the capacity (for chase demand approach) or demand (for demand management approach) line at the appropriate point at which the change is to take place. The ideal situation would be when the capacity and demand lines follow each other as closely as possible on the graph. However, the cost of changing the capacity or demand pattern must be taken into consideration. It should also be noted that it may be cost effective to only change capacity in certain blocks and the cost of the change may be dependent on the direction of that change. For example, it may be cheaper to decrease capacity rather than increase capacity for a certain process.

Queuing Theory

Cumulative representations rely on the fact that when supply exceeds demand inventory can be stored for use when demand exceeds supply. In service situations, however, the output of the operation cannot be stored. Waiting time can only be eliminated when customers are asked to arrive at fixed intervals (i.e., an appointment system) and service times are fixed. Thus, waiting time in queues is caused by fluctuations in arrival rates and variability in service times. **Queuing theory** can be used to explore the trade-off between the amount of capacity and the level of demand. Too much capacity and costs will be excessive, but too little capacity will cause long waiting times for the customer and loss of service quality leading to loss of business. In a service context, queuing theory can provide a useful guide in determining expected waiting time for an arriving customer and the average number of customers who will be waiting for service. This permits an estimate of the amount of capacity that will be needed to keep waiting time to a reasonable level taking into account the expected rate and variability of demand. Examples of queuing situations include customers at a bank, aeroplanes circling waiting to land, patients waiting to see a doctor and parts waiting for processing at a machining centre.

> **QUEUING THEORY:** waiting time in queues is caused by fluctuations in arrival rates and variability in service times. Queuing theory can be used to explore the trade-off between the amount of capacity and the level of demand.

Uncertainty in arrival and service times means that even although on average there may be adequate capacity to meet demand, queuing may still occur when a number of successive arrivals or long service times occur. Conversely, idle time will occur when arrival rates or service times decrease. Although this behaviour means that full utilization will not be feasible for this type of system, queuing theory does allow analysis of how much capacity is needed to keep average or maximum queue length or waiting times to an acceptable level. This acceptable level or service quality level will be dependent on the type of operation involved.

Queue systems can be classified into a single-channel queuing system consisting of a single queue of customers who wait until a service facility is available and a multiple-channel queuing system that has parallel server facilities in order to increase the service capacity (Figure 11.7).

Arrivals, representing demand for the use of the facility, enter the system at a particular demand rate. If the service facility is already in use, the arrival waits in a queue until capacity becomes available. Several factors determine the performance of a queuing system. The timing of customer arrivals into the system are usually assumed to occur randomly according to a probability distribution such as the Poisson distribution for arrival times and the exponential distribution for service times (Chase *et al.*, 2003). A priority system may be used to select the next customer to receive service. In most systems the First Come, First Served (FCFS) rule will apply. In some circumstances, arrivals may not join the queue if it is too long when they arrive (baulking), or they may wait for a time, become impatient and leave (reneging).

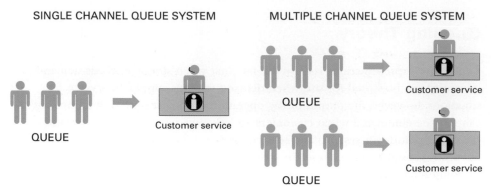

Figure 11.7 Single- and multiple-channel queuing systems

Queuing Theory Equations

There are a number of equations for different queuing structures, but this text will consider the single-server and multiple-server models only. The following assumptions are made when using the following queuing equations:

■ Poisson distribution for arrival rate;
■ exponential distribution for service times;
■ First Come, First Served (FCFS) queue discipline;
■ no limit on queue length (i.e., no reneging);
■ infinite population (i.e., arrival rate is not dependent on outside factors).

The main equations for a single-server queue system are as follows. The mean number of units waiting in the queue:

$$L_q = \frac{\lambda^2}{\mu(\mu - \lambda)}$$

The mean time spent in the queue:

$$W_q = \frac{\lambda}{\mu(\mu - \lambda)}$$

The probability that the server is busy (i.e., server utilization):

$$\rho = \frac{\lambda}{\mu}$$

where λ = Mean arrival rate
        μ = Mean service rate.

Worked Example 11.2

Single-server Queue

A local shop has a single counter/till at which customers are served. Customers arrive at a rate of 24 per hour according to a Poisson distribution and service times are exponentially distributed with a mean rate of 20 customers per hour.

a What is the mean number of customers waiting in the queue?
b What is the mean time a customer spends in the queue?
c What is the probability that the till is busy?

Solution

$$\lambda = 20 \qquad \mu = 24$$

a $L_q = \dfrac{20^2}{24 * (24 - 20)} = 400/96 = 4.17$ customers

b $W_q = \dfrac{20}{24 * (24 - 20)} = \dfrac{20}{96} = 0.2$ hours

c $\rho = \dfrac{20}{24} = 0.83$

The main equations for a multiple-server queue system are as follows. The mean number of units waiting in the queue:

$$L_q = \frac{\lambda\mu(\lambda/\mu)^s}{(s-1)!(s\mu - \lambda)^2} * P_0$$

where

$$P_0 = 1 \left/ \left(\sum_{n=0}^{s-1} \frac{(\lambda/\mu)^n}{n!} + \frac{(\lambda/\mu)^s}{s!(1 - \lambda/s\mu)} \right) \right.$$

The mean time spent in the queue:

$$W_q = L_q/\lambda$$

The probability that the server is busy (i.e., server utilization):

$$\rho = \frac{\lambda}{s\mu}$$

where $\lambda =$ Mean arrival rate
$\mu =$ Mean service rate
$s =$ Number of servers.

P_0 is most easily found by using a lookup table of values of λ/μ and s (see, e.g., Stevenson, 2005).

Worked Example 11.3

Multiple-server Queue

Customers queue in a single line in a department store and are served at one of three tills on an FCFS basis. Customers arrive at a rate of 24 an hour (according to a Poisson distribution) and have a service time that is exponentially distributed with a mean rate of 10 customers served per hour.

a What is the mean number of customers waiting in the queue?
b What is the mean time a customer spends in the queue?
c What is the probability that a till is busy?

Solution

$$\lambda = 24 \qquad \mu = 10 \qquad s = 3$$

P_0 has been given as 0.056.

a $L_q = \dfrac{24 * 10 * (24/10)^3}{(3-1)! * (3*10 - 24)^2} * 0.056 = \dfrac{3317.76}{72} * 0.056 = 2.58$ customers

b $W_q = \dfrac{L_q}{\lambda} = \dfrac{2.58}{24} = 0.1075$ hours

c $\rho = \dfrac{24}{(3*10)} = 0.8$

The mathematical equations used in queuing theory make a number of assumptions about the system. They assume steady state conditions have been reached; that is, the effects of an empty system start-up phase have been overcome and the system has reached a steady state. This may never happen if the mean arrival rate is greater than the service rate. Also, the system may shut down for breaks during the day or may not run long enough to reach equilibrium. The equations can also only be used to describe very simple systems, and business process simulation (Chapter 8) is often used to analyse situations that do not fit adequately the assumed conditions of queuing theory.

CASE STUDY 11.2

Lloyds' Cameras Cut Time in Queues

Lloyds TSB has been using special videocameras to cut the amount of time its customers are spending queuing in branches. The UK's fifth-largest bank has installed special videocameras in 30 of its branches to monitor customer behaviour and track how long people spend queuing. As a result, the amount of time customers wait to be served in these branches has fallen from 1.86 minutes in November 2004 to 1.46

minutes in March as the bank redeploys key staff at busy times of the day. The number of customers who are served within 2 minutes of walking into these branches has risen from 72.4% last November to about 82.6% in March. The average time each customer spends in front of a cashier has remained stable at just over 2.2 minutes. Lloyds TSB has identified queuing time as a major gripe amongst customers.

Graham Lindsay, director of the branch network at Lloyds TSB, said: "We have done customer research and 2 minutes is generally the gratification threshold. Customers resent waiting 5 minutes or more. Levels of customer satisfaction in branches are closely connected to waiting times and efficiency of service." The technology has been developed by Brickstream, the US technology company. There are no comparable figures available from rival banks on how long customers spend queuing. However, at Barclays' annual meeting last month, Roger Davis, head of retail banking, said queuing times had fallen to 3 minutes at Barclays branches.

Source: Jane Croft, FT.com, 8 May 2005
© The Financial Times Ltd

1   How has the use of videocameras enabled Lloyds to cut queue times in its bank branches?

**Case Study 11.2
Question**

The Psychology of Queues

Maister (1985) suggests that although queuing theory has been used successfully to analyse waiting times it does not take into account customer perception of the waiting time itself. Thus, depending on the situation, a customer may or may not feel that a wait time of 10 minutes is acceptable, for instance. Using the concepts of expectation and perception of service levels, Maister has developed a series of propositions about the **psychology of queues** which can be used by service organizations to influence customer satisfaction with waiting times. The propositions are as follows:

> **PSYCHOLOGY OF QUEUES:**
> a series of propositions which can be used by service organizations to instigate policies to influence customer satisfaction with waiting times.

- *Unoccupied time feels longer than occupied time* – the important point here is to try to ensure that unoccupied time is taken up with an activity which is seen as useful by the customer and is related in some way to the forthcoming service.
- *Pre-process waits feel longer than in-process waits* – it is important that human contact is made as soon as possible to convey that the service has started and reduce anxiety in the customer. For example, handing out the menu in a restaurant immediately a customer arrives ensures that they do not feel they have been overlooked.
- *Anxiety makes waits seem longer* – a particular form of this is when parallel queues are used for a service. What usually happens is that the queue you choose to enter suddenly stops moving while the other queues progress rapidly!

Many service organizations (e.g., post offices) have a single-queue system which seems fairer to customers and reduces anxiety by operating a strict FCFS policy.

- *Uncertain waits are longer than known, finite waits* – it is important to inform the customer how long the wait will be. A particular problem with appointment systems is that they create a specific expectation about when a service should begin and if appointments begin to run behind, anxiety increases as the expectation is not met.
- *Unexplained waits are longer than explained waits* – if the customer understands the reason for a wait they will be more satisfied than if no explanation or an explanation which does not provide sufficient justification is given.
- *Unfair waits are longer than equitable waits* – one of the most irritating occurrences for a customer is when someone who has arrived at a later time is served first. This can be eliminated by a single-queue system which operates on a FCFS basis.
- *The more valuable the service, the longer the customer will wait* – if the service is seen to be of little value, the tolerance for waiting will diminish greatly. In particular, post-process waits, when the required service is over, feel longer than in-process or even pre-process waits.
- *Solo waits feel longer than group waits* – when there is group interaction in a waiting line, perhaps initiated by an announcement of a delay, then waiting becomes more tolerable.

Although the FCFS queue discipline has been mentioned as a possible solution to some of the above problems, it cannot always be applied due to factors such as the implications for available space (e.g., for a supermarket customer using a trolley). The single queue also eliminates the possibility of providing custom service points for different customer types (e.g., customer with few items in a supermarket or first-class customers for an airline). Overall, the propositions show that in addition to the actual wait or queue time the context of the waiting line will have a significant effect on the level of customer satisfaction.

CASE STUDY 11.3

Queuing Theory

Last week's debacle over World Cup tickets could have put lives in danger. English football fans, left hanging on the telephone while happy Frenchmen rejoiced over their tickets, felt the same sense of angry injustice that can lead to violent 'road rage' attacks, says the world's leading expert on queuing theory. Richard Larson of the Massachusetts Institute of Technology told a conference in Montreal this week that road rage and related phenomena are an urgent new area for research. An electrical engineer by training, Larson is the leading exponent of a branch of science known as Operations Research (OR). OR keeps the world moving and happy by employing science, maths and computer modelling to overcome the logistical and technical challenges associated with efficiently shifting people, commodities and information around the world.

Larson, who is known in his field as Dr Queue, acts as a consultant to major multi-national companies and government agencies – satisfied customers include Coca-Cola, American Airlines, United Artists Cinemas and the US Department of Justice. Badly managed queues, he says, can tap into a reservoir of anger, hostility and frustration. He cites a new phenomenon: store rage. A fortnight ago, a woman had half her nose cut off by the woman behind her at the express checkout queue of a Milwaukee supermarket – her basket contained more than the permitted 12 items and she had refused to change queues.

Operations researchers manage queues in areas as diverse as air traffic control systems, passenger reservations and parcel delivery. "There are billions of possibilities for this type of operation," says Larson. "These things are too complex for any human mind – you need to employ mathematical modelling, observation, data analysis and computer science." But, he admits, the most useful tool is still common sense: "You need to formulate the problem correctly – if you get that wrong it doesn't matter how sophisticated the maths is." His skill in combining common sense and computer modelling techniques was responsible for saving lives well before the advent of road rage. In the 1970s he pioneered a computer program for finding the most efficient distribution of fire and ambulance crews throughout a city. It has been widely employed throughout the US and Europe. The latest development – the Trauma Resource Allocation Model for Ambulances and Hospitals (TRAMAH) – was presented at the conference this week, and showed how the right distribution of available resources can give a near-perfect emergency response. Using the 27 000 emergency cases in the state of Maryland between 1992 and 1994 as a model, researchers simulated various combinations of positions for trauma centres and helicopters. During this period, 95% of severely injured residents had received access to trauma system resources within 30 minutes and 70% had access within 15 minutes. Using the same number of resources, but changing their locations, the TRAMAH program simulated access within 30 minutes for 99.97% of cases. They also found that taxpayers' money could be saved by cutting some helicopter depots and strategically placing the others – without losing any emergency response capability.

But TRAMAH's developers are aware that scientific advice doesn't always get acted on – local history and political expediency are often much more persuasive in the allocation of emergency resources. "There will be some rural communities that spent 10 years selling brownies so they could buy a helicopter – there's no changing the location of that facility," says Charles Branas, who presented the report. Healthcare managers may not listen to the voice of reason, but in the airline industry the sound of ringing cash tills always catches the ear. United Airlines revealed at the conference that a computer program developed by their operations research office had saved the company $60m in the past year. One hour before United's planes take off, the program analyses the latest weather reports and composes a flight plan that uses current wind conditions to the plane's advantage. "There are millions of possible flight paths for flying from A to B – we came up with an algorithm that searches all those options and gives us the best one," says Bob Bongiorno, the head of United Airlines' operations research department. "It has saved us a huge amount in fuel costs and pilot time and shaved minutes off our flight times."

According to Larson, queue management is easiest to implement in Britain and northern Europe, where there is an acknowledgement of the role of courtesy and FCFS. He told delegates to the conference that the best advice for avoiding road rage was to be found in a British driving manual. "Wherever there's merging traffic, follow the rule: 'let one in and go' – this is the behaviour of fair standing queues, and it seems to be the rule of the road in the UK," he said. Larson has not been to the UK since the 1970s – delegates with more recent experience of British driving no doubt took his observations with a pinch of salt.

Source: 'Science and technology: Why are we waiting?' by Michael Brooks, *The Guardian*, 1 May 1998
© Guardian Newspapers Ltd 1998

**Case Study 11.3
Question**

1   How do queuing theory and the psychology of queuing contribute to queue management?

Appendix: Forecasting

Introduction

Accurate forecasts are an important factor in enabling organizations to deliver goods and services to the customer when required and, thus, achieve a quality service. Forecasting is important in relation to anticipating changing customer requirements and meeting them with new product and service designs (Chapter 7). The ability to measure demand is also a key part of the facility design (Chapter 5), capacity management process (Chapter 11) and supply chain management (Chapter 15).

In order to produce accurate forecasts an organization must collect up-to-date data on relevant information such as prices and sales volumes and choose an appropriate forecasting technique. The accuracy of a forecast is also dependent on the time horizon over which the forecast is derived. Forecasts for short time horizons tend to be more accurate than for longer term forecasts, so one way of improving accuracy is shortening the lead time necessary for the organization to respond to a forecast. This might mean improving operations in terms of the flexibility performance objective.

Forecasting Techniques

Organizations must develop forecasts of the level of demand they should be prepared to meet. The forecast provides a basis for coordination of plans for activities in various parts of the organization. For example, personnel employ the right number of people, purchasing order the right amount of material and finance can estimate the capital required for the business. Forecasts can either be developed through a qualitative approach or a quantitative approach (Figure 11.8).

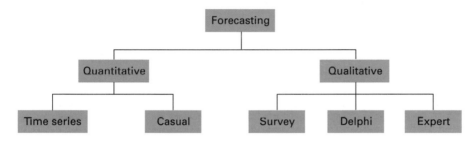

Figure 11.8   Forecasting techniques

Qualitative Forecasting Methods

Qualitative forecasting methods take a subjective approach and are based on estimates and opinions. The following qualitative techniques will be described: market surveys, the Delphi method and expert judgement.

Market Surveys

A market survey collects data from a sample of customers, analyses the responses and makes inferences about the population from which the sample is drawn. They are particularly useful before the launch of a new product when there is limited information on potential customer demand. For the survey to be statistically valid it is necessary to ensure a correct sampling methodology is used and that questions are pertinent and unbiased. Care must also be taken with the analysis of responses. To achieve useful results can be an expensive and time-consuming activity.

Delphi Study

This is a formal procedure which aims to bring together the opinions of a group of experts. A questionnaire is completed by a panel of experts which is then analysed and summaries passed back to the experts. Each expert in the group can then compare their forecast with the summarized reply of the others. This process is repeated, maybe up to six times, until a consensus has emerged within the group on which decision to take. The accuracy of the Delphi method can be good, but the cost and effort of its use may be relatively high.

Expert Judgement

This can take the form of an individual or group judgement. An individual judgement relies entirely on a single person's opinion of the situation – which includes both the knowledge and ignorance of the problem. The technique is unreliable and although it may give a good forecast, it can also give a very bad one.

A group judgement relies on a consensus being found among a group of people. If the difficulty of finding consensus can be overcome this is a more reliable method than an individual judgement. However, it is still relatively unreliable compared with more formal methods and is subject to group processes such as domination of the group by one person and the taking of risky decisions which an individual would not take.

Quantitative Forecasting Methods

QUANTITATIVE FORECASTING METHODS: use a mathematical expression or model to show the relationship between demand and some independent variable or variables. The methods include time series and causal forecasting models.

Quantitative forecasting methods use a mathematical expression or model to show the relationship between demand and some independent variable or variables. The model that is appropriate for forecasting depends on the demand pattern to be projected and the forecaster's objectives for the model. This section will refer to the techniques involved in time series analysis.

A time series is a set of observations measured at successive points in time. Time series analysis attempts to discover a pattern and extrapolate this pattern into the future. There are four components of a time series – trend, cyclical, seasonal and irregular – which are now described:

■ *Trend* – a gradual movement to relatively higher or lower values over time is referred to as the 'trend' (not random fluctuations).
■ *Cyclical* – any recurring sequence of points above and below the trend line lasting for more than 1 year.
■ *Seasonal* – any regularly repeating pattern that is less than 1 year in duration.
■ *Irregular* – deviations of the time series values from those expected by the

trend, cyclical and seasonal components. We cannot attempt to predict its impact on the time series.

To analyse a time series, smoothing methods can be used. Smoothing methods smooth out the random fluctuations caused by the irregular component of the time series. They are only appropriate for a stable time series – one that does not exhibit trend, cyclical or seasonal effects. The Moving Averages and Exponential Smoothing methods are described.

Moving Averages

A moving average is a procedure in which as each new observation becomes available, a new average can be computed by dropping the oldest observation and including the new one. This moving average will then be the forecast for the next period. For example, we might compute a 3-week moving average at the end of each week to smooth out random fluctuations and get an estimate of the average sales per week. To compute a 3-week moving average, at the end of each week we add sales for the latest 3 weeks and divide by 3. An example of a spreadsheet of a moving average forecast is given in Figure 11.9.

Averaging multiple periods helps smooth out random fluctuations so that the forecast or average has more stability or does not fluctuate erratically. A moving average will gain stability if a greater number of periods are used in the average. If the number of periods in the average is too great, however, the average will be so stable that it will be slow to respond to non-random changes in the demand data. Responsiveness is the ability of a forecast to adjust quickly to true changes in the base level of demand. Both responsiveness and stability are difficult to achieve with a forecasting method that looks only at the series of past observations without considering factors that may have caused a change in that pattern.

Exponential Smoothing

In practice, the technique of moving averages as a forecasting technique is not used often because the method of exponential smoothing is generally superior. The most recent observations will usually provide the best guide to the future. The exponential smoothing procedure uses exponentially decreasing weights as the observations get older. This method keeps a running average of demand and adjusts it for each period in proportion to the difference between the latest actual demand figure and the latest value of the average. The equation is:

$$SF_{t+1} = SF_t + \alpha(A_t - SF_t)$$

where SF_{t+1} = Smoothed forecast for time period following t
SF_t = Smoothed forecast for period t
α = Smoothing constant that determines weight given to previous data
A_t = Actual demand in period t.

The smoothing constant is a decimal between 0 and 1 where 0 is most stable and 1 is most responsive. Values between 0.1 and 0.3 are often used in practice. A large value of α gives very little smoothing, while a small value gives considerable smoothing/damping. For a time series with little random variability, larger values of α are better as they react quicker to changes. For a time series with large random variability, lower values of α are best so they do not overreact and adjust the forecasts too quickly. Figure 11.10 provides an example of a spreadsheet of an exponential smoothing forecast.

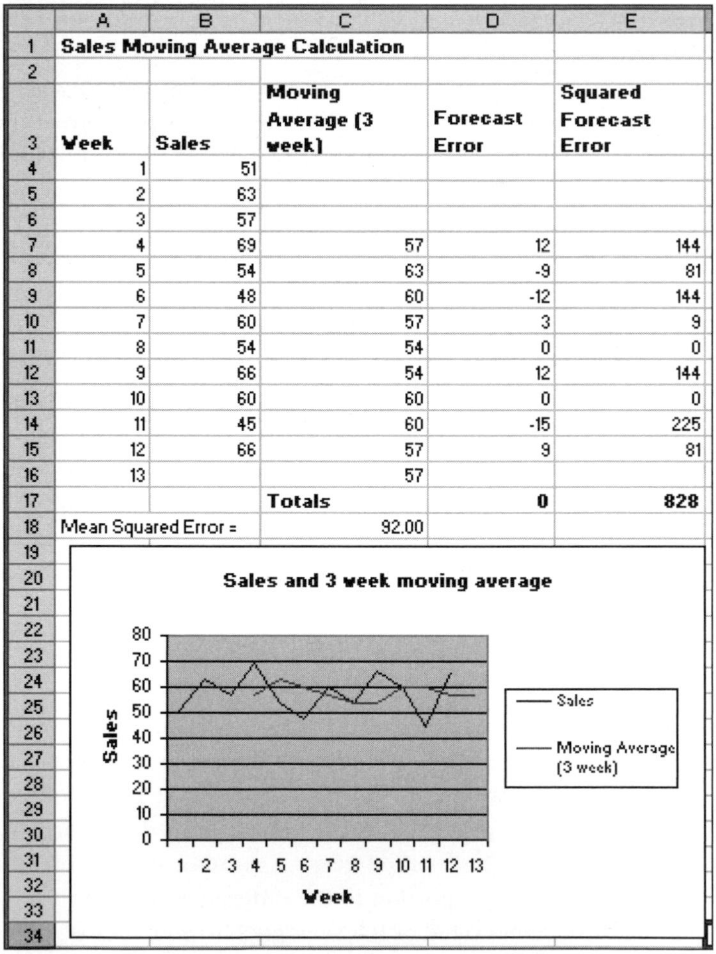

	A	B	C	D	E
1	Sales Moving Average Calculation				
2					
3	Week	Sales	Moving Average (3 week)	Forecast Error	Squared Forecast Error
4	1	51			
5	2	63			
6	3	57			
7	4	69	57	12	144
8	5	54	63	-9	81
9	6	48	60	-12	144
10	7	60	57	3	9
11	8	54	54	0	0
12	9	66	54	12	144
13	10	60	60	0	0
14	11	45	60	-15	225
15	12	66	57	9	81
16	13		57		
17			Totals	0	828
18	Mean Squared Error =		92.00		

Figure 11.9   Example of moving average forecast

	A	B	C	D	E
1	**Sales Exponential Smoothing Calculation**				
2					
3	**Week**	**Sales**	**Exponential Smoothing Forecast (a=0.2)**	**Forecast Error**	**Squared Forecast Error**
4	1	51			
5	2	63	51.00	12.00	144.00
6	3	57	53.40	3.60	12.96
7	4	69	54.12	14.88	221.41
8	5	54	57.10	-3.10	9.59
9	6	48	56.48	-8.48	71.86
10	7	60	54.78	5.22	27.23
11	8	54	55.83	-1.83	3.33
12	9	66	55.46	10.54	111.09
13	10	60	57.57	2.43	5.91
14	11	45	58.05	-13.05	170.42
15	12	66	55.44	10.56	111.44
16	13		57.55		
17			**Totals**	**32.77**	**889.24**
18	Mean Squared Error =		80.84	alpha	0.2

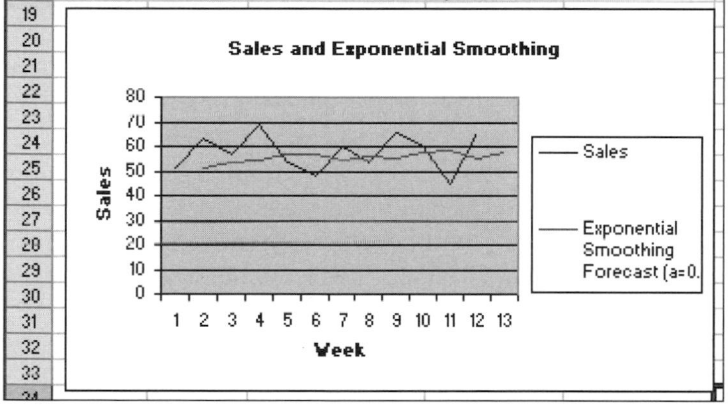

Figure 11.10 Example of an exponential smoothing forecast

The major advantage of using the widely used smoothing methods described are their simplicity and low cost. More accuracy may be obtained with more sophisticated or decomposition methods. Smoothing methods are particularly appropriate for forecasts of thousands of items in inventory systems.

Time Series Decomposition

Often a pattern cannot be recognized in the raw data and so it must be decomposed into the four components of the time series (trend, seasonal, cyclical and random) that show a pattern which is helpful in projecting the data. Time series decomposition is appropriate if seasonal variation is evident in the demand pattern and the effect of seasonality is to be included in the forecast. The technique consists of smoothing past values to eliminate randomness so that the pattern can be projected into the future and used as a forecast. In many instances the patterns can be broken down (decomposed) into sub-patterns that identify each component (e.g., trend and seasonal) separately. Two common forms of the time series that can be used for decomposition are as follows:

$$\text{Additive form} \quad Y_t = T_t + S_t + I_t$$

$$\text{Multiplicative form} \quad Y_t = T_t * S_t * I_t$$

An additive model is appropriate if the magnitude of the seasonal fluctuation does not vary with the level of the series. Multiplicative decomposition is more prevalent with economic series because more seasonal economic series do have seasonal variation which increases with the level of the series. Visual inspection of a plotted series is often used to determine the type of model that most appropriately represents the data. The steps involved in decomposing a series are to compute the seasonal indexes necessary to deseasonalize the data, and if a trend is apparent in the deseasonalized data then use regression analysis to estimate the trend.

To calculate the seasonal indexes a number of smoothing methods are available, the simplest being the moving average. To smooth a quarterly seasonal pattern we can use a four-period moving average. Assuming a multiplicative model, the moving average requires an odd number of observations to ensure the average is centred at the middle of the data values being averaged. For a four-period average the average for Period 3 could be the average of Periods 1–4 or 2–5 giving answers of 21.4 or 22.4. Thus, we add another column which is the average of the two successive values of the four-period average (i.e., the average of 21.4 and 22.4 = 21.9). The moving average graph smooths out both the seasonal and irregular fluctuations in the time series. Divide the observation by the centred moving average to identify the seasonal irregular effect in the time series.

The fluctuations over the 3 years can be assigned to the irregular influence, so we take an average value to compute the seasonal influence as below:

Q1 Seasonal index values $= 0.971, 0.918, 0.908$; therefore,

$$\text{Seasonal index} = \frac{0.971 + 0.918 + 0.908}{3} = 0.93$$

Q2 Seasonal index $= 0.84$
Q3 Seasonal index $= 1.09$
Q4 Seasonal index $= 1.14$

Thus, the best sales in Q4 (14% above average) and worst sales in Q2 (16% below average).

	A	B	C	D	E	F	G	H
1								
2								
3	Year	Quarter	Sales	4-Quarter Moving Average	Centred Moving Average	Seasonal-Irregular Value	Seasonal Index	Deseasonalised Sales
4	1	1	19.2				0.93	20.60
5		2	16.4				0.84	19.58
6		3	24	21.400	21.900	1.096	1.09	21.95
7		4	26	22.400	22.950	1.133	1.14	22.74
8	2	1	23.2	23.500	23.900	0.971	0.93	24.89
9		2	20.8	24.300	24.750	0.840	0.84	24.83
10		3	27.2	25.200	25.300	1.075	1.09	24.88
11		4	29.6	25.400	25.600	1.156	1.14	25.89
12	3	1	24	25.800	26.150	0.918	0.93	25.75
13		2	22.4	26.500	26.700	0.839	0.84	26.74
14		3	30	26.900	27.050	1.109	1.09	27.44
15		4	31.2	27.200	27.350	1.141	1.14	27.29
16	4	1	25.2	27.500	27.750	0.908	0.93	27.03
17		2	23.6	28.000	28.300	0.834	0.84	28.17
18		3	32	28.600			1.09	29.27
19		4	33.6				1.14	29.39
20								

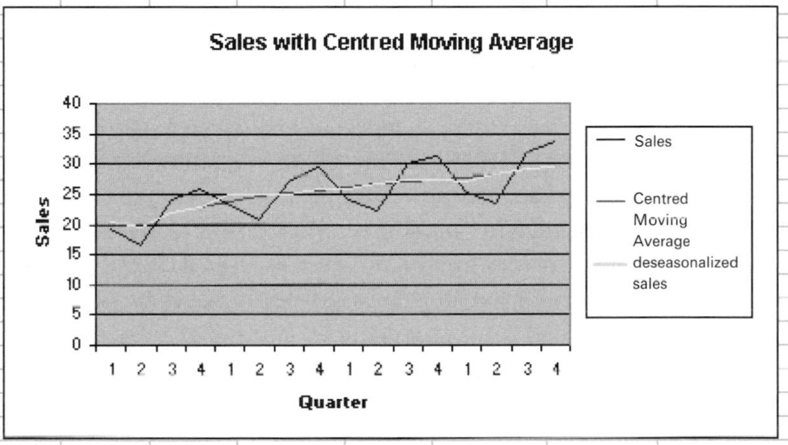

Figure 11.11   **Spreadsheet of deseasonalized sales**

For a multiplicative model, average seasonal indexes must equal 1.0 (i.e., average out over the year). That is:

$$\frac{0.93 + 0.84 + 1.09 + 1.14}{4} = 1.0$$

In this case they do; otherwise, adjust by multiplying each seasonal index by the number of seasons divided by the sum of the unadjusted seasonal indexes. In a multiplicative model we now divide each time series observation by the corresponding seasonal index. Thus, in this case sales are divided by the seasonal index to get the deseasonalized sales figures (Figure 11.11).

There are many decomposition methods, such as Census II and X-12-ARIMA, but these work on the same principles as shown. In practice, a straight line trend model is rarely adequate. Decomposition is a useful tool for understanding the behaviour of a time series, before selection and application of a forecasting method.

Causal Models

Sometimes demand does not exhibit a consistent pattern over time because the level of one or more variables that have an effect on demand had changed during the period when the demand series was collected. Causal modes are used to identify variables, or a combination of variables, which affect demand and are then used to predict future levels of demand. Models that may be used in this way include linear regression, curvilinear regression and multiple regression.

Regression methods are used when it is desirable to find an indicator that moves before the company's sales level changes (a leading indicator) and that has a significantly stable relationship with sales to be useful as a prediction tool. Linear regression is a means of finding and expressing a relationship. Regression analysis is the development of a mathematical equation that predicts the value of a dependent variable from single (simple regression) or multiple (multiple regression) independent variables; for example, sales (dependent) is related to advertising spend (independent). Note that, unlike using regression analysis for trend projection, causal forecasting relates the forecast variable to variables that are supposed to influence or explain that variable. It should be noted that casual forecasts are not necessarily time dependent. A model that relates inputs to outputs facilitates a better understanding of the situation and allows experimentation with different combinations of inputs to study their effects on the forecast (output). Thus, the effect of decisions made today can be forecast in the future.

Causal Forecasting Using Regression Analysis

Scatter graphs are a useful first step in investigating the relationships between two variables. They indicate the strength of the relationship (a small scatter indicates a strong relationship) and the direction of a linear relationship (a positive relationship is when one variable gets larger while the other variable gets larger; a negative relationship is when one variable gets larger while the other variable gets smaller). They also may indicate any points that do not conform to the general pattern (called 'outliers').

To provide a measure of the degree of scatter the correlation coefficient (r) is used which is the ratio of variations in x and y compared with those of x and y

separately. r is a value between -1 and $+1$, with -1 indicating perfect negative correlation, 0 indicating no correlation and $+1$ indicating perfect positive correlation. Please note that correlation does not mean causation. Just because a variable rises with another one this does not imply a direct causation.

If a straight line relationship is present then a simple linear regression method can be used. This is concerned with finding the straight line that best fits the data. The straight line equation is used to formulate the relationship between the two variables:

$$Y = b_0 + b_1 X$$

Thus, the regression method determines the two regression coefficients, b_0 and b_1 and, thus, allows the value of Y to be predicted for a value of X.

The coefficient of determination (r^2) can be used to determine the proportion of variation that is explained by the independent variable in the regression model $(0 = $ no prediction, $1 = $ perfect prediction). The adjusted r^2 gives better results for small samples and a value above 0.5 may be considered acceptable for forecasting purposes.

Worked Example 11.4 shows the procedure using the Microsoft Excel spreadsheet.

Worked Example 11.4

Regression Analysis

Over recent years a company has undertaken five separate advertising campaigns. The figures are as follows:

Advertising (£000s)	Sales (£000s)
2	60
5	100
4	70
6	90
3	80

You have been asked to establish whether there is a relationship (correlation) between advertising spend and sales income and derive a regression formula linking the two variables.

Solution

1 Draw the scatter graph

Select the insert, chart, XY (Scatter) option, select format 1 that shows unconnected points, click next, and then enter the data range and select series by columns, click finish.

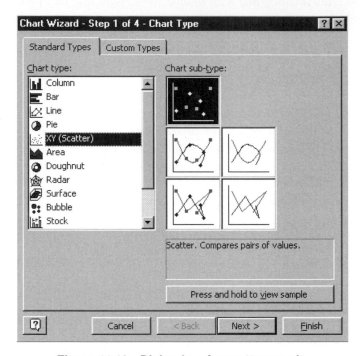

Figure 11.12 Dialog box for scatter graph

2 Inspect the graph to see if there is a linear relationship between the variables

To insert the regression line click on the chart, with the mouse on a data point click on the right-hand mouse button, choose Add Trendline from the options listed, select Linear and in Options select Forecast Backward 2 units, then OK.

A relative measure of the linear association between two variables is Pearson's Coefficient of Correlation (R). A value of $R = +1$ equals a perfect positive correlation, a value of $R = -1$ equals a perfect negative correlation and a value of $R = 0$ equals no correlation. The coefficient of determination (R^2) shows the proportion of the variation in Y which is explained by X. For example, if $R^2 = 0.64$ then 64% of total variation can be accounted for by the regression line.

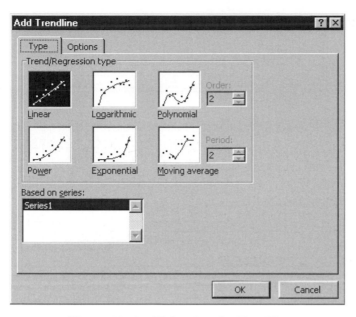

Figure 11.13   Dialog box for Trendline

3. Calculate the regression statistics

To calculate the regression statistics select Tools, Data Analysis, Regression, OK. Input the *X* and *Y* cell ranges. Select the Output Range where you wish the regression statistics to appear.

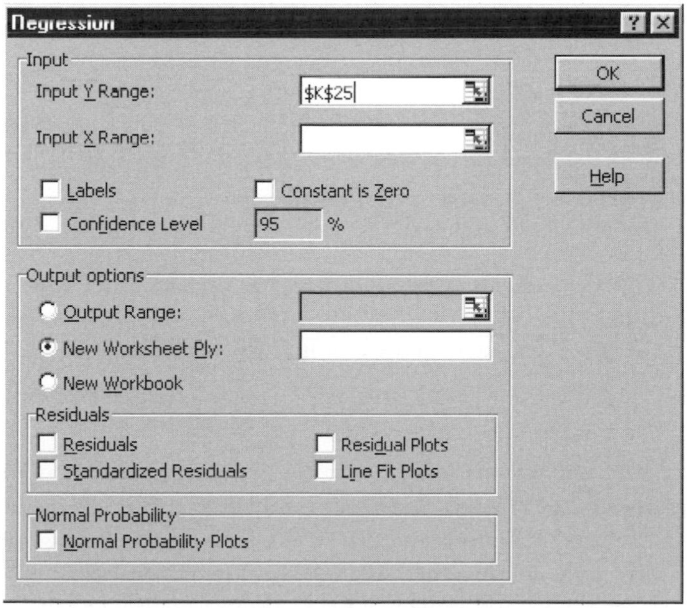

Figure 11.14   Dialog box for regression analysis

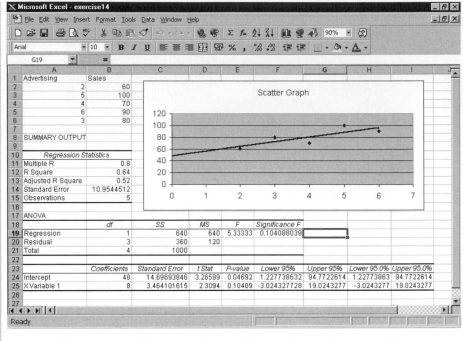

Figure 11.15   Results of regression and correlation analysis

The results of the regression analysis are shown in Figure 11.15.

4   Interpret the Results

- The adjusted r^2 value (cell B13) gives a figure of 0.52 which shows a weak positive relationship between the variables.
- The coefficients of the regression equation are given as intercept (b_0) in cell B24 as 48 and the X variable 1 (b_1) in cell B25 as 8. Thus, the relationship between the variables could be shown by the formula $Y = 48 + 8 * X$; for example, for an advertising spend of 4.5, Sales $= 48 + 8 * 4.5 = 84$.

Simple regression is a special case of multiple regression, which has two or more independent variables. The general form of multiple regression is:

$$Y = b_0 + b_1X_1 + b_2X_2 + \cdots + b_kX_k$$

Thus, if sales were the variable to be forecast, several factors such as advertising, prices, competition, R&D budget and time could be tested for their influence on sales. The coefficients in multiple regression can be calculated using the least squares method (as for simple regression). R^2 can be used to show the proportion of the variation in Y which is explained by X. Multiple regression should be undertaken using the computer (e.g., Excel).

Casual analysis allows the impact of decisions now to be forecast in the future. Correlation is not causation. For example, the number of cola cans sold and the number of deaths by drowning could be correlated, but the number of drownings do not cause the sales of cola. A pair of variables may be correlated because they are both caused by a third 'lurking' variable; for example, in summer both drownings and cola sales increase, thus temperature is a lurking variable.

Summary

1 The main elements in capacity planning decisions are the measurement of capacity and demand and the reconciling of the two to form a feasible plan.

2 The product mix will affect the amount of capacity available as each product or service requires different amounts and different types of capacity at different times.

3 A level capacity plan sets capacity at a uniform level throughout the planning period. A chase demand plan seeks to match production to demand over time. A demand management plan attempts to adjust demand to meet available capacity.

4 Yield management is a collection of demand management approaches used to optimize the use of capacity in service operations where capacity is relatively fixed and the service cannot be stored in any way.

5 Cumulative representations can be used to evaluate a level capacity planning approach by keeping a running total of inventory levels to ensure no stock-outs occur.

6 Queuing theory can provide a useful guide in determining expected waiting time for an arriving customer by using statistical distributions of customer arrivals and service times.

7 Propositions about the psychology of queues can be used by service organizations to influence customer satisfaction with waiting times.

8 Qualitative forecasting techniques include market surveys, Delphi studies and expert judgement. Quantitative methods include time series causal models.

Exercises

1. Explain how capacity management affects organizational performance.
2. Evaluate ways of reconciling capacity and demand in a manufacturing organization.
3. Evaluate ways of reconciling capacity and demand in a service organization.
4. Evaluate the main issues in assessing capacity and demand in service organizations.

5. Customers arrive at an automated teller machine at a rate of 20 per hour according to a Poisson distribution. It serves customers at a mean rate of 15 customers per hour.
   a. What is the mean number of customers waiting in the queue?
   b. What is the mean time a customer spends in the queue?
   c. What is the probability that the till is busy?

6. Customers arrive at a post office counter at a rate of 50 per hour according to a Poisson distribution. There are 8 tills and the service time is at a mean rate of 10 customers per hour. P_0 has been given as 0.006.
   a. What is the mean number of customers waiting in the queue?
   b. What is the mean time a customer spends in the queue?
   c. What is the probability that the till is busy?

7. Discuss how the experience of waiting in a queue can be improved.

8. The table below shows quarterly sales for the past 7 years.

Year	Quarter 1	Quarter 2	Quarter 3	Quarter 4	Total sales
1	6	15	10	4	35
2	10	18	15	7	50
3	14	26	23	12	75
4	19	28	25	18	90
5	22	34	28	21	105
6	24	36	30	20	110
7	28	40	35	27	130

   a. Compute the seasonal indexes for the 4 quarters.
   b. Compute the deseasonalized sales for the 7 years.
   c. Plot the sales and deseasonalized sales on a graph.

References

Chase, R.B., Aquilano, N.J. and Jacobs, F.R. (2003), *Operations Management for Competitive Advantage*, 10th Edition, McGraw-Hill.

Maister, D.H. (1985), The psychology of waiting lines, in: J.A. Czepiel, M.R. Solomon and C.F. Surprenant (eds), *The Service Encounter*, Lexington Press, pp. 113–123.

Stevenson, W.J. (2005), *Operations Management*, 8th Edition, McGraw-Hill/Irwin.

Further Reading

Makridakis, S., Wheelwright, S.C. and Hyndman, R.J. (1998), *Forecasting: Methods and Applications*, 3rd Edition, John Wiley & Sons.

Web Links

http://go.to/forecasting/ Home page for Makridakis forecasting text.

www.forecastingprinciples.com Forecasting Principles.

www.ibf.org Institute of Business Forecasters.

www.ms.ic.ac.uk/iif/index.htm International Institute of Forecasting.

Chapter 12

Inventory Management

■ Types of Inventory
- Inventory Classified by Location
- Inventory Classified by Type

■ Managing Inventory

■ The ABC Inventory Classification System

■ Inventory Models
- Fixed Order Quantity Inventory Systems
- The Re-Order Point (ROP) Model
- The Economic Order Quantity (EOQ) Model
- Fixed Order Period Inventory Systems
- The Fixed Order Inventory (FOI) Model

■ Implementing Inventory Systems

Learning Objectives

After reading this chapter, you should be able to:

1 Describe the different types of inventory.

2 Discuss the purpose of the ABC inventory classification system.

3 Discuss the role of the re-order point inventory model.

4 Discuss the purpose of the EOQ model.

5 Discuss the purpose of the FOI model.

6 Understand the issues involved in implementing inventory systems.

Introduction

Inventory is present in all service and manufacturing processes. In manufacturing, inventory consists of the components that go to make up the product being manufactured. In services, inventory may be used as part of the service delivery system (e.g., disposable implements for a hospital operation) or be part of the tangible component of the service itself (e.g., the brochure for a car insurance policy). Inventory is important because, although it is necessary for customer service, it can also be a major cost to the organization. It has been estimated that a typical firm has about 30% of its current assets and perhaps as much as 90% of its working capital invested in inventory (Stevenson, 2005). Apart from the cost of inventory the use of excessive inventory can lead to other issues such as the disruption of work flow and hiding problems related to product quality and equipment breakdown. Addressing these issues is the focus of the concept of Just-In-Time (JIT) and lean operations covered in Chapter 13.

Inventory management can be considered part of materials management in a service or manufacturing organization. Materials management includes the acquiring of inventory (see procurement section in Chapter 15), the organization of the movement of inventory (see physical distribution management section in Chapter 15) and the assessment of when inventory should be ordered and the amount of inventory which should be ordered (covered in this chapter). Inventory management systems calculate the volume and timing of independent demand items. Independent demand is when demand is not directly related to the demand for any other inventory item. Usually, this demand comes from customers outside the company and so is not as predictable as dependent demand (the management of dependent demand items is covered in Chapter 14).

Types of Inventory

All organizations will carry some inventory or stock of goods at any one time. This can range from items such as stationery to machinery parts or raw materials. Generally, inventory is classified by its location or type.

Inventory Classified by Location

Inventory can be classified by location as raw materials (goods received from suppliers), work in progress (at some point within the operations process) or finished goods (goods ready for dispatch to the customer) (Figure 12.1).

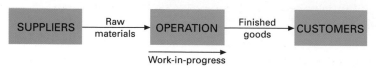

Figure 12.1   Inventory classified by location

The proportion between these inventory types will vary but it is estimated that generally 30% are raw materials, 40% are work in progress and 30% finished goods. Waters (2002) indicates the arbitrary nature of these classifications as someone's finished goods are someone else's raw materials:

RAW MATERIALS INVENTORY:

inventory received from suppliers.

WORK-IN-PROGRESS INVENTORY:

inventory at some point within the operations process.

FINISHED GOODS INVENTORY:

inventory ready for dispatch to the customer.

- **Raw material inventory** may be supplied in batches to secure quantity discounts and reduce material handling. However, smaller and more frequent order quantities translate into less inventory and may be achieved by negotiating smaller batches from suppliers. Variability in supplier lead times may be reduced by specifying longer, but more reliable lead times from suppliers.
- **Work-in-progress inventory** may help uncouple production stages and provide greater flexibility in production scheduling. It can be minimized by eliminating obsolete stock, improving the operation's processes and reducing the number of products or services.
- **Finished goods inventory** may be used to ensure important inventory items are always available to the customer or to avoid disruption caused by changing production output levels. It can be minimized by improving forecasts of customer demand and reducing fluctuations in demand caused by factors such as meeting end-of-period sales targets.

Inventory Classified by Type

The type of inventory can also be used to provide a method of identifying why inventory is being held and so suggest policies for reducing its level. Inventory types include:

- *Buffer/Safety* – this is used to compensate for the uncertainties inherent in the timing or rate of supply and demand between two operational stages. Safety stock is often used to compensate for uncertainties in the timing of supplies from suppliers. It is also used to compensate for uncertainties in supply between operational stages in a process due to factors such as equipment breakdowns.

- *Cycle* – if it is required to produce multiple products from one operation in batches, there is a need to produce enough to keep a supply while the other batches are being produced. This is an example of how differences between the timing of supply and demand can lead to high levels of work-in-progress inventory.

- *De-coupling* – this permits stages in the manufacturing process to be managed and their performance measured independently, to run at their own speed and not match the rate of processing of departments at different points in the process.

- *Anticipation* – this includes producing to stock to anticipate an increase in demand due to seasonal factors. Also, speculative policies such as buying in bulk to take advantage of price discounts may also increase inventory levels. Accurate forecasting can help ensure anticipation inventory reflects any increase in demand. Bulk buying policies will need to take into account the full cost of storing inventory.

- *Pipeline/Movement* – this is the inventory needed to compensate for the lack of stock while material is being transported between stages (e.g., the distribution time from the warehouse to a retail outlet). Thus, pipeline inventory may be the result of delays in the supply chain between customer and supplier. If an alternative supplier can be found then pipeline inventory can be reduced.

Most organizations have a large number of different types of inventory under their control, and operations managers need to assess how they ensure that materials are available when needed, while ensuring inventory costs are not too high. Holding inventory reduces the risk of having no stock and can also reduce ordering costs by ordering larger, but fewer batches of materials, reducing stock-out costs by ensuring disruption to the manufacturing or service delivery system is avoided and reducing acquisition costs by securing quantity discounts. However, these costs need to be set against the costs of holding high levels of inventory. These include the cost of storing and handling inventory items, the lack of responsiveness to customer demands because of the large work-in-progress inventories, the increase in lead times due to inventory queuing, the use of inventory to provide a safety net to unreliable processes that need improving and the capital investment in inventory that will not be used for some time. These issues are explored further in Chapter 13.

The risk of having no stock is particularly important in service systems where the customer expects the immediate consumption of the service and its associated good. For example, in a restaurant, customers will be dissatisfied if certain options are not available on the menu due to lack of produce. More importantly, hospitals need to ensure inventory such as drugs are always available for patients.

Managing Inventory

One of the major issues in inventory management is the level of decentralization required in inventory distribution. Decentralized facilities offer a service closer to the customer and, thus, should provide a better service level in terms of knowledge of customer needs and speed of service. Centralization, however, offers the potential for less handling of goods between service points, less control costs and less overall inventory levels due to lower overall buffer levels required. The Square Root Law (Maister, 1975) states that a firm currently operating out of five warehouses which centralizes to one warehouse can theoretically reduce inventory carried in stock by 55%. The overall demand pattern for a centralized facility will be an average of the variable demand patterns from a number of customers. This will decrease demand variability and, thus, require lower buffer stocks. Thus, there is a trade-off between the customer service levels or effectiveness offered by a decentralized system and the lower costs or efficiency offered by a centralized system. One way of combining the advantages of a centralized facility with a high level of customer service is to reduce the delivery lead time between the centralized distribution centre and the customer outlet. This issue is discussed in more detail in the warehousing section of Chapter 15.

CASE STUDY 12.1

The Tricky Task of Moving from the Warehouse to the Shelves

When Lawrence Christensen worked at Safeway as operations director, he would often find himself smiling over Sainsbury's inability to get its goods on to shelves. "The chairman and I would have a cup of coffee and a chat over breakfast and we would chuckle at what was going on," recalls Mr Christensen. "I never dreamt for one moment that it would be me having to sort it out." But that all changed last year when Wm Morrison bought Safeway and Mr Christensen decided not to stay on at the merged group. He was pondering retirement but was also being doggedly pursued by Justin King, chief executive of Sainsbury, who was in desperate need of someone to sort out the retailer's supply chain. Mr Christensen signed up.

A few weeks in and his – now folkloric – assessment of Sainsbury's supply chain was grim. "There is nothing here I haven't seen before. I just haven't seen it all in the same place at the same time before." As bad practice went, Sainsbury was leading the pack. "It was worse than I thought," says Mr Christensen. The four new automated warehouses – built as part of Sir Peter Davis's £3bn investment programme in Sainsbury's supply chain, IT systems and infrastructure – were not working properly. Suppliers were not packaging their orders to suit the new distribution centres.

The system was clogged and deliveries were coming into stores at the wrong time. Labour was not in the right place at the right time and wastage was high. Stock was languishing in the store room or delivery yard rather than on the shelves.

Sainsbury's was failing to carry out the 'ABC of retailing'. Rival Tesco will count and investigate out-of-stocks every day at every store. Its managers follow the mantra of 'if it is in store it is on the shelf'. Sainsbury was not doing this, says Mr Christensen. Late deliveries meant stock was piling up in the back of the warehouse. Managers were ordering stock 48 hours in advance, fearful that the automated warehouses would not deliver what they wanted on time. It was a disaster. Sir Peter had told shareholders in 2001 that his 'business transformation' programme would deliver a saving of £600m every year by the end of the programme in 2004. In October that year, Mr King said the programme had failed. He wrote off £260m against ineffective supply chain equipment and ineffective IT systems. Sainsbury's was heading for its worst ever loss in its 135-year history.

Six months into the job and Mr Christensen has gone some way in fixing supply issues as the uptick in Sainsbury's sales suggests. TNS market data released today is expected to show Sainsbury's growing faster than Asda – last month's figures put its growth ahead of its US-owned rival for the first time in 10 years. When he joined, Mr Christensen went about identifying the problems. Every Saturday he toured five Sainsbury stores with his wife in tow, talking to managers. He drew up his assessment at the end of last year: stock accuracy was poor; availability was extremely poor; morale was low.

Having made an assessment, Mr Christensen tried to sort out the automated warehouses. "I would never have built them," he says bluntly. "They take away from the flexibility and take a huge amount of time to build and I am not sure if they deliver. But my decision was we could not have another period of disruption." Instead, he drew up an action plan to get the best out of what he had. First, he went back to Witron and Siemens, the two groups behind the equipment and IT systems, to try to make improvements. "We were not talking to each other properly about how the IT systems and warehouses were connected. We are now working more closely together. We went right through Christmas and they have been running for about 4 months without major issues." He put in extra labour to manually sort products where needed and put support chains in for store managers to ensure greater communication between the two sides of the business.

Mr Christensen is now implementing a 'step change' programme across all of Sainsbury stores to improve availability on the shelves. He has put clear systems in place around deliveries, stock auditing and making sure the inventory is correct. "My job isn't done if it is not on the shelf," Mr Christensen says. It is still early days, but in stores that have rolled out Mr Christensen's new practices, things are looking up. He says that where the programme has been fully rolled out – it takes a couple of months for stores to adopt the processes – out of stocks are down by 75%. Only a handful of stores have completed the roll-out, but by the end of this week, all stores will have started.

That said, wastage is still high and availability patchy. "There are still variable store standards," says Clive Black, analyst at Shore Capital. "But at least they have worked out that if you want to sell anything it has to be on the shelf. Christensen has gone back and unravelled some of the problems which has been both difficult and costly. But he has stabilized the ship."

Source: Elizabeth Rigby, FT.com, 5 May 2005
© The Financial Times Ltd

**Case Study 12.1
Question**

1   Why is inventory management so important to Sainsbury's operation?

The ABC Inventory Classification System

**THE ABC
CLASSIFICATION
SYSTEM:**

sorts inventory items into groups depending on the amount of annual expenditure or some other factor.

One way of deciding the importance of inventory items and, thus, an appropriate inventory management method for them is to use the **ABC classification system**. Depending on the classification of the inventory a fixed order quantity or fixed order period inventory system can be chosen for managing that system.

The ABC classification system sorts inventory items into groups depending on the amount of annual expenditure they incur which will depend on the estimated number of items used annually multiplied by the unit cost.

To instigate an ABC system a table is produced listing the items in expenditure order (with largest expenditure at the top), and showing the percentage of total expenditure and cumulative percentage of the total expenditure for each item (Table 12.1).

By reading the cumulative percentage figure, it is usually found, following Pareto's Law, that 10–20% of the items account for 60–80% of annual expenditure. These items are called A items and need to be controlled closely to reduce overall expenditure. The use of forecasting techniques may be used to improve the accuracy of demand forecasts for these items. It may also require a more strategic approach to management of these items which may translate into closer buyer–supplier relationships. A items may be managed using a fixed order quantity system with perpetual inventory checks or a fixed order interval system employing a small time interval between review periods.

The B items account for the next 20–30% of items and usually account for a similar percentage of total expenditure. These items require fewer inventory level reviews than A items. A fixed order interval system with a minimum order level or a fixed order quantity system may be appropriate.

Finally, C items represent the remaining 50–70% of items but only account for less than 25% of total expenditure. Here, a fixed order quantity system may be appropriate or less rigorous inventory control methods can be used, as the cost of

Table 12.1   Example of an ABC classification table

Item	Annual expenditure (Cost * Usage) (000s)	Percentage expenditure (%)	Cumulative expenditure (%)
D-76	800	24.1	24.1
A-25	650	19.6	43.7
C-40	475	14.3	58.1
C-22	450	13.6	71.6
B-18	300	9.0	80.7
G-44	200	8.0	86.7
A-42	150	5.4	91.3
D-21	100	3.0	94.3
H-67	75	2.3	96.5
E-88	65	2.0	98.5
F-23	50	1.5	100.0
Total	3315		

inventory tracking will outweigh the cost of holding additional stock. It is important to recognize that overall expenditure may not be the only appropriate basis on which to classify items. Other factors include the importance of a component part on the overall product, the variability in delivery time, the loss of value through deterioration and the disruption caused to the production process if a stock-out occurs. The fixed order quantity and fixed order interval systems for inventory management are now described.

Inventory Models

Inventory models are used to assess when inventory requires ordering and what quantity should be ordered at that point in time. In a fixed order quantity inventory system, inventory is ordered in response to some event, such as inventory falling to a particular level. The timing of the inventory order can be calculated using a Re-Order Point (ROP) Model. The quantity to order at this point in time may be calculated using the Economic Order Quantity (EOQ) model. In a fixed order period inventory system, inventory is ordered at a fixed point in time (say, once a month). A Fixed Order Inventory (FOI) model can be used to determine the quantity to order at this point in time. These models are now described.

Fixed Order Quantity Inventory Systems

In **fixed order quantity inventory systems** the order quantity is the same each time the order is placed, but the time between orders varies according to the rate of use of the inventory item. When the inventory level has reduced to a certain amount, termed the 're-order point' (ROP), an order for further inventory is made. The ROP can be calculated by the use of a computer system which can also automate the ordering process. An alternative is the two-bin system. Here, inventory is held in two containers, termed 'bins'. When one bin is empty a replenishment order is made and inventory is taken from the other bin until the order arrives. These systems are termed 'perpetual systems' to indicate that the inventory record of the amount of inventory is updated as inventory is used and replenished.

Some systems for less important items only check inventory levels at certain intervals (say, once a week or once a month). When using a fixed order quantity system the point in time when an order should be placed can be determined using the ROP model, and the quantity to order at this time can be determined by the EOQ model. These inventory models are now described.

The Re-Order Point (ROP) Model

The **Re-Order Point (ROP) model** identifies the time to order when the stock level drops to a predetermined amount. This amount will usually include a quantity of stock to cover for the delay between order and delivery (the delivery lead time) and an element of stock to reduce the risk of running out of stock when levels are low (the safety stock).

Safety stock is used in order to prevent a stock-out occurring. It provides an extra level of inventory above that needed to meet predicted demand, to cope with variations in demand over a time period. The level of safety stock used, if any, will vary for each inventory cycle, but an average stock level above that needed to meet demand will be calculated. To calculate the safety stock level a number of factors should be taken into account including:

■ cost due to stock-out;
■ cost of holding safety stock;
■ variability in rate of demand;
■ variability in delivery lead time.

It is important to note that there is no stock-out risk between the maximum inventory level and the re-order level. The risk occurs due to variability in the rate of demand and, due to variability in the delivery lead time, between the ROP and zero stock level.

The re-order level can of course be estimated by a rule of thumb, such as when stocks are at twice the expected level of demand during the delivery lead time. However, to consider the probability of stock-out, cost of inventory and cost of stock-out the idea of a service level is used.

The service level is a measure of the level of service, or how sure the organization is that it can supply inventory from stock. This can be expressed as the probability that the inventory on hand during the lead time is sufficient to meet expected demand (e.g., a service level of 90% means that there is a 0.90 probability that demand will be met during the lead time period, and the probability that a stock-out will occur is 10%). The service level set is dependent on a number of factors such as stockholding costs for the extra safety stock and the loss of sales if demand cannot be met.

The re-order problem is one of determining the level of safety stock that balances the expected holding costs with the costs of stock-out. Equations will be derived for the following four scenarios of constant demand and constant lead time, variable demand and constant lead time, constant demand and variable lead time, and variable demand and variable lead time.

1   Constant Demand and Constant Lead Time

Assuming that the delivery lead time and demand rate are constant there is no risk of stock-out, so no safety stock is required:

$$ROP \text{ (units)} = d * LT$$

where d = Daily demand
           LT = Lead time.

Worked Example 12.1

Constant Demand and Constant Lead Time ROP Model

A company has a demand for an item at a constant of 50 per week. The order delivery lead time is also constant at 3 weeks. What should the ROP be?

Solution

$$d = 50$$

$$LT = 3$$

$$ROP = d * LT = 3 * 50$$

$$= 150 \text{ units}$$

2 Variable Demand and Constant Lead Time

This model assumes that demand during the delivery lead time consists of a series of independent daily demands and, thus, can be described by a normal distribution. The average daily demand rate and its standard deviation (measure of variability) are used to determine the expected demand and standard deviation of demand for the lead time period. Thus, the ROP is:

$$ROP = \text{Expected demand during lead time} + \text{Safety stock}$$
$$= \bar{d} * LT + z * \sqrt{LT} * \sigma_d$$

where $\bar{d}$ = Average demand rate
  LT = Delivery lead time
  σ_d = Standard deviation of demand rate
  z = Number of standard deviations from the mean.

Worked Example 12.2

Variable Demand and Constant Lead Time ROP Model

An office supply company sells paper with a variable demand which can be assumed to be normally distributed with an average of 800 boxes per week and a standard deviation of 250 boxes per week. The delivery lead time has been very consistent at 3 weeks. Determine the recommended re-order level if there is to be no more than a 1% chance that a stock-out will occur in any one replenishment period.

Solution

$$\bar{d} = 800/\text{week}$$
$$\sigma_d = 250/\text{week}$$
$$LT = 3$$

At 1% service level, $z = 2.33$ (from normal distribution table):
$$ROP = \bar{d} * LT + z * \sqrt{LT} * \sigma_d$$
$$= 800 * 3 + 2.33 * \sqrt{3} * 250$$
$$= 2400 + 2.33 * 433$$
$$= 3409 \text{ units}$$

---

3 Constant Demand and Variable Lead Time

Here, the lead time variation is described by a normal distribution and, thus, the expected lead time is normally distributed. Thus, the ROP is:

$$ROP = \text{Expected demand during lead time} + \text{Safety stock}$$

$$= d * \overline{LT} + z * d * \sigma_{LT}$$

where $d =$ Constant demand rate

$\overline{LT} =$ Average lead time

$\sigma_{LT} =$ Standard deviation of lead time

$z =$ Number of standard deviations from the mean.

4   Variable Demand Rate and Variable Lead Time

When both demand rate and lead time are variable, the expected demand during lead time is average daily demand multiplied by average lead time. Both daily demand and lead time are assumed to be normally distributed:

$$ROP = \text{Expected demand during lead time} + \text{Safety stock}$$

$$= \bar{d} * \overline{LT} + z * \sqrt{\overline{LT} * \sigma_d^2 + \overline{d^2} * \sigma_{LT}^2}$$

The Economic Order Quantity (EOQ) Model

The Economic Order Quantity (EOQ) model calculates the fixed inventory order volume required while seeking to minimize the sum of the annual costs of holding inventory and the annual costs of ordering inventory. The model makes a number of assumptions including:

■ stable or constant demand;
■ fixed and identifiable ordering cost;
■ the relationship between the cost of holding inventory and number of items held is linear;
■ the item cost does not vary with the order size;
■ delivery lead time does not vary;
■ no quantity discounts are available;
■ annual demand exists.

Brown *et al.* (2005) are critical of the EOQ method because an approach of ordering a fixed quantity per order item is not seen as relevant in a complex and dynamic market. The assumption of one delivery per order and then the use of that stock over time increases inventory levels and does not fit with the JIT approach. Also, annual demand will not exist for products with a life cycle of less than a year. Another assumption made is that ordering costs are constant with no account taken of the method of ordering (e.g., email, fax, phone), the time spent placing the order or the staffing costs of the person placing the order. However, the EOQ and other approaches in this chapter still have a role in inventory management in the right circumstances if their limitations are recognized.

> **THE ECONOMIC ORDER QUANTITY (EOQ):** calculates the fixed inventory order volume required while seeking to minimize the sum of the annual costs of holding inventory and the annual costs of ordering inventory.

Before the EOQ model is introduced it is useful to know that texts use a number of words to describe the cost of holding inventory and the cost of replacing that inventory. These include:

Inventory held	Inventory replaced
Holding cost	Order cost
Carrying cost	Replenishment cost
Storage cost	Delivery cost

Each order is assumed to be of Q units and is withdrawn at a constant rate over time until the quantity in stock is just sufficient to satisfy the demand during the order lead time (the time between placing an order and receiving the delivery). At this time an order for Q units is placed with the supplier. Assuming that the usage rate and lead time are constant the order will arrive when the stock level is at zero, thus eliminating excess stock or stock-outs. The order quantity must be set at a level which is not too small, leading to many orders and, thus, high order costs, but too large leading to high average levels of inventory and, thus, high holding costs.

The annual holding cost is the average number of items in stock multiplied by the cost to hold an item for a year. If the amount in stock decreases at a constant rate from Q to 0 then the average in stock is $Q/2$ (Figure 12.2).

Thus, if C_H is the average annual holding cost per unit, the total annual holding cost is:

$$\text{Annual holding cost} = \frac{Q}{2} * C_H$$

The annual ordering cost is a function of the number of orders per year and the ordering cost per order. If D is the annual demand, then the number of orders per year is given by D/Q. Thus, if C_O is the ordering cost per order then the total annual ordering cost is:

$$\text{Annual ordering cost} = \frac{D}{Q} * C_O$$

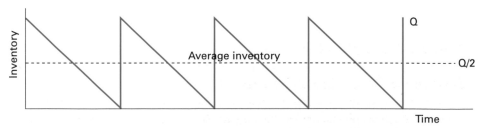

Figure 12.2   Inventory level versus time for the EOQ model

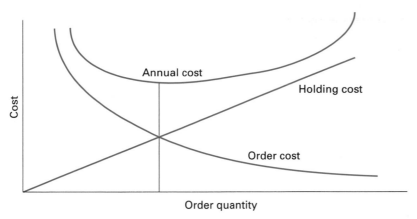

Figure 12.3   Inventory cost versus order quantity for the EOQ model

Thus, the total annual inventory cost is the sum of the total annual holding cost and the total annual ordering cost.

$$\text{Total annual cost} = \frac{Q}{2} * C_H + \frac{D}{Q} * C_O$$

where $Q =$ Order quantity
$C_H =$ Holding cost per unit
$D =$ Annual demand
$C_O =$ Ordering cost per order.

The total cost and its components of ordering and holding cost are shown graphically in Figure 12.3.

From the graph it can be seen that the minimum total cost point is when the holding cost is equal to the ordering cost. Note, however, that in practice the actual order size may differ considerably from the calculated EOQ without major effects on total costs.

Mathematically, when Holding costs = Ordering costs:

$$\frac{Q}{2} * C_H = \frac{D}{Q} * C_O$$

Solving for Q gives:

$$EOQ = \sqrt{\frac{2 * D * C_O}{C_H}}$$

Worked Example 12.3

Economic Order Quantity Model

The annual demand for a company's single item of stock is 1000 units. It costs the company £6 to hold one unit of stock for 1 year. Each time that a replenishment order is made the company incurs a fixed cost of £75.

(i) Determine the EOQ

Suppose that the company's supplier of stock introduces a condition that normally there shall be no more than five orders for replenishment per annum.

(ii) How Much Would the Company Be Prepared to Pay in Order to Avoid Having to Meet This Condition?

Solution

(i)

$$d = 1000$$

$$C_H = 6$$

$$C_O = 75$$

$$EOQ = \sqrt{\frac{2 * D * C_O}{C_H}}$$

$$= \sqrt{\frac{2 * 1000 * 75}{6}}$$

$$= \sqrt{25\,000}$$

$$= 158 \text{ units}$$

(ii) *Total cost at five orders per annum.* Therefore, $1000/5 = 200$ units delivered at one time:

$$\text{Total annual cost} = \frac{Q}{2} * C_H + \frac{D}{Q} * C_O$$

$$= \frac{200}{2} * 6 + \frac{1000}{200} * 75$$

$$= 600 + 375$$

$$= £975$$

Total annual cost at EOQ:

$$\text{Total annual cost} = \frac{158}{2} * 6 + \frac{1000}{158} * 75$$

$$= 474 + 474$$

$$= £948$$

Therefore, the company would be prepared to pay the difference £975 − £948 = £27.

The Economic Order Quantity (EOQ) with Quantity Discounts

Many firms provide discounts for large quantity orders for a number of reasons. These include economies of scale due to smaller setup times and other production efficiencies. Then, the customer must balance the potential benefits of a reduced price against the holding costs incurred by the higher order quantity. The total annual cost with discounts is, thus, the sum of:

$$\text{Holding costs} + \text{Ordering costs} + \text{Purchasing costs}$$

This can be expressed as the following equation:

$$TC = \frac{Q}{2} * C_H + \frac{D}{Q} * C_O + D * C_P$$

where Q = Quantity ordered
D = Annual demand
C_O = Order cost per order
C_H = Holding cost per unit for Q being considered
C_P = Unit price per unit for Q being considered.

Both the unit price and, thus, holding cost vary with an order quantity that is at a different price point. Thus, it may be necessary to calculate the total cost at each price point to find the lowest value. In addition, we need to take into account the fact that we may not be permitted to order the quantity specified at the price discount set. Also, it may be that it would be more economical to purchase just a few more units and achieve a more generous price discount at the next price point.

There are two main scenarios that need to be considered. One is where holding costs are considered constant per unit. In this case there will be a single EOQ for all the cost curves at the different price point. In the second case holding costs are expressed as a percentage of purchase price and so each cost curve will increase the EOQ for each price point.

The procedure for finding the best order quantity is:

1   Begin with the lowest price and solve for the EOQ at this price.
2   If the EOQ is not within the quantity range for this price, go to Step 3. Otherwise go to Step 4.
3   Solve for the EOQ at the next higher price. Go to Step 2.
4   Calculate the total cost for the EOQ that falls within the quantity range and for all the lower price points. Select the quantity with the lowest total cost.

Worked Example 12.4

The Economic Order Quantity Model with Discounts

A company is able to obtain quantity discounts on its order of material as follows:

Price per kilogram (kg)	Kilograms bought
6.00	Less than 250
5.90	250 and less than 800
5.80	800 and less than 2000
5.70	2000 and less than 4000
5.60	4000 and over

The annual demand for the material is 4000 kilograms. Holding costs are 20% per year of material cost. The order cost per order is £6. Calculate the best quantity to order.

Solution

Solving the EOQ at the lowest price ($Q = 4000$ and over):

$$C_O = 6$$
$$C_H = \frac{20}{100} * 5.6$$
$$= 1.12$$
$$C_P = 5.6$$
$$D = 4000$$
$$EOQ = \sqrt{\frac{(2 * 4000 * 6)}{1.12}}$$
$$= 207.$$

The EOQ is not in the quantity range (4000 and above). It is obvious that the EOQ is lower than the price ranges so skip to the highest price.

Solving the EOQ at the highest price ($Q = 250$ and under):

$$C_O = 6$$
$$C_H = \frac{20}{100} * 6 = 1.2$$
$$C_P = 6$$
$$D = 4000$$
$$EOQ = \sqrt{\frac{(2 * 4000 * 6)}{1.2}}$$
$$= 200$$

EOQ is in the quantity range so calculate the total cost at the EOQ and all lower price points.

Q	Order cost	Holding cost	Cost of goods	Total cost
200	120	120	24 000	24 240
250	96	147.5	23 600	23 843.5
800	30	464	23 200	23 694
2000	12	1140	22 800	23 952
4000	6	2240	22 400	24 646

Therefore, the lowest cost and best order quantity is 800.

Fixed Order Period Inventory Systems

For **fixed order quantity inventory systems,** *fixed* quantities of items are ordered at varying time intervals. In a fixed order period inventory system *varying* quantities are placed at fixed time intervals. This means that a higher than normal demand will mean a larger order size rather than a shorter time between orders as in a fixed quantity model. The main attribute of the fixed interval model is that it only requires a periodic review of inventory levels to determine the order quantity required. A graph of inventory level over time for a fixed order interval system is shown in Figure 12.4.

It can be seen that the amount ordered at the fixed interval time period t is determined by the rate of demand during that period. Thus, the order amount A2 is much greater than the order amount A1 due to the relatively high demand during the period leading up to A2. The main advantage of using this system is that it enables a group of related components to be ordered at any one time, saving the cost of repeat deliveries and simplifying stock control. In addition, the need to continuously monitor stock, as in a fixed quantity system, is replaced by a periodic review and so saves monitoring duties.

> **FIXED ORDER PERIOD INVENTORY SYSTEMS:**
> systems in which varying quantities are placed at fixed time intervals.

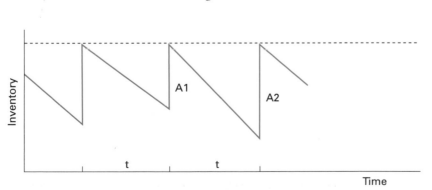

Figure 12.4 Inventory level versus time for the FOP inventory system

Fixed Order Inventory (FOI) Model

**FIXED ORDER
INVENTORY
MODEL:**

calculates the amount to
order given a fixed
interval between
ordering.

The **Fixed Order Inventory (FOI) model** can be used to calculate the amount to order given a fixed interval between ordering. The calculation for the FOI model is dependent on whether demand and delivery lead time are treated as fixed or variable. If it is assumed that deliveries are relatively constant and demand levels are variable, the equation for the amount to order is given as follows:

$$\text{Amount to order} = \text{Expected demand during protection interval}$$

$$+ \text{Safety stock}$$

$$- \text{Amount on hand at reorder time}$$

$$= \bar{d} * (OI + LT) + z * \sigma_d * \sqrt{OI + LT} - A$$

where
$\bar{d} =$ Average demand rate
$OI =$ Order interval (time between orders)
$LT =$ Delivery lead time
$z =$ Number of standard deviations from the mean
$\sigma_d =$ Standard deviation of demand rate
$A =$ Amount of units on hand at re-order time.

A variation on the fixed order interval system is when minimum and maximum levels are set for inventory. Thus, at a periodic interval review point, inventory is replenished up to the maximum level only if the inventory level is below a minimum level. A graph of inventory level over time is shown in Figure 12.5.

This system is suitable for low-cost items where the additional holding cost incurred when holding higher levels of inventory is offset by reductions in the need to order small amounts more frequently.

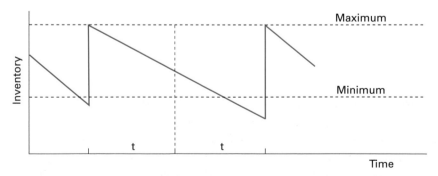

**Figure 12.5 Inventory level versus time for the FOI model with min/max
inventory levels**

Implementing Inventory Systems

In Chapter 15 the use of e-business is discussed in its role of facilitating the outsourcing of supply chain activities to third parties. Inventory management can also be outsourced in this way and, thus, is sometimes referred to as vendor-managed inventory. An example of this is when wholesalers hold stocks for a number of retailers. This allows the retailers to focus on selling activities and order stock from the wholesaler as needed. A number of e-business solutions are available in the area of inventory management which are usually provided as a module within a supply chain management or material management e-business system (Figure 12.6).

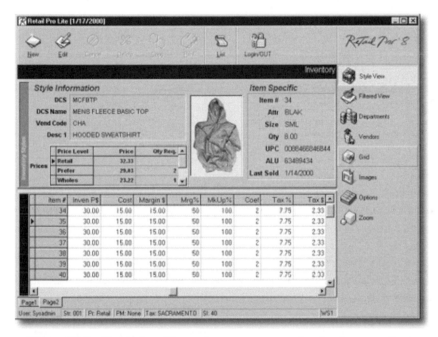

Figure 12.6   Example of inventory management e-business software

CASE STUDY 12.2

Implementing Inventory Systems

Retailers face two big challenges. The first is anticipating what customers want; the second is making sure they have enough of what customers want. Running out of stock is a nightmare. It harms a company's reputation for competence, and unhappy customers create a poor image for a company. Ian Dignum, sales director of Prolog, a marketing support services company, said: "Not all businesses need the same approach. But they all need access to good-quality data telling them which items are selling well, how many are in stock and whether they have enough to meet demand."

Prolog, which handles order processing and fulfilment for several government departments, as well as Corrs Brewers in Burton upon Trent, uses the Mailbrain software package. Dignum said: "If a purchase order is raised on Mailbrain, you can give the order a due-date so customer service staff can tell a customer when the item is likely to be in stock. If you cannot supply this kind of information, you are taking a risk with customer goodwill."

Michael Ross, managing director of Figleaves.com, an online lingerie retailer, agrees that collating sales data and interpreting them correctly is essential for any retailer's success. He said: "In our company every item is barcode-scanned in and out. We even monitor 'pick fails' – when someone goes to pick something off the shelf but it's not there. Every aspect of the business is monitored." Figleaves has its own analytical software, but most companies use established packages. For example, Matt Giles, commercial manager of I Want One Of Those, an online retailer of boys' toys, gadgets and gizmos, said: "Our system is based on Elucid's software. It gives us great data. We can tell the top 20 sellers by hour, day or year. We even know when stock is getting low in relation to purchase frequency."

But knowing which products are selling is one thing, predicting which ones will sell is another. Ross explained the difficulties in his business: "There are two distinct types of lingerie. First, you have your basics; long-running lines that are unlikely to go out of stock. We know how much we are selling each week, how long the deliveries take and the likelihood of deliveries arriving on time. Then, there are the fashion items. You have to predict what demand is likely to be, what styles and sizes are likely to be the most popular. This is hard. It's complicated further by volatility of demand and supply." Although making these decisions can be helped by software, a lot depends on knowing your customer intimately and having an instinct for market trends. That comes with experience and research.

A small, growing company must decide if it can handle inventory management and order fulfilment internally or whether outsourcing would make more sense. It is cheaper to do it internally, but more convenient to outsource. Businesses that keep logistics in-house face the hassle of needing to hire temporary staff at busy times. That cost becomes a millstone if you have overestimated demand. And if your systems cannot cope with increased orders, you risk alienating new customers if service standards drop.

Whether outsourced or done in-house, the key to successful inventory management is integrated systems. Your warehouse and call centre operations must be singing from the same hymn sheet, and your processing system should be able to handle all types of order method – mail, telephone or Internet. These days, most warehouse systems incorporate some form of barcode-scanning linked to an integrated order-handling database. You take a product off the shelf, scan it, and the software automatically updates the figures on how much of that product remains in stock.

Managing suppliers and developing a close relationship with them is another crucial element of inventory management. The more you can share data, the earlier you will be aware of potential supply problems. This is becoming easier now that the computing language XML is becoming standard for database systems. Giles said: "When a newspaper featured our remote-controlled plane, we sold 85 in 2 days. Until then we had been selling about 20 a week. Our supplier realized the importance of keeping the stock going and air-freighted them to us at no extra cost. "It wouldn't have done that if we didn't have an excellent relationship with that company."

Source: 'Keeping suppliers in order' by Matthew Wall, *Sunday Times*, 25 July 2004

Case Study 12.2 Question

1   Discuss the major issues raised in the case study concerning the introduction of an inventory management system.

Summary

1 Inventory management is important because it affects both customer service (inventory is needed to ensure goods and services are available) and costs (the purchase and holding costs of inventory items).

2 Inventory can be classified into buffer/safety, cycle, de-coupling, anticipation and pipeline/movement.

3 The ABC classification system can be used in order to identify appropriate inventory control policies for stock items.

4 The ROP model indicates the level of inventory at which point further inventory should be ordered to avoid a stock-out. The ROP model can take into consideration variable delivery lead time and variable demand characteristics for an item.

5 The EOQ model may be used to calculate a fixed order volume that minimizes total inventory costs. Inventory costs are assumed to consist of holding and ordering costs.

6 The FOI model may be used to calculate inventory order volumes when orders are placed at fixed time intervals.

7 Inventory management systems can be implemented using an e-business platform and are usually supplied as part of an integrated supply chain management system.

Exercises

1. Distinguish between the different types of inventory.
2. Evaluate the EOQ model for inventory control.

3. A typing pool requires 1000 boxes of typing paper each year. Each box is worth £20 and storage costs are 13.5% of stock value a year. The cost of placing an order is £15.

   a. For the order quantities 50, 100, 150, 200 and 250 calculate the storage cost, replenishment cost and total cost.

   b. Plot the costs in (a) on a graph.

   c. Show algebraically that delivery costs and storage costs are equal when 105 boxes are ordered at a time.

4. A company has a demand of 2000 items per annum. Stock ordering costs are fixed at £100 irrespective of the scale of replenishment. It costs £2.50 to hold one item in stock for 1 year. Calculate the EOQ.

5. A company experiences annual demand for 2500 units of the single product that it stocks. The replenishment cost for inventory is fixed at £400 regardless of the size of replenishment. Annual holding costs are £8 per unit. What is the optimum number of replenishments per annum?

6. Computers Ltd has expanded its range of computers and now requires each year, at a constant rate, 200 000 circuit boards which it obtains from an outside supplier. The order cost is £32. For any circuit board in stock it is estimated that the annual holding cost is equal to 10% of its cost. The circuit boards cost £8 each. No stock-outs are permitted.

   a. What is the optimal order size, and how many orders should be placed in a year?

   b. What are the ordering and holding costs and, hence, what is the total relevant inventory cost per annum?

   c. If the demand has been underestimated and the true demand is 242 000 circuit boards per annum, what would be the effect to the order quantity calculated in (a) and still meeting demand, rather than using a new optimal level?

7. The purchasing manager of an electrical components retailer holds a regular stock of light bulbs. Over the past year he has sold, on average, 25 a week and he anticipates that this rate of sale will continue during the next year (which you may assume to be 50 weeks). He buys light bulbs from his supplier at the rate of £5 for 10, and every time he places an order it costs on average £10 bearing in mind the necessary secretarial expenses and the time involved in checking the order. As a guide to the stockholding costs involved, the company usually value their cost of capital at 20% and as the storage space required is negligible, he decides that this figure is appropriate in this case. Furthermore, the prices charged to customers are determined by taking the purchasing and stockholding costs and applying a standard mark-up of 20%.

   a. Currently, the manager is reviewing the ordering and pricing policies and needs to know how many light bulbs he should order each time and what price he should charge. What would be your advice?

   b. If he now finds that he can get a discount of 5% for ordering in batches of 1000 would you advise him to amend the ordering and pricing policy that you have suggested and, if so, to what?

8. The manager of a large fishing tackle shop, open for 50 weeks each year, holds a regular stock of fishing flies. Although the manager has to purchase boxes of these items for £9.60 per box containing 12 flies he is prepared to sell them as single items. Over the past year he has sold, on average, 12 boxes of fishing flies each week and it is likely that this level of sales will continue into the future. Due to telephone, secretarial and transport costs it is estimated that the cost of receiving each order is £16. The annual cost of storage is estimated at 20% of the stock item value and is based on the cost of storage space and the company's cost of capital. The manager of the shop sets a price for his goods by taking the sum of the purchase cost and the appropriately allocated holding cost (storage and delivery) and then applying a mark-up of 50%.

   a. Determine the optimum number of boxes of fishing flies the shop manager should order at a time and the number of orders per year. Show that the selling price per fly that results from this optimum policy is £1.24.

   b. The supplier offers a discount of 4% on the price of each box of flies if the manager is prepared to purchase 500 boxes at a time. It can be assumed that there are no price effects on demand. Show whether or not this discount, assuming it is passed on, is advantageous or not to the customer in terms of shop price.

   c. What percentage discount is required for the order quantity if 500 boxes are to be beneficial to the customers?

References

Brown, S., Lamming, R., Bessant, J. and Jones, P. (2005), *Strategic Operations Management*, 2nd Edition, Elsevier Butterworth-Heinemann.

Maister, D.H. (1975), Centralisation of inventories and the square root law, *International Journal of Physical Distribution*.

Stevenson, W.J. (2005), *Operations Management*, 8th Edition, McGraw-Hill.

Waters, D. (2002), *Operations Management: Producing Goods and Services*, 2nd Edition, Financial Times/Prentice Hall.

Further Reading

Brown, S. (1996), *Strategic Manufacturing for Competitive Advantage*, Prentice Hall.

Kornafel, P. (2004), *Inventory Management and Purchasing: Tales and Techniques from the Automotive Aftermarket*, 1st Books Library.

Shingo, S. (1981), *Study of Toyota Production Systems*, Japan Management Association.

Waters, D. (2004), *Inventory Control and Management*, 2nd Edition, John Wiley & Sons.

Web Links

www.logistics.about.com/od/inventorymanagement/ Links to inventory management resources including background to the Square Root Law.

www.mapics.com MAPICS SA manufacturing software, including inventory management features.

www.inventoryops.com Guide containing extensive links to inventory articles and organizations.

Chapter 13

Lean Operations and JIT

■ **The Philosophy of JIT and Lean Operations**

- Eliminate Waste
- Involvement of Everyone
- Continuous Improvement

■ **JIT and Lean Techniques**

- Cellular Manufacturing
- JIT Supplier Networks
- Total Preventative Maintenance (TPM)
- Setup Reduction (SUR)
- Visual Control
- Push and Pull Production Systems
- *Kanban* Production System
- Levelled Scheduling
- Mixed Model Scheduling

■ **JIT in Service Systems**

■ **Implementing JIT and Lean Operations**

Learning Objectives

After reading this chapter, you should be able to:

1 To describe the two levels of JIT.

2 To explain the main elements of the lean philosophy.

3 To explain the need for JIT techniques.

4 To understand the relevance of the *kanban* production control system to JIT.

5 To discuss the concepts of levelled scheduling and mixed model scheduling.

6 To evaluate the use of JIT in service and administration systems.

7 To discuss the use of JIT and lean operations in service and administrative systems.

8 To evaluate when a JIT and lean implementation are appropriate.

Introduction

Lean operations is a concept that involves eliminating non-value-added activities from the entire supply chain. The term was first used by Womack *et al.* (1990) and is often used interchangeably with the concept of Just-In-Time (JIT). However, JIT traditionally only applies to the organization and its immediate suppliers, whilst lean operations encompasses the entire supply chain – Supply Chain Management (SCM) is covered in Chapter 15. The term 'lean' is meant to emphasize the concept of elimination of waste in all its forms. The concept continues to develop and Bicheno (2004) uses the term 'new lean' to describe an amalgam of traditional lean, theory of constraints (Chapter 11), Six Sigma (Chapter 18) and 'a range of relatively new concepts for measurements, analysis, and transformation'. In this chapter **JIT and lean operations** are considered interchangeably and as an integration of a philosophy and techniques designed to improve performance.

JIT AND LEAN OPERATIONS: integration of a philosophy and techniques designed to improve performance.

The Philosophy of JIT and Lean Operations

Just-In-time (JIT) and lean operations is a philosophy originating from the Japanese auto maker Toyota where Taiichi Ohno developed the Toyota Production system (Ohno, 1995). The basic idea behind JIT is to produce only what you need, when you need it. This may seem a simple idea but to deliver it requires a number of elements to be in place such as high quality and elimination of wasteful activities. Bicheno (1991) states that "JIT aims to meet demand instantaneously, with perfect quality and no waste." To achieve this aim requires a whole new approach, or philosophy, from the organization in how it operates. Three key issues identified by Harrison (1992) as the core of JIT philosophy are eliminate waste, involve everyone and continuous improvement. They are used here to explain the main elements of the lean philosophy.

Eliminate Waste

Waste is considered in the widest sense as any activity which does not add value to the operation. Bicheno (2004) states that although waste is strongly linked to lean, waste elimination is a means to achieving the lean ideal, it is not an end in itself and waste prevention is at least as important as waste elimination. The seven types of waste identified by Ohno (1995) are as follows:

1 *Over-production* – this is classified as the greatest source of waste and is an outcome of producing more than is needed by the next process.
2 *Waiting time* – this is the time spent by labour or equipment waiting to add value to a product. This may be disguised by undertaking unnecessary operations – e.g., generating Work In Progress (WIP) on a machine – which are not immediately needed (i.e., the waste is converted from time to WIP).
3 *Transport* – unnecessary transportation of WIP is another source of waste. Layout changes can substantially reduce transportation time.
4 *Process* – some operations do not add value to the product but are simply there because of poor design or machine maintenance. Improved design or preventative maintenance should eliminate these processes.
5 *Inventory* – inventory of all types (e.g., pipeline, cycle – see Chapter 12) is considered as waste and should be eliminated.
6 *Motion* – simplification of work movement will reduce waste caused by unnecessary motion of labour and equipment.
7 *Defective goods* – the total costs of poor quality can be very high and will include scrap material, wasted labour time and time expediting orders and loss of goodwill through missed delivery dates.

From a customer, rather than an organizational perspective the seven service wastes can be the basis for an improvement programme (Bicheno, 2004):

1 *Delay* on the part of customers waiting for service, for delivery, in queues, for response, not arriving as promised.
2 *Duplication* – having to re-enter data, repeat details on forms and answering queries from several sources within the same organization.

3   *Unnecessary movements* – queuing several times, poor ergonomics in the service encounter.

4   *Unclear communication* and the wastes of seeking clarification.

5   *Incorrect inventory* – out-of-stock, unable to get exactly what is required, substitute products or services.

6   *Opportunity lost* to retain or win customers, failure to establish rapport, ignoring customers, unfriendliness and rudeness.

7   *Errors* in the service transaction, product defects in the product–service bundle, lost or damaged goods.

Involvement of Everyone

JIT aims to create a new culture in which all employees are encouraged to contribute to continuous improvement efforts through generating ideas for improvements and perform a range of functions. In order to undertake this level of involvement the organization will provide training to staff in a wide range of areas, including techniques such as Statistical Process Control (SPC) and more general problem-solving techniques.

Continuous Improvement

CONTINUOUS IMPROVEMENT: a philosophy which believes that it is possible to get to the ideals of JIT by a continuous stream of improvements over time.

Continuous Improvement or *Kaizen*, the Japanese term, is a philosophy which believes that it is possible to get to the ideals of JIT by a continuous stream of improvements over time. Russell and Taylor (2005) adapt the ten principles given in Hiroyuki (1988) into the following principles for implementing a continuous improvement effort:

1   *Create a mind-set for improvement* – do not accept that the present way of doing things is necessarily the best.

2   *Try and try again* – don't seek immediate perfection but move to your goal by small improvements, checking for mistakes as you progress.

3   *THINK* – get to the real cause of the problem. Ask why five times.

4   *Work in teams* – use the ideas from a number of people to brainstorm new ways.

5   *Recognize that improvement knows no limits* – get in the habit of always looking for better ways of doing things.

Chapter 17 deals with the continuous improvement approach in more detail.

JIT and Lean Techniques

A wide variety of JIT techniques are considered to be within the lean philosophy. Concepts such as concurrent design, Design For Manufacture (DFM), mass customization, Failure Mode and Effect Analysis (FMEA) and Value Engineering (VE) are considered in Chapter 7. Additional techniques are considered below:

Cellular Manufacturing

To reduce transportation, machines are often moved from functional departments (i.e., all similar machines are placed together) to a cell which is a close grouping of different types of equipment, each of which performs a different operation – this is termed **cellular manufacturing**. Cell layouts are particularly suited to JIT manufacturing when it is feasible to dedicate equipment to the production of specific products. Equipment can be arranged close together in a U-shaped line to reduce transportation and material handling costs and allow multi-skilled workers to carry out a number of operations simultaneously. Chapter 4 covers cell layouts in more detail.

> **CELLULAR MANUFACTURING:** when equipment is placed in a cell layout which is a close grouping of different types of equipment, each of which performs a different operation.

JIT Supplier Networks

The JIT system requires a continuous stream of small batch supplies to ensure inventory is minimized within the organization. To achieve this, close long-term relationships are formed with a small number of suppliers – these are termed **JIT supplier networks**. Because of the frequency of deliveries in JIT supply, suppliers are usually situated relatively close to the organization. In order to facilitate DFM (Chapter 7) the organization will work with suppliers to improve component design and ensure quality. It is necessary for JIT suppliers to practice JIT supply themselves or to avoid inventory being 'pushed' back to them. Supply chain issues such as these are dealt with in more detail in Chapter 15.

> **JIT SUPPLIER NETWORKS:** formation of close long-term relationships with a small number of suppliers.

CASE STUDY 13.1

Satair

Satair, a supplier of parts and hardware to the aerospace industry, decided to invest in JIT to differentiate itself from competitors, to streamline the supply chain and to cut both its and its customers' costs. "We wanted to offer customers and potential customers lean supply techniques," says Steve Reading, Managing Director. Used by customers or by Satair employees at the business's site, the JIT system handles stock control and fulfilment. Barcodes are swiped as parts are used and the information is relayed back to the system which triggers JIT resupply and invoicing. Full stock usage history at each of the 15 offsite depots is recorded, and parts are also tracked through each stage of the supply chain. "We can see on our computers where every part is at every stage," says Steve. Operations with Satair's biggest customer are completely paperless via links to the customer's MRP system.

Source: www.dti.gov.uk/bestpractice
Crown copyright material is reproduced with the permission of HMSO and the Queen's Printer for Scotland

Case Study 13.1 Question

1   How is Satair helping its customers to implement lean operations?

Total Preventative Maintenance (TPM)

TOTAL PREVENTATIVE MAINTENANCE:

anticipates equipment failures through a programme of routine maintenance which will not only help to reduce breakdowns, but also to reduce downtime and lengthen the life of the equipment.

Total Preventative Maintenance (TPM) combines the practice of preventative maintenance with the ideas of total quality and employee involvement which form part of the JIT and Total Quality Management (TQM) philosophies. The idea behind preventative maintenance is to anticipate equipment failures through a programme of routine maintenance which will not only help to reduce breakdowns, but also to reduce downtime (time not in operation) and lengthen the life of the equipment. It has been realized that the cost of a maintenance programme can be outweighed by the more consistent output of a better quality product.

In a TPM programme all employees are encouraged to use their knowledge to improve equipment reliability and reduce variability in performance. When considering the cost implications of maintenance activities it is important to consider not just the cost of lost production due to poor maintenance but the costs associated with loss of business due to poor customer service.

TPM includes the following activities:

■ *Regular maintenance* activities such as lubricating, painting, cleaning and inspection. These activities are normally carried out by the operator in order to prevent equipment deterioration.
■ *Periodic inspection* to assess the condition of equipment in order to avoid breakdowns. These inspections are normally carried out at regular time intervals by either operator or maintenance personnel.
■ *Preventative repairs*, due to deterioration, but before a breakdown has occurred. Normally carried out by maintenance personnel but ideally by the operators.

TPM thus emphasizes the equipment operator's role in maintenance and considers preventative maintenance to be more than preventative repairs, but the execution of regular maintenance and inspection activities which ensures the equipment is in the best possible environment and is not allowed to deteriorate. This will require a programme of training of operators to maintain equipment over its life span. The TPM approach embraces the philosophy of continuous improvement in that the idea is not just to keep equipment operational but to make improvements to eliminate breakdowns (i.e., zero defects). To do this requires the design of products to include aspects such as the ease of maintenance of equipment used to produce that product.

Preventative maintenance uses a system of routine inspection and replacement of parts. This may lead to the equipment being out of service for periods of inspection or even replacement of parts during what could be productive time. Predictive maintenance uses a system of monitoring performance measures of equipment to predict failures, rather than a periodic check. Thus, by predicting problems in advance the maintenance activity may take place when the machine is not in use saving production output. Also, overtime payments and component expediting costs may be saved.

Predictive maintenance is undertaken using sensors which monitor variables such as vibration at critical points. These readings are tracked by computer which identifies trends in performance. Analysis of particles in lubricants and examination of equipment parts by fibre optics, eliminating the need for disassembly, can also help to predict problems and, thus, help plan maintenance outputs in advance.

The amount of preventative maintenance undertaken can be considered as a trade-off between the cost of preventative maintenance and the cost of breakdown maintenance. The amount of preventative maintenance will depend on a variety of factors such as the age of equipment (see notes on reliability, Chapter 7) but there is a point when too much preventative maintenance (e.g., rebuilding equipment everyday) can be too costly. The relationship between cost and preventative maintenance is shown graphically in Figure 13.1.

Setup Reduction (SUR)

In order to operate with the small batch sizes required by JIT it is necessary to reduce setup time (the time taken to adjust equipment to work on a different component) drastically because of the increased number of setups needed with small batches – this is termed **Setup Reduction (SUR)**. Originally, some operations such as stamping car door panels with a press die were done in very large batch sizes, and the output stored in inventory, because the setup time for the press could be measured in hours or even days. Shigeo Shingo was hired by Toyota to

SETUP REDUCTION (SUR): reduction of time taken to adjust a machine to work on a different component.

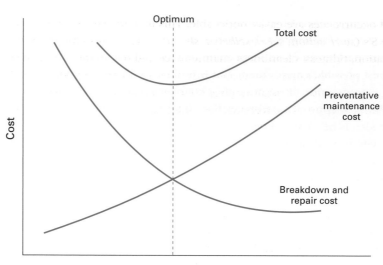

Figure 13.1   Cost versus amount of preventative maintenance

study how press die setup could be reduced and he achieved impressive results. For example, he reduced the setup time on one 1000-ton press from 6 hours to only 3 minutes. The system he developed became known as the Single Minute Exchange of Dies (SMED) and is based on the following principles:

1   *Separate internal setup from external setup* – setup tasks are classified as internal (they must be performed while the machine is stopped) and external (they can be performed in advance whilst the machine is running). Performing external setup tasks during operation and then delaying only for the internal setup tasks can reduce setup times by 30–50%.

2   *Convert internal setup to external setup* – this means ensuring any tasks normally undertaken during the internal setup phase (e.g., gathering tools, preheating an injection mould) are undertaken during the external phase.

3   *Streamline all aspects of setup* – this can be achieved by organizing tools near to the point of use and simplifying or eliminating operations.

4   *Perform setup activities in parallel or eliminate them entirely* – deploying extra people to a setup can reduce setup time by a considerable amount, maybe by more than double. Standardization of parts and raw materials can reduce or even eliminate setup requirements.

VISUAL CONTROL:
maintains an orderly workplace in which tools are easily available and unusual occurrences are easily noticeable.

Visual Control

Visual control is used to facilitate continuous improvement work. Visibility is about maintaining an orderly workplace in which tools are easily available and unusual occurrences are easily noticeable. This is achieved through what is called the five S's (*seiri, seiton, seiso, seiketsu, shitsuke*) which roughly translate as organization, tidiness, cleanliness, maintenance and discipline. To achieve these factors, visibility measures include *andon* signs (coloured lights), control systems such as the *kanban*, and performance charts such as Statistical Process Control (SPC) charts. Chapter 18 covers the SPC method.

Push and Pull Production Systems

In a push production system a schedule pushes work on to machines which is then passed through to the next work centre (Figure 13.2).

In Figure 13.2 materials (M1) and orders for production (O1) are 'pushed' onto Production Stage 1. Production Stage 1 then produces material for Production Stage 2 and the cycle repeats through the production stages. At each production stage a buffer stock (B1, B2, etc.) is kept to ensure that if any production stage fails then the subsequent production stage will not be starved of material. For example, if there is a breakdown at Stage 2 of the production line, Stage 3 will be fed from a buffer stock (B3) until the problem is fixed. The higher the buffer stocks kept at each stage of the line, the more disruption can occur without the production line being halted by lack of material.

The pull system developed by Ohno (1995) comes from the idea of a supermarket in which items are purchased by a customer only when needed and are replenished as they are removed. Thus, inventory coordination is controlled by a customer pulling items from the system which are then replaced as needed.

In a pull system (Figure 13.3) the process starts by an order for the finished product (e.g., car) at the end of the production line (O1). This then triggers an order for components of that item (O2), which in turn triggers an order for further sub-components (O2). The process repeats until the initial stage of

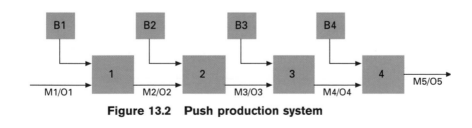

Figure 13.2 Push production system

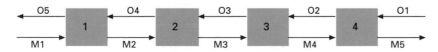

Figure 13.3 Pull production system

production and the material flows through the system as in the 'push' approach. Using the pull system the production system produces output at each stage only in response to demand and eliminates the need for buffer stock.

The aim of the elimination of buffers between production stages is necessary to ensure a responsive system. However, the pull system does not overcome the basic characteristic of a line layout that if one stage fails, all subsequent stages will be starved of work and, in effect, output from the whole production line is lost. This would seem to be a powerful argument for the retention of buffers, but the JIT approach actually argues that the disruption that occurs due to the lack of buffer stock will motivate people to find the root cause of problems. This, over time, will lead to a more reliable and efficient system. Motivation will be generated by the highly visible nature of any problem occurring (it will bring the whole factory to a halt!) and the fact that the problem is now everyone's problem and not just a local difficulty no one else is aware of. In moving from a push to a pull system it is common practice to gradually reduce the buffer levels as the production system reliability is increased. An attempt to move directly to eliminate buffers is likely to cause severe disruption to a system formerly reliant on this safety net.

The pull approach is applied not just to internal production systems, but to the relationship between customers and suppliers in the supply chain. Thus, suppliers in a lean supply chain are required to only supply customers in response to demand and the customer will not keep buffer stocks 'just-in-case' the supplier fails to deliver on time. This reduces inventory and increases responsiveness in the supply chain but does require close cooperation between customer and supplier and reliability in the supplier operations (see Chapter 15).

CASE STUDY 13.2

Goodwin Steel Castings

Goodwin Steel Castings' use of JIT systems has increased profits, reduced timescales and helped develop more competitive products. Faced with an extremely competitive market, steel manufacturer Goodwin Steel Castings decided to introduce just-in-time (JIT) working as part of an investment in technology aimed at improving the efficiency of their systems. Now, from taking orders and production through to process control and customer service, the company has integrated its systems. Since JIT is a demand-led process, Goodwin has worked with clients to ensure it can gauge their needs with maximum accuracy. Many of the company's clients now make their delivery schedules and requirements available on their web sites for Goodwin to retrieve. This information is then translated automatically into project updates which are available online for all customers. As orders are fed through to the foundry, electronic monitors place orders with the business's suppliers. Says General Manager Steven Birks, "The latest stage of our investment in JIT telemetry technology enables us to access information on their websites so we can get valuable management information like trends and historic usage." The main business benefit of integrating JIT technology into Goodwin's supply chain has been faster response times which has led to winning more orders, and the business being able to quote more accurately. The company has also managed to improve efficiency through closer monitoring of manufacturing.

Source: www.dti.gov.uk/bestpractice
Crown copyright material is reproduced with the permission of HMSO and the Queen's Printer for Scotland

1   Why are faster response times important in a JIT system?

**Case Study 13.2
Question**

Kanban Production System

There are a number of ways of implementing a pull production system including the drum buffer rope approach of OPT covered in Chapter 10. One system for implementing a pull system is called a ***kanban* production system**. Each *kanban* (Japanese for 'card' or 'sign') provides information on the part identification, quantity per container that the part is transported in and the preceding and next workstation. *Kanbans* in themselves do not provide the schedule for production but without them production cannot take place as they authorize the production and movement of material through the pull system. *Kanbans* need not be a card, but something that can be used as a signal for production such as a marker, or coloured square area. There are two types of *kanban* system, the single card and the two card.

The single-card system uses only one type of *kanban* card called the conveyance *kanban* which authorizes the movement of parts. The number of containers at a work centre is limited by the number of *kanbans*. A signal to replace inventory at the work centre can only be sent when the container is emptied. Toyota use a dual-card system which in addition to the conveyance *kanban*, utilizes a production *kanban* to authorize the production of parts. This system permits greater control over production as well as inventory. If the processes are tightly linked (i.e., one always follows the other) then a single *kanban* can be used.

In order for a *kanban* system to be implemented it is important that the seven operational rules that govern the system are followed. These rules can be summarized as follows:

■ *Move a kanban only when the lot it represents is consumed* – this means the whole of the batch of parts must be processed before the *kanban* is sent to the preceding process to ask for more parts.

■ *No withdrawal of parts without a kanban is allowed* – no process can move parts without the authorization of a *kanban* request.

> *KANBAN PRODUCTION SYSTEM:*
> to implement a pull system a *kanban* is used to pass information such as the part identification, quantity per container that the part is transported in and the preceding and next workstation.

- *The number of parts issued to the subsequent process must be the exact number specified by the kanban* – this means a *kanban* must wait until sufficient parts are made before the lot of parts is moved.
- *A kanban should always be attached to the physical product* – this means the *kanban* should travel with the parts themselves and be visible.
- *The preceding process should always produce its parts in the quantities withdrawn by the subsequent process* – this means processes should never overproduce parts in any quantity.
- *Defective parts should never be conveyed to the subsequent process* – a high level of quality must be maintained because of the lack of buffer inventory. A feedback mechanism which reports quality problems quickly to the preceding process must be implemented.
- *Process the kanbans in every work centre strictly in the order in which they arrive at the work centre.*
- *If several kanbans are waiting for production they must be served in the order that they have arrived* – if the rule is not followed, there will be a gap in the production rate of one or more of the subsequent processes.

The operation for a dual-card *kanban* system is outlined in Figure 13.4.

1   A production *kanban* arrives at Process B, attached to an empty container. Process B is activated to fill the container.
2   Process B requests inputs from Process A to fulfil 1.
3   A withdrawal *kanban* is sent to Process A to fulfil 2.
4   A full container is sent from Process A to Process B.
5   The production *kanban*, which was attached to the container in 4, is placed on an empty container, activating Process A.
6   Process A requests inputs to fulfil 5. A withdrawal *kanban* is not activated as sufficient stock is present.

The *kanban* system is similar to the re-order point inventory system but has the objective of the continual reduction of inventory. The amount of inventory can be reduced over time by reducing the number of *kanbans* in the system. The formula

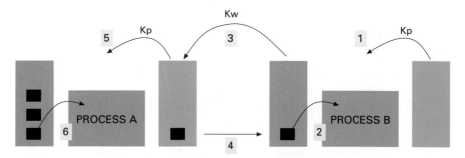

Figure 13.4   Dual-card *kanban* system

suggested by Hall (1989) for the number of *kanbans* at each production stage is given below:

$$y = \frac{D(T_W + T_P)(1 + X)}{a}$$

where
   y = Total number of *kanbans* (production and conveyance) for a part

   D = Planned usage rate (units/day)

   T_W = Average waiting time for replenishment of parts (fraction of a day)

   T_P = Average production time for a container of parts (fraction of a day)

   X = A policy variable corresponding to possible inefficiencies in the system

   a = Capacity of a standard container in units (should usually be less than 10% of daily usage for that part).

Setting X to zero provides just enough inventory ($y \times a$) to cover the time required to produce and move a container of parts.

The system is implemented with a given number of cards in order to obtain a smooth flow. The number of cards is then decreased, decreasing inventory, and any problems which surface are tackled. Cards are decreased, one at a time, to continue the continuous improvement process. It is important to note that a successful implementation of a *kanban* system will require a stable and reliable production system to be in place. That requires prior introduction of many of the lean techniques described here, including setup reduction, total preventative maintenance and levelled scheduling.

CASE STUDY 13.3

Messier-Dowty

Messier-Dowty designs, develops, manufactures and supports landing gear systems for over 19 000 aircraft worldwide. Despite the firm's success, David Johnson, team leader for systems and supplier development, says: "We realized that we were not meeting our customers' expectations. We needed to reach 'zero defect' status, be cost competitive and deliver our products on time every time. To achieve the highest performance standards, we needed a systematic approach." Crucially, the changes needed to be made along the supply chain, improving flow, reducing batch sizes and improving overall quality.

A structured solution was the key: Messier-Dowty introduced a programme of training, diagnostics, workshops and reviews for its own staff and its newly formed 'Supply Chain Group'. Lean systems were introduced to eliminate waste at each stage of production. Following an extensive analysis of production techniques, work flows and key suppliers, the manufacturing process was broken into logical blocks, using *kanban* – a production control system where components are supplied only when demanded and arrive 'just-in-time'. This creates a more accurate replenishment cycle, cuts lead time, makes inventories more precise and, ultimately, reduces costs.

Initially, the changes involved 19 of its suppliers. Rather than take on new staff, Messier-Dowty hired consultants to manage the change. The cost was £38 000, but the programme saved over £350 000 in operating costs in the first year, and £470 000 in the year after. Other members of the Supply Chain Group reported savings of up to £315 000 in the first year with minimal extra expenditure. These saving have then been shared with Messier-Dowty through price cuts. As David Johnson points out:

"While this was never intended to be a cost-saving initiative, it's clear that cutting waste and improving the quality of our performance has created considerable financial benefits."

Dramatic changes have occurred in the speed and reliability of supplies. The *kanban* system means that over 200 supplies are now delivered on time, 100% of the time. Suppliers have also responded positively. Paul Buckley, of Ultra Electronics has noticed that: "Our involvement in the Messier-Dowty supply chain group has focused our attention on improving our manufacturing process by significantly reducing waste. At Ultra we have been working on improvement activities with the aim of sustaining 100% on-time delivery and total customer satisfaction."

At first, not all the suppliers in the group were convinced that the changes would be mutually beneficial. Paul Foulds, from supply company Middlesex Group, says: "Initially there was some scepticism. We'd made attempts at introducing change before, but these initiatives had not been followed through with sufficient conviction. Neither I nor my colleagues knew very much about these techniques at first, but it seemed a practical proposal that offered the opportunity to improve the business while working with one of our major customers."

Central to Messier-Dowty's success was its programme of engagement with suppliers. It trained 57 advocates for the programme internally and 35 advocates among its suppliers to ensure the changes were communicated and managed effectively. Messier-Dowty intends to introduce new suppliers to the initiative at the outset of the business relationship. The firm will continue to work with existing suppliers to eliminate waste, and to monitor and report progress to ensure that the initiative grows with the business.

David Johnson thinks that the results have had a more far-reaching effect than his team at Messier-Dowty could have predicted: "Ultimately, it's a high standard of delivery that satisfies the customer. Focusing on improving our delivery performance has changed the way we do business, and I think we'll be enjoying the benefits for many years to come."

Source: www.dti.gov.uk/bestpractice
Crown copyright material is reproduced with the permission of HMSO and the Queen's Printer for Scotland

Case Study 13.3 Question

1   How has the introduction of lean systems succeeded in improving delivery performance?

Levelled Scheduling

The approach to scheduling which has been followed in traditional manufacturing systems is to make a large number of one product before switching to another. Unfortunately, this approach will lead to high levels of finished goods inventory at some times (the end of a production run) with the possibility of not being able to satisfy customer demand at other times (when long production runs of other goods are being manufactured). A **level assembly schedule** attempts to overcome this problem by producing the smallest reasonable number of units of each product at a time.

> **LEVELLED SCHEDULING:**
> a level assembly schedule produces the smallest reasonable number of units of each product at a time.

Mixed Model Scheduling

Mixed model scheduling attempts to spread the production of several different end items evenly throughout each day. This results in a constant rate of flow all day, rather than in different rates for different products. If, say, three different products are to be produced then the ideal schedule would be to produce the products in sequence throughout the day. Usually, however, the products in the sequence will be needed in different quantities so that the sequence will need to be adjusted to reflect that.

> **MIXED MODEL SCHEDULING:**
> spreads the production of several different end items evenly throughout each day.

When a level assembly schedule has been achieved the production of each item will closely match demand. However, because the flow of component parts must be adjusted to match the rate at which finished goods will be produced it is necessary to match the cycle time (the rate of production) at the work centres with the demand rate.

Worked Example 13.1

Mixed Model Scheduling

If total demand for 3 products is 80 units a day and production is available for 8 hours (480 minutes) a day the cycle time is as follows:

$$\text{Cycle time} = \frac{\text{Working time per day}}{\text{Units required per day}}$$

$$\text{Cycle time} = \frac{480}{80}$$

$$= 6 \text{ minutes/unit}$$

Extending the cycle time calculation for each product, based on a mixed model sequence:

Product	Daily demand	Cycle time (minutes)
A	40	480/40 = 12
B	10	480/10 = 48
C	30	480/30 = 16

One possible assembly sequence could be ACACBACA. One unit of Product A will be produced every 12 minutes on average throughout the day to a level assembly schedule. This means that components must be supplied to Product A to match this cycle time. Also, the system must be coordinated to produce either A, B or C once every 6 minutes. To achieve these results requires that sufficient equipment and labour are configured and setup times minimized.

JIT in Service Systems

JIT is usually associated with manufacturing applications because this is the setting in which it was developed and has been applied most frequently. However, many of the ideas behind JIT can be employed in service settings. For example, Schniederjans (1993) presents introductory JIT implementation strategies that can be applied to almost all administration organizations:

■ Everybody in an administration department should serve as a customer service agent. Service quality is everybody's responsibility in a JIT administration. When poor quality is observed in the delivery of an administration service that can be corrected the individual worker or department that is responsible should be made to implement the correction.
■ Management should be willing to sacrifice production for improved quality and allow workers extra time for JIT activities such as quality control.
■ All employees should be multi-functional to increase worker flexibility and help workers understand more of the operation.
■ Walls and departmental barriers cause greater routing, filing, walking and proofing and should be restructured into various groups of workers or Group Technology (GT) cell workstations with multi-functional skills. Multiple cells allows more than one channel through which work can flow, increasing flexibility to better balance work load with variable capacity. In a departmental system if one department is backlogged other offices will become idle and inefficiencies can occur. Also, elimination of departments decreases much duplication and can substantially reduce the amount of commonly used equipment, filing cabinets and storage areas.

■ Standardizing work procedures can save time in training and improve operational efficiency by removing a job complexity. Standardizing order forms and routing systems can also reduce complexity and helps workers understand processes and, thus, suggest improvements.

Womack and Jones (2005) have developed lean thinking principles for adaptation to the processes of consumption. This involves streamlining the systems for providing goods and services using six principles:

1   Solve the customer's problem completely by ensuring that all the goods and services work, and work together.
2   Don't waste the customer's time.
3   Provide exactly what the customer wants.
4   Provide what's wanted exactly where it's wanted.
5   Provide what's wanted where it's wanted exactly when it's wanted.
6   Continually aggregate solutions to reduce the customer's time and hassle.

Implementing JIT and Lean Operations

JIT and lean operations has been covered in this chapter both as a philosophy and as a set of techniques.

From the viewpoint of JIT as a philosophy of the elimination of waste it can be seen as applicable to all organizations, small or large, manufacturing or service. At this level JIT requires organizational systems to be developed around identifying and eliminating waste. The main implementation issues concern the requirement of a problem-solving culture of trust and cooperation within the workforce. It is also likely that problem identification and problem solving activities will be more successful at a higher volume of output which gives a better chance for learning to occur.

At the level of JIT as a collection of tools and techniques it is more likely to be applicable to medium to high volumes of products which have reached a mature development phase in the market. JIT techniques include the *kanban* production control system. Prerequisites for the implementation of this type of system include aspects such as layout design (e.g., cell manufacturing) (Chapter 5), SUR (Chapter 13), line balancing (Chapter 4) and TQM techniques (Chapter 17) such as SPC (Chapter 18).

CASE STUDY 13.4

From Just-in-Time to 'Just in Case'

Many companies have honed their competitive edge by adopting the just-in-time philosophy that involves producing goods to meet demand exactly in time, quality and quantity. But such highly-tuned systems leave manufacturers vulnerable to disruptions in any of the many links in their supply chain. "More and more, companies are trying to walk that fine line between up-front investment in capabilities, product and inventories before they know what their customers' demand is going to be," says Ed Starr, partner in Accenture's supply chain management practice. "So we have an environment where there's less room for error."

Disruptions in the supply chain can take many forms and range from those that affect single companies or sectors to the entire supply chain. The 2002 strike of dockworkers at US west coast ports paralysed transport of goods across the Pacific, leaving retailers and manufacturers short of goods and Asian producers with exports piling up. Other incidents can have a dramatic impact. As well as killing more than 2000 people, the 1999 earthquake in Taiwan revealed the dependency of the world's PC maker on the country's supply of vital components such as chips, memory and motherboards. Leading chipmakers lost several days' production, mainly because of power shortages, creating a knock-on effect throughout the industry. At the other end of the scale, a single fire in a factory can have an equally disruptive effect on the business of a company.

As well as individual incidents, manufacturers and retailers must face an increasing volatility of demand – particularly in areas such as electronic equipment and fashion – as wider consumer choices turn buyers into ever more fickle customers. Set against these risks is an increasingly competitive business environment, which is driving companies to produce goods more quickly, cheaply and efficiently. "But all the activities that we classify as reducing waste or creating more efficiency amount to eliminating buffers from the systems," says Eitan Zemel, professor of operations management at New York University's Stern School of Business. "We work with less inventory, less spare capacity, less lead time and that makes more elements of the systems critical, so that if something goes down the damage could propagate to a much wider area."

Mr Starr advocates an approach to supply chain operations whereby not all eggs are kept in one basket. This means, for example, not relying on a single supplier. "In business, hedging is the best long-term result," he says. "The challenge is that you can also prove it doesn't frequently turn out to be the best short-term move." Nevertheless, when it comes to the volatility of demand, Mr Starr believes companies can profit from building the ability to react quickly into their business models. He cites the example of Zara, the Spanish fashion chain, which brought some of its manufacturing back in-house because lead times were proving too long to respond to the appetite for new fashions. "They have also set up capabilities to have inputs from customers in their stores and they get that within the next day into what they build and distribute," he says.

To deal with fluctuations in the supply of components for its computers, Dell Computer uses pricing as a fast and flexible tool via its online sales. "Dell may raise the price of the 60-megabyte hard drive price and lower the price of the 80 megabyte – or they'll offer free upgrades," says Yossi Sheffi, professor and head of MIT's Centre for Transportation Studies. "This is a sign that they have bought too much of one and not enough of the other, rather than that they have suddenly become generous." Prof. Sheffi and his colleagues at MIT have launched the Supply Chain Response to Terrorism, a research project that studies the impact of terrorism – as well as other incidents – on global supply chains. "[Flexibility] can provide incredible competitive advantage," he says. "And companies that are building flexibility into their way of doing business can even create variability in the demand by, for example, offering more versions – different coloured phones, for example – and smaller quantities of each."

Prof. Sheffi also believes that lean production techniques are not necessarily incompatible with building security into the supply chain. He cites the experience of Hewlett-Packard. Because in Europe it needs to produce printers for markets, each with its own language – requiring different instructions and software – and power supply, the company redesigned both the machines and its distribution network. It now manufactures standardized printers that are sent to a centralized European distribution centre where the right language and power cords are fitted.

Source: FT.com site, Sarah Murray, 8 March 2004
Reproduced by permission of Sarah Murray

1   What are the advantages and pitfalls of using a JIT approach to supply customers?

**Case Study 13.4
Question**

Summary

1 JIT can be seen on one level as a philosophy and on a second level as a set of tools and techniques.

2 The core of the JIT philosophy are the concepts of elimination of waste, involvement of everyone and continuous improvement.

3 JIT tools and techniques are required to implement lean operations.

4 JIT tools and techniques include design for manufacture, VE and value analysis, cellular manufacturing, JIT supplier networks, TPM, SUR and visual control.

5 JIT planning and control is based on the *kanban* production control system.

6 The techniques of levelled scheduling and mixed model scheduling attempt to match the production of each item with demand.

7 JIT and lean techniques may be applicable to service and administration systems.

8 JIT and lean operations require a problem-solving culture and are more likely to be applicable to medium- to high-volume organizations in mature markets.

Exercises

1. Explain the main elements of the JIT and lean philosophy.
2. Provide an analysis of the techniques used to implement a JIT philosophy in a manufacturing organization.
3. Distinguish between preventative and predictive maintenance.
4. Explain, using an example, how you would utilize the concepts of JIT in a service operations environment.
5. Evaluate the advantages and disadvantages of the JIT approach to production planning.
6. To gain efficiency it is essential to minimize the time it takes to make a car. Compare how this is achieved under traditional and lean operations approaches.
7. Why is the traditional approach to production control termed a 'buffered system'?
8. Discuss how JIT and lean operations can enhance flexibility.

References

Bicheno, J. (1991), *Implementing Just-in-Time*, IFS.

Bicheno, J. (2004), *The New Lean Toolbox: Towards Fast, Flexible Flow*, PICSIE Books.

Hall, R.W. (1989), *Attaining Manufacturing Excellence*, Richard D. Irwin.

Harrison, A. (1992), *Just-in-time in Perspective*, Prentice Hall.

Hiroyaki, H. (1988), *JIT Factory Revolution*, Productivity Press.

Ohno, T. (1995), *Toyota Production System: Beyond Large-Scale Production*, Productivity Press.

Russell, R.S. and Taylor, B.W. (2005), *Operations Management*, 5th Edition, John Wiley & Sons.

Schniederjans, M.J. (1993), *Topics in Just-In-Time Management*, Allyn & Bacon.

Womack, J.P. and Jones, D.T. (2005), Lean consumption, *Harvard Business Review*, March, 1–11.

Womack, J.P., Jones, D.T. and Roos, D. (1990), *The Machine that Changed the World*, Rawson Associates.

Further Reading

Drew, J., McCallum, B. and Roggenhofer, S. (2004) *Journey to Lean: Making Operational Change Stick*, Palgrave Macmillan.

Krafcik, J.F. (1988), Triumph of the lean production system, *Sloan Management Review*, Fall, 41–52.

Schonberger, R. (1982), *Japanese Manufacturing Techniques*, Free Press.

Schonberger, R. (1996), *World Class Manufacturing: The Next Decade*, Free Press.

Web Links

www.nummi.com New United Motor Manufacturing Inc. Joint venture of General Motors Corporation and Toyota Motor Corporation to introduce the Toyota Production System and a teamwork-based working environment to the United States.

www.toyota.com Toyota UK. News and information regarding Toyota.

www.lean.org Lean Enterprise Institute. Details workshops and tools for lean implementation.

www.shingoprize.com Shingo Prize for Excellence in Manufacturing.

Chapter 14

Enterprise Resource Planning

■ Resource Planning

■ Material Requirements Planning

- Master Production Schedule
- Bill Of Materials (BOM)
- Inventory Status File (ISF)
- MRP Calculations
- MRP Reports
- MRP Implementation

■ Manufacturing Resource Planning (MRP II)

■ Distribution Requirements Planning (DRP)

■ Enterprise Resource Planning (ERP)

Learning Objectives

After reading this chapter, you should be able to:

1 Describe the elements in resource planning.

2 Understand the concept of Materials Requirements Planning (MRP).

3 Describe the components of Manufacturing Requirements Planning (MRP).

4 Understand the concept of Manufacturing Resource Planning (MRP II).

5 Understand the concept of Distribution Requirements Planning (DRP).

6 Understand the concept of Enterprise Resource Planning (ERP).

Introduction

This chapter covers the resource planning systems of Materials Requirements Planning (MRP), Manufacturing Resource Planning (MRP II), Distribution Requirements Planning (DRP) and Enterprise Resource Planning (ERP).

MRP systems are used to determine the timing and quantity of material requirements. These systems are usually associated with the management of dependent demand items such as raw materials, components or sub-assemblies. Although most used in manufacturing, it is also seen in services, particularly mass services when an actual product is manufactured as part of the service delivery process (e.g., fast food outlets). MRP aims to ensure that just the right quantity of each item is held at the right time in order to meet the needs of the production schedule taking into account ordering and manufacturing lead times. MRP II systems are a development of MRP and connect the system to other functional areas such as marketing and finance. DRP widens the traditional acquisition, handling and production functions of MRP across the supply chain so that another form of dependent demand can be considered between the producer of goods, the regional distribution centre, the local distribution outlets or retailers and the customer. ERP systems are a further development and provide integration of software applications in different functional areas and provide links to external customers and suppliers in the supply chain.

Resource Planning

The elements involved in resource planning are shown in Figure 14.1.

The first step in resource planning is to generate an **aggregate plan** (also called the 'production plan') which identifies the resources required in the medium term (6–18 months). The **demand profile** consists of the products and services required by the marketing plan, future customer orders and other demand factors such as the manufacture of items for spares. The aggregate plan will specify aspects such as overall production rate, size of the workforce, the amount of subcontracting required to deliver the mix of products or service required to meet the demand profile. The plan will not normally detail the amount of resource necessary for a

AGGREGATE PLAN: specifies aspects such as overall production rate, size of the workforce, the amount of subcontracting required to deliver the mix of products or service required to meet the demand profile.

DEMAND PROFILE: consists of the products and services required by the marketing plan, future customer orders and other demand factors such as the manufacture of items for spares.

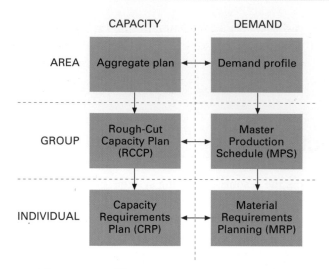

CAPACITY   DEMAND

AREA — Aggregate plan ↔ Demand profile

GROUP — Rough-Cut Capacity Plan (RCCP) ↔ Master Production Schedule (MPS)

INDIVIDUAL — Capacity Requirements Plan (CRP) ↔ Material Requirements Planning (MRP)

Figure 14.1   Elements in resource planning

particular product or service but will provide figures aggregated at the level of product or service families. The plans may be updated on a monthly basis and can incorporate the concepts of lead capacity, lag capacity and the use of inventory to smooth demand (see the capacity timing section in Chapter 5). There are many different aggregate plans that can be formulated to produce a particular output, so each plan should be evaluated in terms of factors such as cost, customer service, operational effectiveness and effect on workforce morale.

The next stage in the planning process is to develop the **Master Production Schedule (MPS)** which shows how many products or services are planned for each time period, based on the resources authorized in the aggregate plan. Thus, the aggregate plan shows how the number of products or services are to be produced in a time period (say, 500 a month) while the MPS specifies the actual products or services to be produced (say, 200 of Service A, 150 of Service B and 150 of Service C, making 500 in total). The MPS is based on information from the aggregate plan (based on the demand profile) and any other forms of demand which require capacity in the short term (e.g., new customer orders). The MPS is then used by the rough-cut capacity planning process to calculate rough estimates of the workload placed by the schedule on key resource constraints. Most operations will have bottleneck resources which constrain the overall production capacity. Checking at this level may save unnecessary detailed planning. If the capacity is not available to meet the MPS, either additional capacity must be secured or the MPS must be adjusted, although this may mean that the marketing plan may not be achieved.

As stated earlier, the aggregate plan takes information from the marketing plan to identify the resources required to deliver the products and services specified. The **Rough-Cut Capacity Plan (RCCP)** takes information from the MPS to evaluate

MASTER PRODUCTION SCHEDULE (MPS): shows how many products or services are planned for each time period, based on the resources authorized in the aggregate plan.

ROUGH-CUT CAPACITY PLAN (RCCP): takes information from the MPS to evaluate the feasibility of the MPS.

the feasibility of the MPS. A third level of checking of capacity is the **Capacity Requirements Plan (CRP)** which takes information from the MRP system to calculate workloads for critical work centres or workers. This allows the feasibility of the MRP system and the use of the critical work centres or workers to be evaluated.

CAPACITY REQUIREMENTS PLAN (CRP): takes information from the MRP system to calculate workloads for critical work centres or workers.

Materials Requirements Planning

Materials Requirements Planning (MRP) is an information system used to calculate the requirements for component materials needed to produce end items. These components have what is called 'dependent demand' (the management of independent demand items is covered in Chapter 12). A dependent demand item has a demand which is relatively predictable because it is dependent on other factors. For example, a fireplace mantel consists of 2 legs and 1 shelf. If daily demand for the mantel, derived from the production schedule, is 50 mantels, then a daily demand of 100 legs and 50 shelves can be predicted. Thus, a dependent demand item can be classified as having a demand that can be calculated as the quantity of the item needed to produce a scheduled quantity of an assembly that uses that item. MRP systems manage dependent demand items by calculating the quantity needed and the timing required (taking into account purchasing and manufacturing lead times) of each item. The components of an MRP system which use and process this information are shown in Figure 14.2.

Each component of the MRP system is now described.

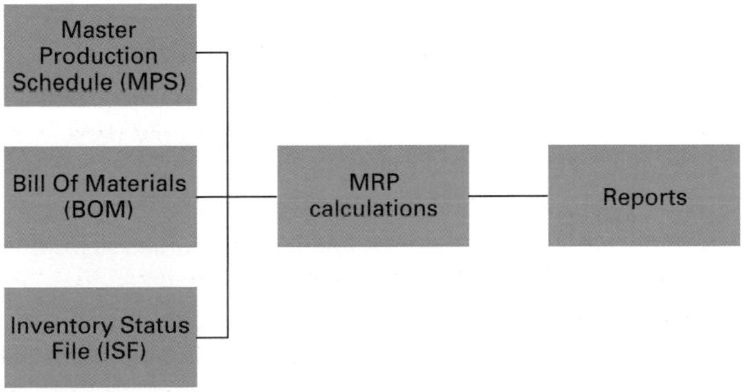

MATERIALS REQUIREMENTS PLANNING (MRP): an information system used to calculate the requirements for component materials needed to produce end items.

Figure 14.2   Components of an MRP system

Master Production Schedule (MPS)

An ideal **Master Production Schedule (MPS)** is one which most efficiently uses the organization's capacity while being able to meet customer due-dates. The master schedule provides a plan for the quantity and timing of when orders are required. The MRP system will use this information and take into account delivery, production and supply lead times and will indicate when materials are needed to achieve the master schedule. The MPS will usually show plans based on time 'buckets' based on, for example, a day or a week. The length of the time bucket will generally be longer (e.g., a month) for planning purposes and become shorter closer to the present time for detailed production planning tasks.

The MPS will usually contain a mix of both plans for customer-ordered items and plans to produce to forecast sales. The forecast is a best estimate of what future demand will be which may be derived from past sales and contact with the customer. These forecasts should be replaced by firm orders as the expected order date approaches. If actual orders exceed the forecast then either the order will be delivered to the customer late or extra capacity must be obtained (e.g., overtime, subcontracting) to meet the customer delivery date.

The mix of forecast and firm orders that a business can work to depends on the nature of the business. A resource-to-order company (e.g., a construction firm) will only allocate resources and materials to a firm order. Purchase-to-order organizations will not order materials until a firm order is made, but will have labour and equipment permanently available. A make-to-stock business, however, will work mainly to forecast demand. Most operations will actually operate with different P : D ratios (Chapter 11) for different product or service types. The mix between firm orders and forecast demand may also vary over time for a certain business. For example, seasonal effects may increase the number of firm orders taken in certain time periods.

Bill Of Materials (BOM)

The **Bill Of Materials (BOM)** identifies all the components required to produce a scheduled quantity of an assembly and the structure of how these components fit together to make that assembly. The BOM can be viewed as a product structure tree, similar to an organization chart (Figure 14.3). In this example the item description is followed by the number of items required in square brackets and the item part number.

The final assembly of the product structure is denoted as level 0, while the structure is 'exploded' to further levels representing sub-assemblies below this. These sub-assemblies are then broken down into further levels until the individual order components are reached. Individual order components can either be a

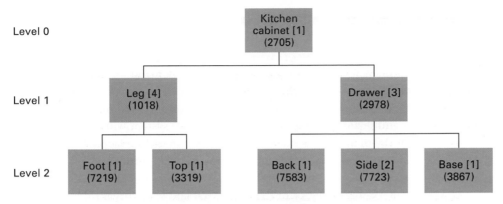

Figure 14.3   Bill Of Materials (BOM) product structure

Table 14.1   Indented Bill Of Materials

Level	Part No.	Quantity	Description
0	2705	1	Kitchen cabinet
1	1018	4	Leg
1	2978	3	Drawer
2	7219	1	Foot
2	3319	1	Top
2	7583	1	Back
2	7723	2	Side
2	3867	1	Base

single component item or sub-assemblies purchased from suppliers and thus treated as a single component. The tree structure shown in Figure 14.3 is useful to show the relationships between components, but to present the structure in a format suitable for processing by the computerized MRP system, an indented BOM is used (Table 14.1).

The MRP system holds information on the number required of any item in the structure and the 'parent' item of which it is a component. Usually, the product structure is stored in a series of single-level BOMs, each of which holds a component part number and a list of the part numbers and quantities of the next lower level. The computer will move through all component BOMs in the product structure to derive a total number of components required for the product. Note the same component may appear in different parts of the product structure if it is used more than once. What is needed is the total number required for each component to make the final assembly. The accuracy of the BOM is obviously vital in generating the correct schedule of parts at the right time.

Inventory Status File (ISF)

The BOM indicates the quantity of components needed derived from the product structure, but this will not be directly translated into demand for components because it is likely that some of the components will be currently held in inventory. The **Inventory Status File (ISF)** provides information on the identification and quantity of items in stock. The MRP system will determine if a sufficient quantity of an item is in stock or an order must be placed. The inventory status file will also contain the lead time, or time between order and availability, for each component.

INVENTORY STATUS FILE (ISF): provides information on the identification and quantity of items in stock.

As with the BOM, the accuracy of the ISF is vital and some organizations use Perpetual Physical Inventory (PPI) checking to ensure that inventory records are accurate. This means a continuous check of inventory records against actual stock, instead of the traditional year end checks for accounting purposes.

MRP Calculations

The time-phased inventory status record can be used to show the inventory data requirements for each stock item. A simplified status record is shown in Table 14.2.

In this case weekly time buckets have been used, which is usual for short-term plans. Longer time buckets may be used for long-term planning purposes. The definition of each row is given below:

■ *Gross requirements* – this row simply states the estimated requirements, in this case per week, for the item described. It is assumed that requirements occur during the time bucket (week) so that the scheduled receipts at the beginning of the week will cover them.

Table 14.2 Time-phased inventory record

		Week				
Item: Sub-assembly 1	0	1	2	3	4	5
Gross requirements		100	0	200	0	30
Scheduled receipts				200		
Projected on hand	100	0	0	0	0	−30

Table 14.3 Inventory status file showing net requirements

				Week		
Item: Sub-assembly 1	0	1	2	3	4	5
Gross requirements		100	0	200	0	30
Scheduled receipts				200		
Projected on hand	100	0	0	0	0	−30
Net requirements						30
Planned order release				30		

■ *Scheduled receipts* – this row indicates when the item becomes available for use, from a previously released order. It is assumed that the receipt of the item occurs at the start of the time bucket period.

■ *Projected on hand* – numbers in this row show the number of units to be available at the end of each time bucket based on the balance of requirements and receipts. The formula for projected-on-hand is shown below:

$$\text{Projected on hand} = \text{Inventory on hand} + \text{Scheduled receipts}$$
$$- \text{Gross requirements}$$

To account for a negative projected on hand, the time-phased inventory status record is extended as in Table 14.3.

■ *Net requirements* – if the projected on hand is negative it is called a net requirement and means there will not be enough of this component to produce the quantities required to meet the MPS. Thus, when a negative projected on hand is shown this will increase the net requirements row by a positive amount equal to the negative on hand.

■ *Planned order release* – the Planned Order Release (POR) row indicates when an order should be released to ensure that the projected-on-hand figure does not become negative (i.e., there are enough items to satisfy the MPS). The POR time must take into consideration the lead time between placing the order and the component becoming available (in the case of Table 14.2 the lead time is 2 weeks). Thus, the planned order release is offset by the required time amount to ensure enough items are available to cover net requirements and, sometimes, to also cover net requirements in future time buckets. It is important that the MRP program works through all the levels of the assembly before calculating the net requirement for a time bucket, as the same item may be needed at different levels of the same assembly or in different assemblies.

Worked Example 14.1

A dentist has scheduled appointments for their surgery over the next 4 weeks.

Week	1	2	3	4
Appointments scheduled	30	60	55	60

Surgical gloves are ordered of 100 pairs at a time and the ordering lead time is 2 weeks. There are 75 pairs of gloves in inventory at the start of Week 1 with another 100 pairs expected to arrive during that week. Use MRP to schedule planned order releases for the gloves.

Item: gloves	0	1	2	3	4
Gross requirements		30	80	75	60
Scheduled receipts		100		100	
Projected on hand	75	145	65	90	30
Net requirements					
Planned order release		100			

Thus, there is a need for an order release in Week 1 to ensure there is sufficient stock in Week 3.

MRP Reports

A number of reports can be generated by the MRP program which include information on the quantity of each item to order in the current and future time period, indication of which due-dates cannot be met, showing when they can be met and showing changes to quantities of currently ordered items. The system can also show the results of simulation of scenarios for planning purposes. For instance, by entering a customer order in the master schedule, the effect of this extra work on overall customer due-date performance can be examined. If capacity restrictions mean that the order cannot be completed by the required due-date, a new due-date can be suggested.

MRP Implementation

MRP can reduce inventory by providing information on the actual inventory required for parent items (rather than stocking enough components for estimated parent demand). It can also help to prioritize orders to ensure delivery due-dates are met, provide information on resource (labour and equipment) requirements for planning purposes and provide financial information on projected inventory expenditure. MRP is most useful in complex scheduling situations when the number of levels of sub-assemblies and components is high.

However, there are a number of limitations of MRP. For instance, when using MRP it is not always possible to assess the feasibility of meeting the due-date quoted to a customer. Repeated changes to order due-dates will entail new plans generated from the MRP system which could lead to ever changing schedules. The need to manufacture in batches negates the advantage of only scheduling inventory when needed. If batches are used extensively the component batch size will be a major factor in manufacturing lead time. Also, if insufficient capacity is available it is necessary to adjust planned order dates or make available additional resources. The knock-on effect may not be clear until the MRP schedule is regenerated. This may lead to a lengthy process of trying to find a feasible schedule. The MRP system has limited ability to assess the robustness of the schedule to random events (e.g., machine breakdown). Changes to the inputs to the MRP stem may be so rapid (customer needs change, design changes, etc.) that the planning function of MRP may be extremely limited. Many of the problems of MRP revolve around the problem of estimating capacity at various time-frames. The aggregate plan, the RCCP and the CRP discussed earlier help with this.

Manufacturing Resource Planning (MRP II)

Manufacturing Resource Planning (MRP II) extends the idea of MRP to other areas in the firm such as marketing and finance (Wight, 1984). Thus, central databases hold information on product structure (i.e., the BOM file) which can be updated due to design changes (e.g., by engineering). By incorporating financial elements into item details, inventory cost information can be utilized by finance departments. At a wider level, information provided by the MRP II system from simulations of business plans can be used to estimate plant investment needs and workforce requirements. This information can then be used to coordinate efforts across departments including marketing, financing, engineering and manufacturing.

> **MANUFACTURING RESOURCE PLANNING (MRP II):** extends the idea of MRP to other areas in the firm such as marketing and finance

Although MRP II overcame many of the problems of MRP systems, there are still problems with MRP II implementations. A major problem remains the issue of ensuring the accuracy of information such as inventory records and BOMs to ensure a usable system. Some MRP II systems are so complex they often require installation by external agencies who may not understand the business needs of the company. Companies were also faced with expensive modifications to systems that did not provide all the functionality required for the business. The MRP systems are based around meeting performance targets in terms of meeting customer due-dates. However, conflicting objectives, such as financial targets, may override these, so undermining the planning process defined by the MRP implementation.

Distribution Requirements Planning (DRP)

MRP is traditionally associated with managing dependent demand items which form an assembly which has as independent demand (i.e., the demand is not dependent on other items). However, if the concept of MRP is widened from the traditional acquisition, handling and production functions across the supply chain to the customer then another form of dependent demand can be considered between the producer of goods, the regional distribution centre, the local distribution outlets or retailers and the customer. **Distribution Requirements Planning (DRP)** manages these linkages between all these elements on the supply chain beginning with an analysis of demand at each customer service location. These demands are aggregated across distribution centres to form a gross requirement which is fed into the MPS. Independent demand items are incorporated into the MRP logic by having a safety stock level below which a replenishment order is triggered. The order amount is determined by a lot sizing calculation. This method is called 'time phased order point'.

DISTRIBUTION REQUIREMENTS PLANNING (DRP): manages linkages between elements of the supply chain beginning with an analysis of demand at each customer service location.

Enterprise Resource Planning (ERP) systems

Enterprise Resource Planning (ERP) systems provide a single solution from a single supplier with integrated functions for major business areas such as production, distribution, sales, finance and human resources management. They are normally purchased as an off-the-shelf package which is then tailored. ERP is particularly relevant in the integration of supply chains in enabling organizations in the supply chain to access one another's databases. ERP systems may access other members of the supply chain via Electronic Data Interchange (EDI) facilities (Chapter 15). The Internet is also increasingly used as a platform to allow secure access to information by members of the supply chain. These systems are sometimes referred to as c-commerce (collaborative commerce). Like ERP, e-business systems facilitate the integration of the supply chain, and

ENTERPRISE RESOURCE PLANNING (ERP): provide a single solution from a single supplier with integrated functions for the major business areas.

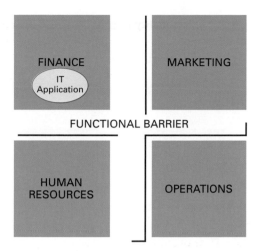

Figure 14.4   An IT application within an information island

many ERP vendors have repositioned themselves as suppliers of e-business solutions.

The main reason for implementing an ERP system is that it can replace a number of separate IT applications using incompatible data (sometimes known as 'information islands') in different functional parts of the company (Figure 14.4).

There are two main reasons for the existence of information islands. First, some organizations had grown through the merger of firms, each with their own systems which were incompatible with one another. The second reason is that in many organizations the selection of software applications became devolved, with the end-users in individual departments making their own purchasing decisions. This often led to separate applications from different vendors in different departments, often with poor data transfer between applications. The goal of ERP is to achieve integration across the organization (Figure 14.5). Here, the applications are integrated across the organization in terms of their technology architecture, application and data architecture and business process architecture (Chaffey, 2004).

This integration of applications across the organization fits with the process view that organizations have used in improvement approaches such as Business Process Reengineering (BPR) (Chapter 17). Using a process view the organization is seen as a family of processes (such as order fulfilment), rather than as a set of departments. ERP is seen as a way of implementing a process view in the organization through the use of software.

Although many successful ERP implementations exist there are potential disadvantages to ERP systems, the most prominent of which is the potential high costs of installing a system which replaces all the previous departmental applications. The cost of an ERP system can be in the millions of euros and so it may not be a feasible option for many small and medium-sized organizations.

Figure 14.5   An IT application integrated across the organization

However, scaled-down versions of ERP software is appearing for small and medium-sized enterprises (see Case Study 14.2).

The move to an ERP system with a common database can also mean that working practices have to change. This has implications for the cost of training personnel in new ways of working and any loss of performance that may derive from the need to adapt to the ERP system, rather than utilize applications developed to departmental requirements.

CASE STUDY 14.1

ERP and Cross-culture Management

In the past few years, Enterprise Resource Planning (ERP) systems have worked their way up companies' shopping lists because, in the right hands, they can improve operational processes – a priority for global organizations trying to manage operations in a number of different countries. However, global software projects bring with them a range of classic cross-border and inter-company challenges. Local staff may want to retain their current technology because it works and because they dislike change, so there is nearly always resistance to introducing new software. Many high-profile cross-border ERP systems have failed because local business units did not want the technology – while a lack of high-level backing at head office allowed local businesses to get away with dissent and, at worst, downright refusal to implement the systems. Boards did not put into place appropriate change management structures and processes to get all the organization's business units to behave as if they were one. Some senior managers will be more receptive to new ideas than others and will feel less threatened by ideas that are different from their own. These open-minded executives are the people who will operate most successfully in an international environment. They will become frustrated when they do not succeed and will gain considerable satisfaction when they manage to conduct good business with fellow professionals who come from different backgrounds. To make sure the majority of staff work successfully, the role of senior management must change from structuring workers' tasks to shaping their behaviour. If it does not, then managing the cultural complexity increasingly found in today's global organizations is going to become much more difficult for them.

Source: Sunday Business Group, *The Business*, 12 January 2002

1   What is the relationship between ERP and globalization?

**Case Study 14.1
Question**

In common with other investment decisions that operations managers have to make in terms of people and equipment, it is important that decisions are based on achieving strategic objectives. It is unlikely that one ERP software supplier will provide all the most up-to-date and relevant application software for a particular company. If alternative software is available that may provide a competitive advantage then a decision to forego the advantages of integration may have to be taken. It should also be considered that the main reason for ERP, in terms of achieving integration of systems, can usually be achieved at a price, in terms of the time of cost of writing integration software. The major choice facing an organization is to renew IT systems in a number of 'big bangs' with the installation of detailed specified major systems or to develop systems that contain a mix of new and old (legacy) systems in a more incremental manner. Either of these choices may make sense and can incorporate the advantages of the other.

ERP systems may allow some customization (without requiring a whole new system) through the use of Application Programming Interfaces (APIs) which allow programmers some access to the ERP software package. Mixed systems can provide compatibility by defining standards at the communications interface level. Thus, the internal operation of software can be tailored to local needs, but all software must work to a common interface. However, the choice made should be directed by the need to improve strategic performance, in regard to the performance objectives such as lower prices, higher quality, lower lead times, which gives the organization a competitive advantage in the market place.

CASE STUDY 14.2

Implementing ERP

Despite the snail's pace at which some industries cottoned on to e-business, even the most conservative sectors eventually came to see some potential benefit. Take the chemicals industry. On the surface, the sector seems untouched by the new-fangled ways of the Internet. To a large extent, it is. But within that, there are pockets of progress. For Oxford Chemicals, a manufacturer of aroma chemicals for the niche food and fragrance industry, the decision to collaborate more closely with customers and agents was cemented 2 years ago, after its IT contractor at the time threatened to withdraw support for the manufacturer's ERP systems.

With Nestle and ICI-owned Quest among its customers, Oxford Chemicals wanted to use technology literally to forge stronger links with its client base, and also to snatch a competitive advantage from rivals who didn't. For a company producing up to 450 products a year, with the capacity to produce 200 more, the existing ERP system had gone as far as it could. It would never be in a position to give the company the computing power it would need to win more international business, and had started to threaten the Teesside firm's growth.

"The ERP system was difficult to interrogate, making it impossible to identify the root causes of problems," explains Oxford Chemicals' managing director, Dr Richard Smith. "Basically, we were never 100% sure that our figures were accurate. And when we looked at our future plans, we knew the old system didn't have the collaborative features, like e-business with external partners, nor would it allow us to integrate other IT systems on the site," he adds. So the decision to upgrade was made, but it was never going to be straightforward.

"Being a smaller company, we needed a system we could implement quickly and which would allow us to continue work as we implemented it," recalls Smith.

The company opted for the SAP R3 system, after the vendor introduced a scaled-down version of its ERP systems for SMEs. Implemented by SAP systems integrator Plaut Consulting, the system took 3 months to fully integrate into Oxford Chemicals' existing network, but it took orders, issued invoices and dispatched goods on the new system the day it went live. The manufacturer had limited resources, and was able to negotiate with Plaut for an off-the-shelf SAP system pre-configured to the standard business processes of the chemical industry and around 70% pre-configured for Oxford Chemicals' specific requirements, at a cost of £200 000. The system now links the customer services department to inventory and manufacturing elements of the enterprise. "We now have a much clearer picture of what our customers require and how quickly we can meet those requirements," claims Smith.

"Now, when a customer places an order by fax, phone or email, customer service staff can immediately give them a lead time for delivery, whether or not the material to produce the goods is in stock. In the latter case, the SAP can calculate the additional time needed by us to order materials and produce the goods. In short, it drives the placing and manufacture, and leads the scheduling of production in the company."

Smith is loath to put any of the benefits of the new ERP system in financial terms. "One main improvement at Oxford Chemicals since we introduced the new system is that we've been able to lower the number of admin staff and increase numbers in the doing and making areas. In other words, we have more customer-facing staff and less who have to process admin. The system has made the tasks less arduous, allowing staff to improve customer service and make more products."

He added that inventory had been cut, stock turns had been improved and the monthly reporting burden reduced by 50% in terms of the days required to produce reports and accounts. The next phase of Oxford Chemicals' systems development will include linking directly into the SAP systems of customers and agents, here and abroad. So far, this has been successful with one client, the Duckworth Group, one of Britain's largest flavouring and fruit compound manufacturers. Duckworth now places orders from its purchasing system, which are electronically transferred directly to the sales order system at Oxford Chemicals using a tool from SAP called Business Connector. On receipt of the order, the sales order system automatically sends an acknowledgment back to the purchasing department.

But other link-ups will be delayed until it is possible to integrate even more closely – right into the manufacturing process – by adding new SAP application modules to the ERP system. "When material is in stock to produce the requested goods, it automatically sends an invoice. But when it is not in stock, and it has to be manufactured, that information cannot as yet be sent back. The second half of next year should see other linkages," says Smith. Oxford Chemicals is also a member of Elemica, an online trading exchange for the chemical industry, and plans to integrate its ERP system first with the exchange itself, then with individual members. In a bid to offer more than the ability to place orders over the Internet, Oxford Chemicals is also trying out a Web-based link with an agent who has access to the manufacturer's customer and orders databases from its web site. Linked to the back office, the agent can pull up the histories and status of recent sales. "We'll roll this out to all our agents next year, and then offer it to our major customers, eventually allowing every customer to place orders directly over the Web," says Smith.

Source: 'Business solutions: Wake up and smell the ERP', by Wale Azeez, *Guardian Special Supplement*,
31 October 2002
Reproduced by permission of Wale Azeez

1   Discuss the incremental approach to ERP described in the case study.

**Case Study 14.2
Question**

Summary

1 Resource Planning involves developing an MPS which is derived from the medium-term aggregate plan of resource requirements and the demand profile. The feasibility of the MPS is checked by the RCCP and the CRP.

2 MRP is a computer software package which provides resource planning facilities. It is used to calculate demand for component materials needed to produce end items.

3 MRP calculations are based on how many products or services are planned (held in the MPS), the product structures (held in the BOM) and current inventory levels (held in the ISF).

4 MRP II extends the concept of MRP to other areas in the organization such as marketing and finance to form an integrated business system.

5 DRP extends the concept of MRP across the supply chain to producers and distributors of goods.

6 ERP provides an integrated solution to resource planning across the supply chain and across business functions such as production, distribution, sales, finance and human resources management.

Exercises

1. Identify and explain the role of the main components of an MRP system.
2. A company makes a product with a product code S40. Each S40 consists of two sub-assemblies A10 and B5. Sub-assembly A10 consists of part 1765 (two required) and part 1867 (one required). Part 1867 is in turn made from part 8644 (one required) and part 2888 (five required). Sub-assembly B5 consists of part 2887 (two required) and part 2888 (four required).
   a. Draw a tree diagram showing the product structure of product S40.
   b. Show an indented bill of materials for product S40.
3. A company has the following master schedule for its most popular dining table:

Week	1	2	3	4	5	6
Tables	400	300	450	300	450	400

   Each table has four legs which have a production lead time of 2 weeks. 3500 legs are available as projected on-hand inventory. An order for 2000 legs has already been released and is scheduled to arrive in Week 2. The legs may be produced in any quantity. Use MRP to schedule planned order releases.
4. What are the main factors in the successful implementation of an MRP system?
5. Evaluate the advantages and disadvantages of the MRP approach to production planning.
6. An electrical retailer operates two regional warehouses, both of which are supplied from a central distribution centre. Delivery time from the distribution centre to the warehouses is 1 week. A particular model of dishwasher has a production lead time to the distribution centre of 2 weeks. It is shipped in standard quantities of 50 units. Use DRP to determine planned order releases for each warehouse and for the distribution centre using the following data:

	Week				
Warehouse 1	0	1	2	3	4
Gross requirements		30	30	40	20
Scheduled receipts					
Projected on hand	10				

	Week				
Warehouse 2	0	1	2	3	4
Gross requirements		20	30	30	30
Scheduled receipts					
Projected on hand	40				

7. Discuss the advantages and disadvantages of implementing an ERP system
8. Discuss the use of ERP software to replace software packages used in single areas of the organization, such as operations, marketing and accounting.

References

Chaffey, D. (2004), *E-Business and E-Commerce Management*, 2nd Edition, Financial Times/Prentice Hall.

Wight, O. (1984), *Manufacturing Resource Planning: MRP II*, Oliver Wight.

Further Reading

Bocij, P., Chaffey, D., Greasley, A. and Hickie, S. (2006), *Business Information Systems: Technology, Development and Management for the E-Business*, 3rd Edition, Pearson Education.

Web Links

www.bpic.co.uk Portal for resources for MRP and ERP installations.

www.manufacturingtalk.com Portal for resources for manufacturing, including MRP and ERP.

ERP Vendors

www.sap.com SAP (mySAP ERP).

www.baan.com SSAGlobal (SSA ERP).

www.peoplesoft.com Peoplesoft Inc. (Peoplesoft Enterprise).

www.oracle.com Oracle (Oracle Enterprise Manager).

Chapter 15
Supply Chain Management

■ Supply Chain Design
- Fluctuations in the Supply Chain
- Supply Chain Integration

■ Activities in the Supply Chain
- Procurement
- Physical Distribution Management

Learning Objectives

After reading this chapter, you should be able to:

1 Identify the elements of a supply chain management system.

2 Understand how demand fluctuations can occur in supply chains.

3 Describe the varying degrees of cooperation and integration in the supply chain.

4 Understand the role of procurement in the supply chain.

5 Describe an e-procurement system.

6 Discuss the area of physical distribution management in terms of material handling, warehousing, packaging and transportation.

Introduction

The **supply chain** consists of the series of activities that moves materials from suppliers, through operations to customers. Each product or service will have its own supply chain, which may involve many organizations in processing, transportation, warehousing and retail. A representation of the structure of a supply chain is shown in Figure 15.1.

Activities on the input side to the organization are termed 'upstream' or 'supply side' and are divided into tiers of suppliers. **Upstream suppliers** that supply the

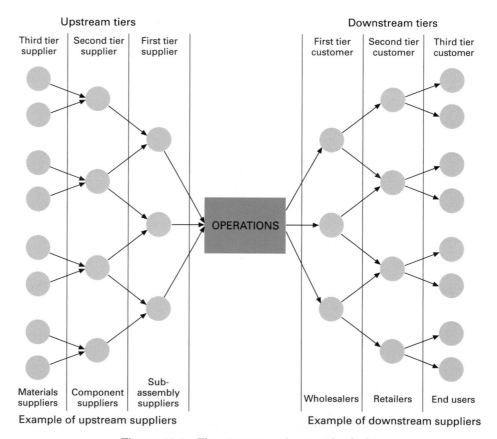

Figure 15.1   The structure of a supply chain

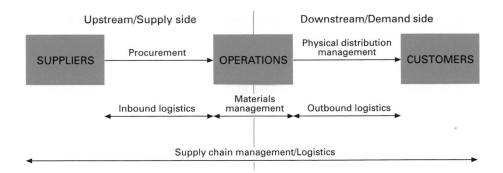

Figure 15.2   Terms used to describe the management of the supply chain

organization directly are termed 'first tier' and suppliers that supply first-tier organizations are termed 'second tier' and so on. Examples of upstream suppliers are component and sub-assembly suppliers.

Activities on the output side are termed 'downstream' or 'demand side' and are divided into tiers of customers. Examples of **downstream customers** are wholesalers and retailers. There will be a separate supply chain for each product or service an organization produces and this structure is sometimes referred to as the 'supply network' or 'supply web'.

The terms used in the area of supply chain management are defined in a number of ways and so the most common terms are first defined as they will be used in this text (Figure 15.2). **Supply Chain Management** and **logistics** are terms used to refer to the management of the flow of materials through the entire supply chain. Sometimes logistics or business logistics refer to activities in the downstream portion of the chain. **Inbound (or inward) logistics** is used to describe the activity of moving material in from suppliers and **outbound (or outward) logistics** is used to describe the activity of moving materials out to customers. The movement of materials within the organization is termed **materials management** (materials management can also be used to refer to the management of upstream supply chain activities). Materials management activities are specifically addressed in this text in Chapters 12–14. In this chapter supply chain activities are presented around the areas of procurement which are the operations interface with upstream activities and physical distribution management with downstream activities such as warehousing and transportation.

Supply Chain Design

This section discusses the strategic issue of how the supply chain should be designed to optimize performance. Other strategic issues regarding supply chain

DOWNSTREAM CUSTOMERS: customers of the organization such as wholesalers and retailers.

SUPPLY CHAIN MANAGEMENT: management of the flow of materials through the entire supply chain.

INBOUND LOGISTICS: the activity of moving material in from suppliers.

OUTBOUND LOGISTICS: the activity of moving materials out to customers.

MATERIALS MANAGEMENT: the movement of materials within the organization.

design are facility location and long-term capacity planning (both covered in Chapter 5). One of the key issues in supply chain design is that organizations need to cooperate with one another in order to provide customer satisfaction. One of the reasons for that cooperation is to limit the fluctuations in demand occurring in these networks that affect performance. The reasons behind these fluctuations will be discussed, before exploring various ways in which the supply chain network can be configured to promote cooperation.

Fluctuations in the Supply Chain

BULLWHIP EFFECT: occurs when there is a lack of synchronization in supply chain members. Even a slight change in consumer sales will ripple backwards in the form of magnified oscillations in demand upstream

The behaviour of supply chains that are subject to demand fluctuations has been described as the 'Forrester effect' or **bullwhip effect** as described by Forrester (1961). The effect occurs when there is a lack of synchronization in supply chain members, when even a slight change in consumer sales will ripple backwards in the form of magnified oscillations in demand upstream. To demonstrate this effect Figure 15.3 shows a spreadsheet of the relationship between four members of a supply chain, the customer, retailer, wholesaler and manufacturer. As can be seen, a slight change in customer demand, rising from 100 units to 108 units in Week 2, has an ever increasing effect on demand at each stage of the upstream demand. Note also that it takes until Week 6 for the supply chain to revert to the stable pattern shown in Week 1, despite customer demand reverting to 100 units from Week 3 onwards.

The calculations used in the spreadsheet are as follows:

■ Demand = Orders made by next tier in supply chain
■ Opening stock = Closing stock from previous week
■ Closing stock = Demand for that week
■ Orders = Demand + (Closing stock − Opening stock)

The bullwhip effect occurs because each tier in the supply chain increases demand by the current amount, but also assumes that demand is now at this new level, so increases demand to cover the next week also. Thus, each member in the supply chain updates their demand forecast with every inventory review. Thus, in Week 2 an increase in customer demand of 8 units is translated into an order from the retailer to the warehouse of 16 units (8 units to cover this week and 8 units to cover next week's demand), who then orders 32 units from the manufacturer, who then orders 64 units from the supplier and so on. Thus, each member in the supply chain is replenishing each level in the supply chain above it, rather than being linked directly to customer demand.

There are other factors which increase variability in the supply chain. These include a time lag between ordering materials and getting them delivered, leading

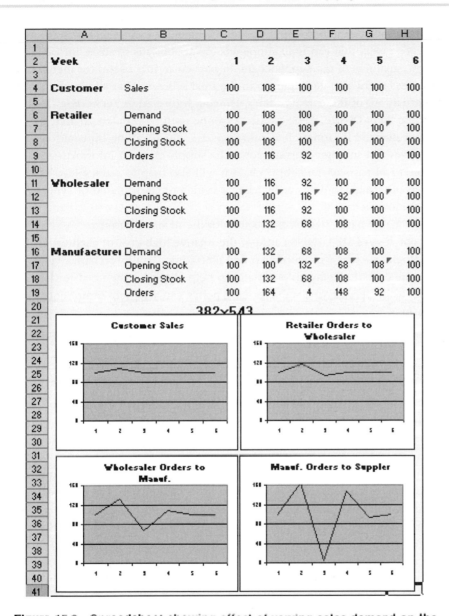

	A	B	C	D	E	F	G	H
1								
2	**Week**		**1**	**2**	**3**	**4**	**5**	**6**
3								
4	**Customer**	Sales	100	108	100	100	100	100
5								
6	**Retailer**	Demand	100	108	100	100	100	100
7		Opening Stock	100	100	108	100	100	100
8		Closing Stock	100	108	100	100	100	100
9		Orders	100	116	92	100	100	100
10								
11	**Wholesaler**	Demand	100	116	92	100	100	100
12		Opening Stock	100	100	116	92	100	100
13		Closing Stock	100	116	92	100	100	100
14		Orders	100	132	68	108	100	100
15								
16	**Manufacturer**	Demand	100	132	68	108	100	100
17		Opening Stock	100	100	132	68	108	100
18		Closing Stock	100	132	68	108	100	100
19		Orders	100	164	4	148	92	100

Figure 15.3 **Spreadsheet showing effect of varying sales demand on the supply chain**

to over-ordering in advance to ensure sufficient stock are available to meet customer demand. Also, the use of order batching (when orders are not placed until they reach a predetermined batch size) can cause a mismatch between demand and the order quantity. Price fluctuations such as price cuts and quantity discounts also lead to more demand variability in the supply chain as companies buy products before they need them.

In order to limit the bullwhip effect certain actions can be taken.
The major aspect that can limit supply chain variability is to share information amongst members of the supply chain. In particular, it is useful for members to have access to the product demand to the final seller, so that all members in the chain are aware of the true customer demand. Information Technology such as Electronic Point-Of-Sale (EPOS) systems can be used by retailers to collect customer demand information at cash registers which can be transmitted to warehouses and suppliers further down the supply chain. If information is available to all parts of the supply chain it will also help to reduce lead times between ordering and delivery by using a system of coordinated or synchronized material movement.

Using smaller batch sizes will also smooth the demand pattern.
Often, batch sizes are large because of the relative high cost of each order. Technologies such as e-procurement and Electronic Data Interchange (EDI) can reduce the cost of placing an order and so help eliminate the need for large batch orders. Finally, the use of a stable pricing policy can also help limit demand fluctuations.

Supply Chain Integration

Organizations in a supply chain can have varying degrees of cooperation and integration. In order of increasing ownership the options are a market relationship, strategic partnerships and alliances, virtual organization and vertical integration (Figure 15.4).

At the level of an individual product or service the amount of integration in the supply chain can be characterized as an analysis of the costs and risks in either making a component in-house or buying it from a supplier, termed a 'make-or-buy decision'. However, this approach does not take into account what may be critical strategic issues involved in deciding what the organization should do itself and what can be done by other firms. At a strategic level, supply chain integration decisions should be related to the way that the organization competes in the market place. For example, if speed of delivery is an order winner, then it may be necessary to make certain components in-house to ensure a fast and reliable supply.

DEGREE OF INTEGRATION

Figure 15.4   Supply chain relationships by degree of integration

One way of looking at supply chain integration decisions is to use the technique of value chain analysis (Porter and Millar, 1985) which views the decision in terms of which set of activities (e.g., design, assembly) should be undertaken, rather than from the viewpoint of products or services. This approach allows consideration of the fact that the outsourcing of one product or service may have cost implications for other products and services which are produced using the same resources. Thus, the impact of economies of scope are taken into account, as well as economies of scale (see Chapter 5 for more information on economies of scale and economies of scope).

However, value chain analysis aims to configure activities in order to minimize cost, given a firm's competitive strategy, and not specifically define where (i.e., inside or outside the firm) activities should occur. It is suggested that the degree of ownership should be directed by the capability or core competences (Chapter 2) that the organization requires to support the current and future strategy. This decision will need to be made within the constraints of the financial resources available to the organization in acquiring supply chain elements and the challenge of the coordination of activities within the supply chain.

The different degrees of integration in the supply chain are now discussed.

Market Relationships

Cooperation can simply mean the act of conducting a transaction between two organizations. In **market relationships**, each purchase is treated as a separate transaction and the relationship between the buyer and seller lasts as long as this transaction takes. There can be some additional arrangements around this relationship such as the use of EDI facilities to share information, combining orders in a single delivery to reduce transportation costs, agreements on packaging standards to improve materials handling and other factors. This approach does have a number of advantages by permitting flexibility in that suppliers can be changed or discontinued if demand drops or a supplier introduces a new product. Other advantages include the use of competition between suppliers to improve performance in aspects such as price, delivery and quality. However, there can be disadvantages in this arrangement in that either side can end the relationship at any time. A supplier withdrawal requires the often lengthy task of finding a new supplier. From a supplier perspective the withdrawal of a buyer may cause a sudden drop in demand on the operations facility, leading to disruption and idle resources.

> **MARKET RELATIONSHIPS:** here each purchase is treated as a separate transaction and the relationship between the buyer and seller lasts as long as this transaction takes.

Strategic Partnerships and Alliances

When an organization and supplier are trading successfully they can decide to form a **strategic alliance or strategic partnership**. This involves a long-term

> **STRATEGIC PARTNERSHIPS AND ALLIANCES:** these involve long-term relationships in which organizations work together and share information regarding aspects such as planning systems and development of products and processes.

relationship in which organizations work together and share information regarding aspects such as planning systems and development of products and processes. There may also be agreement on such aspects as product costs and product margins. The idea of a partnership or alliance is to combine the advantages of a market place relationship which encourages flexibility and innovation with the advantages of vertical integration which allows close coordination and control of such aspects as quality.

From a supplier viewpoint a long-term strategic partnership may give them the confidence to invest in resources and focus on a product line to serve a particular customer. Lambert *et al.* (1996) categorizes the factors that make a successful partnership as:

- *Drivers* – these are compelling reasons for forming partnerships, such as cost reduction, better customer service, or security.
- *Facilitators* – these are supportive corporate factors that encourage partnerships, such as compatibility of operations, similar management styles and common aims.
- *Components* – these are the joint activities and operations used to build and sustain a relationship, such as communication channels, joint planning, shared risk and rewards, and investments.

Some factors may mitigate against the formation of a partnership. For instance, for low-value items the use of a partnership may not be worthwhile. Also, a company may not want to share sensitive information or lose control of a particular product or process.

CASE STUDY 15.1

BASF and Aker Kvaerner

BASF and Aker Kvaerner benefit from an innovative alliance for maintaining one of the UK's largest chemical plants. BASF is the world's leading chemical company. It has production facilities in 39 countries and trades in 170 countries. Its strategy at its Seal Sands plant on Teesside in the UK has been to marry technological and commercial innovation through partnering. One of the ways it has done this is through a partnership with the maintenance arm of Aker Kvaerner, a provider of services to the engineering and construction sectors. Throughout the history of the Seal Sands plant the maintenance provision has been managed by BASF but outsourced to a number of different providers. Whilst the company names have changed, many of the employees had worked on the site for more than 20 years. Although the general belief for many years was that the service was world-class, in reality an emphasis on cost control was stifling development and long-term improvements. BASF decided to shake things up by looking at partnering. Its first step was to define what it meant by a partnership: "a long-term, mutually beneficial relationship where resources, knowledge, skills and values are shared with the purpose of enhancing each partner's competitive position." When BASF settled on Aker Kvaerner to provide the whole maintenance service for the site, the main reason was the approach of its senior management team. BASF saw the team as having the ability to see beyond traditional approaches and to adopt the new ways of working enthusiastically. The core of the agreement is a performance-based contract whereby Aker Kvaerner is paid according to a set of Key Performance Indicators (KPIs). Where Aker Kvaerner achieves or exceeds performance, BASF's productivity and profitability are enhanced. BASF then shares its additional gains with Aker Kvaerner.

Source: www.dti.gov.uk/bestpractices
Crown copyright material is reproduced with the permission of HMSO and the Queen's Printer for Scotland

1 What steps did BASF take to encourage a successful strategic partnership?	**Case Study 15.1** **Question**

The Virtual Organization

The form of an organization's relationship within its supply chain is increasingly being affected by developments in e-business systems. **E-business** involves electronically mediated information exchanges, both within an organization and between organizations. Evans and Wurster (1997) describe how information can impact the value chain in three ways:

■ *Reach* – a business can share information with more stakeholders or gain a larger audience at a relatively low cost.
■ *Customization* – information can be more readily tailored for sharing with a large number of partners.
■ *Dialogue* – interaction between the parties is two-way rather than the traditional push of information. For example, it is possible for a supplier to anticipate a retailer's product requirements from examining their inventory forecast rather than awaiting a faxed order.

Thus, the implication of e-business developments is that it becomes easier to outsource more and more supply chain activities to third parties and the boundaries between and within organizations become blurred. This development is known as virtualization and companies that follow this route are known as **virtual organizations**. The objective is that the absence of any rigid boundary or hierarchy within the organization should lead to a more responsive and flexible company with greater market orientation. Kraut *et al.* (1998) suggests that the features of a virtual organization are:

E-BUSINESS:
this involves electronically mediated information exchanges, both within an organization and between organizations.

VIRTUAL ORGANIZATION:
an organization in which e-business is used to outsource more and more supply chain activities to third parties so that the boundaries between and within organizations become blurred.

- Processes transcend the boundaries of a single form and are not controlled by a single organizational hierarchy.
- Production processes are flexible with different parties involved at different times.
- Parties involved in the production of a single product are often geographically dispersed.
- Given this dispersion, coordination is heavily dependent on telecommunications and data networks.

DIS-INTERMEDIATION: using e-business to alter the supply chain structure by bypassing some of the tiers.

E-business can also be used to alter the supply chain structure by bypassing some of the tiers using a process known as **disintermediation**. Figure 15.5 shows a traditional demand side supply chain from operations through a wholesaler and retailer to the customer. Disintermediation is shown omitting both the wholesaler and retailer. This process is facilitated by the use of Web-based **e-commerce** systems which involve electronically mediated information exchanges between organizations. By omitting these stages in the supply chain, the producer is able to reduce their costs.

E-COMMERCE: this involves electronically mediated information exchanges between organizations.

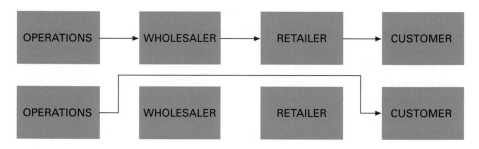

Figure 15.5   Disintermediation in the supply chain

RE-INTERMEDIATION: the creation of new intermediaries between customers and suppliers in the supply chain.

Perhaps a more significant phenomenon using e-commerce systems is the use of **reintermediation**, the creation of new intermediaries between customers and suppliers in the supply chain. Figure 15.6 demonstrates the change in structure when an intermediary is placed between operations and suppliers in the supply chain. Reintermediation removes the inefficiency of checking all the suppliers by placing an intermediary between purchaser and seller. This intermediary performs the price evaluation stage of fulfilment since its e-procurement or ERP system (Chapter 14) has links updated from the different suppliers. The next section on procurement will cover these systems in more detail.

VERTICAL INTEGRATION: the amount of ownership of the supply chain by an organization.

Vertical Integration

Complete integration is achieved by an organization when they take ownership of other organizations in the supply chain. The amount of ownership of the supply chain by an organization is termed its level of **vertical integration**. When an

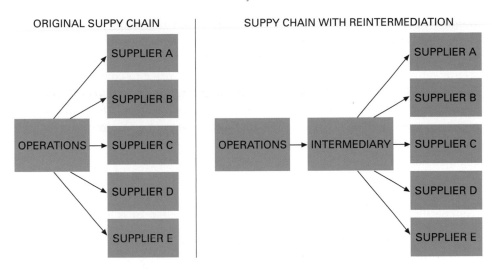

Figure 15.6   Reintermediation in the supply chain

organization owns upstream or supply-side elements of the supply chain it is termed backward vertical integration. For ownership of downstream or demand-side elements of the supply chain it is termed forward vertical integration (see Figure 15.7). When a company owns elements of a different supply chain (e.g., a holding company which has interests in organizations operating in various markets), the term used is 'horizontal integration'.

One potential advantage of vertical integration is the ability to secure a greater control of the competitive environment. Although a market-based economy is based on the idea of competition, many firms will attempt to reduce competition

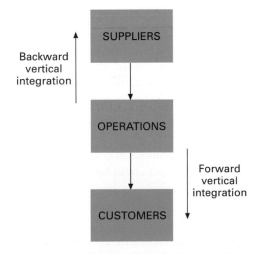

Figure 15.7   Types of vertical integration

and, thus, provide an opportunity to increase profits. For example, a manufacturer can use forward integration to buy retailers to limit the availability of competing product ranges. Backward integration, implemented by owning suppliers, can secure supplies of components whose availability and price to competitors can be controlled. Another factor is that technological innovations in one part of the organization are available to other elements in the supply chain. Thus, product and process improvements can be disseminated quickly. Also, improved communication can help coordinate planning and control systems in the supply chain to improve delivery speed and dependability.

Another reason for vertical integration is to keep distinctive competence or capability in house and not available to competitors. If an activity is seen as strategically important, or it utilizes specialized knowledge, or is in an area where the company has superior performance to competitors, then it is likely that the company will want to keep that activity as part of its supply chain.

There are, however, a number of disadvantages of vertical integration and perhaps the major reason for outsourcing is the cost incurred in owning major elements of the supply chain. The resources required to own elements of the supply chain are resources that cannot be dedicated to the activities that represent the core tasks of the organization. This means there is a risk in that trying to do everything will mean that the company is not competitive against companies who are focusing their resources and skills on particular elements of the supply chain. For example, the activity of warehousing may not be a core task for a manufacturer. By outsourcing this function the facilities of a third party are available who can share storage costs amongst a number of companies and invest in up-to-date warehouse technologies in order to increase efficiency. Another factor is the increased flexibility available when using a number of suppliers to meet fluctuations in demand. This means the organization only buys the capacity it needs and does not have idle capacity in house.

In summary, there are a number of factors that need to be taken into account when deciding the amount of vertical integration that is appropriate for an organization. First, the amount of vertical integration that can feasibly be undertaken will be dependent on the financial resources of the organization. It is unlikely that smaller firms will be able to own large sections of the supply chain, but even large organizations may find this difficult. For example, a car manufacture may source an engine for a new car from a third party rather than invest millions of euros in developing a new design. Apart from cost, the time taken to acquire supply chain capabilities may be a barrier. It may also be felt that resources used for vertical integration could be better spent elsewhere (e.g., R&D or marketing). Finally, an organization needs to consider that it is unlikely that they will be able to undertake all the activities in the supply chain well and may leave certain aspects to specialist suppliers.

Even if the organization has the capability to undertake further activities in the supply chain it may not make sense to take ownership of them. The virtual organization concept using e-business systems described earlier may allow efficient coordination of supply chain activities without the need for ownership of them. Disadvantages of non-ownership of supply chain elements include the potential high cost of switching partners, loss of intellectual property which may provide the competitive advantage of the firm, and the termination of partnerships if the strategic interests of the supply chain partners diverge.

CASE STUDY 15.2

Implementing Supply Chain Software

Why is it that almost every time a big company buys fancy new supply chain software it seems to end in tears? The seller of the IT will have no doubt wooed the company by saying it will save millions by having its order processing, inventory management and purchasing all handled automatically. The seller may even flog the management a whizzy supply chain 'optimization' system, which aims to link up all the purchasing, manufacturing and sales processes with the company's customers and suppliers, and their customers and suppliers. However, instead of a smooth transition to savings' heaven, it frequently seems that something goes wrong and the company ends up losing money.

Last month, furniture chain MFI dispatched two top executives after revealing that its new system from SAP and IBM had been implemented poorly, leaving customers waiting for weeks for deliveries that were incomplete on arrival. The executives weren't the only ones to go: half the year's pre-tax profit will also disappear, according to analysts' forecasts. Ten days earlier it had emerged that dozens of British Airways planes had been sitting idle in repair hangars since July waiting for the right nuts and bolts. The reason? 'Teething problems' with a new supply chain management system. Also, last month, Electrocomponents said glitches with its new supply chain system would hit full-year results. The company – which sells a multitude of components from exit signs to plug fuses – had tested the system in France. It worked perfectly well, it's just that staff there couldn't work out how to use it properly. They didn't order enough stock, so the customers, who are used to having deliveries in 24 hours, were left without their widgets for days. As Electrocomponents prepares to roll out the system in the UK – where it makes half its turnover – the management is spending an extra £11m on more staff and excess inventory just in case it messes up again. It will be painful, but it shows a refreshing realism.

A report last year by technology research house Forrester looked at 25 major supply chain optimization projects and found that 68% had gone over budget – on average by 74%. The main problem, according to the report's author George Lawrie, was that the companies using the new IT systems had failed to recognize that things can and do go wrong all the time in a supply chain. Many companies go for the one-size-fits-all option, thinking they will magically solve all of their supply chain problems. However, a rigid IT system may not allow enough slack to cope when the inevitable problems occur, such as late deliveries from suppliers. In such circumstances a tightly controlled planning system can fall apart, so companies need to ensure they can cope if the unexpected happens – and they don't necessarily need a fancy piece of software to do that.

Imagine a company sells tractors in two colours: red and green. It buys an IT system that links with its customers and suppliers to work out how many red and how many green tractors it needs to produce to maximize profits. The shiny new system ensures the tractors leave its factory in Ukraine in time to get on the ship it uses (it only uses one because it is now so lean and efficient). On day 1 the ship gets loaded up and everything seems to be going well but, wait a minute, the paint machine broke down, so the tractors aren't painted. The ship has to leave right away though, because otherwise something else will go wrong further along the chain and the software system won't be able to cope. Before the company got itself into such difficulties someone might have asked whether, instead of buying that impressive new IT system, the money could have been better invested in making sure the paint machine works.

Source: 'Don't get stranded by supply chain IT', *The Daily Telegraph*, 5 October 2004
Reproduced by permission of Telegraph Group Ltd

Case Study 15.2 Question

1   Discuss the issues of the implementation of supply chain IT systems as described in the case study. How might they be overcome?

Activities in the Supply Chain

In this section supply chain activities are presented around the areas of procurement (which is the operations interface with upstream activities) and physical distribution management (which deals with downstream activities such as warehousing and transportation).

Procurement

PROCUREMENT:
acquisition of all the materials needed by an organization.

The role of **procurement** is to acquire all the materials needed by an organization in the form of purchases, rentals, contracts and other acquisition methods. The procurement process also includes activities such as selecting suppliers, approving orders and receiving goods from suppliers. The term 'purchasing' usually refers to the actual act of buying the raw materials, parts, equipment and all the other goods and services used in operations systems. However, the procurement process is often located in what is called the 'purchasing department'.

Procurement is an important aspect of the operations function as the cost of materials can represent a substantial amount of the total cost of a product or service. There has recently been an enhanced focus on the procurement activity due to the increased use of process technology, both in terms of materials and information processing. In terms of materials processing the use of process technology such as Flexible Manufacturing Systems (FMS) (Chapter 6) has meant a reduction in labour costs and, thus, a further increase in the relative cost of materials associated with a manufactured product. This means that the control of material costs becomes a major focus in the control of overall manufacturing costs for a product.

Worked Example 15.1

Procurement Costs

The simple example below demonstrates the importance of procurement costs to the profitability of the organization.

Scenario 1

A company sells a product for €11, of which €6 is on raw materials and €4 on operations:

$$\text{Profit} = 11 - (6 + 4) = €1 \text{ per unit}$$

Scenario 2

The procurement function has negotiated a 10% discount on material costs:

$$\text{Profit} = 11 - ((6 \times 0.9) + 4) = 11 - 9.4 = €1.6 \text{ per unit}$$

Thus, a 10% drop in material costs has led to an increase in profit of 60%.

Another issue that has increased the importance of procurement is that the efficient use of automated systems requires a high quality and reliable source of materials to be available. This is also the case with the adoption of production planning systems such as JIT which require the delivery of materials of perfect quality, at the right time and the right quantity.

Steps in Procurement

Figure 15.8 outlines the main steps in the purchasing process and the relationship between operations, purchasing and suppliers in the process.

The procurement process begins with the department requiring the goods or services issuing a purchase requisition which authorizes the purchasing function to buy the goods or services. The requisition will usually include a description of what is to be purchased, the amount to be purchased and a requested date for

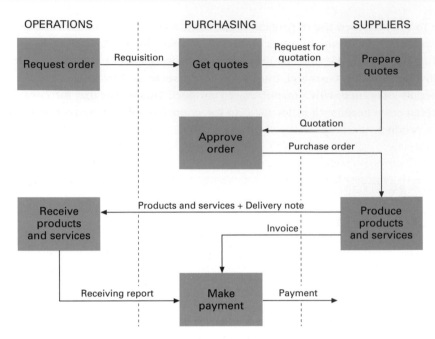

Figure 15.8 Steps in the procurement process

delivery. Other information provided will be the account to which the purchase cost will be charged, the delivery address and the approval of an appropriate person of the transaction.

The purchasing department will receive the request and prepare a 'request for quotation' document to a suitable supplier or suppliers. The quotation will require a price, any other payment terms such as quantity discounts, a delivery date and any other conditions stipulated by the supplier. When a supplier has been chosen (see section 'Choosing Suppliers') then they are issued with a purchase order which represents a legal obligation by the buyer to pay for the items requested. The purchase order will usually include information specifying the item to be purchased, its price and delivery date.

The supplier will then produce the goods or service and deliver them to the relevant department and provide an invoice form requesting payment. When the organization is satisfied the good or services and the invoice details are satisfactory a payment will be issued to the supplier.

Choosing Suppliers

Before choosing a supplier, the organization must decide whether it is feasible and desirable to produce the good or service in house. Buyers in purchasing departments, with assistance from operations, will regularly perform a make-or-buy analysis to determine the source of supply. Often goods can be sourced internally at a lower cost, with higher quality or faster delivery than from a supplier. On the other hand, suppliers who focus on delivering a good or service can specialize their expertise and resources and, thus, provide better performance. Strategic issues may also need to be considered when contemplating the outsourcing of supplies. For instance, internal skills required to offer a distinctive competence may be lost if certain activities are outsourced. It may also mean that distinctive competences can be offered to competitors by the supplier.

If a decision is made to use an external supplier, the next decision relates to the choice of that supplier. Criteria for choosing suppliers for quotation and approval include the following:

■ *Price* – as stated in the introduction, the cost of goods and services from suppliers is forming an increasingly large percentage of the cost of goods and services which are delivered to customers. Thus, minimizing the price of purchased goods and services can provide a significant cost advantage to the organization.

■ *Quality* – to be considered as a supplier, it is expected that a company will provide an assured level of quality of product or service. This is because poor-quality goods and services can have a significant disruptive effect on the performance of the operations function. For example, resources may have to be deployed checking for quality before products can be used, poor-quality products that get into the production system may be processed at expense before faults arc found and poor-quality goods and services that reach the customer will lead to returns and loss of goodwill.

■ *Delivery* – in terms of delivery, suppliers who can deliver on time, every time – in other words, show reliability – are required. The ability to deliver with a short lead time and respond quickly once an order has been placed can also be an important aspect of performance.

The process of locating a supplier will depend on the nature of the good or service and its importance to the organization. If there are few suppliers capable of providing the service then they will most likely be well known to the organization. If there are a number of potential suppliers and the goods are important to the organization then a relatively lengthy process of searching for suppliers and the evaluation of quotations may take place.

Most organizations have a list of approved suppliers they have used in the past, or are otherwise known to be reliable. However, it is important to monitor suppliers in order to ensure that they continue to provide a satisfactory service. A system of supplier rating, or vendor rating, is used to undertake this. One form of vendor rating is a checklist which provides feedback to the supplier on their performance and suggestions for improvement. Another approach is to identify the important performance criteria required of the supplier (e.g., delivery

Table 15.1 Advantages of single sourcing and multi-sourcing	
Advantages of single sourcing	*Advantages of multi-sourcing*
Stronger relationship between parties, leading to greater commitment to success	Reduces risk of loss of supply from single supplier
Opportunities for savings due to economies of scale with larger order quantities	Can be used to reduce price by encouraging competition between suppliers
Facilitates better communication and reduces administration overhead	Provides more flexibility in meeting changes in demand
Easier to maintain confidential terms of business	A range of suppliers can give access to a wider knowledge about goods and services

reliability, product quality and price). The supplier can then be rated on each of these performance measures against historical performance and competitor performance.

When choosing suppliers a decision is made whether to source each good or service from an individual supplier, termed 'single sourcing' or whether to use a number of suppliers, termed 'multi-sourcing'. Although the trend toward alliances and partnerships between firms leads towards single-sourcing, there are certain advantages to the multi-sourcing approach also (Table 15.1).

Procurement Information Systems

There are a number of steps in the procurement process which has implications in terms of time, cost and reliability. One problem is the time lapse between a department requesting a good or service and receiving it. This is due to the time it takes to undertake all the steps involved, including supplier selection and the exchange of documentation. The cost involved in employing personnel to undertake these tasks can be particularly onerous for companies who procure many low-cost goods and services. In this situation the purchasing costs are likely to be a relatively high proportion of total costs. Another issue is the reliability of a process in which personnel have to coordinate between a number of suppliers and complete and track a large amount of documentation. In order to improve the procurement process an electronic purchasing system was developed called Electronic Data Interchange (EDI).

Electronic Data Interchange (EDI)

Electronic Data Interchange (EDI) can be defined as the exchange, using digital media of structured business information, particularly for sales transactions such as purchase orders and invoices, between buyers and sellers. A complementary technology is Electronic Funds Transfer (EFT) which allows the automated digital transmission of money between organizations and banks. EDI has traditionally been carried out over specialist computer networks, but, recently, Internet EDI systems which can lower costs by using the public Internet network have been carried out as well. EDI can improve the procurement process by reducing the time information is in transit, reducing data entry errors and reducing costs such as staff time. Many EDI systems have adopted the use of the **eXtensible Markup Language (XML)** which allows documents to be easily transferred between computer systems and applications software. An XML document created using one application can be used with other programs without the need to convert it or process it in any other way. XML lends itself to applications that include e-commerce and e-procurement. The use of XML in e-procurement systems is likely to replace many EDI-based applications over the coming years.

> **ELECTRONIC DATA INTERCHANGE (EDI):**
> the exchange, using digital media of structured business information, particularly for sales transactions such as purchase orders and invoices, between buyers and sellers.

> **EXTENSIBLE MARKUP LANGUAGE (XML):**
> a data description language that allows documents to store any kind of information.

CASE STUDY 15.3

Chance & Hunt

Chance & Hunt has employed technology right across its business – including EDI – which has allowed an extensive degree of supply chain integration. The company, which markets and distributes chemicals, wanted to improve its telemetry system for managing its clients' inventories – with the aim of offering a better service and cutting costs. The idea was that automatic exchange of business information with clients could bring dramatic efficiency savings and help cement long-term relationships. The company's solution was to invest in the infrastructure to provide remote network access, online credit card purchasing – an industry first – and an integrated EDI ordering system that checks stock and links to the warehouse. The system constantly monitors client inventories checking stock levels against optimum levels. Should stocks fall below this level, the system delivers alerts to the client budget holders and relevant sales staff, before channelling orders back to Chance & Hunt's internal systems.

Source: www.dti.gov.uk/bestpractice
Crown copyright material is reproduced with the permission of HMSO and the Queen's Printer for Scotland

1   What business benefits do you think would be gained from the use of EDI described in the case study?

**Case Study 15.3
Question**

E-procurement

E-procurement refers to the electronic integration and management of all procurement activities including purchase request, authorization, ordering, delivery and payment between purchaser and supplier. E-procurement can achieve significant savings and other benefits which directly impact the customer.

■ Faster purchase cycle times leading to a need for less material in inventory.
■ Less staff time spent in searching and ordering products and reconciling deliveries with invoices.
■ Savings also occur through automated validation of pre-approved spending budgets for individuals or departments, leading to fewer people processing each order, and in less time.
■ A reduction in the cost of physical materials such as specially printed order forms and invoices.
■ Enables greater flexibility in ordering goods from different suppliers according to best value.

E-procurement also tends to change the role of buyers in the purchasing department. By removing administrative tasks such as placing orders and reconciling deliveries and invoices with purchase orders, buyers can spend more time on value-adding activities. Such activities may include more time spent with key suppliers to improve product delivery and costs, or analysis and control of purchasing behaviour.

E-procurement can be classified in terms of business and consumer models of Internet access. **Business-to-Consumer (B2C)** transactions are between an organization and consumers, whilst **Business-to-Business (B2B)** is used to describe transactions between an organization and other organizations. Although the use of the Internet by consumers for purchasers has received most media attention, the majority of commerce over the Internet is actually between businesses, using the B2B model and most e-procurement is undertaken in this way.

A risk of implementing an e-procurement system, typical of many e-business implementations, is the difficulty in integrating information systems. Figure 15.9 shows how different types of information system cover different parts of the procurement cycle. The different types of systems are described below:

■ *Stock control system* – this relates mainly to production-related procurement; the system highlights when re-ordering is required when the number in stock falls below re-order thresholds.
■ *CD- or Web-based catalogue* – paper catalogues have been replaced by electronic forms that make it quicker to find suppliers.

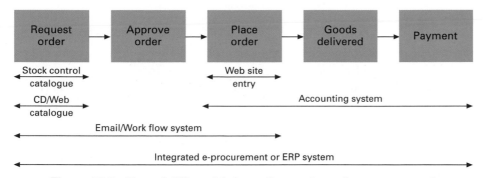

Figure 15.9   Use of different information systems for procurement

■ *Email- or database-based workflow systems* – integrate the entry of the order by the originator, approval by manager and placement by buyer. The order is routed from one person to the next and will wait in their inbox for actioning. Such systems may be extended to accounting systems

■ *Order entry on web site* – the buyer often has the opportunity to order directly on the supplier web site, but this will involve rekeying and there is no integration with systems for requisitioning or accounting.

■ *Accounting systems* – networked accounting systems enable staff in the buying department to enter an order which can then be used by accounting staff to make payment when the invoice arrives.

■ *Integrated e-procurement or ERP systems* – these aim to integrate all the facilities above and will also include integration with suppliers' systems.

Apart from the use of the appropriate technology the introduction of an information system should address change in terms of its implications for people and processes. The introduction of e-procurement will require people to change the way that they work in order to secure the benefits of the information system. It may also require changes to current supplier–customer relationships and both of these issues can lead to resistance and dissatisfaction. There is also a need to avoid replacing poor manual procurement processes with poor automated procurement processes. This may mean the use of a process-centred design effort, using techniques such as process mapping, as part of the e-procurement implementation. Another point to consider is that no matter how efficient the electronic e-procurement systems are, the success of the procurement process will still depend on the efficiency, derived from their operations capability, with which the suppliers in the supply chain can deliver the physical goods or services requested.

Perhaps the major barrier to the use of e-procurement is in the difficulty of linking systems with suppliers whose systems may be incompatible or non-existent. It may be that small firms may find themselves increasingly excluded by buyers due to their lack of investment in the required information technology infrastructure. For organizations that are attempting to provide an integrated e-procurement or ERP implementation one of the main issues is gaining access to the price catalogues of suppliers. One approach is to house electronic catalogues from different suppliers inside the company and use a firewall for security. These catalogues can be updated by either an occasional link beyond the firewall or the delivery of a CD version from the supplier. An alternative approach is to 'punch out' through the firewall to access the catalogue either on a supplier's site or intermediary site such as a B2B marketplace. A B2B market place provides a web site that connects buyers and sellers to enable trading in a private and secure environment. For example, it is reported that IBM has saved $1.7bn since 1993 by being able to divulge sensitive price and inventory information over a private exchange (i.e., a web site with regulated access) built for 25 000 suppliers and customers (Computerworld, 2001).

CASE STUDY 15.4

Access-to-Retail

The Access-to-Retail concept was inspired when the company's owners were developing a supply chain system for a single, multi-national company. They suspected that supply chain management requirements were largely the same whatever the industry or size of company. The market research the company undertook confirmed this, and it developed an online platform open to all that would support buyers and sellers of all types in their supply chain transactions. The objective was then to sell the concept into the market place.

Says Operations Director, Philip Rakusen, "It is important to understand we were building a 'closed' system purely to support supply chain arrangements between companies who are already doing business. The first and vital phase was to set up focus groups of potential users, to understand their needs in-depth. There were a great many issues to consider, from how the system could be made available to an independent store with one PC; to the degree of interaction bigger companies would require with their corporate systems. As well as the technicalities we also had to determine users' attitudes and what they wanted from the system."

At the core of the resulting solution is a secure Web-based trading platform, accessible to registered users. This allows companies to do business with their customers and suppliers electronically. Crucially, access to the platform is via the Web and requires no special technology. Indeed, the bulk of the software is housed on Access-to-Retail's server, so any business can hook into the basic service with an ordinary PC and Web link. Registered users simply log in using a secure password and start trading.

The centrepiece of the solution is the electronic catalogues created from a standard online template, using a simple password-protected interface. Products and promotional offers can be updated this way at any time and, once complete, can be forwarded to all their customers who have registered with the service. Customer relationship management facilities are also built in, with an online database identifying buyers logging in and personalizing prices accordingly. Promotional offers can also be forwarded to individual customers.

The company has made the experience for buyers as simple and intuitive as possible. Once buyers have logged on to the service, a menu appears, naming all of their suppliers currently using the platform to trade. Selecting a supplier then brings up the relevant product catalogue, along with a useful product search facility. The buyer simply adds items to the shopping basket or brings up their order history if they just want the same items again. Once complete, one mouse click will then forward the order electronically.

A key technical consideration was ease of implementation for larger users requiring compatibility with other systems. XML was chosen as the core technology, as this is now the de facto standard for data transfer in supply chain management. An 'open systems' philosophy was also adopted so that the product could be integrated with users' existing inventory, sales and finance systems, without complex software engineering.

Bearing in mind many users would be small to medium-sized companies, the team also forged strategic partnerships with other systems companies who could provide bolt-on applications to the system. This ensured that customers seeking a complete e-management solution from scratch would be well catered for. The company has successfully created a secure, Web-based trading platform for customers, manufacturers and distributors of all sizes. The basic computer technology required to use the system allows Access-to-Retail to market the product to small retailers, who are used to less sophisticated technology.

Access-to-Retail is also cutting sellers' labour and error costs by as much as 5% of turnover, as electronic orders feed directly into its inventory systems with no rekeying. It has an enhanced Web presence too and its sales operations are more productive, with representatives able to concentrate on account development rather than order taking.

Access-to-Retail offers the service to buyers completely free of charge. The service provides fast online access to buyers' suppliers, useful online tools such as a favourite file for fast re-ordering, and add-on software products if they want integrated stock management on their PCs. Those with EPOS systems can download and integrate the product catalogues for one-click ordering.

Philip is clear that the product is still in its ascendancy. "Everyday we learn more about users' needs and we are constantly evolving the system, as new technologies or applications become apparent. We are first in the market and need to keep the initiative." There is also the challenge of remaining buyer-led. Even though the service is free to them, it is their presence that attracts the fee-paying sellers. "We need to have a strong throughput of orders for prospective customers to be convinced," says Philip, "so we make sure we look after buyers' needs." The challenge also remains to show smaller to medium-sized companies the value of electronic supply chain management and what's now possible. There has to be a strong element of market education in the company's marketing collateral.

Source: www.dti.bestpractice
Crown copyright material is reproduced with the permission of HMSO and the Queen's Printer for Scotland

Case Study 15.4 Question	1 What are the main implementation issues discussed when providing a Web-based trading platform?

Physical Distribution Management

> **PHYSICAL DISTRIBUTION MANAGEMENT:** the movement of materials from the operation to the customer.

Physical distribution management, sometimes called 'business logistics', refers to the movement of materials from the operation to the customer. Four main areas of physical distribution management are materials handling, warehousing, packaging and transportation.

Materials Handling

> **MATERIALS HANDLING:** the movement of materials, either within warehouses or between storage areas and transportation links.

Materials handling relates to the movement of materials, either within warehouses or between storage areas and transportation links. The aim of materials handling is to move materials as efficiently as possible. The type of materials handling systems available can be categorized as manual, mechanized and automated. A manual handling system uses people to move material. This provides a flexible system, but is only feasible when materials are movable using people with little assistance. An example is a supermarket where trolleys are used to assist with movement, but the presence of customers and the nature of the items make the use of mechanization or automation not feasible. Mechanized warehouses use equipment such as forklift trucks, cranes and conveyor systems to provide a more efficient handling system, which can also handle items too heavy for people. Automated warehouses use technology such as Automated Guided Vehicles (AGVs) and loading/unloading machines to process high volumes of material efficiently. More information on process technologies is provided in Chapter 6.

Warehousing

> **WAREHOUSING:** the use of locations to hold a stock of incoming raw materials used in production or hold finished goods ready for distribution to customers. Warehousing is also used to store work-in-progress items or spares for equipment.

When producing a tangible item it is possible to provide a buffer between supply and demand by holding a stock of the item. Many organizations have specific locations to hold this stock, termed a **warehouse** or 'distribution centre'. Most warehouses are used to hold a stock of incoming raw materials used in production or hold finished goods ready for distribution to customers. Warehouses are also used to store work-in-progress items or spares for equipment.

Because of the need to process goods and services through the supply chain as quickly as possible to serve customer demand, warehouses are not simply seen as long-term storage areas for goods, but provide a useful staging post for activities such as sorting, consolidating and packing goods for distribution along the supply chain. Consolidation occurs by merging products from multiple suppliers over time, for transportation in a single load to the operations site. Finished goods sourced from a number of suppliers may also be grouped together for delivery to a customer in order to reduce the number of communication and transportation links between suppliers and customers. The opposite of consolidation is break-bulk where a supplier sends all the demand for a particular geographical area to a local warehouse. The warehouse then processes the goods and delivers the separate orders to the customers.

One of the major issues in warehouse management is the level of decentralization and, thus, the number and size of the warehouses required in inventory distribution. Decentralized facilities offer a service closer to the customer and, thus, should provide a better service level in terms of knowledge of customer needs and speed of service. Centralization, however, offers the potential for less handling of goods between service points, fewer control costs and fewer overall inventory levels due to the lower overall buffer levels required. The overall demand pattern for a centralized facility will be an aggregation of a number of variable demand patterns from customer outlets and so will be a smoother overall demand pattern, thus requiring lower buffer stocks (see Figure 15.10). Thus, there is a trade-off between the customer service levels or effectiveness offered by a decentralized system and the lower costs or efficiency offered by a centralized system. One way of combining the advantages of a centralized facility with a high level of customer service is to reduce the delivery lead time between the centralized distribution centre and the customer outlet. This can be accomplished by using the facility of EDI or e-procurement systems discussed in the procurement section.

The warehouse or distribution system can be itself outsourced and this will often be the only feasible option for small firms. The choice is between a **single-user or private warehouse** which is owned or leased by the organization for its own use and a **multi-user or public warehouse** which is run as an independent business. The choice of single-user or multi-user warehouse may be seen as a break-even analysis with a comparison of the lower fixed costs, but higher operating costs of a multi-user warehouse, against the high fixed costs and lower operating cost of a single-user warehouse. However, the cost analysis should be put into a strategic context. For example, the warehouse and distribution system may enable a superior service to be offered to customers. It may also be seen as a barrier to entry to competitors due to the time and cost of setting up such a system.

SINGLE-USER OR PRIVATE WAREHOUSE:
a warehouse owned or leased by the organization for its own use.

MULTI-USER OR PUBLIC WAREHOUSE:
a warehouse run as an independent business.

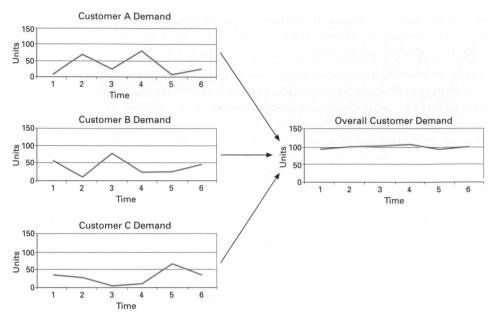

Figure 15.10   Aggregating customer demand in a centralized warehouse facility

Packaging

Packaging provides a number of functions including identifying the product, giving protection during transportation and storage, making handling easier and providing information to customers. The emphasis put on each of these factors will depend on the nature of the product, with protection being a major factor for some products. In terms of packaging materials we have a choice that includes cardboard, plastic, glass, wood and metal. The choice between these is dependent on how they meet the functional needs of the product and their relative cost.

Transportation

Distribution is an important element of the supply chain and can account for as much as 20% of the total costs of goods and services. The amount of cost will depend largely on the distance between the company and its customers and the method of transportation chosen. There are five main methods of transportation to choose from (shown in Table 15.2).

Table 15.2   Transportation methods

Transport mode	Normal usage
Rail	Provides fast movement of bulky products, but total transportation time lengthened by the need to use alternative transport between train station nodes and destination point.
Road	Provides flexible point-to-point service for most products of any size. Most popular method of transportation but reliability of delivery time can be affected by traffic congestion.
Air freight	All types of products can be moved long distances quickly. Most suited to lightweight products and overseas destinations. Requires handling facilities which slows overall transportation time.
Water	Can carry all types of products either inland on canal systems or by sea travel. Provides slow transportation, but relatively low cost and especially useful for carrying bulky items internationally.
Pipeline	Transportation of liquids and gases such as water, oil and gas. After high initial cost of laying pipeline provides a reliable transportation method with low operating costs.

Summary

1 A supply chain management system is made up of procurement, materials management and physical distribution management elements.

2 Demand fluctuations occur in a supply chain when there is a lack of synchronization between supply chain members.

3 Supply chain integration can range, in order of increasing integration, from a market relationship to a strategic partnership, to a virtual organization and to vertical integration. A market relationship permits flexibility but can be ended by either organization at any time. A strategic partnership or alliance involves a long-term relationship in which the organizations work together and share information. A virtual organization is where information technology is used to allow outsourcing of supply chain activities and the boundaries between and within organizations become blurred. Vertical integration is when an organization takes ownership of other organizations in the supply chain

4 The role of procurement is to acquire all the materials needed by an organization in the forms of purchases, rentals, contracts and other acquisition methods.

5 E-procurement refers to the electronic integration and management of all procurement activities.

6 Physical distribution management refers to the movement of materials from the operation to the customers. It covers the areas of materials handling, warehousing, packaging and transportation.

Exercises

1. Describe the elements of a supply chain.
2. Explain the term 'bullwhip effect'. How can it be overcome?
3. Evaluate the main supply chain relationships in terms of their degree of integration.
4. Discuss the increasing importance of procurement.
5. What are the key factors in choosing suppliers?
6. What is the impact of e-commerce on procurement activities?
7. Locate e-procurement software suppliers on the Internet and evaluate the benefits claimed for this software.
8. Discuss the relative merits of the centralization and decentralization of warehouse facilities.

References

Computerworld (2001) 'Private exchanges drive B2B success', by Pimm Fox, 7 May. Available online at www.computerworld.com

Evans, P. and Wurster, T.S. (1997), Strategy and the new economics of information, *Harvard Business Review*, September.

Forrester, J.W. (1961), *Industrial Dynamics*, MIT Press.

Kraut, R., Chan, A., Butler, B. and Hong, A. (1998), Coordination and virtualisation: The role of electronic networks and personal relationships, *Journal of Computer Mediated Communications*, 3(4).

Lambert, D.M., Emmelhainz, M.A. and Gardner, J.T. (1996) Developing and implementing supply chain partnerships, *International Journal of Logistics Management*, 7(2), 1–17.

Porter, M.E. and Millar, V.E. (1985), How information gives you competitive advantage, *Harvard Business Review*, July/August, 149–160.

Further Reading

Murray, E.A. and Mahon, J.F. (1993), Strategic alliances: Gateway to the new Europe?, *Long Range Planning*, **26**(4), 102–111.

Stevenson, W.J. (2005), *Operations Management*, 8th Edition, McGraw-Hill.

Susaki, T. (1993), What the Japanese have learned from strategic alliances, *Long Range Planning*, **26**(6), 41–53.

Waters, D. (2003) *Logistics: An introduction to Supply Chain Management*, Palgrave Macmillan.

Web Links

www.supply-chain.org The Supply Chain Council. Numerous papers and news items regarding supply chain management.

www.lmi.org Logistics Management Institute. Provides a database of reports regarding logistics issues.

www.steelauction.com Web auction for steel industry.

www.verticalnet.com Web auction site for industrial equipment.

www.transportation.com Web auction site for transportation equipment.

www.ism.ws Institute for Supply Management. Conferences, guides and tools in the area of supply chain management.

Chapter 16

Project Management

■ Project Management Activities
- Project Estimating
- Project Planning
- Project Control

■ Projects and Organizational Structure
- The Project Structure
- The Functional Structure
- The Matrix Structure

■ The Role of the Project Manager

■ Network Analysis
- Critical Path Method (CPM)
- Gantt Charts
- Capacity Loading Graphs
- Project Cost Graphs
- Project Crashing
- Project Evaluation and Review Technique (PERT)
- Project Network Simulation
- Software for Network Analysis
- Benefits and Limitations of the Network Analysis Approach

Introduction

Projects are unique, one-time operations designed to accomplish a specific set of objectives in a limited time-frame. Examples of projects include a building construction or introducing a new service or product to the market. Large projects may consist of many activities and must, therefore, be carefully planned and coordinated if a project is to meet cost and time targets. However, not all aspects of implementation can be controlled or planned, but the chance of success can be increased by anticipating potential problems and by applying corrective strategies. Network Analysis can be used to assist the project planning and control activities.

Project Management Activities

The project management process includes the following main elements of estimate, plan and control.

Project Estimating

At the start of the project a broad plan is drawn up assuming unlimited resources. Once estimates have been made of the resources required to undertake these

PROJECT ESTIMATING: estimating the type and number of resources required to undertake a project.

activities it is then possible to compare overall project requirements with available resources. If highly specialized resources are required then the project completion date may have to be set to ensure these resources are not overloaded. This is a **resource-constrained** approach. Alternatively, there may be a need to complete a project in a specific time-frame (e.g., due-date specified by customer). In this case alternative resources may have to be utilized (e.g., subcontractors) to ensure timely project completion. This is a **time-constrained** approach.

The next step is to generate estimates for the time and resources required to undertake each task defined in the project. This information can then be used to plan what resources are required and what activities should be undertaken over the life cycle of the project. Statistical methods should be used when the project is large (and therefore complex) or novel. This allows the project team to replace a single estimate of duration with a range within which they are confident the real duration will lie. This is particularly useful for the early stage of the project when uncertainty is greatest. The accuracy of the estimates can also be improved as their use changes from project evaluation purposes to approval and day-to-day project control. The PERT approach described later in this chapter allows optimistic, pessimistic and most likely times to be specified for each task from which a probabilistic estimate of project completion time can be computed.

Once the activities have been identified and their resource requirements estimated it is necessary to define their relationship to one another. There are some activities that can only begin when other activities have been completed, termed a 'serial relationship'. Other activities may be totally independent and, thus, they have a parallel relationship. Both these relationships are shown graphically in Figure 16.1.

For a project of a reasonable size there may be a range of alternative plans which may meet the project objectives. Project management software can be used

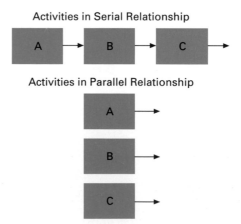

Figure 16.1   Serial and parallel relationship of activities

to assist in choosing the most feasible schedule by recalculating resource requirements and timings for each operation.

Project Planning

The purpose of the project planning stage is to ensure that the project objectives of cost, time and quality are met. It does this by estimating both the level and timing of resources needed over the project duration. These steps may need to be undertaken repeatedly in a complex project due to uncertainties and to accommodate changes as the project progresses. The planning process does not eradicate the need for the experience of the project manager in anticipating problems or the need for skill in dealing with unforeseen and novel incidences during project execution. However, the use of plans which can be executed sensibly will greatly improve the performance of the project.

The project management method uses a systems approach to dealing with a complex task in that the components of the project are broken down repeatedly into smaller tasks until a manageable chunk is defined. Each task is given its own cost, time and quality objectives. It is then essential that responsibility is assigned to achieving these objectives for each particular task. This procedure should produce a Work Breakdown Structure (WBS) which shows the hierarchical relationship between the project tasks (Figure 16.2) A typical WBS will have at the top level the project and at the bottom level the individual work package. A work package is an individual work element that can be accurately defined, budgeted, scheduled and controlled. Between the top and bottom levels various categories can be defined. These categories are usually organized in a product-oriented fashion but may be task-oriented for service operations such as design or management.

> **PROJECT PLANNING:** ensures the project objectives of cost, time and quality are met. It does this by estimating both the level and timing of resources needed over the project duration.

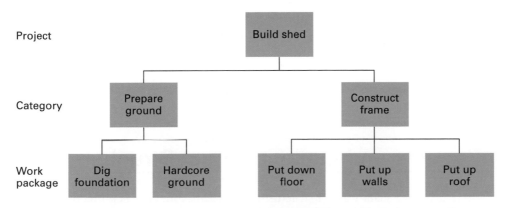

Figure 16.2 Work Breakdown Structure (WBS) for building a shed

Project Control

Project control involves the monitoring of the project objectives of cost, time and quality as the project progresses. It is important to monitor and assess performance as the project progresses in order that the project does not deviate from plans to a large extent. Milestones or time events are defined during the project when performance against objectives can be measured. The amount of control will be dependent on the size of the project. Larger projects will require development of control activities from the project leader to team leaders. Computer project management packages can be used to automate the collection of project progress data and production of progress reports.

The type of project structure required will be dependent on the size of the team undertaking the project. Projects with up to six team members can simply report directly to a project leader at appropriate intervals during project execution. For larger projects requiring up to 20 team members, it is usual to implement an additional tier of management in the form of team leaders. The team leader could be responsible for either a phase of the development or a type of work. For any structure it is important that the project leader ensures consistency across development phases or development areas as appropriate. For projects with more than 20 members it is likely that additional management layers will be needed in order to ensure that no one person is involved with too much supervision.

The two main methods of reporting the progress of a project are by written reports and verbally at meetings of the project team. It is important that a formal statement of progress is made in written form, preferably in a standard report format, to ensure that everyone is aware of the current project situation. This is particularly important when changes to specifications are made during the project. In order to facilitate two-way communication between team members and team management, regular meetings should be arranged by the project manager. These meetings can increase the commitment of team members by allowing discussion of points of interest and dissemination of information on how each team's effort is contributing to the overall progression of the project.

Projects and Organizational Structure

There are three main ways of structuring an organization: project, functional and matrix. The reasons for choosing a particular structure are outlined below.

The Project Structure

This consists of an organization which not only follows a team approach to projects, but has an organizational structure based on teams formed specifically for projects. The approach delivers a high focus on completing project objectives but can involve duplication of resources across teams, an inhibition of diffusion of learning across teams, a lack of hierarchical career structure and less continuity of employment. Examples of organizations which utilize this approach include many professional service firms such as management consultancies.

The Functional Structure

Here, a project is given to the most appropriate functional department. Thus, the organizational structure remains in the standard hierarchical form. The approach ensures there is limited disruption to the normal organizational activities but can lead to a lack of focus on project objectives. A lack of coordination can result, especially if outside help is required, and there can be a failure to meet customer needs if other departmental activities are taking priority over project work.

The Matrix Structure

Here, a series of project teams are overlaid on a functional structure in an effort to provide a balance between functional and project needs. There are three different forms of matrix structure:

- *Functional matrix* – here, the project manager reports to functional heads to coordinate staff across departments.
- *Balanced matrix* – here, the project manager manages the project jointly with functional heads.
- *Project matrix* – here, functional staff join a project team for a fixed period of time.

The Role of the Project Manager

The project manager, sometimes known as a 'team leader' or 'project coordinator', bears the ultimate responsibility for the success or failure of the project. One of the functions of the project manager is to provide clearly defined goals to project participants and to ensure that adequately skilled and experienced human resources are employed on the project. Throughout the project it is necessary to manage the elements of time, cost and quality. Because of the unique nature of projects and the potentially high number of interrelated tasks involved, an effective way is needed to communicate project plans and progress across the project team. Network Analysis methods can provide a valuable aid to the monitoring and control of projects and will be described below.

Network Analysis

NETWORK ANALYSIS:
the use of network-based techniques for the analysis and management of projects.

Network analysis refers to the use of network-based techniques for the analysis and management of projects. This section describes two network analysis techniques of the Critical Path Method (CPM) and the Project Evaluation and Review Technique (PERT). The CPM method described here was developed by DuPont during the 1950s to manage plant construction. The PERT approach was developed by the US Navy during the development of the Polaris Submarine-Launched Ballistic Missile System during the same decade (Sapolsky, 1972). The main difference between the approaches is the ability of PERT to take into consideration uncertainty in activity durations.

In order to undertake network analysis it is necessary to break down the project into a number of identifiable activities or tasks. This enables individuals to be assigned responsibility to particular tasks which have a well-defined start and finish time. Performance objectives of time, cost and quality can be associated with each activity. The next stage is to retrieve information concerning the duration of the tasks involved in the project. This can be collated from a number of sources, such as documentation, observation and interviewing. The accuracy of the project plan will depend on the accuracy of these estimates. The next step is to identify any relationships between tasks in the project. For instance, a particular task may not be able to begin until another task has finished. Thus, the task waiting to begin is dependent on the former task. Other tasks may not have a dependent relationship and can, thus, occur simultaneously.

CRITICAL PATH METHOD (CPM):
used to show the activities undertaken during a project, the dependences between these activities and the project duration.

Critical Path Method (CPM)

Critical Path Method (CPM) diagrams are used extensively to show the activities undertaken during a project and the dependences between these activities. Thus, it is easy to see that Activity C, for example, can only take place when Activity A and Activity B have completed. There are two methods of constructing critical

Early start	Duration	Early finish
	Task name	
Late start	Slack	Late finish

Figure 16.3   Activity on Node notation

path diagrams, Activity On Arrow (AOA) where the arrows represent the activities and Activity On Node (AON) where the nodes represent the activities. The issues involved in which one to utilize will be discussed later. The following description on critical path analysis will use the AON method. For AON notation, each activity task is represented by a node with the format shown in Figure 16.3.

Thus, a completed network will consist of a number of nodes connected by lines, one for each task, between a start and end node. An example of a completed network is shown in Figure 16.4.

Once the network diagram has been constructed it is possible to follow a sequence of activities, called a 'path', through the network from start to end. The length of time it takes to follow the path is the sum of all the durations of activities on that path. The path with the longest duration gives the project completion time. This is called the 'critical path' because any change in duration in any activities on this path will cause the whole project duration to either become shorter or longer. The following four steps show how to identify the critical path.

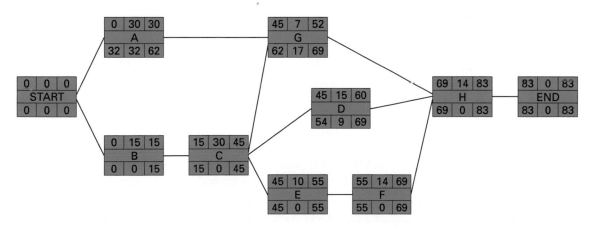

Figure 16.4   Activity on Node network diagram

1 Calculate the Earliest Start/Finish Times (Forward Pass)

From the duration of each task and the dependency relationship between the tasks it is possible to estimate the earliest start and finish time for each task as follows. You move left to right along the network, forward through time:

1 Assume the start (i.e., first) task begins at Time = 0.
2 Calculate the earliest finish time where:

$$\text{Earliest finish} = \text{Earliest start} + \text{Duration}$$

3 Calculate the earliest start time of the next task where:

$$\text{Earliest start} = \text{Earliest finish of task immediately before}$$

If there is more than one task immediately before, take the task with the latest finish time to calculate the earliest start time for the current task.

4 Repeat Steps 2 and 3 for all tasks.

2 Calculate the Latest Start/Finish Times (Backward Pass)

It is now possible to estimate the latest start and finish time for each task as follows. You move right to left along the network, backward through time:

1 Assume the end (i.e., last) task end time is the earliest finish time (unless the project end time is given).
2 Calculate the latest start time where:

$$\text{Latest start} = \text{Latest finish} - \text{Duration}$$

3 Calculate the latest finish time of the previous task where:

$$\text{Latest finish} = \text{Latest start of task immediately after}$$

If there is more than one task immediately after, take the task with the earliest start time to calculate the latest finish time for the current task.

4 Repeat Steps 2 and 3 for all tasks.

3 Calculate the Slack/Float Times

The slack or float value is the difference between the earliest start and latest start (or earliest finish and latest finish) times for each task. To calculate the slack time:

1 Slack = Latest start − Earliest start *OR* Slack = Latest finish − Earliest finish.
2 Repeat Step 1 for all tasks.

4   Identify the Critical Path

Any tasks with a slack time of 0 must obviously be undertaken on schedule at the earliest start time. The critical path is the pathway connecting all the nodes with a zero slack time. There must be at least one critical path through the network, but there can be more than one. The significance of the critical path is that if any node on the path finishes later than the earliest finish time, the overall network time will increase by the same amount, putting the project behind schedule. Thus, any planning and control activities should focus on ensuring tasks on the critical path remain within schedule.

Worked Example 16.1

Critical Path Method

A particular project comprises the following activities.

Activity	Duration (days)	Immediate predecessor(s)
A	30	–
B	15	–
C	30	B
D	15	C
E	10	C
F	14	E
G	7	A, C
H	14	D, F, G

(a)   Draw an AON diagram for this project.
(b)   Calculate the earliest start, earliest finish, latest start, latest finish and slack times for each activity.
(c)   Identify the critical path.

Solution

(a) The AON diagram is constructed by using the predecessor information contained in the table to connect the nodes as appropriate. For instance, Activity G has two predecessors, A and C, so both these nodes must point to the start of Activity G. The completed network diagram is shown in Figure 16.4.

   (b) The earliest start/finish times are calculated by a forward pass (left to right) through the network. For instance, Activity A has an earliest start of 0 and duration of 15, therefore its earliest end is $15 - 0 = 15$; Activity G has an earliest start of 45 (i.e., earliest finish of activities immediately before: A = 30, C = 45). The latest start/finish times are calculated by a backward pass (right to left) through the network.

For instance, Activity H has a latest end of 83 and duration of 14, therefore its latest start is $83 - 14 = 69$; Activity C has a latest end of 45 (i.e., latest start of task immediately after: $G = 62$, $D = 54$, $E = 45$). The slack time is the difference between the earliest and latest start times for each activity. For instance, the slack time for Activity G is 17 (i.e., Latest start − Earliest start $= 62 - 45 = 17$).

(c) The critical path is the path or paths through the network with all nodes having a zero slack time. In this case there is one critical path: B, C, E, F, H.

The Activity-On-Arrow Method

The format for the AOA method will now be described. The symbol used in this method is shown in Figure 16.5.

Rather than considering the earliest and latest start and finish times of the activities directly, this method uses the earliest and latest event times as below:

■ *Earliest event time* − this is determined by the earliest time at which any subsequent activity can start.
■ *Latest event time* − this is determined by the latest time at which any subsequent activity can start.

Thus, for a single activity the format would be as shown in Figure 16.6.

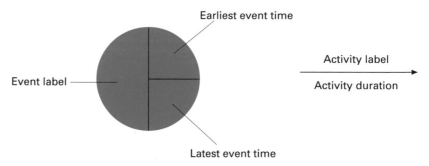

Figure 16.5   Activity-on-Arrow notation

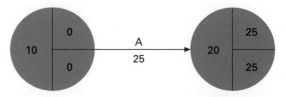

Figure 16.6   Calculating event times for an Activity-on-Arrow network

As stated earlier there are two methods of constructing network diagrams. Historically, there has been a greater use of the AOA method, but the AON method is now being recognized as having a number of advantages including:

■ Most project management computer software uses the AON approach.
■ AON diagrams do not need dummy activities to maintain the relationship logic.
■ AON diagrams have all the information on timings and identification within the node box leading to clearer diagrams.

Gantt Charts

Although network diagrams are ideal for showing the relationship between project tasks, they do not provide a clear view of which tasks are being undertaken over time and, particularly, how many tasks may be undertaken in parallel at any one time. The **Gantt chart** provides an overview for the project manager to allow them to monitor project progress against planned progress and so provides a valuable information source for project control.

To draw a Gantt chart manually, undertake the following steps:

1 Draw a grid with the tasks along the vertical axis and the timescale (up to the project duration) along the horizontal axis.
2 Draw a horizontal bar across from the task identifier along the left of the chart starting at the earliest start time and ending at the earliest finish time.
3 Indicate the slack amount by drawing a line from the earliest finish time to the latest finish time.
4 Repeat Steps 2 and 3 for each task.

A Gantt chart for the AON network shown in Figure 16.4 is shown in Figure 16.7.

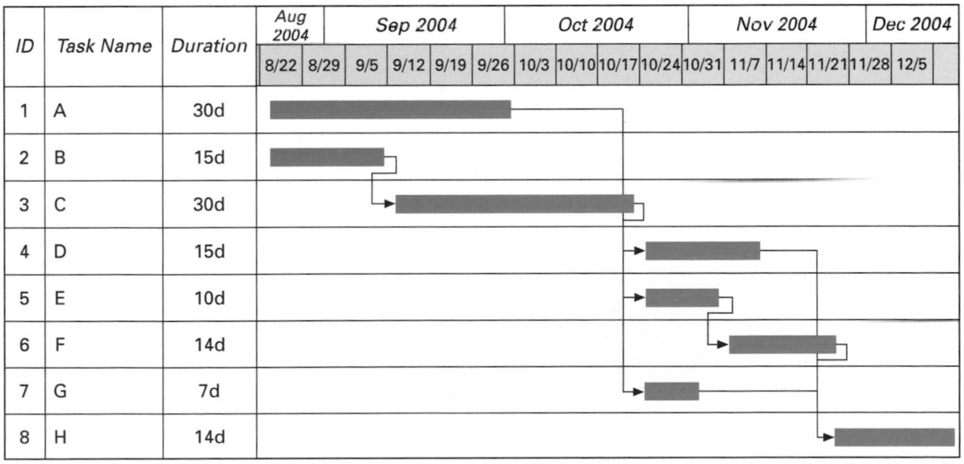

> **GANTT CHART:**
> provides a view of which tasks are being undertaken over time. This allows monitoring of project progress against planned progress and so provides a valuable tool for project control.

ID	Task Name	Duration	Aug 2004 8/22	8/29	Sep 2004 9/5	9/12	9/19	9/26	Oct 2004 10/3	10/10	10/17	10/24	10/31	Nov 2004 11/7	11/14	11/21	11/28	Dec 2004 12/5
1	A	30d																
2	B	15d																
3	C	30d																
4	D	15d																
5	E	10d																
6	F	14d																
7	G	7d																
8	H	14d																

Figure 16.7   Gantt chart

Capacity Loading Graphs

The basic network diagram assumes that all tasks can be undertaken at the earliest start times derived from the critical path calculations. However, the capacity available, for what may be a number of parallel tasks requiring the same type of resource, is usually limited. In order to calculate the capacity requirements of a project over time the capacity requirements associated with each task are indicated on the Gantt chart. From this a **capacity loading graph** can be developed by projecting the loading figures on a time graph. To manually construct a capacity loading graph, undertake the following steps (see Figure 16.8):

CAPACITY LOADING GRAPHS: indicate the type and level of capacity required at a point in time.

1 Draw a Gantt chart for the project. Each task bar should indicate the capacity requirements for that task.

2 Draw a capacity loading graph immediately below the Gantt chart. The graph should have an identical horizontal timescale. The vertical axis should be scaled to the estimated highest capacity loading level from the Gantt chart.

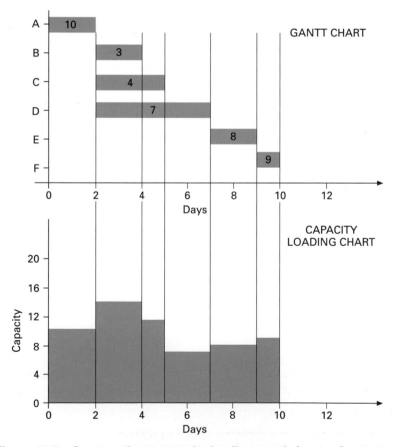

Figure 16.8 Constructing a capacity loading graph from a Gantt chart

3 Start at time 0.

4 Calculate the capacity loading requirement by totalling the loading figures for all parallel tasks. Move along the timescale until a task finishes or a new task begins.

5 Mark the capacity loading level on the graph.

6 Repeat Steps 4 and 5 for each change in loading figure.

Project Cost Graphs

The previous discussion has concentrated on the need to schedule and control activities in order to complete the entire project within a minimum time-span. However, there are situations in which the project cost is an important factor. If the costs of each task are known then it is possible to produce a **project cost graph** which will show the amount of cost incurred over the life of the project. This is useful in showing any periods when a number of parallel tasks are incurring significant costs leading to the need for additional cash-flow at key times. In large projects it may be necessary to aggregate the costs of a number of activities, particularly if they are the responsibility of one department or subcontractor. As a control mechanism the project manager can collect information on cost to date and percentage completion to date for each task to identify any cost above budget and take appropriate action without delay. Conversely, costs below budget may be an indication of a project running late. The performance measures used to do this are called the **earned value** or Budgeted Cost of Work Performed (BCWP) and show, for any day in the project, how much work has actually been done in terms of budgeted costs. This measure can be compared with the Budgeted Cost of Work Scheduled (BCWS) to find the Schedule Variance (SV):

$$SV = BCWP - BCWS$$

and the Actual Cost of Work Performed (ACWP) to find the Cost Variance (CV):

$$CV = BCWP - ACWP$$

PROJECT COST GRAPHS: provide an indication of the amount of cost incurred over the life of a project.

EARNED VALUE: also termed the Budgeted Cost of Work Performed (BCWP), shows for any day in the project how much work has actually been done in terms of budgeted costs.

Project Crashing

Within any project there will be a number of time–cost trade-offs to consider. Most projects will have tasks which can be completed with an injection of additional resources, such as equipment or people. Reasons to reduce project completion time include:

■ reduce high indirect costs associated with equipment;
■ reduce new product development time to market;

■ avoid penalties for late completion;
■ gain incentives for early completion;
■ release resources for other projects.

The use of additional resources to reduce project completion time is termed **crashing the project**. The idea is to reduce overall indirect project costs by increasing direct costs on a particular task. One of most obvious ways of decreasing task duration is to allocate additional labour to a task. This can be either an additional team member or through overtime working. To enable a decision to be made on the potential benefits of crashing a task, the following information is required:

■ the normal task duration;
■ the crash task duration;
■ the cost of crashing the task to the crash task duration per unit time.

The process by which a task is chosen for crashing is by observing which task can be reduced for the required time for the lowest cost. As stated before, the overall project completion time is the sum of the task durations on the critical path. Thus, it is always necessary to crash a task which is on the critical path. As the duration of tasks on the critical path are reduced, however, other paths in the network will also become critical. When this happens, it will require the crashing process to be undertaken on all the paths which are critical at any one time.

Worked Example 16.2

Project Crashing

Software Ltd has established a project team to undertake some important market research work. It is possible to reduce the expected or 'normal' times for certain activities in units of 1 week (but not in fractions of a week), but at an extra cost. The relevant information is given below.

Activity	Predecessor	Normal Duration (weeks)	Normal Cost of weeks (£)	Crash Duration (weeks)	Crash Extra cost per week saved (£)
A	–	5	4 000	3	2 000
B	–	4	3 000	4	–
C	A	2	6 000	1	15 000

Activity	Predecessor	Normal		Crash	
		Duration	Cost of weeks	Duration	Extra cost per week saved
		(weeks)	(£)	(weeks)	(£)
D	C	4	1 000	4	–
E	B	5	4 000	3	3 000
F	B	5	7 000	1	7 000
G	B, C	4	4 000	2	20 000
H	F	3	5 000	2	10 000

In addition to the costs shown there is a cost of retainer fees and administration overheads of £10 000 for each week that the project lasts:

(a) What is the normal expected duration of the project, and its total cost? What is the critical path?
(b) What would be the cost of completing the project using the normal durations?
(c) What would be the duration of the project if costs are to be minimized?

Solution

(a) Construct the AON diagram by using the predecessor information in the table. From the diagram the duration of the project is 12 weeks. The critical path is B, F, H.

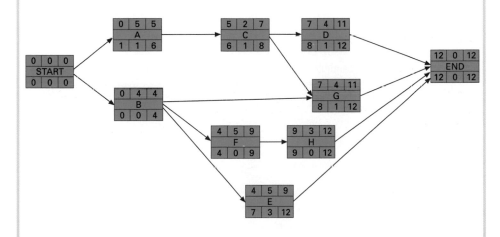

(b) The total project cost:

$$\text{Cost of activities} + \text{Other costs} = £34\,000 + 12 \times £10\,000$$

$$= £154\,000$$

(c) The minimum cost solution can be found by looking at the normal time solution:

- Ignore B and D because they cannot be reduced.
- Ignore C, G and H because it is too expensive to reduce these activities. This leaves A, E and F.
- F is the only activity on the critical path, so reduce this activity from 5 weeks to 4 weeks. This costs £7000 but saves £10 000, net saving £3000.
- Reduce E by 2 and A by 2, thus reducing the overall project duration to 9 weeks. This costs 2 × £9000 but saves 2 × £10 000, net saving of £2000.
- No more time can be saved for less than the relevant cost.
- Therefore, the optimal duration is 9 weeks and optimal cost is £149 000.

CASE STUDY 16.1

Fast Homes – Courtesy of Prefabrication

On a muddy building site in the flat Cambridgeshire countryside, a crane swings a prefabricated concrete slab over a half-finished house and a team of workers slot it in to form part of the ground floor ceiling. A three-storey house built using prefabricated methods employed by Bovis Homes in the new village of Cambourne can be weathertight within 10 days compared with the $5\frac{1}{2}$ weeks required by conventional techniques. "This allows electricians and plumbers to get to work sooner and means the house can be completed in less than half the 22 weeks normally needed," says David Lowther, Bovis's research and development director.

Bovis and a handful of other housebuilders see prefabrication as the way forward while the government is keen for the building industry to modernize its production techniques. But, despite years of trials and the use of timber frame construction methods in Scotland, Scandinavia and the US, prefabrication remains controversial. The home-buying public associates it with post-war austerity and with the draughty, condensation-prone, system-built high-rises of the 1960s and 1970s. The verdict in the City is that prefabrication is a useful way of speeding up production and improving the housebuilders' return on capital. But the industry has yet to show that faster build times justify the higher costs, and prefabrication is not a reason for giving a company a higher rating.

Malcolm Harris, Bovis chief executive, believes 'factory-finished components' – a term he prefers to prefabrication – is essential to overcome skill shortages among trades such as bricklayers and to boost quality. Units made in advance in a factory can be built to much tighter tolerances than are possible on a muddy, windy building site. This results in fewer complaints. After trials Bovis is using its modern techniques at Cambourne, a development that will grow to 3300 homes over the next 10 years. Houses are being built with inner walls made of 'aircrete' blocks that are stuck together with glue. The blocks, made from relatively light aerated concrete, are the size of about

10 bricks, allowing walls to be built more quickly. Unlike traditional mortar, the glue can be used in freezing conditions, which means construction can continue throughout the winter. The selling points of concrete over timber are that it feels more solid and is fireproof, rot-proof and provides better insulation.

Once the walls and floors are up, the roof trusses can be fixed and covered with waterproof felt, allowing work on installing the electrics, plumbing and internal finishes to be carried out. Bovis's plan is to build complete roof units on the ground – where work can go ahead faster and more safely than on the top of a house – and lift them into place. If the tiling industry can develop lightweight roof tiles, Bovis's aim is to fix the tiles as well before lifting the roof into position. With the roof in place, factory-made one-piece dormer windows are lifted by crane into position. Underneath, completed door and window units are fitted in the gaps left in the walls.

Once the inner wall is up and work is going on inside, the bricklayer can be brought in to build a brick outer 'skin' so the house looks just like its traditional counterparts. "The beauty of this method is that it removes the bricklayer from the critical path of building the house," says Mr Harris.

Bovis is not alone in shifting to prefabrication, although it buys the components rather than making them itself. Two other large housebuilders, Westbury and Wilson Connolly, have in-house operations making timber frame units. But while Westbury is increasing production, Wilson Connolly is cutting back because it has not achieved savings. The problem with prefabrication is that it is more expensive than traditional methods – though costs should come down as more experience is gained and volumes increase. Faster build times mean a higher return on capital invested but, for companies with manufacturing arms, moving to factory production requires the housebuilders to forecast demand in a notoriously cyclical market, analysts warn.

"Bovis is a good way of investing in new production techniques without absorbing all of the risks involved in manufacturing," said Mark Howson, analyst at ABN Amro. Bovis shares rose $12\frac{1}{2}$p to $329\frac{1}{2}$p after it unveiled its prefabrication plans to analysts last week, it has since risen to 336p, but there are no signs that a commitment to prefabrication is a guarantee of a premium over conventional housebuilders.

Source: FT.com, Charles Batchelor, 21 November 2001
© The Financial Times Ltd

**Case Study 16.1
Question**

1   Discuss the strategies used in this case to reduce the project completion time of new homes.

PERT:
takes into account the fact that most task durations are not fixed by using a statistical distribution to describe the variability inherent in the tasks.

Project Evaluation and Review Technique (PERT)

The **Project Evaluation and Review Technique (PERT)** approach attempts to take into account the fact that most task durations are not fixed but vary when they are executed. Thus, PERT provides a way of incorporating risk into project schedules.

It does this by using a beta probability distribution to describe the variability inherent in the processes. The probabilistic approach involves three time estimates for each activity:

■ *optimistic time* – the task duration under the most optimistic conditions;
■ *pessimistic time* – the task duration under the most pessimistic conditions;
■ *most likely time* – the most likely task duration.

To derive the average or expected time for a task duration the following equation is used:

$$\text{Expected duration} = \frac{\text{Optimistic} + (4 * \text{Most likely}) + \text{Pessimistic}}{6}$$

Greater risk is reflected in the spread between 'Optimistic' and 'Most likely' and, in particular, between 'Most likely' and 'Pessimistic'. For an activity with no risk the values of 'Optimistic', 'Most likely' and 'Pessimistic' would be the same. To calculate the degree of uncertainty associated with the duration of a task we compute the task variance:

$$\text{Variance} = \frac{(\text{Pessimistic} - \text{Optimistic})^2}{36}$$

By summing the variance for each task on a path through the network it is possible to calculate the variance for the path. The square root of the variance is taken to calculate the standard deviation for a particular network path.
The combination of the expected time and standard deviation for the network path allows managers to compute probabilistic estimates of project completion times. The probability of completing any path through the network in a specified time is calculated using the following equation:

$$z = \frac{\text{Specified time} - \text{Expected time}}{\text{Path standard deviation}}$$

Thus, if the Specified time = 20 and the Expected time = 19, with a Path standard deviation of 1.00, $z = (20 - 19)/1.00$, therefore $z = 1$. Looking up the value of z on a standardized normal curve gives an area under the curve of 0.8413. Thus, the probability of finishing the project in 20 weeks is 84.13%. The project manager can then make an informed decision about the use of a time buffer or reserve to the project schedule to increase the likelihood of the project completing on time.

A point to bear in mind with these estimates is that they only take into consideration the tasks on the critical path and discount the fact that slack on tasks on a non-critical path could delay the project. Therefore, the probability that the project will be completed by a specified date is the probability that all paths will be completed by that date, which is the product of the probabilities for all the paths.

Worked Example 16.3

PERT

Stone Ltd has just accepted a project that can be broken down into the following eight activities.

		Estimated duration (days)		
Activity	Predecessor	Optimistic	Most likely	Pessimistic
A	–	4	11	12
B	–	45	48	63
C	B	13	33	35
D	B	25	29	39
E	A, C	14	21	22
F	D, E	18	32	34
G	A, C	17	19	27
H	G	15	20	25

The project must be completed in 141 days, otherwise severe penalties become payable. You are required to find the critical path and to estimate the probability of the critical path time exceeding 141 days.

Solution

First, calculate the mean and standard deviation for each activity:

$$\text{Mean} = \frac{(\text{Optimistic} + 4 * \text{Most likely} + \text{Pessimistic})}{6}$$

$$\text{Standard deviation} = \frac{(\text{Pessimistic} - \text{Optimistic})^2}{36}$$

Activity	Mean	Standard deviation
A	10	1.33
B	50	3
C	30	3.67
D	30	2.33
E	20	1.33
F	30	2.67
G	20	1.67
H	20	1.67

Next, draw the AON network diagram:

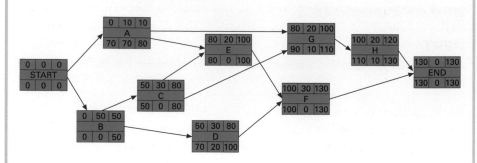

This gives a critical path of B, C, E, F giving an expected time of 130 days. Assuming that the distribution of the total project time is normal, the probability of the project time exceeding 141 days can be found as follows.

There are five routes through the network:

Route	Mean duration	Standard deviation	141 day − Mean	Z	Probability within 141 days (%)
BCEF	130	5.6	11	1.96	97.5
BDF	110	4.6	31	6.63	100
BCGH	120	5.3	21	3.96	100
AEF	60	3.3	81	24.55	100
AGH	50	2.7	91	33.7	100

Since the only route likely to exceed 141 days is BCEF, the probability that the company will become liable to pay the penalties is $(100 - 97.5) = 2.5\%$.

Project Network Simulation

In addition to the use of PERT, another method for measuring the consequence of risk on project completion times is the use of **project network simulation**. In order to use the PERT approach it must be assumed that the paths of a project are independent and the same tasks are not on more than one path. If a task is on more than one path and its actual completion time was much larger than its expected time it is obvious that the paths are not independent. If the network consists of these paths and they are near the critical path time then the results will be invalid. Simulation can be used to develop estimates of a project's completion time by taking into account all the network paths. Probability distributions are constructed for each task derived from estimates provided by such data collection methods as observation and historical data. A simulation then generates a random number within the probability distribution for each task. The critical path is then determined and the project duration calculated. This procedure is repeated a number of times (maybe more than 100) until there is sufficient data in order to construct a frequency distribution of project times. This distribution can be used to make a probabilistic assessment of the actual project duration. If greater accuracy is required the process can be repeated to generate additional project completion estimates which can be added to the frequency distribution.

Apart from the use of PERT and simulation to provide a measure of the consequence of risk on project completion times, other methods include decision trees and payoff tables. See Nicholas (2004) for more details.

Software for Network Analysis

For projects of any size or in a commercial situation computer software will be used to assist in constructing the network diagram and calculating network durations. From a critical path network and with the appropriate information, it is usually possible for the software to automatically generate Gantt charts, resource

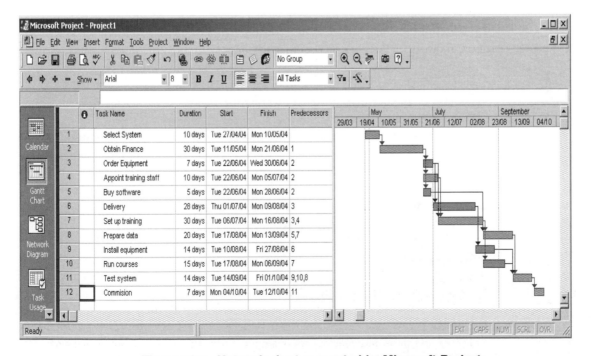

Figure 16.9 Network chart generated by Microsoft Project

loading graphs and cost graphs. A screen display for Microsoft Project charts is shown in Figure 16.9.

Benefits and Limitations of the Network Analysis Approach

A number of benefits can be attained by using the network analysis approach in project management. First, it requires a structured analysis of the number and sequence of tasks contained within a project, so aiding understanding of resource requirements for project completion. It also provides a number of useful graphical displays which assist understanding of such factors as project dependences and resource loading. It also gives a reasonable estimate of the project duration and the tasks which must be completed on time to meet this duration (i.e., the critical path). The network also acts as a control mechanism to monitor actual progress against planned progress on the Gantt chart. It also provides a means of estimating any decrease in overall project time by providing extra resources at any stage. Finally, it can be used to provide cost estimates for different project scenarios.

There are, however, a number of limitations to bear in mind when using network analysis. Its use is no substitute for good management judgement in such areas as prioritizing and selecting suppliers and personnel for the project. Also, any errors in the network such as incorrect dependency relationships or the omission of tasks may invalidate the results. The task times are forecasts and are, thus, estimates which are subject to error. PERT and simulation techniques may reduce time estimation errors, but at the cost of greater complexity which may divert management time away from more important issues. Time estimates for tasks may be greater than necessary to provide managers with slack to ensure they meet deadlines ('sandbagging') or too short for a realistic estimate ('blue skies'). Also, the method assumes activities are independent. Actually, the duration of one activity may be dependent on the duration of another. The method assumes a precise breaking point between activities. In reality, one activity may start before a predecessor activity has finished. Finally, activities just off the critical path may become critical after it is too late to do anything about them.

Summary

1 Projects are unique, one-time operations designed to accomplish a specific set of objectives in a limited time-frame.

2 The main elements of project management are estimate, plan and control.

3 There are three main ways of structuring an organization: project, functional and matrix.

4 The role of the project manager is to provide clearly defined goals and ensure adequate resources are employed on the project.

5 The steps in the network analysis technique briefly comprise identifying the project activities, estimating activity durations, identifying activity relationships, drawing the network diagram and identifying the critical path.

6 Project risk analysis can be undertaken using methods such as PERT and simulation.

7 The network analysis technique can provide an estimate of project performance under a number of scenarios. It is not, however, a substitute for good project management.

Exercises

1. Discuss the project management activities of estimate, plan and control.
2. What assumptions does the network analysis method make?
3. A company has identified the following activities that will make up a project:

Activity	Duration (hours)	Immediate predecessor(s)
A	1	–
B	1	A
C	3	B
D	2	B
E	2	D
F	1	E
G	3	C
H	2	F, G
I	1	H
J	1	I
K	1	I
L	1	J, K

a. Draw an AON diagram for this project.
b. Calculate the earliest start, earliest finish, latest start, latest finish and slack times for each activity.
c. Identify the critical path.

4. A company has identified the activities and resource requirements for the following project:

Activity	Duration (days)	Immediate predecessor	Members required (day)
A	3	–	4
B	4	–	3
C	9	–	4
D	4	A, B	7
E	5	B	8
F	6	D, C	9
G	6	E, C	5
H	10	F, G	2

a. Draw an AON diagram for this project.

b. Calculate the earliest start, earliest finish, latest start, latest finish and slack times for each activity.

c. Identify the critical path.

d. Draw a Gantt chart of the project indicating the slack times for each activity.

e. Draw a capacity loading graph based on the Gantt chart.

5. The following describes the introduction of a new product to be manufactured by a firm. The product has been developed and market-tested by the R&D centre, but the manufacturing processes required to produce the product have yet to be developed. The process engineering group has been assigned the responsibility of the design project and have been given a target of 60 days to arrive at an overall process design. Although 60 days seemed very short to the process engineers at first, after some discussion it was concluded that they could probably pull it off because the product and its processes were so similar to the present processing technologies in use at their plant. These activities, their precedence relationships and their durations were estimated by the engineers as follows:

Activity	Description	Precedence	Duration (days)
A	Initial product design study	–	12
B	Preliminary product redesign for production	A	10
C	Preliminary facility redesign for product	A	15
D	Preliminary process technologies study	A	9
E	Facility modification for product redesign	B	6
F	Intermediate facility redesign	C, E	12
G	Intermediate product redesign	B	14
H	Specific process machinery design	B, D	21
I	Final facility, product and process design	F, G, H	10

a. Draw an AON diagram for this project.

b. Calculate the earliest start, earliest finish, latest start, latest finish and slack times for each activity.

c. Identify the critical path.

6. The HairCare company manufactures a range of hair care products, including a range of hair-styling gels. A competitor has recently introduced a new hair gel, which in the last 6 months has taken a significant share of the market, with adverse effects on HairCare's sales. The management at HairCare has decided that a competitive product must be introduced as quickly as possible and has asked Walter Dobie, the management accountant, to draw up a plan for developing and marketing the new product. As the first step in planning the project, Walter has identified the following major tasks which will be involved in the new product launch. He has also estimated how long each task will take and the order in which the tasks must take place:

Activity	Description	Precedence	Estimated duration (weeks)
A	Design new product	–	8
B	Design packaging	–	4
C	Organize production facilities	A	4
D	Obtain production materials	A	2
E	Manufacture trial batch	C, D	3
F	Obtain packaging	B	2
G	Decide on test market area	–	1
H	Package trial batch	E, F	2
I	Distribute product in test area	H, G	3
J	Conduct test market	I	4
K	Assess test market	J	3
L	Plan national launch	K	4

a. Draw an AON diagram for this project and determine how long it will be before the new product can be launched.

b. Calculate the slack time available for all the activities.

c. The time taken to complete tasks A, B, D, K and L is somewhat uncertain and so the following optimistic and pessimistic estimates have also been made to supplement the most likely figure given above. The additional estimates are:

Activity	Optimistic time (weeks)	Pessimistic time (weeks)
A	5	13
B	2	6
D	1	4
K	2	6
L	2	8

What is now the expected time for the product to be launched and what is the probability of this time exceeding 35 weeks (you should assume that the overall project duration follows a normal distribution)?

7. A computer system has recently been installed in the accounts department of a manufacturing company. The activities involved in introducing the system are listed below together with their normal durations and costs. Since it would be possible to shorten the overall project duration by crashing certain activities at extra cost, the relevant details are also included. In addition, there will be a weekly charge of £2500 to cover overheads.

Activity	Predecessor	Normal		Crash	
		Duration (weeks)	Cost	Duration (weeks)	Cost
A	–	3	3 000	2	4 000
B	–	6	6 000	–	–
C	A	4	8 000	1	11 000
D	B	2	1 500	–	–
E	A	8	4 000	5	5 000
F	B	4	3 000	2	5 000
G	C, D	2	2 000	–	–
H	F	3	3 000	1	6 000

The crash time represents the shortest time in which the activity can be completed given the use of more costly methods of completion. Assume that it is possible to reduce the normal time to the crash time in steps of 1 week and that the extra cost will be proportional to the time saved:

a. Using the normal durations and costs construct an activity network for the introduction of the new computer system. Determine the critical path and associated cost.

b. Activities E and F have to be supervised by the chief accountant who will not be available for the first 7 weeks of the project period. Both activities, however, can be supervised simultaneously. Determine whether or not this will affect the completion date and, if so, state how it will be affected.

c. Assuming the chief accountant will be available whenever required and that all resources necessary to implement the crashing procedures will also be available, determine the minimum cost of undertaking the project.

8. Explain the following terms associated with project management:
   a. Critical path.
   b. Slack time.
   c. Crashing.
   d. PERT.

References

Nicholas, J.M. (2004), *Project Management for Business and Engineering: Principles and Practice*, 2nd Edition, Elsevier Butterworth-Heinemann.

Sapolsky, H.M. (1972), *The Polaris System Development: Bureaucratic and Programmatic Success in Government*, Harvard University Press, pp. 118–119.

Further Reading

Cadle, J. and Yeates, D. (2004), *Project Management for Information Systems*, 4th Edition, Pearson Education.

Hughes, B. and Cotterell, M. (2002), *Software Project Management*, 3rd Edition, McGraw-Hill.

Lock, D. (2003) *Project Management*, 8th Edition, Gower.

Maylor, H. (2002), *Project Management*, 3rd Edition, Financial Times/ Prentice Hall.

Moser, S., Henderson-Sellers, B. and Misic, V.B. (1999), Cost estimation based on business models, *Journal of Systems and Software*, 49(1), 33–42.

Web Links

www.ogc.gov.uk/prince/index.htm PRINCE2 official site.

www.pmi.org Project Management Institute. Contains information regarding news and events in the area of project management.

www.projectnet.co.uk Project Manager Today. Links to books and events in the area of project management.

www.comp.glam.ac.uk/pages/staff/dwfarthi/projman.htm Dave W. Farthing's Software Project Management Web link page contains many links to project management resources.

www.projectmanagement.com Contains many articles regarding project management.

www.primavera.com Primavera Systems Inc. Software product Primavera Project Planner.

Chapter 17

Quality

■ Defining Quality

■ Total Quality Management (TQM)

- ● The Principles of Total Quality Management
- ● The Cost of Quality
- ● Quality Standards and Awards

■ Six Sigma Quality

- ● Improving Effectiveness
- ● Improving Efficiency
- ● The DMAIC Methodology
- ● Implementing Six Sigma

■ Statistical Process Control (SPC)

- ● Chance Causes of Variation
- ● Assignable Causes of Variation
- ● Control Charts for Variable Data
- ● Control Charts for Attribute Data
- ● Investigating Control Chart Patterns
- ● Determining the Sample Size for Variable and Attribute Control Charts
- ● Tolerances, Control Limits and Process Capability

■ Acceptance Sampling

- ● The Operating Characteristic Curve
- ● Producer's and Consumer's Risk
- ● Average Outgoing Quality (AOQ)
- ● Sampling Plans

Learning Objectives

After reading this chapter, you should be able to:

1 Understand the philosophy of Total Quality Management (TQM).

2 Understand customer expectations of quality.

3 Describe the TQM implementation models of the quality gurus.

4 Evaluate the costs of quality.

5 Understand the objectives of the ISO 9000 quality standard.

6 Describe the concept of Six Sigma improvement.

7 Understand the use of acceptance sampling.

Introduction

Quality is increasingly seen as important to competitive success due in part to the high cost of quality failures which are incurred through aspects such as inspection and loss of customer goodwill. Quality is one of the five performance objectives and, as such, having a high-quality product or service often represents an essential element in being considered by the customer, even if the main competitive factor is another aspect of performance such as price (Chapter 2 covers the relationship between performance objectives and competitive factors). Quality is a particular challenge for service organizations in that both the tangible and intangible aspects of the service (e.g., the food and the service at a restaurant) must meet quality standards in order to earn repeat customers. The quality of the intangible aspect of the service may be difficult to measure and often depends on an unpredictable interaction between the service provider and customer. The issue of simultaneity in services (the characteristic that services are produced and consumed simultaneously) which means the service provider and customer will interact during the service delivery process is covered in more detail in Chapter 1.

This chapter considers topics relevant to the pursuit of high quality. Total Quality Management (TQM) is a philosophy and approach which aims to ensure that high quality is a primary concern throughout the organization. The realization that a high level of quality can deliver competitive advantage is reflected in the widening use of Six Sigma initiatives. Statistical process control is a particularly important technique in ensuring that the process of delivering the product/service is performing satisfactorily. Acceptance sampling is relevant to organizations when the cost of inspection is high relative to the cost of a defective product being identified.

Defining Quality

In order to understand programmes such as Total Quality Management (TQM), it is first necessary to consider more closely the meaning of quality itself. If the objective of a business is to produce goods and services that meet customer needs then the concept of quality should be related to how well these needs are met from the customer's point of view. Feigenbaum (2005) defines quality around the notion of the combination of product and service characteristics through which the product or service will meet customer expectations. However, since different customers will have different product needs and requirements it follows that they will have different quality expectations. Garvin (1984) defines eight dimensions of quality or quality characteristics which the customer looks for in a product:

- performance;
- features;
- reliability;
- conformance;
- durability;
- serviceability;
- aesthetics;
- other perceptions.

The customer will trade off these quality characteristics against the cost of the product in order to get a value for money product. From the producer's point of view it is important that marketing can identify customer needs and then operations can meet these needs at the quality level expected. Once the product design has been determined then quality during the production process can be defined by how closely the product meets the specification required by the design. This is termed the quality of conformance and the ability to achieve this depends on a number of factors such as the performance level of the machinery, materials and training of staff in techniques such as statistical process control. In addition, the product cost is an important design consideration and the production process needs to produce items at a cost that conforms to the product price. Thus, the organization must consider quality both from the producer and customer point of view and product design must take into consideration process design in order that the design specification can be met.

QUALITY OF CONFORMANCE: how closely the product meets the specification required by the design.

TOTAL QUALITY MANAGEMENT (TQM): a philosophy and approach which aims to ensure that high quality, as defined by the customer, is a primary concern throughout the organization and that all parts of the organization work towards this goal.

Total Quality Management

Total Quality Management (TQM) is a philosophy and approach which aims to ensure that high quality, as defined by the customer, is a primary concern throughout the organization and all parts of the organization work towards this goal. TQM does not prescribe a number of steps that must be followed in order to achieve high quality but rather should be considered a framework within which organizations can work. The TQM process will be dependent on factors such as customer needs, employee skills and the current state of quality management within the organization.

The Principles of Total Quality Management

TQM has evolved over a number of years from ideas presented by a number of people termed 'quality gurus'. People such as W. Shewhart developed many of the technical methods of statistical control such as control charts and sampling methods which formed the basis of quality assurance. In the early 1970s, however, this technical focus was subsumed by more of a managerial philosophy. A.V. Feigenbaum introduced the concept of total quality control to reflect a commitment of effort on the part of management and employees throughout an organization to improving quality. There is a particular emphasis on strong leadership to ensure everyone takes responsibility for control and there is an emphasis on quality improvement as a continual process – giving rise to the term 'continuous improvement'. TQM encompasses both the techniques of quality assurance and the approach of total quality control. A number of implementation models have been put forward by quality gurus, like Deming (1985), Juran (2001) and Crosby (1996).

Deming proposed an implementation plan consisting of 14 steps which emphasizes continuous improvement of the production process to achieve conformance to specification and reduce variability. This is achieved by eliminating common causes of quality problems such as poor design and insufficient training and special causes such as a specific machine or operator. He also places great emphasis on statistical quality control techniques and promotes extensive employee involvement in the quality improvement program.

Deming's (1985) 14 steps are summarized as follows:

1   Create a constancy of purpose toward product improvement to achieve long-term organizational goals.
2   Adopt a philosophy of preventing poor-quality products instead of acceptable levels of poor quality as necessary to compete internationally.
3   Eliminate the need for inspection to achieve quality by relying instead on statistical quality control to improve product and process design.
4   Select a few suppliers or vendors based on quality commitment rather than competitive prices.
5   Constantly improve the production process by focusing on the two primary

sources of quality problems, the system and workers, thus increasing
productivity and reducing costs.

6   Institute worker training that focuses on the prevention of quality problems
and the use of statistical control techniques.

7   Instil leadership among supervisors to help workers perform better.

8   Encourage employee involvement by eliminating the fear of reprisal for
asking questions or identifying quality problems.

9   Eliminate barriers between departments, and promote cooperation and a
team approach to working together.

10   Eliminate slogans and numerical targets that urge workers to achieve higher
performance levels without first showing them how to do it.

11   Eliminate numerical quotas that employees attempt to meet at any cost
without regard for quality.

12   Enhance worker pride, artisanry and self-esteem by improving supervision
and the production process so that workers can perform to their
capabilities.

13   Institute vigorous education and training programmes in methods of quality
improvement throughout the organization, from top management down, so
that continuous improvement can occur.

14   Develop a commitment from top management to implement the previous
13 points.

Juran (2001) put forward a ten-step plan in which he emphasizes the elements of
quality planning (designing the product quality level and ensuring the process can
meet this), quality control (using statistical process control methods to ensure
quality levels are kept during the production process) and quality improvement
(tackling quality problems through improvement projects).

Crosby (1996) suggested a 14-step programme for the implementation of TQM.
He is known for changing people's perceptions of the cost of quality when he
pointed out that the costs of poor quality far outweigh the cost of preventing poor
quality, a view not traditionally accepted at the time.

Oakland (2005) sees the approaches of the quality guru as essentially
complementary and has suggested his own 11-step process.

The main principles of TQM covered in these plans can be summarized in the
following three statements:

1   *The customer defines quality and, thus, their needs must be met* – earlier it
was stated that the organization must consider quality both from the producer
and customer point of view. Thus, the product design must take into
consideration the production process in order that the design specification
can be met. A customer perspective is required so that the implications for
customers are considered at all stages in corporate decision making.

2 *Quality is the responsibility of all employees in all parts of the organization* – in order to ensure the complete involvement of the whole organization in quality issues TQM uses the concept of the internal customer and internal supplier. This recognizes that everyone in the organization consumes goods and services provided by other organizational members or internal suppliers. In turn, every service provided by an organizational member will have an internal customer. The implication is that poor quality provided within an organization will, if allowed to go unchecked along the chain of customer/ supplier relationships, eventually lead to the external customer. Therefore, it is essential that each internal customer's needs are satisfied. This requires a definition for each internal customer about what constitutes an acceptable quality of service. It is a principle of TQM that the responsibility for quality should rest with the people undertaking the tasks which can either directly or indirectly affect the quality of customer service. This requires not only a commitment to avoid mistakes but actually a capability to improve the ways in which they undertake their jobs. This requires management to adopt an approach of empowerment. This involves providing people with training and the decision-making authority necessary in order that they can take responsibility for the work they are involved in and learn from their experiences.

3 *A 'continuous improvement' culture must be developed to instil a culture which recognizes the importance of quality to performance* – continuous improvement is discussed later in this chapter.

The Cost of Quality

All areas in the production system will incur costs as part of their TQM programme. For example, the marketing department will incur the cost of consumer research in trying to establish customer needs. Quality costs are categorized as either the cost of achieving good quality (the cost of quality assurance) or the cost of poor-quality products (the cost of not conforming to specifications).

The Cost of Achieving Good Quality

The costs of maintaining an effective quality management programme can be categorized into **prevention costs** and **appraisal costs**. Prevention costs reflect the quality philosophy of doing it right the first time and includes those costs incurred in trying to prevent problems occurring in the first place. Examples of prevention costs include:

PREVENTION COSTS: reflect the quality philosophy of 'doing it right the first time' and includes those costs incurred in trying to prevent problems occurring in the first place.

APPRAISAL COSTS: are associated with controlling quality through the use of measuring and testing products and processes to ensure conformance to quality specifications.

■ the cost of designing products with quality control characteristics;
■ the cost of designing processes which conform to quality specifications;
■ the cost of the implementation of staff training programmes.

Appraisal costs are the costs associated with controlling quality through the use of measuring and testing products and processes to ensure conformance to quality specifications. Examples of appraisal costs include:

■ the cost of testing and inspecting products;
■ the costs of maintaining testing equipment;
■ the time spent in gathering data for testing;
■ the time spent adjusting equipment to maintain quality.

The Cost of Poor Quality

This can be seen as the difference between what it actually costs to provide a good or service and what it would cost if there was no poor quality or failures. This can account for 70% to 90% of total quality costs and can be categorized into internal failure costs and external failure costs. Internal failure costs occur before the good is delivered to the customer. Examples of internal failure costs include:

■ the scrap cost of poor-quality parts that must be discarded;
■ the rework cost of fixing defective products;
■ the downtime cost of machine time lost due to fixing equipment or replacing defective product.

External failure costs occur after the customer has received the product and primarily relate to customer service. Examples of external failure costs include:

■ the cost of responding to customer complaints;
■ the cost of handling and replacing poor-quality products;
■ the litigation cost resulting from product liability;
■ the lost sales incurred because of customer goodwill affecting future business.

The Quality–Cost Trade-off

The classical economic trade-off between costs shows that when the cost of achieving good quality (i.e., prevention and appraisal costs) increases, the cost of poor quality (internal and external failure costs) declines. This relationship is shown graphically in Figure 17.1.

Adding the two costs together produces the total cost curve. The optimal quality level is, thus, at the point when quality costs are minimized. However, many Japanese organizations did not accept the assumptions behind the traditional

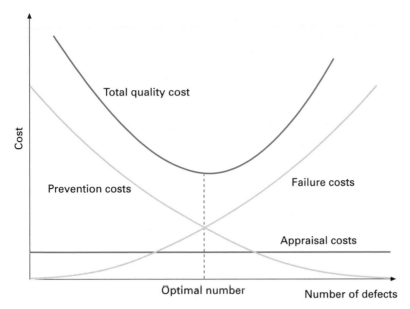

Figure 17.1   The traditional quality–cost trade-off

model and aimed for a zero-defect performance instead. The two views on the costs of quality can be seen by comparing the 'traditional' (Figure 17.1) and 'zero defect' (Figure 17.2) cost of quality graphs. According to the traditional view, the cost of prevention rises substantially as the zero-defect level is approached. This is based on the assumption that the last errors are the hardest to find and correct.

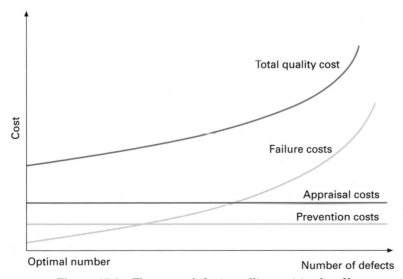

Figure 17.2   The zero-defect quality–cost trade-off

The zero-defect approach assumes that it costs no more to remove the last error as the first. It may take longer to determine what the source of the last error is but the steps to correct it are likely to be simple. While there is debate about the shape of the cost–quality curves and if zero defects is really the lowest cost way to make a product, it is beyond doubt that the new approach to quality performance is beneficial.

Many of the benefits of a quality programme are difficult to measure. These include the positive reputation from customers that follows from good quality and increased motivation and productivity gains from a quality improvement programme. However, the establishment of a zero-defect approach does have many implications for the organization. It means that all involved in the delivery of the product or service must not only strive to minimize errors but eliminate them, by a change in how they are undertaking their tasks if necessary. This means identifying and removing the cause of errors in order to obtain a right first time performance every time. This will require a proactive role from workers involved in the processes in finding solutions to quality problems. It is not enough for management to issue directives on quality, the workforce must be given the tools and training to improve the processes which they are the most familiar with. There must also not be a blame culture when defects are found but a recognition of the need to work together to solve the cause of the problem.

There must also be an increased awareness of the cost of quality through widely available statistics. Suppliers also need to be educated in order to ensure quality problems are not 'imported' into the organization. Other aspects include the need to ensure that quality is designed into the product to eliminate costly problems later at the manufacturing stage.

Quality Standards and Awards

ISO 9000:
a group of QMSs laid down by the International Organization for Standardization.

ISO 9000 provides a quality standard between suppliers and customers developed by the International Organization for Standardization (www.iso.ch). Having a pre-defined quality standard reduces the complexity of managing a number of different quality standards when a customer has many suppliers. Many countries have adopted ISO 9000 and, thus, it is particularly useful in standardizing the relationship between customers and suppliers on a global basis. The ISO 9000 model contains eight quality management principles on which to base a Quality Management System (QMS):

1 Customer focus.
2 Leadership.
3 Involvement of people.
4 Process approach.

5   Systems approach to management.

6   Continual improvement.

7   Factual approach to decision making.

8   Mutually beneficial supplier relationships.

The most recent ISO 9000 series of standards for QMSs comprises the following:

- ISO 9000 : 2000 – fundamentals and vocabulary of QMSs;
- ISO 9001 : 2000 – requirements of QMSs;
- ISO 9004 : 2000 – detailed guidelines for performance improvement in QMSs.

The standard is general enough to apply to almost any good or service, but it is the specific organization or facility that is registered or certified to the standard. To achieve certification, a facility must document its procedures for every element in the standard. These procedures are then audited by a third party periodically. The system thus ensures that the organization is following a documented, and thus consistent, procedure which makes errors easier to find and correct.

Other programmes which attempt to provide national and international standards for quality are the European Quality Award (EQA), the EFQM Excellence Model®, the Baldrige Award and the Deming Prize. The EQA was launched in 1992 by members of the European Foundation for Quality Management (EFQM) and is a yearly competition in which companies are scored in various categories such as leadership, processes and key performance results. The EFQM has also developed an Excellence Model® which allows a company to compare the way they run their business with best practice. A checklist is provided covering the areas of leadership, policy and strategy, people, partnerships and resources, processes, customer results, people results, society results and key performance results. The Baldrige Award was established in the USA in 1987 and seeks to recognize and encourage quality improvements. It measures performance in the seven areas of leadership, strategic planning, customer and market focus, measurement, analysis and knowledge management, human resource focus, process management and business results. The Deming Prize was established in 1951 by Japan and is awarded annually to companies that have distinguished quality management programmes.

CASE STUDY 17.1

Yell

With some 3400 employees, Yell is an international directories business operating in the classified advertising market. Its vision is to be the best business information bridge between buyers and sellers, regardless of channel, time or location in the markets in which they operate. The company aims to put buyers in touch with sellers through an integrated portfolio of simple to use advertising solutions – including printed (Yellow Pages), online (Yell.com) phone products and services.

Yell started introducing quality management in the late 1980s by adopting a TQM approach, and this approach became integrated into the way Yell manages its business. The company has used tools such as the EFQM Excellence Model®, Six Sigma, ISO 9001 : 2000, ISO 14001 : 1996, OHSAS 18001 : 1999 and Investors in People (IiP) to review and refine its overall management approach. A critical enabler of activities has been Yell's commitment to effective leadership, involvement and communication. Its focus now is on becoming the best in everything the company does.

Yell sets the scope and direction for its system of management through its vision and business purpose. It also defines the way this will be achieved through strong and clear values. Together, these provide the framework for all their activities. Yell brings this alive for people, through a structured approach that focuses on both the process and the people:

☐ alignment of goals and objectives through a systematic planning process;
☐ integration of policies and processes through a key process framework;
☐ enablement of activity through effective leadership, involvement and communication.

Senior managers generate the policy and strategy through an annual planning process, and work closely with members of the Strategic Planning team to ensure alignment with vision, purpose and strategic goals. All managers and their people are involved in the effective deployment of strategy by agreeing business initiatives and departmental plans and budgets. This is a highly interactive process with managers using a Scorecard approach to help them to align objectives with strategy.

Policy and strategy are delivered through a key process framework, which provides the top level architecture for their process management system. It consists of a value chain of customer-facing processes supported by five internal management processes. 'Providing Strategic Direction' is the first part of the Key Process Framework.

Strategy is communicated via face-to-face presentations to managers, which they then communicate to their team. This is supported by an 'objectives' intranet site where people can trace their progress. In addition, the theme for objectives is revised each year, to provide renewed focus; in the *You Make Us Unique* objectives brochure every employee's name was featured in the design. Other themes have included 'Breaking Boundaries', 'Superbrand-Superfuture' and 'Accelerating Performance'.

Against the backdrop of regulatory conditions and the changing economy between 2001 and 2004, Yell has achieved consistent annual UK revenue growth of approximately 5%. This is matched in its growth in customer base by approximately 5% and by continuous improvement in processes and customer services. The company has achieved positive trends, sustained high performance and good comparisons with other organizations; for example, errors in over 1 million individually produced adverts have been reduced by several per cent over the past 10 years to just 0.1%.

Yell UK is considered to be a benchmark in its approach to engaging with its people. For example, the objectives communication process is supported by a communication approach called 'Storytellers', which is highly interactive and encourages all employees to think strategically about their contribution to Yell. The company also runs an 'Uncles Programme', where senior managers meet with geographically dispersed teams and talk about business strategy and individual concerns. Senior managers go outside their own function and it keeps them in touch with front line issues as well as enabling them to explain strategic decisions.

Yell is very proud of its record on communicating individual responsibilities, and carries out a census survey amongst its employees once a year. The most recent survey achieved a 94% response rate. Since 1998 they have averaged over 97% for people saying that they clearly understand what is expected of them.

In 1999 Yell won the European Quality Award, and in 2004 became the first company to win the award for a second time. Yell also received two Special Prizes for 'Leadership' and 'People Development and Management'.

One of the challenges the company has faced was the proliferation of Areas For Improvement (AFIs). When Yell began its quality journey, and following any of its many assessments, they highlighted a daunting number of AFIs. This led to the introduction of a prioritizing approach, with improvement activities that are followed through until completed – with the focus clearly on actions and outcomes. Achievements are always recognized and this is communicated throughout the organization.

The company has also been very careful not to establish a 'flavour of the month'. The focus of the approach was placed upon improvement and not introducing 'another' initiative. This was also achieved by integrating tools such as the EFQM Excellence Model®, ISO 9001 and IiP into the overall management system.

Source: www.dti.gov.uk/bestpractice
Crown copyright material is reproduced with the permission of HMSO and the Queen's Printer for Scotland

1 What is Yell trying to achieve with its use of quality management standards and techniques?

**Case Study 17.1
Question**

Six Sigma Quality

Six Sigma is a quality improvement initiative launched by Motorola in the USA in the 1980s. The initiative was originally conceived by Motorola to achieve quality levels which are within six sigma control limits, corresponding to a rate of 3.4 defective parts per million (p.p.m.). However, Six Sigma has developed beyond a defect elimination program to become a companywide initiative to reduce costs through process efficiency and increase revenues through process effectiveness. The relationship between efficiency, effectiveness and organizational performance measured by revenue is shown in Figure 17.3.

SIX SIGMA:

a companywide initiative to reduce costs through process efficiency and increase revenues through process effectiveness.

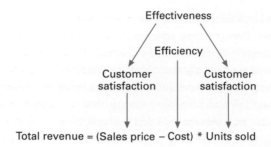

Figure 17.3   The relationship between effectiveness, efficiency and revenue

Revenue is given by the difference between the sales price and cost of the good or service (i.e., the profit margin) multiplied by the volume of the units sold or services delivered (i.e., the market share). The model shows how an increase in effectiveness leads to an increase in customer satisfaction which enables an increase in sales price (increasing profit margin) and an increase in units sold (increasing market share). An increase in efficiency will allow a reduction in cost (increasing profit margin) and again increasing total revenue. An increase in efficiency can also allow the sales price to be reduced keeping the profit margin constant, but leading to an increase in market share. Six Sigma contains plans for both increasing effectiveness and efficiency leading to increased revenues and, thus, improving company performance.

Improving Effectiveness

The level of effectiveness of the organization is reflected in the level of customer satisfaction. This means that efforts to improve effectiveness will focus on identifying and meeting internal and external customer requirements. In order to identify customer requirements and translate them into product and service characteristics Six Sigma advocates the use of Quality Functional Deployment (QFD). QFD asks customers not only about their critical requirements but also about the desired target values and limits for these requirements. Internal customer requirements must be aligned with those of the external customer. This is because external customers ultimately generate the revenues by being prepared to pay for a good or service at a price and at a volume that generates sufficient revenues. More details on QFD are given in Chapter 7.

Improving Efficiency

The aim of every process improvement approach using Six Sigma is to achieve measurable cost savings through a focus on decreasing process variation in terms of dispersion, predictability and centring. Dispersion relates to the amount (or width) of variation in the process. Predictability means that the measured characteristic belongs to the same statistical distribution over time. Centring refers to how well the mean of the distribution is aligned with the target value over time. An ideal process would be predictable, with a low dispersion and well centred.

Process variation is inherent in any process and needs to be analysed and the source identified in order to reduce its effect and, thereby, increase quality and reduce costs. One tool for reducing process variation is Statistical Process Control (SPC), which is covered in Chapter 18. Once identified, variation is usually divided into two types; common cause or random variation (which is inherent in the design of the process itself) and special cause or non-random variation which can be attributed to identifiable causes (e.g., poor material entering the process). The first step in reducing overall variation is to eliminate special cause variation and then, if necessary, reduce common cause variation by a new process design. A five-step methodology of Define, Measure, Analyse, Improve and Control (DMAIC) is used for both improving process performance and for improving process or product design.

The DMAIC Methodology

The **DMAIC methodology** emphasizes the use of statistical tools to gather data at each of the five stages of define, measure, analyse, improve and control.

> **THE DMAIC METHODOLOGY:** uses statistical tools to gather data at each of the five stages of define, measure, analyse, improve and control.

- *Define* – identify a potential area of improvement and define the project scope and processes involved. Assign a project team.
- *Measure* – decide what characteristics of the process require improvement. Identify the critical input variables that can be controlled and affect the output. Define what constitutes unacceptable performance or a defect. Collect sufficient data on process performance.
- *Analyse* – use the data collected in the measure phase to document current performance. Use control charts to judge whether the process is in control. The process performance can be benchmarked against similar internal or external processes.
- *Improve* – eliminate the root causes of non-random variation to achieve improvements in predictability, dispersion and centring. If no special causes can be found the improvement effort may need to focus on the design of the product or process.
- *Control* – verify and embed the change through the use of techniques such as control charts. Share experiences to transfer knowledge between process improvement teams.

Implementing Six Sigma

The DMAIC methodology is one aspect of a framework for implementation of the Six Sigma concept. Other aspects of this framework include top management commitment, stakeholder involvement, and training and measurement. Top management commitment is required in order to implement Six Sigma in all parts of the organization. Six Sigma requires the involvement of stakeholders such as employees, suppliers and customers. Employees are required to be trained and implement the concept and suppliers must deliver high-quality inputs to the organization. The whole rationale behind Six Sigma is to understand and meet the needs of customers, so their involvement is also vital. Training is important in order to implement the statistical tools necessary for Six Sigma and is based on various levels of expertise. These levels are often denoted by the terms White Belts, Green Belts, Black Belts, Master Black Belts and Champions in order of increasing training duration and level. In terms of measurement Six Sigma focuses on the measure of variation and uses the metric of defects per million opportunities (d.p.m.o.). As stated earlier the goal is to reduce variation to within Six Sigma control limits, corresponding to a rate of 3.4 defective p.p.m.

To summarize, the Six Sigma approach emphasizes a measurable improvement in revenues through increasing effectiveness and efficiency. It uses the DMAIC methodology to ensure process improvement efforts are based on factual data. It uses customer-focused improvements to ensure change increases revenue and uses training to ensure the appropriate tools are used for specific improvement projects.

CASE STUDY 17.2

Six Sigma at LG Electronics

Young-Ho Ham is standing with a man in a white coat who is holding up a series of wires which end in electrodes, the other ends plug into an ominous-looking machine bearing the word 'Polygraph'. Just as things are beginning to look a little worrying, and Young-Ho's smile a little sinister, the truth is revealed. "We tape the electrodes on to the muscles of the back and monitor the strain the back undergoes as it makes certain movements. So we can synthesize how much tension is created by, say, emptying a washing machine," the senior designer explains.

I'm in the Design Centre, a massive hi-tech building in central Seoul, built for (and by) the Korean company, LG. It's only when you're in LG's territory that you realize how huge this company is. Along with the building section of LG that put up this skyscraper, the company's logo is emblazoned everywhere you turn. LG has its own petrol stations, 24-hour convenience stores and fashion outlets. It makes the majority of the escalators and lifts you'll come across. And that's before you get as far as the electronics half of the company; for example, the company is the world's biggest manufacturer of air conditioners.

The Design Centre isn't just about making sure that the gadgets LG Electronics comes up with are ergonomically efficient and don't break your back every time you use them (although it's good to know that's a priority). It's not just about whether they look good – although there are rooms full of colour swatches, samples of fabrics and plastics and metals which will be expected to work together functionally and aesthetically in the company's next hi-fi, mobile phone or fridge-freezer. It's also the place where they talk a lot about Six Sigma.

This is the method whereby a manufacturing company can reduce its costs, and customers can get more reliable products. Six Sigma dictates that the failure rate for products should be no more than a really tiny figure (e.g., five or six per million). This means that a company like LG will produce many prototypes (pricey) so that the released product is virtually foolproof (saves a fortune in product recalls). They take it pretty seriously. In 2000, S.S. Kim, president and CEO of LG Digital Appliances, won the Presidential Award 'for his remarkable Six Sigma Activity', presented by the President of Korea.

LG was first known in Britain as Goldstar (LG stands for Lucky Goldstar, although it's never spelt out) when it secured a niche in the market by being pricier than Dixon's and Curry's in-house brands like Matsui but cheaper than practically everybody else (e.g., its 42-in plasma TV sells for around £3000). The company changed its name in 1995 and since then has been slowly repositioning itself to replace associations like 'bargain basement' with ones more like 'competitively priced quality'. It's a fair reflection of the company's products which are consistently highly specced and well priced: its flagship offerings include plasma and LCD flatscreen displays which are exceptionally good value, and the range of kitchen goods also includes innovative and impressive technology like the Solar Dom Lightoven, where conventional heating is assisted by halogen light to speed cooking time and save energy.

Then there is the Internet-enabled range: your fridge, washing machine, microwave and even air conditioner can all be connected to the Net so that you can control them remotely, or so they can perform diagnostic programs and contact an engineer if anything's going wrong (though they haven't got as far as arranging for someone to be at home to open the door when the engineer calls . . .).

The fridge includes a built-in touch-screen TV which also allows you to surf the Net, leave video notes for other members of your household and, providing you input the sell-by dates of your food, reminds you when it's about to spoil. The company recognizes that not everyone will want these products yet, but one day, maybe . . .

So, the Design Centre also includes futuristic prototypes of remarkable products such as the Magic Mirror, which is – yes, that's right – a mirror, but also displays information such as the weather for that day, news headlines and your appointments. (Next, perhaps, it will tell you if your clothes suit you.) And products which are more down to earth are given surprising new twists such as the fridge-freezer with a removable wine cooler section which can be wheeled out to become a separate wine bar.

As to whether such a gadget would be to everyone's tastes ... well, perhaps they could use the Polygraph machine to find the truth there as well.

Source: 'Fast Forward; Heart and Seoul; They take their electronics seriously in Korea – sometimes a little too seriously. David Phelan pays a visit to LG', by Dave Phelan, *The Independent*, 7 December 2002
© Independent News and Media Ltd

Case Study 17.2 Question

1   What is the relationship between the company's use of Six Sigma and its market position of competitively priced quality?

Statistical Process Control (SPC)

STATISTICAL PROCESS CONTROL (SPC): a sampling technique that checks the quality of an item which is engaged in a process.

Statistical Process Control (SPC) is a sampling technique which checks the quality of an item which is engaged in a process. Thus, SPC should be seen as a quality check for process rather than product design. Quality should be built in to the product during the design stage (techniques which can assist this are covered in Chapter 7). SPC works by identifying the nature of variations in a process, which are classified as being caused by 'chance' causes or 'assignable' causes.

Chance Causes of Variation

All processes will have some inherent variability due to factors such as ambient temperature, wear of moving parts or slight variations in the composition of the material that is being processed. The technique of SPC involves calculating the limits of these **chance cause variations** for a stable system, so any problems with the process can be identified quickly. The limits of chance cause variations are called 'control limits' and are shown on a control chart, which also shows sample data of the measured characteristic over time. There are control limits above and below the target value for measurement, termed the Upper Control Limit (UCL) and Lower Control Limit (LCL), respectively. An example control chart is shown in Figure 17.4.

CHANCE CAUSES OF VARIATION: inherent variability in processes due to factors such as ambient temperature, wear of moving parts or slight variations in the composition of the material that is being processed.

The behaviour of the process can, thus, be observed by studying the control chart. If the sample data plotted on the chart shows a random pattern within the UCL and LCL then the process is 'in-control'. However, if a sample falls outside the control limits or the plot shows a non-random pattern then the process is 'out-of-control'.

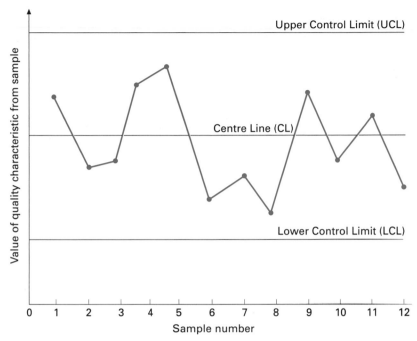

Figure 17.4   Statistical process control chart

Assignable Causes of Variation

If an 'out-of-control' process is discovered, then it is assumed to have been caused by an **assignable cause of variation**. This is a variation in the process which is not due to random variation but can be attributed to some change in the process, which needs to be investigated and rectified. However, in some instances the process could actually be working properly and the results could have been caused by sampling error. There are two types of error which can occur when sampling from a population:

■ *Type I error* – an error is indicated from the sample output when none actually occurs. The probability of a type I error is termed α.
■ *Type II error* – an error is occurring but has not been indicated by the sample output. The probability of a type II error is termed β.

Thus, type I errors may lead to some costly investigation and rectification work which is unnecessary. It may even lead to an unnecessary recall of 'faulty' products. Type II errors will lead to defective products as an out-of-control process goes unnoticed. Customer compensation and loss of sales may result if defective products reach the market place. The sampling methodology should ensure that

ASSIGNABLE CAUSES OF VARIATION: variations in the process which are not due to random variation but can be attributed to some change in the process, which needs to be investigated and rectified.

the probability of type I and type II errors should be kept as low as reasonably possible.

Control Charts for Variable Data

Control charts for variable data display samples of a measurement that can take a value from a range of possible values. Values will fall in or out of a range around a specified target value. Examples of variable data could be customer transaction time in a bank or the width of an assembly component. Two control charts are used in measuring variable data. The $\overline{X}$ Chart shows the distance of sample values from the target value (central tendency) and the R Chart shows the variability of sample values (dispersion).

$\overline{X}$ Chart

The $\overline{X}$ (x-bar) chart consists of a series of tests on a sample of data to check that the mean value of the process aligns with the target value. The sample size tends to be small: four or five. The $\overline{X}$ chart uses the central limit theorem which states that the sample means will be normally distributed if the process distribution is also normal. Otherwise, if the process does not follow a normal distribution the distribution of the sample means will be normally distributed if the sample size is sufficiently large. Thus, to construct control limits for an $\overline{X}$ chart, the following calculations can be used:

$$UCL = \mu + z * \sigma_x$$
$$LCL = \mu - z * \sigma_x$$

where $\mu =$ Process average
$\sigma_x = \sigma/\sqrt{n}$
$\sigma =$ Process standard deviation
$n =$ Sample size
$z = 3$ (for a Three Sigma chart).

When the process mean, μ, is not known, the average of the sample means, $\bar{\bar{x}}$, can be used instead and substituted in the previous equation.

A z value of 3 corresponds to a normal probability of 99.74%. Sometimes, the z value is 2, giving a probability of 95%, thus giving more narrow control limits. A smaller value of z increases the risk that the process sample will fall outside the control limits due to normal random variations. Conversely, a large value of z means that non-random changes may not be discovered. Traditionally, control charts use $z = 3$, called '3-sigma' (3σ) or 3 standard deviation limits.

Using $\overline{X}$ with R Charts

Usually, the $\overline{X}$ and R charts are used together and in this case the sample range is used as a measure of process variability. Thus, the control limits can be calculated as follows:

$$CV = \overline{\overline{X}}$$

$$UCL = \overline{\overline{X}} + A_2\overline{R}$$

$$LCL = \overline{\overline{X}} - A_2\overline{R}$$

where $\overline{\overline{X}} =$ Average of sample means
   $\overline{R} =$ Average sample range

Values of A_2 vary with the sample size and are shown in Table 17.1.

Table 17.1   Factors for determining control limits for X and R charts

Sample size n	Factor for $\overline{X}$ Chart A_2	Factor for R Chart D_3	Factor for R Chart D_4
2	1.88	0	3.27
3	1.02	0	2.57
4	0.73	0	2.28
5	0.58	0	2.11
6	0.48	0	2.00
7	0.42	0.08	1.92
8	0.37	0.14	1.86
9	0.34	0.18	1.82
10	0.31	0.22	1.78
11	0.29	0.26	1.74
12	0.27	0.28	1.72
13	0.25	0.31	1.69
14	0.24	0.33	1.67
15	0.22	0.35	1.65
16	0.21	0.36	1.64
17	0.20	0.38	1.62
18	0.19	0.39	1.61
19	0.19	0.40	1.60
20	0.18	0.41	1.59
21	0.17	0.43	1.58
22	0.17	0.43	1.57
23	0.16	0.44	1.56
24	0.16	0.45	1.55
25	0.15	0.46	1.54

R Chart

Control limits for range limits are found using the following calculations:

$$CV = \overline{R}$$

$$UCL = D_4\overline{R}$$

$$LCL = D_3\overline{R}$$

where $\overline{R} =$ Average sample range.

Values of D_3 and D_4 vary with the sample size and can be found in Table 17.1.

It is usual to plot both an $\overline{X}$ and a separate R chart for a process to provide perspectives on both movements in the process mean and movements in process dispersion, respectively.

Worked Example 17.1

Control Charts for Variable Data

As part of its process control activities a bakery wishes to monitor the weight of dough portions being measured out prior to baking. Below are given the weight of 13 samples each of 5 portions. Plot these data onto the appropriate charts and comment on the stability or otherwise of the process.

Sample/Weight (grams)

1	2	3	4	5	6	7	8	9	10	11	12	13
375	375	375	373	375	378	375	379	378	374	378	374	379
378	374	375	376	379	373	373	374	378	376	376	379	380
376	376	378	377	376	376	377	376	375	373	380	379	379
378	379	377	376	378	375	376	376	377	376	379	376	377
377	376	376	375	376	378	377	379	378	377	377	379	379

Solution

The first step is to calculate the mean ($\overline{X}$) and range (R) for each sample.

Sample	1	2	3	4	5	6	7	8	9	10	11	12	13
$\overline{X}$	376.8	376	376.2	375.4	376.8	376	375.6	376.8	377.2	375.2	378	377.4	378.8
R	3	5	3	4	4	5	4	5	3	4	4	5	3

Then calculate the mean of the means:

$$\overline{\overline{X}} = 376.6 \quad \text{and} \quad \overline{R} = 4$$

For the Means Chart

Sample size is 5; therefore, A_2 is 0.58 (lookup value in Table 17.1):

$$LCL = 376.6 - 0.58 \times 4$$
$$= 374.28$$
$$CV = 376.6$$
$$UCL = 376.6 + 0.58 * 4$$
$$= 378.92$$

For the Ranges Chart

Sample size is 5; therefore, $D_3 = 0$ and $D_4 = 2.11$ (lookup values in Table 17.1):

$$LCL = 4 \times 0$$
$$= 0$$
$$CV = 4$$
$$UCL = 4 \times 2.11$$
$$= 8.44$$

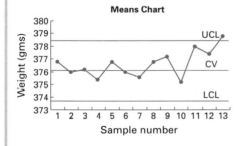
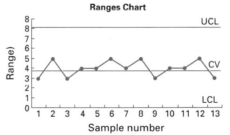

From the means chart it can be seen that the machine is overfilling.

Control Charts for Attribute Data

Attribute control charts measure discrete values such as whether a component is defective or not. Thus, there are no values, as in a variable control chart, from which a mean and range can be calculated. The data will simply provide a count of how many items conform to a specification and how many do not.

Two control charts will be described for attribute data: the p-chart shows the proportion of defectives in a sample and the c-chart shows the number of defectives in a sample.

p-chart

The p-chart is used when it is possible to distinguish between defectives and non-defectives for each sample item and, thus, calculate the number of defectives as a percentage of the whole (i.e., the proportion).

A p-chart takes samples from a process over time and the proportion of defective items is calculated to see if it falls within the control limits on the chart. Assuming a significant sample size and a 3-sigma chart the calculations can be based on a normal distribution to calculate the control limits as follows:

$$CV = p$$

$$UCL = p + 3\sqrt{\frac{p(1-p)}{n}}$$

$$LCL = p - 3\sqrt{\frac{p(1-p)}{n}}$$

where p = Population proportion defective (process mean)
n = Sample size.

When the process mean p is not known, the proportion defective $\bar{p}$ can be calculated from the samples and substituted in the previous equation.

Worked Example 17.2

Control Charts for Attribute Data

The following table gives the results of daily inspections of 500 units of a standard design electronic device produced during the month of June 1998:

Date in June	3	4	5	6	7	10	11	12	13	14
Rejects	10	14	18	10	14	21	17	12	15	16
Date in June	17	18	19	20	21	24	25	26	27	28
Rejects	16	25	26	12	14	17	15	9	10	14

(a) Estimate the total proportion of rejects during this month.
(b) Establish a single set of control limits for the daily fraction of rejects based on these figures and plot a control chart, showing the daily results.
(c) Comment on the stability of the manufacturing process. What appears to have happened to cause the sudden change between 19 and 20 June?
(d) Based on the records of this month, what would you recommend as the central value p to use for the following month's control chart for fraction rejects?

Solution

(a) The number of inspections in June 1998 is 500 units per day for 20 days, totalling 10 000 units. During this month a total of 305 units are rejected. Hence, the proportion rejected p is:

$$p = \frac{305}{10\,000}$$

$$= 0.0305 \ (3.05\%)$$

(b) The control limits are as follows:

$$p = 0.0305$$

$$n = 500$$

$$UCL = 0.0305 + 0.02306$$

$$= 0.0536$$

$$CV = 0.0305$$

$$LCL = 0.0305 - 0.02306$$

$$= 0.0074$$

The proportion of rejects over the 20 working days of June 1998 are as follows:

Date	3	4	5	6	7	10	11	12	13	14
Proportion defective	0.02	0.028	0.036	0.02	0.028	0.042	0.034	0.024	0.030	0.032
Date	17	18	19	20	21	24	25	26	27	28
Proportion defective	0.032	0.050	0.052	0.024	0.028	0.034	0.030	0.018	0.020	0.028

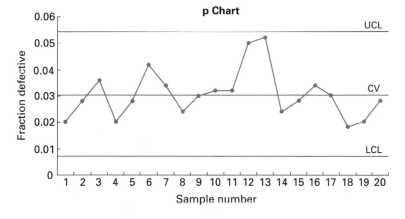

(c) The manufacturing process appears to be under control for the first half of June, and again over the last few days of the month. However, it seems clear that the process was interrupted between the 19th and 20th of June. It seems likely that the process controller decided that the process had gone out of control during the 18th and 19th of June, with two consecutive observations so close to the UCL. This fault was rectified so that the later results were an improvement.

(d) When recommending a central value for the following month it would seem sensible to only use those days in June when the process was stable. Hence, the results of the 18th and 19th of June would be ignored. The recommended value for p for the following month is:

$$p = \frac{305 - (25 + 26)}{10\,000 - 1000}$$

$$= \frac{254}{9000}$$

$$= 0.0282$$

Alternatively, we might use the results of just the last 7 days of June (the days after adjustment) to form the basis of the recommendation. This gives:-

$$p = \frac{91}{3500}$$

$$= 0.026$$

c-chart

A c-chart counts the actual number of defects when the proportion cannot be calculated. For example, if the quality of paint on a car body panel is being inspected, the number of blemishes (defects) can be counted, but the proportion cannot be calculated because the total number is not known. The Poisson distribution is theoretically used to represent the probability of a defect from an extremely large population, but the normal distribution is used as a substitute for the c-chart. Assuming a 3-sigma chart the control limits can be calculated as follows:

$$CV = c$$

$$UCL = c + 3\sqrt{c}$$

$$LCL = c - 3\sqrt{c}$$

where　　$c =$ Mean number of defects per sample.

When the process mean c is not known, the sample mean $\bar{c}$ can be estimated by dividing the number of defects by the number of samples and substituting in the previous equation.

Investigating Control Chart Patterns

Apart from the plots on the control charts that lie outside the control limits it is still possible that the process may be out-of-control due to non-random behaviour within the control limits. If the behaviour is random then the plots should follow no discernible pattern and occur either side of the centre line. There are several guidelines for identifying non-random behaviour. A selection of these guidelines are shown in Figure 17.5.

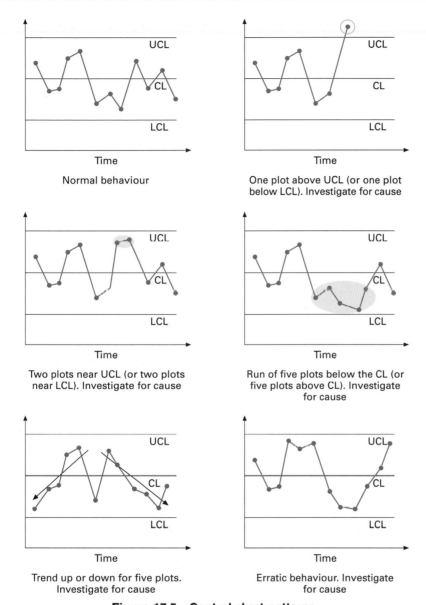

Figure 17.5   Control chart patterns

Run Patterns

It is possible to use a z pattern test or run test to determine the probability of certain plot patterns occurring. The general form of the calculation for the z test is as follows:

$$z_{\text{TEST}} = \frac{\text{Observed runs} - \text{Expected runs}}{\sigma}$$

where σ = Standard deviation.

From this the following calculation is derived for a run of sample values that consistently go up or down within the control limits:

$$Z_{U/D} = r - \frac{[(2N-1)/3]}{\sqrt{(16N-29)/90}}$$

where $r =$ Observed number of runs
         $N =$ Sample size.

For a run of sample values which are above or below the centre line, the calculation is as follows:

$$Z_{A/B} = r - \frac{[(N/2)+1]}{\sqrt{(N-1)/4}}$$

where $r =$ Observed number of runs
         $N =$ Sample size.

The z test values are compared with a z value for a particular level of variability. At a 95% probability level the z value will be ± 1.96. This means if the $Z_{A/B}$ or $Z_{U/D}$ is not within ± 1.96 then there is a 95% chance that the variability is not due to random variation.

Worked Example 17.3

Control Chart Patterns

A company wants to perform run tests to see if there is a pattern of non-randomness exhibited within the control limits. It wants to use a test statistic consistent with a 95% probability that the non-random patterns exist. The following run pattern has been identified:

Sample	Above/Below	Up/Down
1	B	–
2	A	U
3	B	D
4	A	U
5	B	D
6	B	D
7	A	U
8	B	D
9	A	U
10	B	D

Solution

$$r = 9$$

$$N = 10$$

$$Z_{A/B} = \frac{9 - ((10/2) + 1)}{(10 - 1)/4}$$

$$= 2.00$$

$$r = 8$$

$$N = 10$$

$$Z_{U/D} = \frac{8 - ((20 - 1)/3)}{(160 - 29)/90}$$

$$= 1.38$$

At a 95% probability $z = \pm 1.96$. The above/below test is slightly over this limit at $+2.00$, indicating that there may be some non-random pattern in the samples and the process should be checked.

Determining the Sample Size for Variable and Attribute Control Charts

It is important to note that the required sample size for each plot for a variable or attribute control chart is quite different. For $\overline{X}$ and R charts, sample sizes are usually 4 or 5 and can be as low as 2. This is because even 2 observations should provide a reasonable measure of the sample range and sample average.

For p-charts and c-charts, sample sizes are usually in the hundreds to achieve a useful quality measure. For example, a proportion defective of 5% would require 5 defective items from 100. In practice, sample size is also kept to a minimum to save operator time in observation. This will also permit more observation points to be implemented which will assist in finding the cause of any quality problem. Also, observations of output from a mix of machines may make it difficult to identify which machine is the source of the error.

Tolerances, Control Limits and Process Capability

It is important to distinguish between the above terms, referring to the variability of process output. They can be defined as follows:

■ *Tolerance* – a specified range of values (e.g., from customer needs) in which individual units of output must fall in order to be acceptable.

■ *Control limits* – statistical limits on how sample statistics (e.g., mean, range) can vary due to randomness alone.

■ *Process capability* – the inherent variability in a process.

The relationship between control limits and process capability can be expressed in the following formula:

$$\text{Control limits} = \text{Process mean} \pm z * \frac{\text{Process capability}}{\sqrt{n}}$$

where $z =$ Number of standard deviations from the mean

$n =$ Sample size.

Thus, it can be seen that control limits are based on the variability of samples of process output whose variability is a function of the process capability. Tolerances, however, are product/service specifications and are not specified in terms of the process by which the product/service is generated. Thus, a process which is performing statistically in-control may not necessarily be conforming to the external tolerance specifications imposed. Therefore, it is essential to ensure that the process is capable of meeting the required specifications and then ensure it can meet this tolerance consistently over time using process control. Conversely, if the natural variation of the process exceeds the designed tolerances of the product the process cannot produce the product according to specifications as the process variations which occur naturally, at random, are greater than the designed variation. To avoid this situation it is important that process capability studies are undertaken during the product/service design stage.

Acceptance Sampling

ACCEPTANCE SAMPLING:

consists of taking a random sample from a larger batch or lot of material to be inspected. The quality of the sample is assumed to reflect the overall quality of the lot.

Acceptance sampling consists of taking a random sample from a larger batch or lot of material to be inspected. The quality of the sample is assumed to reflect the overall quality of the lot. If the sample has an unacceptable number of defects the whole lot will be rejected. The point at which the defect level becomes unacceptable is based on an agreement between the customer and supplier of the goods. Because acceptance sampling is based on the traditional approach which assumes that a number of defects will be produced by a process, it is usually associated with the receiving inspection process from external suppliers.

Although the acceptable defect rate may be quoted as a percentage, the comments on Six Sigma quality levels in the Statistical Process Control (SPC) section apply here also. Thus, many organizations who take a Total Quality Management (TQM) approach would expect defect levels measured in p.p.m. Indeed, if suppliers have successfully achieved a TQM philosophy and are in a stable partnership with the supplier the receiving inspection process may be eliminated.

Acceptance sampling is, however, still relevant to organizations which have not yet achieved TQM quality levels and has also been traditionally used when the cost of inspection (e.g., destructive testing, sampling food, etc.) is high relative to the cost of the defective being identified. As in SPC when the product is inspected to see if it conforms to a specification, the measurement can be variable or in the form of an attribute.

Sampling design includes the following aspects:

■ the Operating Characteristic curve;
■ producer's and consumer's risk;
■ average outgoing quality.

The Operating Characteristic Curve

Because we are only using a sample to estimate the actual number of defects in the lot, this may lead to errors in accepting or rejecting a lot due to sampling error. For example, if there is a target of 2% fraction defectives in a lot, a particular sample may contain a higher percentage than this even though the whole lot may not. Therefore, the lot will be incorrectly rejected.

The Operating Characteristic (OC) curve indicates how effective the sampling plan is in discriminating between good and bad lots by showing the probability of accepting a lot for different quality levels for a given sample size and acceptance level. The shape and location of the OC curve is determined by the sample size (n) and the acceptance level (c) for the sampling plan. A selection of OC curves for different values of n and c is shown in Figure 17.6. Note that when the sample size is the same as the lot size the curve is a vertical line indicating 100% inspection with no risk.

Producer's and Consumer's Risk

As discerned for the OC curve, sampling error may mean either that a good lot is rejected (type I sample error) or that a bad lot is accepted (type II sample error). The Acceptable Quality Level (AQL) is the maximum percentage (fraction defective) that is considered acceptable. The probability of rejecting a lot that has an acceptable quality level is termed the producer's risk and is related to α, the probability of a type I error. Due to sampling error there may be a sample taken that does not accurately reflect the quality level of the lot and, thus, a lot that does not meet the AQL is passed on to the customer. The upper limit of defective items

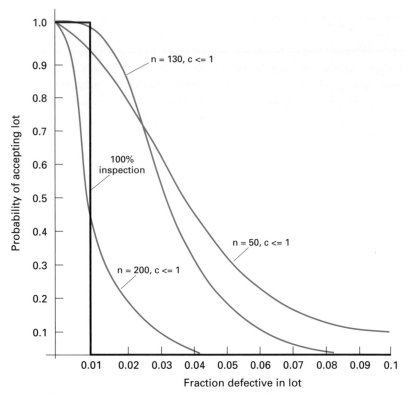

Figure 17.6 OC curves for different sample size (*n*) and acceptance number (*c*)

which the customer will accept is termed the Lot Tolerance Percent Defective (LTPD). The probability of accepting a lot in which the quality level (fraction defective) exceeds the LTPD is termed the 'consumer's risk' and relates to β, the probability of a type II error.

Usually, the customer will prefer the quality of lots to be as good or better than the AQL but is willing to accept some lots with quality levels no worse than the LTPD. A common scenario is to have producer's risk (α) at 5% and consumer's risk (β) at 10%. This means the customer expects to reject lots that are good or better than the AQL about 5% of the time and to accept lots that exceed the LTPD about 10% of the time.

A sampling plan is devised from these measures by using the OC curve. The α and AQL measures specify a point on the probability of acceptance axis and the β and LTPD measures define a point on the proportion defective axis. However, a trail and error process is required to determine the sample size (*n*) and acceptance number (*c*) to achieve these performance measures. This involves determining the probabilities of accepting a lot for various lot percentage defective values. A typical OC curve is shown in Figure 17.7.

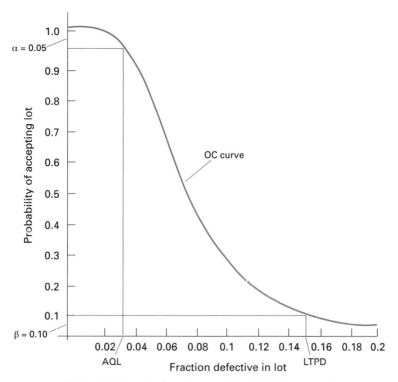

Figure 17.7 An Operating Characteristic curve

From Figure 17.7 it can be seen that if a lot has 3% defective items, for example, the probability of accepting a lot is 0.95. If management defines the AQL at 3%, then the probability that the lot will be rejected (α) is 1 minus the probability of accepting a lot (i.e., $1 - 0.95 = 0.05$). If management is willing to accept lots with a percentage defective up to 15% (LTPD), this corresponds to a probability that the lot will be accepted (β) of 0.10.

To avoid the time-consuming task of using a trial and error method to construct OC curves, standardized tables called 'Dodge–Romig Inspection tables' can be used based on a given set of risks. Also, computer software is available which will develop sampling plans based on values for AQL, LTPD, α and β.

Average Outgoing Quality (AOQ)

Even though the probability of accepting a lot containing defects may be very small, all lots, whether they are accepted or not, will pass on some defects to the customer. The expected number of these defective items is measured by the AOQ.

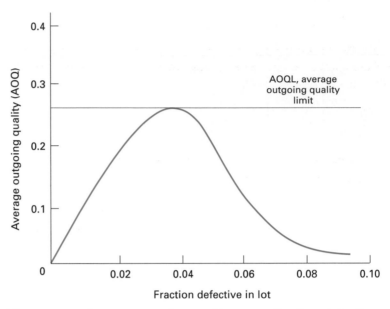

Figure 17.8   Average outgoing quality versus fraction defectives

Thus:

$$AOQ = pP_a\frac{N-n}{N}$$

where $p =$ Percentage defectives (horizontal axis in OC chart)
   $P_a =$ Possibility of accepting a lot (vertical axis in OC chart)
   $N =$ Lot size
   $n =$ Sample size.

Values for AOQ against fraction defectives are shown in Figure 17.8.

From Figure 17.8 it can be seen that the AOQ rises to a point from the origin and then falls back again. The peak is termed the Average Outgoing Quality Limit (AOQL) and represents when the sampling plan does its worst job of upgrading quality. That is, below this there are few defects accepted, above this there are more defects, but they are rejected and replaced. Each sampling plan will have a different AOQ curve and the AOQL can be used to select a suitable sampling plan.

Sampling Plans

The method of sampling or sampling plan can take a number of forms including the following.

Single Sampling Plan

For a single sample attribute plan the method consists of selecting a sample at random from a larger lot and determining whether the goods are defective or not (i.e., a discrete decision).

Double Sampling Plan

In a double sampling plan a smaller sample is taken than in a single sampling plan. If the quality is very good or very bad the lot is accepted or rejected as before. If the result is inconclusive then a second sample is taken and the lot is rejected or accepted on the combined results of the two samples. The technique should allow an overall saving of inspection costs by the use of a smaller sample which will usually provide a definite result.

Multiple Sampling Plan

Here, an initial sample (which can be as small as 1 unit) is taken. If the number of defectives is above or below a specified limit the lot is rejected or accepted as appropriate. If the number of defectives is between these limits, a second sample is taken and the total number of defects is compared with an increased set of upper and lower limits. The process repeats until the lot is accepted or rejected. Multiple sampling plans are particularly appropriate when inspection costs are relatively high. For example, for destructive testing when the cost of testing the whole sample would be prohibitive.

Variable Sampling Plan

A variable sampling plan takes samples from a measure that can take a range of values, as opposed to an attribute plan which is a discrete value. Variable sampling plans are constructed in a similar way to attribute plans but, instead of the binomial and Poisson distribution, a normal distribution is assumed (especially for a sample size greater than 30). This means the trial and error approach to develop the plan is not needed, but standardized variable tables are available to develop plans for various AQL values.

Summary

1 TQM is a philosophy which aims to ensure high quality is a primary concern for the organization.

2 Different customers will have different product needs and requirements and, thus, different quality expectations.

3 Deming proposes an implementation plan which emphasizes continuous improvement to achieve conformance to specification. Crosby proposes a TQM implementation plan that emphasizes changing people's perception of the cost of quality.

4 Quality costs can be categorized as either the cost of achieving good quality or the cost of poor quality.

5 ISO 9000 provides a quality standard between suppliers and customers.

6 Six Sigma is a companywide initiative to reduce costs through process efficiency and increase revenues through process effectiveness.

7 SPC is a sampling technique which checks the quality of an item which is engaged in a process.

8 Acceptance sampling consists of taking a random sample from a larger batch or lot of material to be inspected.

Exercises

1. What is the purpose of TQM?
2. Contrast the traditional quality/cost trade-off with the zero defects quality/cost trade-off.
3. Use the Web to compare the Baldrige Award and the European Quality Award.
4. Explain the relationship between Six Sigma and process management.
5. The following table gives the number of defectives in successive samples of 100 final assemblies removed at random from that day's production.

Day	Number of defectives	Day	Number of defectives
1	6	11	11
2	8	12	8
3	7	13	13
4	10	14	14
5	11	15	15
6	5	16	12
7	13	17	7
8	9	18	34
9	9	19	29
10	10	20	8

   a. Estimate the total proportion of rejects.
   b. Establish a single set of control limits for the daily fraction of rejects based on these figures and plot a control chart, showing the daily results.
   c. Comment on the stability of the manufacturing process.

6. The following table gives the means and ranges, from a sample size of 10, for the diameter of a machined part.

Mean	Range R	Mean	Range R	Mean	Range R
0.52	0.03	0.5	0.11	0.57	0.1
0.53	0.1	0.53	0.08	0.52	0.07
0.57	0.09	0.52	0.05	0.52	0.12
0.49	0.08	0.48	0.09	0.51	0.11
0.48	0.12	0.54	0.03	0.49	0.09

Use the data to set up a control chart for means and for ranges.

7. A machine produces components to a specified average length of 9.03 cm. Every hour a random sample of five components is selected from the process and their lengths measured. After 10 hours the data given below have been collected:

Sample number	Measurements (cm)				
1	9.00	9.10	9.00	9.05	8.95
2	9.10	9.10	9.00	9.05	9.05
3	9.00	9.05	9.00	9.05	9.00
4	9.00	9.00	8.95	9.00	9.05
5	9.00	9.10	9.05	9.05	9.00
6	9.00	9.10	9.10	9.05	9.00
7	9.00	9.10	9.05	9.15	9.05
8	9.00	9.10	9.10	9.00	9.05
9	9.00	9.00	8.95	9.00	9.00
10	9.00	9.05	9.00	9.10	8.95

Use the data to set up a control chart for means and for ranges.

8. Explain the concepts of producer's risk and consumer's risk in acceptance sampling.

References

Crosby, P.B. (1996), *Quality is Still Free: Making Quality Certain in Uncertain Times*, McGraw-Hill.

Deming, W.E. (1985), Transformation of Western style management, *Interfaces*, **15**(3), May/June, 6–11.

Feigenbaum, A.V. (2005), *Total Quality Control*, 4th Edition, McGraw-Hill.

Garvin, D.A. (1984), What does quality really mean, *Sloan Management Review*, **26**(1), 25–43.

Juran, J.M. (2001), *Juran's Quality Handbook*, 5th Edition, McGraw-Hill.

Oakland, J.S. (2005), *TQM: Text with Cases*, 3rd Edition, Butterworth Heinemann.

Further Reading

Besterfield, D.H. (2003), *Quality Control*, Prentice Hall.

Dodge, H.F. and Romig, H.G. (1959), *Sampling Inspection Tables: Single and Double Sampling*, 2nd Edition, John Wiley & Sons.

Taguchi, G., Chowdhury, S. and Wu, Y. (2005), *Taguchi's Quality Engineering Handbook*, John Wiley & Sons.

Web Links

www.iso.ch International Organization for Standardization (ISO). Site providing details on ISO 9000 and other standards.

www.baldrige.nist.gov National Institute of Standards and Technology. Details of the Baldrige Award.

www.efqm.org/model_awards/eqa/intro.asp European Foundation for Quality Management. Details of the European Quality Award.

www.qfdi.org QFD Institute. Contains newsletters and forums in the area of QFD.

www.qualitydigest.com Quality Digest. Access to magazine, news and tips on quality management.

www.quality.co.uk Quality Network. Resources on benchmarking, ISO 9000 and environmental management.

www.asq.org American Society for Quality. Publications and courses in the area of quality management.

www.quality.nist.gov National Institute of Standards and Technology. Contains details of Baldrige National Quality Programme.

www.ukas.com UK Accreditation Service. Accredits the certification bodies which oversee the implementation of quality management systems based on ISO 9001 : 2000.

www.quality-foundation.co.uk British Quality Foundation. A not for profit organization that promotes business excellence to the private, public and voluntary sectors.

Chapter 18

Improvement

■ Continuous Improvement (CI)

- ● Environment
- ● Involvement
- ● Problem-solving Skills

■ The Learning Organization

- ● Adaptive Learning
- ● Reconstructive Learning
- ● Process Learning

■ Business Process Reengineering (BPR)

- ● The relationship between BPR and CI Approaches

■ Systems Thinking

■ Balanced Scorecard

■ Activity-Based Costing (ABC)

■ Benchmarking

> ## Learning Objectives
>
> After reading this chapter, you should be able to:
>
> 1 Understand the role of environment, involvement and problem solving in the implementation of continuous improvement.
>
> 2 Understand the need for organizational learning.
>
> 3 Understand the concept of Business Process Reengineering (BPR).
>
> 4 Understand the concept of systems thinking.
>
> 5 Describe the use of the balanced scorecard.
>
> 6 Describe the use of activity-based costing.
>
> 7 Understand the concept of benchmarking.

Introduction

This chapter covers the topic of operations improvement in the organization. The focus of improvement should be directed towards appropriate areas of the operation where any increase in performance will help the organization meet its strategic goals. In this text the five performance objectives of quality, speed, dependability, flexibility and cost are used to measure operations performance in relation to its strategy (Chapter 2). Once priorities for improvement have been identified then the improvement approaches in this chapter can be used to implement the changes needed to improve performance in the required areas. In this chapter the approaches of continuous improvement, business process reengineering, organizational learning, systems thinking, balanced scorecard and activity based costing are discussed.

Continuous Improvement

CONTINUOUS IMPROVEMENT: concerns incremental changes within the organization whose cumulative effect is to deliver an increased rate of performance improvement.

Continuous improvement programmes are associated with incremental changes within the organization whose cumulative effect is to deliver an increased rate of performance improvement. Continuous improvement requires creating the right environment in which the importance of the approach is recognized and rewarded. This means ensuring the involvement of all the members of the organization and ensuring that these members have the problem-solving skills necessary to achieve worthwhile improvements. The issues of environment,

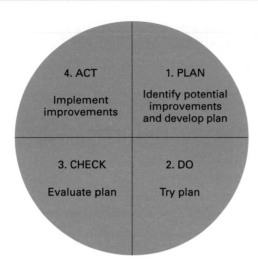

Figure 18.1   The Plan–Do–Check–Act (PDCA) cycle

involvement and problem-solving skills will now be explored in relation to continuous improvement implementation.

Environment

In order to create the right environment in which improvement can take place it is important to have a set of procedures for the improvement process which formalizes actions so that progress can be monitored and measured. A procedure for an improvement study could follow the steps of the Plan–Do–Check–Act (PDCA) cycle (Figure 18.1) as follows:

1   What changes are needed in order to gain continual improvement?
2   Analyse appropriate data. Carry out suggested changes to the process.
3   Evaluate the results of the changes to the process.
4   Make the changes permanent, or try another step (i.e., go to Step 1).

Involvement

The idea behind continuous improvement is to utilize the skills and knowledge of all the workforce in a sustained attempt to improve every aspect of how the organization operates. It is useful to disseminate information around the organization regarding progress on various performance measures in order to emphasize the importance of the improvement effort. This can be done using meetings, newsletters and boards displaying charts. The most common objectives used are the QCDSM measures of Quality, Cost, Delivery, Safety and Morale.

Suggestion Schemes

The idea behind suggestion schemes is to offer the person closest to the work activity the opportunity to suggest improvements to the process. Suggestions by employees are evaluated and if they are assessed as providing a significant saving then a cash award may be paid by the employee. The award could be a fixed amount for all suggestions or a percentage of net savings over a specific time period. Suggestion schemes are most likely to be successful when employees are given training in aspects such as data collection and the scheme is promoted, rather than the size of any award payments.

Continuous Improvement Teams

Process improvement teams or quality circles use the different skills and experiences of a group of people in order to solve problems and, thus, provide a basis for continual improvement. In order to do this the team should be aware of the tools available for measuring and, thus, improving performance such as Statistical Process Control (SPC) (Chapter 17). Expertise outside the group can also be used to contribute to group effectiveness. A quality circle is a small group of people (6–12) who meet voluntarily on a regular basis. Process improvement teams are usually made up of experienced problem solvers from departments affected by the process and are appointed by management. The use of a group can be particularly effective at working through a cause and effect diagram to find the root cause of a particular problem. An example cause and effect diagram is shown in Figure 18.2.

The idea of a cause and effect diagram is to work back from the quality problem and identify individual causes on lines radiating from each category branch associated with the problem in each major category (categories may differ from those shown in the example).

Problem-solving Skills

Information Technology has had a particular impact on the level of problem solving and, thus, decision-making skills required in the organization. The decision-making activity is often classified in order that different decision processes and methods can be adopted for the common features of decisions within these choices. Decision types can be classified into strategic, tactical and operational

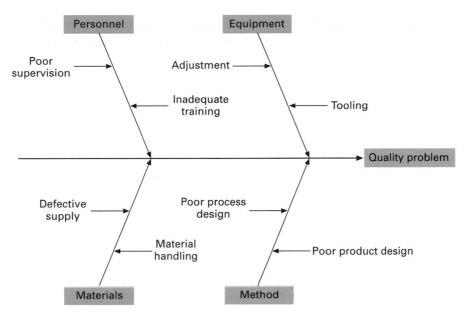

Figure 18.2 Cause and effect diagram

relating to top, middle and supervisory management levels, the main variables across these levels being the time-span over which decisions are taken and the amount of money involved in the choice of option. However, these classifications fail to recognize the changes that are taking place with the introduction of information systems (see Case Study 18.1).

CASE STUDY 18.1

In the Age of the Smart Machine

Shoshana Zuboff (1988) in her book *In the Age of the Smart Machine* describes the changes that took place within continuous process factories in the United States which changed to computer-controlled systems. The extra information produced by these systems required a different kind of conceptual grasp by the person concerned in order to recognize patterns and understand the consequences of actions on the overall process. This represents a major change from just the monitoring of information on a computer screen. In other words, these more sophisticated computer applications, rather than simply replacing repetitive and mechanical tasks, often serve as a sophisticated decision support tool that is most valuable in the hands of a sophisticated user with broad responsibilities. This implies that the link between information and management level may become increasingly inappropriate as the job scope and responsibility of many people within the organization increases with the advent of information systems.

**Case Study 18.1
Question**

1   What are the implications of the findings in the case study for operations managers?

The Learning Organization

**THE LEARNING
ORGANIZATION:**
creates an environment
which builds knowledge
within the organization
and can utilize that to
improve performance.

Continuous improvement is associated with the concept of the **learning organization** which aims to create an environment which builds knowledge within the organization and can utilize that to improve performance. The need for organizational learning has been identified as a consequence of the need for organizations to continually produce innovations in order to maintain a competitive edge. The ability to generate a continuous stream of ideas for improvement and implement them is seen as a sustainable competitive advantage for organizations. To consider how an organization learns is really to consider how learning of individuals within that organization takes place and how the results of that learning are integrated into the practices, procedures and processes of the organization. The transfer of knowledge from individuals to organizational systems means that the knowledge becomes independent of the individual and is possessed by the organization and is replicable by individuals within that organization.

Probst and Büchel (1988) state that the outcome of an organizational learning process is qualitatively different from the sum of the individual learning processes. This is because learning is the outcome of human interactions and the sharing of experiences between individuals. For example, a decision made by a group can have outcomes which are totally different from the outcomes of the sum of individual decisions. There are a range of definitions of the levels of organizational learning. Probst and Büchel distinguish between three different levels of adaptive, reconstructive and process learning which are now described.

Adaptive Learning

This is when an organization adapts to its environment by means of members of that organization identifying problems in the environment, developing strategies for dealing with them and implementing these strategies. Thus, the organization is making a correction in order to align behaviour towards existing goals.

Reconstructive Learning

Reconstructive or double-loop learning occurs when there is a more significant change in the relationship between the organization and its environment for which a process of adaptation is insufficient. Here, changes at the more fundamental level of the values of individuals or groups within the organization must be changed in order to align behaviour towards attainment of an organization's goals. In fact, this questioning of the organization's 'theories of action' leads to a questioning of the original organizational goals, which are then changed.

Process Learning

A formidable obstacle to the successful learning process is defensive routines which individuals, groups and organizations have built up to protect them from the threat of change (Argyris, 1999). This means that even if individuals recognize the need for learning, these defensive routines prevent this from occurring. Thus, a process of 'learning to learn' – the study of the process of learning itself – must take place. This process is the highest level of learning and is, in fact, the act of learning to understand adaptive and reconstructive learning.

Business Process Reengineering (BPR)

Business Process Reengineering (BPR) calls for an analysis of a business from a process rather than a functional perspective and a redesign of these processes to optimize performance. Davenport (1993) provides the following five-step approach to a BPR study:

> **BUSINESS PROCESS REENGINEERING (BPR):** calls for an analysis of a business from a process rather than a functional perspective and a redesign of these processes to optimize performance.

1 *Identifying processes for innovation* – the organization should select a process or processes which are critical to the organization and so provide a potentially large increase in performance in return for the reengineering effort. The scope and number of process redesign projects must be compatible with the organization's ability and experience to undertake them.
2 *Identify change levers* – the three main enablers or levers of change are Information Technology (IT), information and organizational/human resource.

Table 18.1	Categories in which IT can provide process innovation
Automational	For example, robotics in manufacturing, work flow in services
Informational	The ability of IT to provide additional information about a process which can be used for improvement (see Zuboff, 1988)
Sequential	Transform process execution (e.g., concurrent engineering)
Tracking	Knowing the status of components (e.g., mail delivery systems)
Analytical	Providing additional information for decision making
Geographical	Using a worldwide communications system (e.g., linked CAD)
Integrative	Case management approach – needs database of information from around the organization
Intellectual	Database of company knowledge of processes
Disintermediating	Connects buyers and sellers without intermediaries

Information Technology (IT)

Davenport provides the following categories in which IT can provide process innovation (Table 18.1).

Information

Much information is not manipulated by IT resources in the organization, but may still be a powerful lever in making process innovation possible. Examples include the visible display of information on the shop floor in lean production organizations and the market information used by executives in making strategic decisions.

Organizational/Human Resource

The need to align the organizational culture with technological change is discussed in Chapter 9 on job design. For example, many process innovations will lead to increased worker empowerment which may require an adjustment in organizational culture to ensure successful implementation. The successful use of teams is also essential in implementing cross-functional processes.

3   *Developing process vision* – it is essential that the process innovation effort is consistent with the organization's strategy. A process vision consists of measurable objectives and provides the link between strategy and action.

A shared vision is essential to ensure true innovation, rather than standard improvement efforts such as simplification and rationalization. A vision allows conventional wisdom about how processes are undertaken to be questioned. Key activities in developing a process vision include assessing existing business strategy for process direction, consulting with process customers, benchmarking process performance targets and developing process performance objectives and attributes.

4   *Understanding existing processes* – this step is necessary to enable those involved in the innovation activities to develop a common understanding of the existing processes, understand complexities, avoid duplicating current problems and provide a benchmark against which improvement can be measured. Traditional process-oriented approaches such as flowcharting can be used for this task, but do not contain the elements necessary for the implementation of radical change.

5   *Designing and prototyping the new processes* – the design of new processes requires a team with a mix of members who can deliver creative and innovative process solutions and ensure that they are implemented.
Key activities in the design and prototype phase are the brainstorming of design activities, assessing the feasibility of these alternatives, prototyping the new process design, developing a migration strategy and implementation of the new organizational structure and systems. Simulation Modelling can be a valuable tool in assessing new process design (Chapter 8).

The Relationship between BPR and CI Approaches

In this chapter the improvement approaches of continuous improvement and BPR have been covered. Continuous improvement programmes are associated with incremental changes within the organization whose cumulative effect is to deliver an increased rate of performance improvement. The important point about continuous improvement is that it can deliver improvements that are difficult to copy by competitors. For instance, a culture which recognizes and delivers quality and reliability is a long term project which may not show immediate financial benefit.

In order to catch up or overtake competitors it has been realized that continuous improvements may not be enough, and that step changes in performance are required. These are associated with innovations in areas such as product design or process design. The technique of BPR has been widely cited as an approach which locates suitable areas for change and delivers improvements to them.

These two approaches share orientation to process as the unit of improvement, orientation to strategy execution rather than strategy itself, belief in the

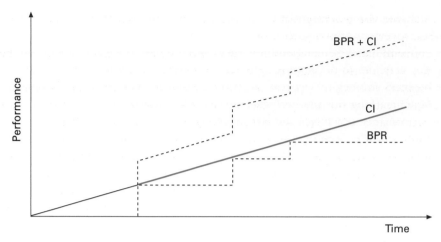

Figure 18.3   Combining Business Process Reengineering (BPR) and Continuous Improvement (CI) initiatives

importance of measurement and analysis and focus on external criteria (e.g., benchmarking) as the basis for judging improvement. When BPR and CI coexist within an organization they should be perceived as being related aspects of an overall performance improvement initiative. Figure 18.3 shows how the two approaches could be combined in an improvement initiative to outperform an organization using only one of the approaches.

In the 1990s many organizations attempted major or breakthrough change by attempting to implement radical process redesigns under the banner of BPR. It was found that many of these efforts failed but the use of a process perspective was seen as useful and so companies are now more likely to try process improvement to enable more limited changes. The concept of Business Process Management (BPM) is used to refer to the variety of methods and technologies that are used to enable a process-oriented change (Chapter 8).

Systems Thinking

SYSTEMS THINKING: this approach does not break down the organization into parts in order to understand it, but uses the idea of holism to study the whole before that of the parts.

Improvement approaches such as total quality management, continuous improvement, learning organizations and process reengineering have been criticized for being too simplistic and not creative enough (Jackson, 2003). It is argued they are too simplistic in that they concentrate on only part of the organization and miss the crucial interactions between the parts. **Systems thinking** does not break down the organization into parts in order to understand it, but uses the idea of holism to study the whole before that of the parts. This ensures that the parts are working and are related together in order that they serve the purposes of the whole organization.

Systems thinking is an approach for seeing the structures that underlie complex situations and, thus, for identifying what causes patterns of behaviour. In an organizational setting it is postulated that there are four levels of the systems view operating simultaneously of events, patterns of behaviour, underlying structures and mental models (Maani and Cavana, 2000). Events are reports that only touch the surface of what has happened and offer just a snapshot of the situation. Patterns of behaviour look at how behaviour has changed over time. Underlying structures describe the interplay of the different factors that bring about the outcomes that we observe, and mental models represent the beliefs, values and assumptions held by individuals and organizations that underlie the reasons for doing things the way we do them.

Balanced Scorecard

Linked to the topic of operations improvement is the area of performance measurement which involves choosing the measures which will be used to determine if improvement has taken place. Traditionally, performance measures in operations have focused on indicators such as **productivity** (Maani and Cavana, 2000) which divides the value of the output by the value of the input resources consumed:

PRODUCTIVITY: divides the value of the output by the value of the input resources consumed.

$$\text{Productivity} = \frac{\text{Output}}{\text{Input}}$$

Productivity is used at both the organizational and national level as a comparative measure of performance. From the equation it can be seen that productivity can be increased by either increasing output without a proportionate increase in input or decreasing input without a proportionate decrease in output. Productivity can be a valid tool for the operations manager and provides an indication of the level of utilization of resources. However, it can be difficult to find appropriate input and output parameters for the calculation, and the measure also fails to consider performance from a wider viewpoint encompassing customer and other stakeholder needs.

BALANCED SCORECARD: a measurement system that incorporates performance measures across the four perspectives of financial, stakeholder, business process, and innovation and learning.

The **balanced scorecard** approach (Kaplan and Norton, 1996) is an attempt to incorporate the interests of a broader range of stakeholders through performance measures across four perspectives of financial, stakeholder/customer, business process, and innovation and learning. The idea of the scorecard is to provide managers with a multiple perspective of the goals that need to be met for organizational success. In Operations the five performance objectives (see Chapter 2) of quality, dependability, speed, flexibility and cost are intended to provide a more customer-based and strategic perspective to performance measurement.

Activity-Based Costing (ABC)

A key factor in improving performance is to identify where cost is being incurred within an operation. **Activity-Based Costing (ABC)** (Turney, 1996) provides a way of allocating costs to manufacturing and services activities in order that a company can determine how much it costs to make a certain product or deliver a service. In ABC there are three main drivers of cost, named the 'cost driver', 'resource driver' and 'activity driver':

ACTIVITY-BASED COSTING:

provides a way of allocating costs to manufacturing and services activities in order that a company can determine how much it costs to make a certain product or deliver a service.

■ The cost driver relates to the amount of resources needed to perform an activity and can be reduced by, for example, redesigning the process.
■ The resource driver relates to the type of resources needed for an activity and can be reduced, for example, by using different personnel, information technology or equipment.
■ The activity driver relates to the number of times the process occurs and can be reduced, for example, by training to improve the reliability of a process.

Thus, an investigation of a combination of resource drivers, activity drivers and cost drivers for an activity can improve process performance by identifying why cost has been incurred from these three perspectives.

CASE STUDY 18.2

Activity-based Costing at a Police Force

In Chapter 8 we outlined a study that was undertaken of the costs involved in operating a custody suite at a police force in the UK. The custody suite is involved in the processing of arrested persons and their subsequent release, interview or detention. Like most service operations the custody operation is characterized by having a large part of the resources available as labour. Unfortunately, this often leads to a situation of management of resources by inputs (i.e., budgets). Thus, the number of resources (e.g., people, capital) deployed are based on historical budgets with a large proportion classified as overhead and fixed with an annual addition for inflation. Departments are then managed by tracking variances in expenditure from budgeted amounts. In this case an ABC approach was taken in order to identify where cost was being incurred as a first step to improving performance.

In terms of cost drivers, a major source of cost was found to be the time taken to undertake the paper-based booking-in process which occurs for all arrested persons. In order to reduce the amount of resource needed for this the booking-in process was redesigned using BPR and a proposal for computerization put in place.

The resource drivers in this case relate primarily to the pay rates of personnel involved in the arrest process. A civilianization programme, which involves using trained civilians for activities formerly undertaken by police personnel, was proposed.

In this case the activity driver relates to the timing and frequency of arrests. The activity driver is dependent on environmental factors such as the crime rate and government policy on crime as well as factors under the control of the police. It was found, however, that a high proportion of arrests were for minor theft offences involving children which could possibly be processed using alternative methods.

1 What are the benefits of the ABC analysis of the custody suite?	**Case Study 18.2** **Question**

Benchmarking

Benchmarking can be defined as the continuous measurement of an organization's products and processes against a company recognized as a leader in that industry. The analysis of competitor products is an older technique which forms part of the product design process (Chapter 7). Benchmarking was initially restricted to the comparison of direct competitors in the manufacturing sector. Now it is practised in the service sector (e.g., banks), in all functional areas (e.g., marketing) and in comparison with a wide variety of competitors from which lessons can be learnt (i.e., not just the best in class). Because of the widespread use of the technique and the requests by many organizations to visit the same high-performance firms, many benchmarking data are held in databases for general use. A number of models for implementing a benchmarking programme have been developed. The main activities involved in benchmarking are summarized below:

> **BENCHMARKING:**
> the continuous measurement of an organization's products and processes against a company recognized as a leader in that industry.

- *Planning* – understand your own processes, identify key processes and form benchmarking teams.
- *Analysis* – conduct research on possible competitors and formulate questions to elicit the required information. Establish a relationship with a partner organization and collect and share information.
- *Implementation* – implement and monitor improvements suggested by analysis.

It is important that the relevant processes in the organization are benchmarked before comparison with a competitor. Processes are benchmarked in terms of metrics (numeric measurements) and procedures (process flows). For example, a payment process could be measured by the time taken from receiving the request to delivery of the payment. The technique would also measure the type and number of personnel involved in each step of the process. One problem with some benchmarking programmes has been the focus on developing metrics and the lack of energy put into implementing changes suggested by the benchmarking process. Other problems are the difficulty in obtaining competitor information and the fact that if the process is simply used to emulate a competitor, competitive advantage may be short lived as the competitor makes further improvements.

CASE STUDY 18.3

Injection Moulds: Quietly Building Reputation as a World Leader

Benchmarking and the sharing of best practices are among the mantras management experts most urge industry to adopt in the struggle to improve Portugal's low level of productivity. Emulating the strategies of thriving companies and sectors is seen as one of the most reliable paths to success. The frontrunners setting the pace are neither often big nor high profile. Portugal's engineering and tooling sector, for example, has quietly gained a reputation as a global leader in building injection moulds for the production of plastic goods, from the dashboards of the world's best-selling cars to stylish furniture gracing the trendiest European homes. The sector is based in Marinha Grande and Oliveira de Azeméis, two central Portuguese towns about 100 km apart, which grew into important glass-making centres in the 18th century. In the 1940s the sector evolved from glass to engineering injection moulds for the plastic industry. The size limitations of the domestic market led the industry to focus on export markets. Today, overseas customers account for about 85% of total sales. Main markets include France, Germany, Spain, the US, the UK and Scandinavia – countries where Portuguese companies supply moulds for the world's leading producers of household goods, telecommunications and office equipment, electrical appliances, cosmetics, pharmaceuticals and packaging.

Since the early 1990s, the auto industry, which has progressively replaced metal parts with components made from new, sophisticated plastics, has increasingly shown a preference for Portuguese engineering and today accounts for about 50% of total sales in Azeméis. In these two small towns about 300 mould-making companies employing 7500 workers play an overlooked but important role in shaping the look and feel of the modern world. Not only do they engineer the moulds from which millions of everyday plastic utensils are made, but they often contribute to their design as well. Electrolux, Samsonite, General Electric, Fisher Price, Hasbro, Black & Decker, Thermos, IBM, Rubbermaid, General Motors/Opel, Volkswagen, Renault, Sony, Nokia, Moulinex, Hoover and BMW are among the industry's leading customers. One of the keys to the success of Portuguese companies has been to see themselves not just as simple suppliers of moulds, but as partners who provide an integrated service to support the plastics-processing industry from the conception and design of a new product to the end of a manufacturing run of hundreds of thousands of units.

"Designing a part and designing a mould are two very different things," says Henrique Neto, chairman of Marinha Grande-based Iberomoldes, one of the world's leading injection mould groups. "By inputting our mould-making skills into the equation, we ensure that products are designed to guarantee maximum efficiency and minimum cost through all the subsequent stages, from mould engineering to injection." Working partnerships to which Portuguese companies bring their engineering and tooling experience can result in big advantages for manufacturers. In one collaboration, a company proposed a simpler way of fixing a door panel to a car's bodywork. This resulted in a cut of 150 000 in the original €1.4m cost of the mould. It also reduced the injection cycle for each part from 60 to 50 seconds – a huge saving for a company producing 200 000 units a year.

"The know-how we contribute in this way often produces savings in the manufacturing process that cover the entire cost of the mould," says Leonel Gomes, chairman of LN-Moldes. The mould industry also stands out in Portugal for the priority it gives to investment in research and training. Low levels of spending on R&D and training are important causes of the country's low level of productivity and industrial competitiveness. But the mould sector has consistently invested a higher percentage of earnings – about 20% – in technology and training than any of its overseas competitors. Each year hundreds of teenage schoolchildren are given hands-on experience of the industry in a fun and entertaining environment. The programme helps attract a constant flow of bright young people to the sector, rejuvenating the industry's human resources and ensuring that its accumulated know-how is passed on to coming generations. The industry maintains especially close ties with the engineering faculty at Minho University in northern Portugal. The faculty focuses on advanced courses in mould-making and plastics processing, including masters programmes with a special emphasis on rapid prototyping and rapid tooling.

The long history of mould-making in Portugal has also led to the natural development of a 'horizontal cluster', another important success factor that involves cooperation and networking between companies, research institutions and training facilities. The flow of workers between companies helps spread qualifications, skills and knowledge acquired from companies or specialized institutions throughout the sector. Innovation and technology spill over from company to company, building up a research and development network as businesses, institutions and universities exchange skills and know-how. The cluster has even extended beyond Portugal's boundaries through the pioneering use of technology. The industry's Round-the-Clock project, for example, uses information technology to link engineering and mould-making facilities in different time zones around the world, enabling non-stop collaborative work on designing and building moulds 24 hours a day.

Source: FT.com site, by Peter Wise, 20 October 2004
© The Financial Times Ltd

**Case Study 18.3
Question**

1   What best practices does the article identify regarding the Portuguese mould-making sector?

Summary

1   Implementation of continuous improvement requires attention to the organizational environment, involvement of organizational members and development of problem-solving skills.

2   Organizational learning has been identified as a consequence of the need for organizations to continually produce innovations in order to maintain a competitive edge.

3   BPR calls for an analysis of a business from a process rather than a functional perspective and then the reengineering of these processes to optimize performance.

4   Systems thinking uses the idea of holism to study the whole before that of the parts. This ensures that the parts are working and are related together in order that they serve the purposes of the whole organization.

5   The balanced scorecard incorporates performance measures for improvement across the perspectives of financial, customer, business process, and innovation and learning.

6   Activity-based costing assists in determining how much it costs to make a certain product or deliver a service.

7   Benchmarking can be defined as the continuous measurement of an organization's products and processes against a company recognized as a leader in that industry.

Exercises

1. Discuss the main issues involved in the implementation of a continuous improvement effort.
2. Describe the three different levels of organizational learning.
3. Search on the Web for consultancy organizations and examine their methodologies and claims for BPR.
4. Discuss the factors behind the integration of the BPR and CI improvement approaches.
5. Compare and contrast the BPR and CI improvement approaches.
6. Identify the need for using a balanced scorecard rather than measuring performance using a measure such as productivity.
7. Why is ABC a useful tool for the operations manager?
8. Discuss the role of benchmarking.

References

Argyris, C. (1999), *On Organizational Learning*, 2nd Edition, Blackwell Publishers.

Davenport, T.H. (1993), *Process Innovation: Reengineering Work through Information Technology*, Harvard Business School Press.

Jackson, M.C. (2003), *Systems Thinking: Creative Holism for Managers*, John Wiley & Sons.

Kaplan, R.S. and Norton, D.P. (1996), *The Balanced Scorecard: Translating Strategy into Action*, Harvard Business School Press.

Maani, K.E. and Cavana, R.Y. (2000), *Systems Thinking and Modelling: Understanding Change and Complexity*, Pearson Education, New Zealand.

Probst, G. and Büchel, B. (1997), *Organizational Learning: The Competitive Advantage of the Future*, Prentice Hall.

Turney, P.B.B. (1996), *Activity Based Costing: The Performance Breakthrough*, Kogan Page.

Zuboff, S. (1988), *In the Age of the Smart Machine: The Future of Work and Power*, Heinemann.

Further Reading

Greasley, A. (2005), Using system dynamics in a discrete-event simulation study, *International Journal of Operations and Production Management*.

Hammer, M. and Champy, J. (1993), *Re-engineering the Corporation: A Manifesto for Business Revolution*, Harper Business.

Harmon, P. (2003), *Business Process Change: A Manager's Guide to Improving, Redesigning, and Automating Processes*, Morgan Kaufman.

Holloway, J., Lewis, J. and Mallory, G. (eds) (1995), *Performance Measurement and Evaluation*, Sage Publications.

Senge, P.M. (1990), *The Fifth Discipline: The Art and Practice of the Learning Organization*, Century Business.

Web Links

www.apqc.org Amercian Productivity and Quality Center. This site provides information on such topics as benchmarking, knowledge management and performance measurement.

www.benchnet.com The Benchmarking Exchange. Contains best practice survey reports on benchmarking.

www.prosci.com BPR Online Learning Centre. Contains tutorials and many articles on BPR.

www.kaizen-institute.com Kaizen Institute. Contains tips for implementing continuous improvement.

Appendices

GLOSSARY

ABC classification system   Sorts inventory items into groups depending on factors such as the amount of annual expenditure.

Acceptance sampling   Consists of taking a random sample from a larger batch or lot of material to be inspected. The quality of the sample is assumed to reflect the overall quality of the lot.

Activity-based costing (ABC)   A way of allocating costs to manufacturing and services activities in order to determine how much a company spends to make a certain product or deliver a service.

Actual capacity   The capacity remaining after loss of output due to both planned and unplanned factors. Unplanned factors include equipment breakdown and absenteeism. See also *Effective capacity*.

Aggregate plan   A plan that specifics aspects such as overall production rate, size of the workforce and the amount of subcontracting required to deliver the mix of products or service required to meet the *Demand profile*.

Agile operations   The ability to respond quickly to changing market demand in order to retain current markets and gain new market share by developing the capability of resources.

Anthropometric data   Information concerning factors related to the physical attributes of a human being, such as the size, weight and strength of various parts of the human body.

Appraisal costs   Costs associated with controlling quality through the use of measuring and testing products and processes to ensure conformance to quality specifications.

Assignable causes of variation   Variations in the process that are not due to random variation but can be attributed to some change in the process, which needs to be investigated and rectified. See also *Chance causes of variation*.

Automated material handling (AMH) systems   Systems designed to improve efficiency in the movement, storage and retrieval of materials.

Autonomous work groups   Groups that are able to decide on their own working methods and handle problems as they arise. They will typically be responsible for the whole delivery of a product or service.

Balanced scorecard   A measurement system that incorporates performance measures across four perspectives: financial, stakeholder, business process, and innovation and learning.

Balancing capacity   Equalizing the capacity of a number of sequential processes.

Batch process   A process that covers a relatively wide range of volume and variety combinations. Products are grouped into batches whose batch size can range from 2 to 100 s. See also *Continuous process*, *Jobbing process*, *Mass process*, *Project process*.

Benchmarking   The continuous measurement of an organization's products and processes against a company recognized as a leader in that industry.

Bill of materials (BOM)   A document that identifies all the components required to produce a scheduled quantity of an assembly and the structure of how these components fit together to make that assembly.

Budgeted cost of work performed (BCWP)   *See* Earned value.

Bullwhip effect   The results of a lack of synchronization between *Supply chain* members, where even a slight change in consumer sales will ripple backwards in the form of magnified oscillations in demand upstream.

Business level strategy   Strategy at the organizational or strategic business unit (SBU) level in large companies, which is concerned with the products and services that should be offered in the market. See also *Functional level strategy*.

Business process management (BPM)   The analysis and improvement of business processes.

Business process reengineering (BPR)   The analysis of a business from a process rather than a functional perspective and the redesign of processes to optimize performance.

Business process simulation   The use of computer software, in the context of a process-based change, to simulate the operation of a business.

Business-to-business (B2B)   Transactions between an organization and other organizations.

Business-to-consumer (B2C)   Transactions between an organization and consumers.

Buy-side e-commerce Web-based transactions between a purchasing organization and its suppliers. See also *Sell-side e-commerce*.

Capacity loading graph A graph showing the type and level of capacity required at a point in time.

Capacity requirements plan (CRP) The calculation of workloads for critical work centres or workers based on information from the *MRP* system.

Cell layout Cells are created from placing together resources which service a subset of the total range of products or services.

Cellular manufacturing The placing of equipment in a *Cell layout* that is a close grouping of different types of equipment, each of which performs a different operation.

Centre of gravity method A way of determining the location of a distribution centre by minimizing distribution costs. The relative coordinates of the distribution points are placed on a map and the location of the distribution centre should be at the centre of gravity of the coordinates.

Chance causes of variation The inherent variability in processes due to factors such as ambient temperature, wear of moving parts or slight variations in the composition of the material that is being processed. See also *Assignable causes of variation*.

Chase demand A capacity-planning strategy that seeks to match output to the demand pattern over time. Capacity is altered by such policies as changing the number of part-time staff, increasing staff availability through overtime working, changing equipment levels and subcontracting.

Competitive factors A range of factors such as price, quality and delivery speed, derived from the marketing strategy, on which the product or service wins orders.

Computer numerically controlled (CNC) machines Machine tools that can be controlled by computer.

Computer-aided design (CAD) The ability to create drawings on a computer screen to assist in the visual design of a product or service.

Computer-aided engineering (CAE) The ability to design simulated tests and run them on drawings in a *CAD* system.

Computer-aided manufacturing (CAM) An extension of the use of *CAD*, which electronically transmits the design held in the CAD system to computer-controlled machine tools.

Computer-aided process planning (CAPP)   An extension of the use of *CAD*, which electronically transmits a process plan of how parts will be manufactured to a machine tool. It can also sequence parts through a number of process steps.

Computer-integrated manufacture (CIM)   The automation of the product and process design, planning and control, and manufacture of the product.

Concurrent design   When contributors to the stages of the design effort provide their expertise together throughout the design process as a team.

Continuous improvement   Incremental changes within the organization whose cumulative effect is to deliver an increased rate of performance improvement.

Continuous process   An operation that produces a very high volume of a standard product, usually by a continuous flow, rather than in discrete items, such as oil and gas. See also *Batch process, Jobbing process, Mass process, Project process.*

Control chart for attribute data   Measures discrete values such as whether a component is defective or not. Thus, there are no values, as in a *Control chart for variable data*, from which a mean and range can be calculated. The data will simply provide a count of how many items conform to a specification and how many do not.

Control chart for variable data   Displays samples of a measurement that can take a value from a range of possible values. Values will fall in or out of a range around a specified target value.

Corporate level strategy   Long-range guidance on the direction of the whole organization.

Cost   The finance required to obtain the inputs and manage the transformation process which produces finished goods and services.

Critical path method (CPM)   A way of mapping the activities undertaken during a project, the dependencies between these activities and the project duration.

Cumulative representation   A running total of inventory, which should always meet or exceed cumulative demand. It is used to ensure no stock-outs occur when using a *Level capacity* plan.

Customer relationship management (CRM)   Systems designed to integrate the range of information systems that contain data about the customer.

Cycle time   The time taken to produce or deliver one unit of output.

Degree of customer contact   The amount of interaction between the service provider and customer during the service delivery process.

Demand management   A capacity-planning strategy that attempts to adjust demand to meet available capacity. This can be achieved by strategies such as varying price of goods and services, advertising and using appointment systems. See also *Level capacity*.

Demand profile   Consists of the products and services required by the marketing plan, future customer orders and other demand factors such as the manufacture of items for spares.

Demand-side influences   Factors influencing customer services that vary according to location and are, therefore, taken into account when making the location decision. See also *Supply-side influences*.

Dependability   Consistently meeting a promised delivery time for a product or service to a customer.

Design capacity   The theoretical output of a process as it was designed.

Design for manufacture (DFM)   A concept that views product design as the first step in the manufacture of that product.

Design of experiments (DOE)   A way of testing a number of design options under various operating and environmental conditions in order to identify which factors affect a product's performance.

Disintermediation   Using *E-business* to alter the *Supply chain* structure by bypassing some of the tiers. See also *Reintermediation*.

Distribution requirements planning (DRP)   The management of linkages between elements of the *Supply chain*, beginning with an analysis of demand at each customer service location.

DMAIC methodology   The use of statistical tools to gather data at each of the five stages of Define, Measure, Analyse, Improve and Control.

Downstream customers   Customers of the organization such as wholesalers and retailers. See also *Upstream suppliers*.

Earned value   How much work has actually been done in terms of budgeted costs for any day in the project. Also termed 'budgeted cost of work performed' (BCWP).

E-business   Electronically mediated information exchanges, both within an organization and between organizations.

E-commerce   Electronically mediated information exchanges between organizations.

Economic analysis   The comparison of estimates of production and delivery costs with estimates of demand.

Economic order quantity (EOQ) A model that calculates the fixed inventory order volume required while seeking to minimize the sum of the annual costs of holding inventory and the annual costs of ordering inventory.

Economies of scale Savings that result if a facility is expanded and fixed costs remain the same, so that the average cost of producing each unit will fall until the best operating level of the facility is reached and the lowest average unit cost met.

Economies of scope Savings that result from the ability to produce many products in one highly flexible production facility more cheaply than in separate facilities.

Effective capacity The capacity remaining after loss of output due to planned factors such as maintenance and training. See also *Actual capacity*.

Efficiency The proportion of time a process is in use compared with its *Effective capacity*. See also *Utilization*.

Electronic commerce See *E-commerce*.

Electronic data interchange (EDI) The exchange, using digital media, of structured business information, particularly for sales transactions such as purchase orders and invoices between buyers and sellers.

Empowerment When employees of an organization are given more autonomy, discretion and responsibility for decision making.

Enterprise resource planning (ERP) A system that provides a single solution from a single supplier with integrated functions for the major business areas.

E-procurement The electronic integration and management of all procurement activities, including purchase request, authorization, ordering, delivery and payment between purchaser and supplier.

Ergonomics The collection of information about human characteristics and behaviour in order to understand the effect of design, methods and environment.

Extensible Markup Language (XML) A data description language that allows documents to store any kind of information.

Facility location The geographical location of capacity supplied by the organization.

Failure mode and effect analysis (FMEA) A systematic approach to identifying the cause and effect of product failures. The idea of FMEA is to anticipate failures and deal with them at the design stage.

Finished goods inventory Inventory ready for dispatch to the customer.

Fixed order inventory model   A way of calculating the amount to order based on a fixed interval between ordering.

Fixed order period inventory system   A system in which orders for varying quantities are placed at fixed time intervals.

Fixed order quantity inventory system   A system in which orders for the same quantity are placed, but the time between orders varies according to the rate of use of the inventory item.

Fixed-position layout   Used when the product or service cannot be moved and so the transforming process must take place at the location of product creation or service delivery.

Flexibility   The ability of the organization to change what it does quickly. In terms of products or services this can relate to introducing new designs, changing the mix, changing the overall volume and changing the delivery timing.

Flexible manufacturing cell (FMC)   Systems that integrate individual items of automation to form an automated manufacturing system.

Flexible manufacturing systems (FMS)   These extend the facilities of an FMC by incorporating automatic parts loading and unloading facilities and an automated guided vehicle system for parts movement.

Focus   The alignment of particular market demands with individual facilities to reduce the level of complexity generated when attempting to service a number of different market segments from an individual organization.

Form design   The product aesthetics, such as look, feel and sound.

Functional design   Design that meets the performance characteristics specified in the product concept.

Functional level strategy   Long-range plans made by the functions of the business (e.g., operations, marketing, finance) which support the competitive advantage being pursued by the *Business level strategy*.

Gantt chart   A valuable tool for *Project control*, which allows monitoring of project progress against plan by providing a view of which tasks are being undertaken over time.

Global organization   The extension and coordination of internal operations to create new value through a consolidation of manufacturing, reduced delivery costs and *Economies of scale*.

Group technology   The process of grouping products for manufacture or services for delivery.

Heterogeneity The interaction of the customer, service provider and surroundings causing variability in the performance of the service.

Human capital management system (HCMS) A Web-based software application that manages human resource functions such as payroll, recruitment and staff deployment across the organization.

Inbound logistics The activity of moving material in from suppliers.

Infrastructural decisions The systems, policies and practices that determine how the operation's structural elements are managed.

Input/output control Attempt to make queue times more consistent and predictable by managing the size of the queues at processes.

Inventory status file (ISF) Information on the identification and quantity of items in stock.

ISO 9000 A group of quality management standards laid down by the International Organization for Standardization.

JIT and lean operations An integration of a philosophy and techniques designed to improve performance.

JIT supplier network A formation of close long-term relationships with a small number of suppliers.

Job characteristics model Linking job characteristics with the desired psychological state of the individual and the outcomes in terms of motivation and job performance.

Job enlargement The horizontal integration of tasks to expand the range of tasks involved in a particular job.

Job enrichment The vertical integration of tasks and the integration of responsibility and decision making.

Job rotation A form of *Job enlargement* that involves a worker changing job roles with another worker on a periodic basis.

Jobbing process The process for making a one-off, or low volume, product to a customer specification. The product moves to the location of transforming resources such as equipment. See also *Batch process*, *Continuous process*, *Mass process*, *Project process*.

Just-in-time See *JIT and lean operations*.

***Kanban* production system** To implement a pull system, a *kanban* is used to pass information such as the part identification, quantity per container that the part is transported in, and the preceding and next workstation.

Lag capacity   Capacity that is added only when there is extra demand which would utilize the additional resources. See also *Lead capacity*.

Layout design   The arrangement of facilities in a service or manufacturing operation.

Lead capacity   Extra capacity above forecast demand, which allows an operation to maintain a capacity 'cushion'. This tries to ensure that capacity is sufficient even if demand increases above forecast. See also *Lag capacity*.

Lean operations   See *JIT and lean operations*.

Learning curves   Provide an organization with the ability to predict the improvement in productivity that can occur as experience of a process is gained.

Learning organization   A working environment that builds knowledge within the organization and uses that knowledge to improve performance.

Level capacity   A capacity-planning strategy that sets processing capacity at a uniform level throughout the planning period regardless of fluctuations in forecast demand. This means production is set at a fixed rate, usually to meet average demand, and inventory is used to absorb variations in demand. For a service organization, output cannot be stored as inventory so a level capacity plan involves running at a uniformly high level of capacity. See also *Demand management*.

Levelled scheduling   Producing the smallest reasonable number of units of each product at a time.

Line balancing   Aims to ensure that the output of each production stage in a line layout is equal and maximum efficiency is attained.

Loading   Determining the available capacity for each stage in a process and allocating a work task to that stage.

Locational cost–volume analysis   Identifying when a particular location is superior for a particular volume level by analysing the mix of fixed and variable costs.

Long-term capacity planning   Determining how much long-term capacity should be supplied by the organization. This decision needs to be made within a long-term plan which provides a fit with the operations strategy of the organization.

Maintainability   The cost of servicing the product or service when it is in use.

Make-to-order   A planning policy that acquires the raw material used to construct the product on the receipt of a customer order. See also *Make-to-stock*.

Make-to-stock   A planning policy that produces to a forecast of demand for the product. See also *Make-to-order*.

Manufacturing resource planning (MRP II) Extends the idea of MRP (*Materials requirements planning*) to other areas in the firm such as marketing and finance.

Market analysis Evaluating the design concept with potential customers through interviews, focus groups and other data collection methods.

Market relationships Where each purchase is treated as a separate transaction and the relationship between the buyer and seller lasts as long as this transaction takes.

Market-based operations strategy A method of determining organizational strategy based on decisions regarding the markets and the customers within those markets that it intends to target. See also *Resource-based operations strategy.*

Mass customization An attempt to combine high-variety and high-volume output in order to provide the customer with customized products at a relatively low price.

Mass process A process that produces products of high volume and low variety. The process of production will essentially be the same for all the products and so it is cost effective to use specialized labour and equipment. See also *Batch process, Continuous process, Jobbing process, Project process.*

Mass service Processes that operate with a low variety and high volume. There will be little customization of the service to individual customer needs and limited contact between the customer and people providing the service.

Master production schedule (MPS) Shows how many products or services are planned for each time period, based on the resources authorized in the *Aggregate plan.*

Match capacity Obtaining capacity to match forecasted demand.

Materials handling The movement of materials, either within warehouses or between storage areas and transportation links.

Materials management The movement of materials within the organization.

Materials requirements planning (MRP) An information system used to calculate the requirements for component materials needed to produce end items.

M-business The integration of Internet and wireless communications technology.

Method study Dividing and analysing a job in order to reduce waste, time and effort.

Mixed model scheduling Spreading the production of several different end items evenly throughout each day.

Motion study   The study of the individual human motions that are used in a job task with the purpose of trying to ensure that the job does not include any unnecessary motion or movement by the worker.

Network analysis   The use of network-based techniques for the analysis and management of projects.

Operations management   The management of the processes that produce or deliver goods and services.

Operations performance objectives   The five objectives by which operations performance is measured: quality, speed, dependability, flexibility and cost.

Optimized production technology (OPT)   An operations control system that is based on the identification of bottlenecks within the production process.

Outbound logistics   The activity of moving materials out to customers.

P : D ratio   The comparison of the demand time D (from customer request to receipt of goods/services) with the total throughput time P of the purchase, make and delivery stages.

Perishability   Because a service is a process, not a physical thing that can be stored, it must be consumed when it is produced.

Programme evaluation and review technique (PERT)   A form of *Network analysis* that takes into account the fact that most task durations are not fixed by using a statistical distribution to describe the variability inherent in the tasks.

Physical distribution management   The movement of materials from the operation to the customer.

Predetermined motion times   Generic times for standard micromotions such as reach, move and release, which are common to many jobs.

Prevention costs   Costs arising from the quality philosophy of 'doing it right the first time', such as those incurred by trying to prevent problems occurring.

Private or single-user warehouse   A warehouse owned or leased by the organization for its own use. See also *Public or multi-user warehouse*.

Process activity chart   A device used to analyse the steps of a job or how a set of jobs fit together into the overall flow of a process.

Process layout   A layout in which resources (such as equipment and people) that have similar processes or functions are grouped together.

Process mapping   The use of a flowchart to document the process, incorporating process activities and decision points.

Process technology Used to help transform the three main categories of transformed resources: materials, customers and information.

Procurement The acquisition of all the materials needed by an organization.

Product layout A layout in which the resources required for a product or service are arranged around the needs of that product or service.

Production design Design that takes into consideration the ease and cost of manufacture of a product.

Production flow analysis (PFA) A *Group technology* technique that can be used to identify families of parts with similar processing requirements.

Productivity The value of the output divided by the value of the input resources consumed.

Professional service Service characterized by high levels of customization, in that each service delivery will be tailored to meet individual customer needs, high levels of customer contact and a relatively high proportion of staff supplying the service in relation to customers.

Project control The monitoring of the project objectives of cost, time and quality as the project progresses.

Project cost graph Provides an indication of the amount of cost incurred over the life of a project.

Project crashing The use of additional resources to reduce project completion time.

Project estimating Estimating the type and amount of resources required to undertake a project.

Project network simulation A method of estimating a project's completion time without the assumptions that all paths of a project are independent and the same tasks are not on more than one path.

Project planning Ensuring that the project objectives of cost, time and quality are met by estimating both the level and timing of resources needed over the project duration.

Project process Used to make a one-off product to a customer specification. A feature of a project process is that the location of the product is stationary. See also *Batch process, Continuous process, Jobbing process, Mass process.*

Psychology of queues A series of propositions that can be used by service organizations to instigate policies to influence customer satisfaction with waiting times.

Public or multi-user warehouse   A warehouse run as an independent business. See also *Private or single-user warehouse.*

Qualitative forecasting methods   Methods that take a subjective approach and are based on estimates and opinions. They include market surveys, the Delphi method and expert judgement. See also *Quantitative forecasting methods.*

Quality   Quality covers both the product or service itself and the processes that produce the product or service.

Quality functional deployment   A structured process that translates the voice of the customer (what the customer needs) into technical design requirements (how these needs are met).

Quality loss function   A simple cost estimate which shows how customer preferences are oriented towards consistently meeting quality expectations and that a customer's dissatisfaction (i.e., quality loss) increases geometrically as the actual value deviates from the target value

Quality of conformance   How closely the product meets the specification required by the design.

Quantitative forecasting methods   Methods that use a mathematical expression or model to show the relationship between demand and some independent variable or variables. They include time series and casual forecasting models. See also *Qualitative forecasting methods.*

Queuing theory   Waiting time in queues is caused by fluctuations in arrival rates and variability in service times. Queuing theory can be used to explore the trade-off between the amount of capacity and the level of demand.

Raw materials inventory   Inventory received from suppliers.

Reintermediation   The creation of new intermediaries between customers and suppliers in the *Supply chain*. See also *Disintermediation.*

Reliability   The probability that a product or service will perform its intended function for a specified period of time under normal conditions of use.

Re-order point (ROP) model   Identifying the time to order when the stock level drops to a predetermined amount.

Resource-based operations strategy   A method of evaluating operations capability based on an assessment of the operation's tangible and intangible resources and processes. See also *Market-based operations strategy.*

Resource-constrained project   A project requiring highly specialized resources, meaning that the completion date will have to be set to ensure these resources are not overloaded. See also *Time-constrained project.*

Resource-to-order When it is not necessary to activate a planning system and acquire resources until a delivery date for an order is received.

Reverse engineering A systematic approach to dismantling and inspecting a competitor's product to look for aspects of design that could be incorporated into the organization's own product.

Robot A programmable machine that can undertake tasks that may be dangerous, dirty or dull for people to carry out.

Robust design The process of designing in the ability of the product to perform under a variety of conditions and so reduce the chance of product failure.

Rough-cut capacity plan (RCCP) This takes information from the *Master production schedule* to evaluate its feasibility.

Scheduling The allocation of a start and finish time to each order while taking into account the *Loading* and *Sequencing* policies employed.

Sell-side e-commerce *E-commerce* transactions between a supplier organization and its customers. See also *Buy-side e-commerce*.

Sequencing The sequential assignment of tasks or jobs to individual processes.

Service blueprinting A charting device for processes, which documents the interaction between the customer and the service provider.

Service package The combination of goods and services that comprise a service.

Service shop process A process that operates with a medium amount of variety and volume. There will be, therefore, a mix of staff and equipment used to deliver the service.

Set-up reduction (SUR) The reduction of the time taken to adjust a machine to work on a different component.

Simultaneity Describes services that are produced and consumed at the same time.

Six sigma A companywide initiative to reduce costs through process *Efficiency* and increase revenues through process effectiveness.

Sociotechnical systems A job design approach that suggests that the social and technical sub-systems within the organization should be designed in parallel to achieve an overall optimum system.

Speed The time delay between a customer request for a product or service and receipt of that product or service.

Stakeholder Anyone with an interest in the activities of an organization, such as employees, customers and government.

Statistical process control (SPC) A sampling technique which checks the quality of an item that is engaged in a process.

Strategic partnerships and alliances Long-term relationships in which organizations work together and share information regarding aspects such as planning systems and development of products and processes.

Structural decisions Decisions that concern aspects of the organization's physical resources such as service delivery systems and capacity provision.

Subcontracting networks Long-term contractual arrangements made with suppliers to supply goods and services.

Supply chain The series of activities that moves materials from suppliers, through operations to customers.

Supply chain management Management of the flow of materials through the entire *Supply chain*.

Supply network design The configuration of the organization's relationship with its suppliers and the decision about which activities the organization should undertake internally and which should be subcontracted to other agencies.

Supply-side influences Factors influencing costs that vary according to location and are, therefore, taken into account when making the location decision. See also *Demand-side influences*.

Systems thinking An approach that uses the idea of holism to study the whole organization instead of breaking it down into parts in order to understand it.

Tangibility The quality of goods that are physical things you can touch. A service is intangible and can be seen as a process that is activated on demand.

Technical analysis Determining whether the technical capability to manufacture the product or deliver the service exists.

Time study The use of statistical techniques to arrive at a standard time for performing one cycle of a repetitive job.

Time-constrained project A project that must be completed within a specific time-frame and, therefore, may need to use alternative resources. See also *Resource-constrained project*.

Total preventative maintenance A programme of routine maintenance that will not only help to reduce breakdowns, but also to reduce downtime and lengthen the life of the equipment. See also *Prevention costs*.

Total quality management (TQM) A philosophy that aims to make high quality, as defined by the customer, a primary concern throughout the organization and to ensure that all parts of the organization work towards this goal.

Trade-off   A situation where to excel in one objective results in a poor performance in one or more other objectives.

Upstream suppliers   Those who supply the organization with goods or services. See also *Downstream customers*.

Utilization   The proportion of time a process is in actual use compared with its design capacity. See also *Efficiency*.

Value chain   The set of processes used to create value for a customer.

Value engineering (VE)   The elimination of unnecessary features and functions that do not contribute to the value or performance of the product.

Vertical integration   The amount of ownership of the *Supply chain* by an organization.

Virtual organization   An organization is which *E-business* is used to outsource more and more *Supply chain* activities to third parties so that the boundaries between and within organizations become blurred.

Visual control   The maintenance of an orderly workplace in which tools are easily available and unusual occurrences are easily noticeable.

Warehousing   The use of locations to hold a stock of incoming raw materials used in production or hold finished goods ready for distribution to customers. Warehousing is also used to store *Work-in-progress inventory* or spares for equipment.

Weighted scoring   The process by which a list of factors that are relevant to the location decision is compiled and each factor given a weighting that indicates its relative importance compared with the other factors. Each location is then scored on each factor and this score is multiplied by the factor value. The alternative with the highest score is chosen.

Work measurement   Determining the length of time it will take to undertake a particular task.

Work sampling   A method for determining the proportion of time a worker or machine spends on various activities; work sampling can be very useful in job redesign and estimating levels of worker output.

Work study   Measuring the performance of jobs through two elements: *Method study* and *Work measurement*.

Workforce schedule   This determines the daily workload for each member of staff.

Work-in-progress inventory   Inventory at some point within the operations process.

Yield management The use of *Demand management* strategies aimed at maximizing customer revenue in service organizations. It is particularly appropriate when the organization is operating with relatively fixed capacity and it is possible to segment the market into different types of customers.

ABBREVIATIONS

ABS	Activity-Based Costing
ACWP	Actual Cost of Work Performed
AFIs	Areas For Improvement
AGV	Automated Guided Vehicle
AMH	Automated Material Handling
AOA	Activity On Arrow
AON	Activity On Node
AOQ	Average Outgoing Quality
AOQL	Average Outgoing Quality Limit
API	Application Programming Interface
AQL	Acceptable Quality Level
AS/RS	Automated Storage and Retrieval Systems
ATM	Automatic Teller Machine
AU	Autonomy
B2B	Business-to-Business
B2C	Business-to-Consumer
BCWP	Budgeted Cost of Work Performed
BCWS	Budgeted Cost of Work Scheduled
BOM	Bill Of Materials
BPI	Business Process Improvement

BPM	Business Process Management
BPR	Business Process Reengineering
BPS	Business Process Simulation
C2B	Consumer-to-Business
C2C	Consumer-to-Consumer
CAD	Computer-Aided Design
CAE	Computer-Aided Engineering
CAM	Computer-Aided Manufacturing
CAPP	Computer-Aided Process Planning
CI	Continuous Improvement
CIM	Computer-Integrated Manufacture
CIPS	Chartered Institute of Purchasing and Supply
CNC	Computer Numerically Controlled
CPM	Critical Path Method
CR	Critical Ratio
CRM	Customer Relationship Management
CRP	Capacity Requirements Plan
CV	Cost Variance
CVP	Cost–Volume–Profit model
DDS	Customer Due-Date
DFM	Design For Manufacture
DFMA	Design For Manufacture and Assembly
DIP	Document Image Processing
DKC	Donkey Kong Country
DMAIC	Define, Measure, Analyse, Improve and Control
DOE	Design of Experiments
d.p.m.o.	Defects per million opportunities
DRP	Distribution Requirements Planning
DSS	Decision Support System

E2E	Employee-to-Employee
EDI	Electronic Data Interchange
EFT	Electronic Funds Transfer
EIS	Executive Information System
EISAM	European Institute for Advanced Studies in Management
EOQ	Economic Order Quantity
EPOS	Electronic Point-Of-Sale
EQA	European Quality Award
EFQM	European Foundation for Quality Management
ERP	Enterprise Resource Planning
ESIA	Eliminate, Simplify, Integrate and Automate
EUROMA	European Operations Management Association
FB	Feedback
FCFS	First Come, First Served
FMC	Flexible Manufacturing Cell
FMEA	Failure Mode and Effect Analysis
FMECA	Failure Mode, Effect and Criticality Analysis
FMS	Flexible Manufacturing System
FOI	Fixed Order Inventory
GT	Group Technology
HCM	Human Capital Management
HCMSs	Human Capital Management Systems
HR	Human Resources
ICT	Information Communications Technology
IiP	Investors in People
IRR	Internal Rate of Return
IRS	Information Reporting System
ISF	Inventory Status File
ISO	International Organization for Standardization

IT	Information Technology
JIT	Just-In-Time
KPI	Key Performance Indicator
LAN	Local Area Network
LCL	Lower Control Limit
LG	Lucky Goldstar
LPT	Longest Process Time
LTPD	Lot Tolerance Percent Defective
MC	Machining Centre
MDF	Medium Density Fibreboard
MPS	Motivating Potential Score
MPS	Master Production Schedule
MRP	Materials Requirements Planning
MRP II	Manufacturing Resource Planning
MTBF	Mean Time Between Failures
MTTR	Mean Time To Repair
NES	Nintendo Entertainment System
NPV	Net Present Value
p&l	Profit and loss
OAS	Office Automation System
OC	Operating Characteristic
OPT	Optimized Production Technology
OR	Operations Research
PDA	Personal Digital Assistant
PERT	Programme Evaluation and Review Technique
PFA	Production Flow Analysis
PLC	Product/service Life Cycle
PMTS	Predetermined Motion Time System
POR	Planned Order Release

p.p.m.	Parts per million
PPI	Perpetual Physical Inventory
QCDSM	Quality, Cost, Delivery, Safety and Morale
QFD	Quality Functional Deployment
QLF	Quality Loss Function
QMS	Quality Management System
R&D	Research and Development
RCCP	Rough-Cut Capacity Plan
ROP	Re-Order Point
RTA	Road Traffic Accident
SBU	Strategic Business Unit
SCM	Supply Chain Management
SME	Small- or Medium-sized Enterprise
SMED	Single Minute Exchange of Dies
SOT	Shortest Operating Time
SPC	Statistical Process Control
SPT	Shortest Process Time
SSM	Service System Mapping
SUR	Setup Reduction
SV	Skill Variety
SV	Schedule Variance
TCP/IP	Transmission Control Protocol over Internet Protocol
TI	Task Identity
TPM	Total Preventative Maintenance
TPS	Transaction Processing System
TQM	Total Quality Management
TRAMAH	Trauma Resource Allocation Model for Ambulances and Hospitals
TS	Task Significance
UCL	Upper Control Limit

UNCTAD	UN Conference on Trade and Development
VA	Value Analysis
VAN	Value-Added Network
VE	Value Engineering
VIM	Visual Interactive Modelling
WAN	Wide Area Network
WBS	Work Breakdown Structure
WFMS	Workflow Management System
WIP	Work In Progress
WLAN	Wireless Local Area Network
WWW	World Wide Web
XML	eXtensible Markup Language

INDEX